HARRY THE K

THE REMARKABLE LIFE OF HARRY KALAS

RANDY MILLER

FOREWORD BY
MIKE SCHMIDT

SPECIAL INTRODUCTION
RYAN HOWARD

RUNNING PRESS
PHILADELPHIA • LONDON

DEDICATIONS

To Gram, thank you for my best childhood memories, steering me down the right path in life and everything else. You are missed every day.

To Miller, thank you for taking me into your home, being a provider, all the games of catch and supporting my career.

To Diane, thank you for always being there and inspiring my stronger Christian faith.

To Howard, thank you for taking friendship to another level by making the editing portion of this project your life.

To my father, thank you for the encouragement and turning me into such a passionate sports fan that I found a way to make it my career.

To Jim Isler—wherever you are—thank you for giving a 15-year-old, sports-crazed teen his first sports writing job for the *Jeannette News-Dispatch* in 1980.

To GS, thank you for hiring me not once, not twice, but three times.

To Jodi Campbell Soup, Lou Michael and the rest of my family, thank you for caring.

To Les, Herm and Dave, thank you for being trusted and loyal friends for so many years.

To Joseph, Babylon John, Bill, Luigi, Maury, Macho Man, Sir Bob, the Smiths and everyone else who has touched my life—you know who you are—thank you for the friendship.

To Jim Fregosi, Terry Francona, Larry Bowa and Charlie Manuel, thank you for teaching me so much baseball during my first 14 years as a Phillies beat writer.

To Relentless, Jasmine and Detective Sergeant McCabe, thank you for the time and support in helping me share HK's amazing life story.

Printed in the United States

9 8 7 6 5 4 3 2
Digit on the right indicates the number of this printing

Library of Congress Control Number: 2009938626

ISBN 978-0-7624-3896-9

Cover and Interior Design: Joshua McDonnell
Editor: Greg Jones
Photo research by Sue Oyama & Randy Miller

Unless noted, all photos courtesy of the Kalas family

Running Press Book Publishers
2300 Chestnut Street
Philadelphia, PA 19103-4371

Visit us on the web!
www.runningpress.com

CONTENTS

FOREWORD

Good guys—genuinely good, loveable, friendly guys—are hard to find. Men who live life to serve, men who are blessed with the ability to live without animosity, jealousy, or a judgmental nature, men who bring a joyous smile to you every day, are hard to find. These are natural traits, but they are seldom found in one person. I came to know Harry Kalas in 1972. Thirty-seven years later, in writing a testimonial for his memorial, I finally realized how much he meant to me, and to the city of Philadelphia.

I came to the Phillies as a call-up in 1972. The broadcast team of Harry Kalas, Andy Musser and Richie Ashburn were to me just that, the broadcasters, the guys who described the games on radio and TV. I didn't see them or their work as being a big deal. I would grow to understand the exact opposite was true.

Harry Kalas came to Philadelphia, from his first major-league job in Houston, just in time to open Veterans Stadium in 1971. I came a year later. We'd share a special friendship for 37 years, not long enough for me.

In 1974, I married Donna Wightman, and she was a big reason that season was my coming-out party. After struggling through the previous year, I won Opening Day with a ninth-inning walk-off home run and never slowed down.

I was not the focal point of the Kalas/Schmidt friendship. It was Donna, a natural entertainer who had a short career of professional singing before I lured her away. When the Phils' broadcast network, led by Harry, experienced her engaging personality, the pre-game show, *Phillies Digest*, was created. Harry, with Donna as his co-host, had a blast with this magazine-themed show and another wonderful friendship was formed.

Not only were Harry and I close as professionals, but we enjoyed vacation time together. We hosted a 10-day excursion to Hawaii in 1975. Honolulu, where Harry met first wife Jasmine and served in the military, was very close to his heart. Together, we saw parts of the island only he could have shown us.

As time went on, our careers went on the upswing and the mid-1970s were tremendously exciting. With Harry, Richie and Andy at the mike, we played and they broadcasted some of the most exhilarating baseball ever—my four-home-run game in Chicago, the 23-22 victory at Wrigley Field, many close pennant-race games. . . . Philadelphia baseball was back. As we headed into a new decade, we expected the memories to mount.

Our friendship only grew stronger. Toward the end of the 1970s, Harry came upon what would become one of his broadcasting trademarks, his soon-to-be famous home run call, "Outta Here!" The story is that he picked up the idea around the batting cage one day after hearing Larry Bowa use the phrase watching Greg "the Bull" Luzinski hit one out. It didn't catch on right away, but as we became one of the best teams in baseball, with exciting players who hit lots of long balls, Harry tailored each call to us individually. It always ended with "Outta here, home run, Bake McBride" . . . or whomever.

Harry, Richie, and Andy, with Chris Wheeler added in 1977, made a loveable foursome. Quirky, humorous and fun, but with a strong passion and astute knowledge of the game, the broadcast team became the darlings of Philadelphia.

With Richie offering his daily musings sporting his pipe, hats, tennis garb and hilarious stories, with Harry playing the straight-man role, and with Andy and Wheels providing support, the team was a perfect sideshow. Especially Harry and Richie, who would become lifelong buddies, a friendship that was cut short by the untimely passing of Richie in 1997 in New York. It's been said that Harry never got over losing Richie—"His Whiteness," as Harry called him. They were best of friends, doing what they loved together.

Until 2007, the only consistently successful years for the Phillies were almost 25 years in the past. Of course, there were some great teams in between—the 1993 Kruk-Dykstra-Daulton boys, for one—but from 1979 to 1983 all of us were on a roll. In 1979, we obtained Pete Rose as a free agent and the ghosts of playoffs past went away. Though the Pittsburgh Pirates won the World Series that season, Pete showed us why a team needs a vocal leader and someone who had been on the winning end of postseason games. Pete was it—he'd won championships with the Cincinnati Reds in 1975 and '76. As for Harry and Richie, Pete was perfect, too. Harry and Pete spent lots of time together, as they both loved horseracing. For Richie, well, he and Pete and I had more knockdown, drag-out gin games than you could imagine. Pete fit right in. He was a great teammate. And for Harry's team, what better a player could they have for their broadcasts?

In 1980, the Phillies went through a period of gut-wrenching baseball from the end of September through October. It was like nothing ever before—we just seemed to survive every obstacle thrown in front of us. We got through Montreal to take the division, Houston to win the pennant, and Kansas City to win the first World Series in franchise history, culminating in one of Harry's finest moments to that date. The 1980 victory parade was indescribable. It concluded with floats carrying us players into JFK Stadium in front of 100,000 people, where Harry, as only he could, addressed the crowd and introduced each of us with a small comment. His presence behind the mike, his professionalism and timing set the tone for a moment in Phillies' history never to be equaled, until 2008.

The success in the early 1980s continued as the "Wheeze Kids" were born. That 1983 pennant-winning team was unique. From Cincinnati's Big Red Machine and free agency to us came Joe Morgan and Tony Perez. Now we had Pete, Joe and Tony together on the Phillies, a broadcaster's dream. What a ride we had in 1983. Little did we know it would be our last. The old Reds were all let go that offseason and we were left to rebuild the franchise from within.

Harry, with his crew, was trucking right along, logging season after season of wonderful broadcasts featuring memorable calls of momentous home runs and record-setting performances. He would put his biggest stamp to date on my 500th home run in 1986, a call that will forever grace my life and career—"Swing and a long drive, there it is! Number 500, home run number 500 for Michael Jack Schmidt!" It is a home run call that will go down in history as one of the greatest ever. His stamp on that home run gave it everlasting life.

Similar stamps were put on Steve Carlton's 3,000th strikeout and Pete Rose's all-time NL-leading hit. Harry was master of ceremonies for every occasion honoring me at Veterans Stadium following my retirement in 1989. His voice and smile had graced every special moment of my baseball career.

I was away from baseball and Harry's life from 1990 until I returned for some coaching at spring training in 2000. The broadcast team had changed dramatically, now including my ex-teammate Larry Andersen and some faces unknown to me. But Harry was still the anchor. In the 1990s, I had been a fan from afar. Starting in 2000, upon returning to the Phillies family in a small way, I got to see Harry more often. Nothing had changed. He still greeted me the same way with a unique nickname: "In the game today." That's how he referred to me for most of my career, which meant in his opinion that I was the best player "in the game today." This was a major compliment coming from a Hall of Fame broadcaster.

Harry's career continued to spiral upward with the Phillies, plus his work with NFL Films, broadcasting football and national commercials. Harry's baritone voice and smooth style was "Facenda-like." His voice was popular year round. Harry Kalas truly was a man for every season.

Our relationship was distant as my visits to Philly were few and far between, but I spoke to him often enough to stay current. He became the link of a new generation of Phillies and their fans, and what a run he was about to have. Starting in 2005, as Rollins, Utley and Howard became the nucleus, Harry would begin reliving his days of 1980. They took a big step each year. In 2008, they finally reached the Series and won it. His final-out victory call and performance as Master of Ceremonies at the end of the parade were vintage Harry.

Over the 2008 offseason, Harry's health became an issue, and it was evident as he tried to throw out the first pitch during the 2009 World Series ring-ceremony game. He couldn't get the pitch to home plate, but everyone thought this would pass. Everyone, including me, took him for granted. No one ever imagined what a Phillies game would be without Harry Kalas. On April 12, he called Matt Stairs' tie-breaking homer in the top of the 9th and Chase Utley's fielding play in the bottom of the inning that ended the game. They were Harry's last calls, and on April 13, in Washington D.C., he died of heart failure.

His death was a tremendous blow to us all. The reality of his departure made us all reflect on his value to the city, its fans, and to the Phillies organization. He was a special man, and he left a wonderful legacy, one of which we should all be mindful. For me personally, his friendship, his passion, his unselfishness, and most of all, his smile will be forever linked to my existence as a Phillies player.

—MIKE SCHMIDT

Philadelphia Phillies (1972-89)

1980 World Champion

Three-time National League MVP

Baseball Hall of Famer

SPECIAL INTRODUCTION

Growing up in St. Louis, baseball to me was the voice of Jack Buck. Listening to Cardinals baseball, there was no other voice. He was the epitome of Cardinals baseball. Jack brought an entirely different feel to the game. When I was younger, Jack made me feel everything was going to be OK, even when the team was losing. The Cardinals were either going to come back and win, or everything was going to be all right. He provided comfort.

Harry Kalas reminded me a lot of Jack Buck.

When I was called up from the minor leagues to play for the Philadelphia Phillies for the first time in 2004, Harry came up to me and said, "Congratulations. Welcome." When I heard Harry speak, I thought to myself, "No way, that's the dude from Campbell's Chunky Soup commercials and NFL Films!"

As I continued to play in Philadelphia, as I got to know Harry better, I would think to myself, "I'm having a living legend call my games." And behind the scenes, he was the greatest guy, the nicest guy. He would always stop by my locker to say hello. Every once in awhile he would ask for an autograph for someone, which was cool. I would think, "That's a Hall of Famer asking me for an autograph." I thought about asking Harry for an autograph once or twice, but I couldn't pull myself to do it. I didn't want to bother him.

I would go home and watch when they'd replay Phillies games on television late at night. Hearing Harry call my home runs truly was something special. To hear Harry go, "It's a long drive, it's deep, it's outta here, home run Ryan Howard!" That was just the greatest feeling. Being able to hit the home run and hear Harry call it—it was awesome. He had a whole aura about him. Everyone on the team felt he was part of us.

As everyone knows, Harry had a great voice, too. I'd hear him talk before a game and think, "Harry's ready to go. He's in game mode right now." Then when the game is over, you would see Harry back at the hotel and his voice was still the same. I would think, "You don't have to talk like that anymore. The game's over. You can talk regular now." We put on our uniforms and get ready for the games, and I used to think Harry did the same thing with his voice in the booth. But that was his normal voice.

Listening to Harry call games, he reminded me of Jack Buck. He made the crowd feel good. He never bashed anyone. Even when he was telling it how it was, there was that hope and comfort that everything was going to be OK.

—**RYAN HOWARD**
Philadelphia Phillies (2004-present)
2008 World Champion
2006 National League MVP
2005 Rookie of the Year

PREFACE: THE HARRY THAT I KNEW

It was past last call and time to hit the sack when I shuffled through the revolving doors of my Milwaukee hotel on a September weeknight in 1999. Silence and light from a dimmed but still spectacular chandelier greeted me as I entered the lobby of The Pfister. This ancient, 23-story treasure, built in 1883 three blocks from the shores of Lake Michigan, radiated the feel of old European grandeur, with its 32-foot-high lobby ceiling, Victorian art collection and grand marble staircase.

I was in my fourth season in what would become a long run covering Major League Baseball for a living. The Philadelphia Phillies were in Milwaukee for a series, and I'd reported on their game that night at County Stadium against the hometown Brewers. After filing my newspaper stories, I headed to a local pub for a late-night snack and drinks with another reporter. Once back at the hotel, we were headed for the elevators when we passed a closed hotel bar in an open area of the lobby. The Lobby Lounge lights were down low, too, and the bartender had departed, but two older gentlemen were still seated in the lounge, talking from barstools with empty beer mugs in front of them.

Phillies broadcaster Harry Kalas waved us over. He introduced us to his friend, whom he'd known from his days working Notre Dame basketball and football games in the 1980s. It was 1:30 in the morning and Harry, 63 at the time, wanted to keep talking about that night's game. He always did enjoy discussing the strategy of each and every baseball game. Thirty minutes later, Harry was holding court sharing a couple of his favorite baseball stories. I'd heard them before, but his old friend hadn't and listening to Harry tell them never got old.

Midway through one of Harry's tales, a clean-cut and sharp-dressed fellow in his mid-20s walked in and asked if the bar was open.

"Sorry, pal," Harry said.

The man perked up. He was a Philly guy in town on business. He wasn't much of a baseball fan, but needed to hear Harry say only a couple of words to recognize one of the country's most identifiable voices.

"Oh my God, Harry, my old college roommate is not going to believe I met you," the man said. "When we were at Villanova, he used to impersonate you all the time. The guy worships you."

"What's your buddy's name?" Harry asked.

"George Myers," the stranger replied.

Harry noticed the visitor had a cell phone clutched in one of his hands. "George Myers, huh?" he said. "Get him on the phone."

"Huh? Are you serious?"

Harry nodded.

By then, it was 3 a.m., back in Philadelphia where George lived, and he was probably fast asleep. But the young man phoned his friend anyway. When a groggy Myers picked up, his friend quickly explained where he was and what was going on, then added "Harry told me to call you and I swear I'm not making this up."

The guy had to figure Harry would make his half-asleep friend's night by saying "hello." Typically, he did better than that. Harry took the phone in his hand and launched into broadcasting mode:

"It's the ninth inning, 2-1 ballgame here at Villanova University. The 'Cats are down a run. Two down. George Myers is coming up. He's the last hope. And here's the pitch. . . ."

At this point, Harry turned up the volume on his voice, as he would in a real game, and this time his hollering call bounced off the hotel lobby walls, producing an unforgettable echo.

"Swing and a long drive, watch that baby, outta here! Home run, George Myers! Villanova University wins the game, 3-2!"

When finished with his dramatic home run call, Harry paused for a second for effect, and then said, "Nice talking to you, pal," before handing the phone back to the now-startled Philly guy. Harry shook the fellow's hand one more time, then turned back to his guests and picked up the story that he'd been telling right where he had left off.

Watching Harry that night gave me a lasting snapshot of a man who earned his way into the hearts of so many Philadelphia sports fans—just by being himself.

I first met Harry Kalas on Opening Day 1996, my first day on a new job as a Phillies beat writer for three suburban Philadelphia newspapers—the *Bucks County Courier Times*, *Doylestown Intelligencer* and *Burlington County Times*. I introduced myself in a hallway near the press elevator and remember being struck that day by how friendly and soft-spoken Harry was to me and everyone else.

Even though I grew up across the state in Jeannette, 26 miles to the east of Pittsburgh, I certainly knew of Harry Kalas. I've been a sports junkie my whole life, so I'd heard many of his NFL Films narrations and watched him do Notre Dame football on Sunday replays. During my college years at the University of Pittsburgh, I distinctly remember being enthralled by the way Harry Kalas pronounced the name of Notre Dame's star running back in the early-to-mid 1980s. When Harry would say it on telecasts, I would try to turn my voice into a baritone and repeat it the same way: "Touchdown, Allen Pinkett!"

I learned pretty quickly that Harry Kalas was so much more than a popular broadcaster with a great voice. I doubt that I've ever met a more genuine, humble and kind man. Over the years, I came to know Harry pretty well by being around him almost every day for seven-plus months each year. He frequently had dinner with writers before Phillies games and often would pick our brains to see what inside information we could share—not always to use on the air, but mostly because he was genuinely interested in the team and in us. But it was more fun to let Harry do the talking, especially when he was storytelling in a hotel bar—and even more fun when Harry sat next to the piano singing at Lefty O'Doul's in San Francisco.

There's an old cliché about "no crying in baseball," and it may be true, but I've dealt with some very sad days during my time covering the Phillies. The Phillies played the first games in Denver after the April 1999 Columbine High School massacre in nearby Littleton, Colo. That weekend, I saw the pain from the shootings up close when a sports writer friend from *The Denver Post* and I took a Sunday morning drive to a park that sits next to Columbine. A group of Columbine students sat in the grass in a circle praying. A few feet away, we spotted a pickup truck that belonged to one of the students who had been killed. The vehicle was covered with cards, letters, book bags and lit candles. It wasn't easy concentrating on writing about a baseball game a few hours later.

Another tough day came in the fall of 2006 when former Phillies pitcher Cory Lidle lost his life at age 34 by accidentally flying his private plane into a Manhattan apartment building. Cory and I not only were friendly, but he had talked me into being his first passenger after obtaining his pilot's license the previous spring. Two days before his fatal crash, we were on the phone talking about making a second flight together. Writing his obituary was a daunting task.

Probably the hardest time that I've ever had focusing on work was after Harry Kalas' sudden death on April 13, 2009 in a Washington Nationals broadcast booth. Harry had made me feel like a friend, as he did with most everyone around him. Maybe 15 minutes before Harry's fatal heart attack, he was in the Phillies' clubhouse jotting down the lineups and exchanging greetings with writers. I can't say what happened was a total shock—Harry was 73 and just two months removed from heart surgery. But right away I knew that this sudden departure of a Philadelphia icon would be the biggest story I'd cover in my 25-plus years in newspapers.

The idea for this book developed about a month after Harry's death. I was intrigued about doing something to honor a man whom I greatly respected. After thinking it through, I decided to write Harry's life story. Over the next six months, I interviewed more than 160 people for this project, many of them on multiple occasions. I probably talked to Harry's two wives 50 times each, and I can't thank each enough—not only for their support, but also for their enthusiastic efforts to help. Some of our phone conversations would last two or three hours, but the time would fly hearing Harry stories. I think sharing their memories in great detail helped their grieving.

Eileen Kalas, Harry's second wife, provided me with phone numbers for dozens of key contacts, including Harry's brother, his childhood and college friends, NFL Films and Westwood One radio people, agents, and many others. She also encouraged me to track down Jasmine Kalas, Harry's first wife. Eileen knew that Jasmine never had gotten over the pain of losing Harry, who moved out in January 1987 after starting an affair with Eileen in September 1985, and that she blamed Eileen for much of her troubles. But Eileen insisted.

"Jasmine was a part of Harry's life for a long time, so you need to talk to her," Eileen told me.

She was right. Jasmine was an immense help offering stories of her life with Harry from the time they began dating in 1961 through their 31 years of marriage. She's a sweet woman with a cheerful and infectious personality. She was under orders from her two sons not to discuss Eileen, but if she ever made mention of her in passing, Jasmine always referred to Harry's second wife as "your friend." I used to joke with Jasmine trying to get her to say Eileen's name. She did slip a couple of times, which would lead to her pretending to be mad and saying, "Oh, you got me!"

Eileen was simply fantastic to me. She welcomed me into her old home in Media, Pa., to spend a full day and night going through Harry's scrapbooks and photo albums. I went back a second time and could have made more visits, had I needed them. On July 10, Eileen phoned me five minutes after midnight to be the first to wish me a happy 45th birthday. Then she playfully got on me for not remembering hers the day before. If I went a week to 10 days without contacting her, she'd usually call to tell me to keep plugging away and assure me that she was available for more help. Other times, Eileen would leave me voicemail offering a phone number of someone new that I should contact.

Within a few months of Harry's death, Eileen sold their home and relocated to Delaware. Her future plans are to move to Hawaii sometime in 2010, at least for a year. I would tease Jasmine that Eileen should move in with her so that they could make a reality television show together, *The Kalas Wives.* Jasmine always responded with that infectious giggle of hers.

Harry's friendship-turned-feud with longtime broadcast partner Chris "Wheels" Wheeler was one of the toughest parts of this project. I was covering the Phillies through it all and knew there were serious issues between the two. But I did not understand the extent and depth of their differences until I investigated the situation. I decided to devote an entire chapter to this saga in hopes of explaining what happened. Wheels certainly wished that I had ignored this part of Harry's life, but nevertheless was cooperative before and after learning that several of Harry's supporters had made some damaging accusations against him. I tried very hard to be fair to all parties.

Harry Kalas' many years of heavy drinking also left me with some difficult decisions. I spent many nights awake in bed wondering which stories I should use and which I should leave out. I wanted to tell Harry's story, yet not hurt his image. I decided to include details of his 1996 DUI and some of his infidelities because each already had been reported. Through interviews with

Harry's friends, family members, colleagues, and even his psychologist Dr. Jack Porter, I attempted to make some sense of a beloved man who made some mistakes, to reveal how he dealt with them and, ultimately, how he became an even better man late in life.

Harry's lifelong quest to help others surely inspired many of his friends to be so supportive of this project. Harry's broadcast partners in Hawaii tracked down and provided important information for me, as did some of Harry's high school and college friends. It was easy getting people to talk about Harry Kalas.

In September 2009, almost five months after Harry's death, I did book interviews before a San Francisco Giants-Phillies game at Citizens Bank Park with two of baseball's best-known sportscasters. Bob Costas was working the game for the MLB Network and Jon Miller, the ESPN *Sunday Night Baseball* play-by-play man, was in town doing Giants' radio, his full-time job. I was told to meet Costas in his booth 30 minutes before the first pitch. When I arrived, I was informed by an MLB Network engineer that we'd have to do it after the game.

I said we could try for another time because I knew after the game wouldn't work. I'd be on deadline for about an hour doing newspaper work, and Costas would be long gone by the time I finished. Disappointed, I was walking away as Costas was returning to the booth from a trip to the restroom.

"You won't have time after the game, will you?" Costas asked.

"I'll be writing, but it's no problem," I told him. "Thanks anyway."

Costas cracked opened the door to his broadcast booth, peeked his head in and whispered, "Tell them I'm still in the bathroom." Costas immediately turned on his 'A' game and offered up five minutes worth of elegant words about a man whom he respected and liked.

A few minutes later, I ventured into the Giants radio booth. Jon Miller finished up a conversation with a friend, and then motioned me over. Sitting in front of his mike, Miller answered a few questions on Harry and then told a few stories. Fifteen minutes later, the radio engineer told Miller, "We're on in one minute." Miller kept talking. "Thirty seconds." He kept talking. At this point, I started getting nervous. With a few seconds to spare, Jon Miller finally wrapped up his last story on Harry and began his Giants radio intro as I exited the booth.

I'm grateful to Bob Costas and Jon Miller for giving me a few of their valuable minutes, but I know why they did it. Even when pressed for time, it was unthinkable for them to pass on a chance to honor the memory of a true legend and treasure in their profession.

I hope that this labor of love sharing Harry's life story does justice to the man Philadelphians and America's sports fans were so fortunate to have in their lives for 39 years. Harry the K truly was one of a kind.

—RANDY MILLER

INTRODUCTION: HIGH HOPES

Cases of champagne had been sprayed, poured and sipped, leaving the new kings of baseball with wet hair, damp clothes, sticky skin and a good buzz. It was after 11 o'clock on October 29, 2008, a cold and windy autumn night in Philadelphia, more than an hour after Brad Lidge's slider in the dirt produced a swing-and-miss that won the 2008 World Series for the Phillies over the Tampa Bay Rays. Late-night parties broke out around a region used to watching everyone else's teams celebrate championships.

Thousands of fans remained at Citizens Bank Park hours after the game and deep into the night, cheering and watching Phillies players pose for pictures and snap some of their own. Most everyone there refused to leave until the festivities were christened with the typical Phillies celebration encore act. Every time they'd won a big game over the past two decades, their Hall of Fame announcer punctuated the moment by crooning a chorus of "High Hopes," his personal theme song.

What a night it was for Harry Kalas, who at the age of 72 finally got to call the final out to a World Series title game for his beloved "Fightins." And what a World Series it had been for the man known affectionately as "Harry the K," whose oldest son worked the Series as a member of the Tampa Bay Rays' broadcast team.

Todd Kalas, a 42-year-old bachelor, went looking for his father after finishing his post-game duties in the losing clubhouse. Todd wanted to offer congratulations and hug his father goodbye before hopping on a team bus to the airport for a late-night flight home. With time short, Todd walked around the crowded ballfield, shifting his head from one side to the other searching for one of Philadelphia's most recognizable faces. Harry wasn't there. Todd headed indoors to continue his search in the press dining room and then in the Phillies broadcast booth. There still was no sight of Harry. He scribbled a quick note and left it on a ledge in the radio booth, then left.

"Congratulations, Dad, you guys deserved it," read Todd's note. "You've got bragging rights for awhile."

Too late for Todd, Harry finally made his appearance, striding onto the playing field in a black Phillies World Series Champions hat with a curled bill pushed down over his eyes. Dan Baker, the Phillies' public address announcer since 1972, introduced Harry with the kind of enthusiasm ring announcers use to present boxers before championship bouts. The fans still in the stands broke into a chant: "Har-ry! Har-ry! Har-ry!" Harry grabbed the mike from Baker and started speaking to the crowd. Not surprisingly, he started by thanking Phillies fans for their support. But the fans wanted to hear something else.

"Sing it," one Phillies fan called out.

After working the crowd a little bit more, Harry posed a question to his audience: "Do you know what this team had?"

"High hopes," fans screamed in response.

As the grounds crew tugged home plate out of the ground, Harry stood a few feet in front of the Phillies dugout and started singing in his famous bass baritone:

"When you're down
Lift your head off the ground
There's a lot to be learned
So look around
Once there was a silly old ant
Thought he'd move a rubber tree plant
Anyone knows that ants can't
Move a rubber tree plant
But he had high hopes. . . ."

Harry wasn't in tune, especially at the end, and he butchered the lyrics. Few, if any, in the crowd knew. For sure, nobody cared. Besides, Harry had been singing it this way for years. Like *American Idol* judge Simon Cowell encourages contestants, Harry made the song his own.

"I like it my way," Harry once told his second wife.

"That was Harry," Eileen Kalas said. "He had to put his own spin on it."

Noted songwriter Sammy Cahn, who penned *Married . . . With Children's* theme song "Love and Marriage," wrote "High Hopes" for a 1959 film, *A Hole in the Head.*" In the comedy, 12-year-old child star Eddie Hodges sang "High Hopes" from a park bench with Frank Sinatra. The tune became an immediate hit and won an Oscar for Best Original Song at the 1959 Academy Awards. The next year, "High Hopes" was adopted by John F. Kennedy for his 1960 Presidential campaign. JFK had Sinatra sing alone and change the lyrics:

"Everyone is voting for Jack
'Cause he's got what all the rest lack
Everyone wants to back Jack
Jack is on the right track
'Cause he's got high hopes. . . ."

Interestingly, a song about a different Harry had previously been used during another Presidential campaign. Harry S. Truman chose the popular 1921 foxtrot tune "I'm Just Wild About Harry" as the theme of his successful 1948 White House run.

Sinatra re-recorded "High Hopes" for a second time in 1961, this time with a children's choir, for his album *All the Way*. Later, Sinatra sang it solo, which is the best remembered version.

Harry was a big Sinatra fan. During his drives to and from the Phillies ballpark, he often sang along while listening to "Ol' Blue Eyes" on his car stereo.

Harry saw Sinatra perform live once. During a baseball offseason in the 1990s, Harry and Eileen got great seats for a Sinatra concert in Atlantic City. Harry sobbed happy tears while singing along with Frank, who kept forgetting the words to his songs. The night ended with disappointment. A friend lined up a post-concert meeting between Harry and Sinatra, but it was called off when Sinatra's wife became ill. Another bummer was that Sinatra didn't sing "High Hopes." But Harry didn't complain. He rarely complained about anything.

For most of his adult life, Harry did a lot of singing—especially during late-night visits to drinking establishments, such as Lefty O'Doul's in San Francisco and The Lodge in Chicago on his annual travels with the Phillies. People started associating Harry with "High Hopes" when he sang it at one of his March spring training birthday bashes during the 1970s. "It became a staple for his parties and expanded from there," Todd Kalas recalled.

Tragedy struck as Harry performed a rendition of "High Hopes" at the New York Sheridan piano bar sometime that same decade. Halfway through the song, an older gentleman standing at the bar collapsed from a heart attack and stopped breathing. By the time that medical help arrived, it was too late. Harry was shaken that a life was lost. But by the next day, he returned to his usual self-deprecating, witty outlook that inspired him to always try to make the best of everyone and everything, even death. Telling the story to his broadcast partners, he concluded, "It must have been my singing."

Over the years, it become a favorite Harry bar story and took on a life of its own. Exaggerating to improve the tale, Harry turned the victim into a homeless man. Then he was homeless and naked. Then he was homeless, naked and committed suicide by slashing his wrists as he listened to Harry sing.

"I've tried to find the most accurate description of that story, just for myself, and it's part of Harry's legend," said Video Dan Stephenson, the Phillies' longtime videographer. "It's the old Whitey Ashburn clause: never let the facts get in the way of a good story."

"It's a true story," said Jasmine Kalas, Harry's first wife. "A guy died. Harry told me about it right away. But he wasn't naked and didn't kill himself. He was just a patron who came in for a drink and happened to have a heart attack while Harry was singing."

Harry kept singing that song nevertheless. It fit his personality. He'd sing it in bars, at parties and sometimes when nobody expected it.

One of Jim Eisenreich's favorite memories of his playing days with the Phillies was when Harry broke into "High Hopes" at three in the morning on a bus ride from the airport to Veterans Stadium following a long flight. "We were all sleeping, then everybody joined in," Eisenreich said. "Harry was just one of the guys."

Eisenreich was an outfielder on the 1993 Phillies, Harry's favorite team of all time. That club won a National League pennant, but the best moment of the season for many players came after a division-clinching victory in Pittsburgh. With most of the team celebrating in a smallish Three Rivers Stadium training room, Harry walked in and belted out "High Hopes."

"That was his song, and for him to come in there and lead the whole team to that . . . my God, it's my greatest Harry Kalas moment," said Larry Andersen, a reliever on the 1993 Phillies who went on to become one of Harry's broadcast partners from 1997 to 2009.

Harry's most enduring version of "High Hopes" came in 2002 on the night before he was inducted into the broadcaster's wing of the Baseball Hall of Fame in Cooperstown. Harry broke away from an official function to make an appearance at a party the Phillies were throwing in his honor. Harry jumped in with the band and sang two verses, the first of which was shown following every Phillies home victory in 2009 after his death that April.

"High Hopes" was more than a song to Harry. It represented his whole attitude toward baseball and life. When the Phillies had lousy teams, he believed that things would turn around quickly. He also found the good in all types of people. He had many, many friends, including people of all different races, religions and economic classes.

Harry's broadcasting talents were legendary. In Philadelphia, he became the voice of the franchise and an indelible part of the team's greatest moments of the modern era, a figure as important—and perhaps even more important—to fans than any Phillies player. Harry called Phillies games as the club climbed the National League ladder during the 1970s, rising from perennial basement dwellers to annual pennant contenders. Harry was there when the franchise finally won its first World Series in 1980, very much a part of the team and the moment, even though Major League Baseball rules at the time only permitted network broadcasters to work the game. When the Phillies won again in 2008, Harry was there, this time broadcasting. Harry was always there, living and telling the Phillies' day-to-day story for almost four decades.

Harry's legendary voice was far from his defining characteristic. Talk to the people who knew him best or even those who may have just met him once, and you'll hear the same thing again and again about his character.

"If you want to say there was one mark in Harry's life, it was that he was a great guy," retired Philadelphia sportscasting legend Al Meltzer said. "Everybody loved him."

But Harry had his vices. By high school, he'd become hooked on three of his lifelong addictions—alcohol, cigarettes and carousing.

"He smoked too much, he drank too much, but I loved him anyway," San Diego Padres Hall of Fame broadcaster Jerry Coleman said.

Harry dressed with a distinctive flair, too. He started wearing colorful jackets and white shoes when they were in style in the early 1970s, and stayed with them for the rest of his life.

"Harry had the powder blue blazer and the Clark Griswald white shoes," said former Phillies pitcher Randy Wolf, referring to Chevy Chase's movie character in *Vacation*. "Awesome. I would call them 'the Griswald shoes.' But it wasn't out of disrespect. That was HK. No one ever made fun of HK. We respected him too much."

The son of a minister, Harry spent most of his childhood in Naperville, Ill. By the age of 10, Harry had attended his first Major League Baseball game—the White Sox against the Washington Senators at Comiskey Park in Chicago. Before the game, Senators outfielder Mickey Vernon gave Harry a tour of the dugout and a baseball. That day, Harry became a die-hard fan of the Senators and Vernon and of baseball. It was his fall-in-love-with-baseball moment.

By high school, Harry was telling people that he planned to become a Major League Baseball broadcaster. Around this time, Harry's voice started changing into a rich baritone that resembled his father's voice from behind the pulpit. That voice and unrelenting passion for the game gave Harry a fighting chance to achieve his baseball broadcasting dream. But he was set on reaching his goal by doing it his way—having as much fun as possible along life's journey.

In college, Harry's pursuit of good times threatened to derail his plans. He started out at Cornell College, a strict Methodist school in Iowa that was the alma mater of his father, Reverend Harry H. Kalas. He was greatly influenced during his freshman year by a blind speech professor, but bad grades and suspensions for broken rules convinced Cornell to encourage Harry not to return for his sophomore year. Harry transferred to the University of Iowa, one of the best broadcasting schools in the country, where he learned to mix business with pleasure. He drank a lot of beer over the next four years, the final three living in a fraternity house, but he also set up a career in broadcasting by excelling as a sportscaster at the campus radio station.

On his college graduation day, Harry was drafted into the Army. He got lucky. Of all places, he was stationed in Honolulu. Two years later, Harry gained an early discharge from the Army and got hired as the play-by-play broadcaster for the inaugural season of the Hawaii Islanders, a minor league franchise in the Pacific Coast League. Harry called Islanders' games for four seasons, working home games at Honolulu Stadium and recreating road games from radio station studios. During his first season with the Islanders, Harry met a beautiful Hawaiian woman of Japanese descent named Jasmine Kishie Kimura. She became Harry's serious girlfriend in 1961, then his wife in 1963. Though Harry's time in Hawaii was not lengthy, more than 40 years later his lasting impact on the state was reflected upon his death through Internet blog postings containing warm recollections from old-time Hawaii Islanders fans.

By 1965, Harry was in the big leagues as the third man in the broadcasting booth for the Houston Astros. He established himself as a young up-and-comer, despite only broadcasting a few innings each game and receiving no guidance from Astros' lead broadcaster Gene Elston. Harry and Jasmine became the parents of their two children while in Houston, sons Todd and Brad. In 1971, Harry left Houston for a new job in Philadelphia, where he found two of the other great loves of his life: the Phillies and broadcast partner Richie "Whitey" Ashburn.

"Best professional move I ever made," said Harry, who would go on to call more than 6,000 games over 39 seasons with the Phillies.

Harry Kalas arrived in Philadelphia amid controversy. Bill Campbell, the Phillies broadcaster whom Harry replaced, was very popular. But with help from Ashburn, Harry quickly won over hard-to-please Phillies fans. Harry and Whitey went on to establish their own show within the game. They were broadcasters and a comedy team, with Harry playing the straight man setting up Ashburn's one-liners, rants and off-the-wall analysis. They gave fans a reason to keep watching and listening, even during down seasons. Their wonderful act lasted 27 years, stretching from the day Harry arrived in Philadelphia in 1971 to the day Ashburn died in 1997. Harry and Whitey also became the best of friends. Away from the ballpark, they drove to spring training together and hung out at Philadelphia Country Club. Whitey, who was nine years older, played big brother by encouraging Harry to slow down on his drinking. When Whitey's daughter was killed in a car accident, Harry stayed up all night comforting his friend.

In Philadelphia, Harry became known as "Harry the K." Larry Christenson, a Phillies pitcher from 1973 to 1983, takes credit for coming up with the nickname, which would be used more frequently by fans than friends. Harry was the first to call Christenson "LC," a nickname that stuck. Using the same tone he applied to his famous "outta here" home run calls, Harry stretched out each syllable, making "LC" sound poetic. Doing his best Harry impersonation, Christenson greeted his friend the same way, "Harrr-eeee the Kaaayyy." It stuck, too.

Harry the K's reign in Philadelphia led to many business opportunities outside baseball. He started doing voiceovers for NFL Films in 1975, a side gig that would last the rest of his life and make his voice recognizable to sports fans throughout the country. Harry also served as the voice of Notre Dame football and basketball for a time, as well as for Philadelphia Big Five college basketball, and for national commercials such as Coors Light and Campbell's

Chunky Soup, as well as other products.

"I know it sounds ridiculous, but Harry was bigger than every player on the team," former Phillies pitcher Ricky Bottalico said. "There was an aura about Harry, and when you were around him you felt that aura. Everybody loved him. Everybody copied his voice. For your peers to do your voice—it's the ultimate compliment."

Harry was in his 22nd year of marriage to Jasmine when he met Eileen Vanwey on September 1, 1985. They started an affair, which led to a divorce and a second marriage for Harry. During divorce proceedings, which took over six years to complete, Harry and Eileen had a child, Kane. During his time with Eileen, Harry got himself into trouble; he had a DUI and confessed to other marital infidelity.

"His personal life turned into a mess, but he was a fun-loving guy," said Jim Bunning, Hall of Fame pitcher and U.S. Senator from Kentucky.

Harry eventually quit drinking, sought out counseling and saved his marriage to Eileen.

In 1997, Harry had a falling out with Chris Wheeler, his longtime Phillies broadcast partner and close friend. Things grew uglier when Eileen took the feud to the press. Harry and Wheeler never did patch things up, but they continued to work well together in Harry's final seasons.

Harry wasn't a perfect man, but he was considered a very good man. Harry put the brotherly love back in Philadelphia, a blue-collar city with passionate sports fans that had a reputation for being tough on its players, sometimes way too tough. Harry saw only the good in the fans and the players, just as he did in all people.

"If you didn't love Harry, something was wrong with you," said Ron Reed, a Phillies reliever in the 1970s.

Phillies fans adored Harry, too. When Harry was inducted into the Baseball Hall of Fame in 2002, thousands of Phillies fans drove 265 miles from Philadelphia to Cooperstown, N.Y., for the ceremony. During his acceptance speech, Harry read a poem he'd written especially for Phillies fans.

On the final day of the 2007 season, the Phillies clinched a playoff berth for the first time since 1993. Harry provided the perfect ending to a wild on-field celebration by singing "High Hopes." Harry did it again in 2008 after the Phillies won the National League East on the next-to-last day of the season. On October

27, 2008, the night Harry finally got to broadcast the final out of a Phillies world championship, he put his stamp on this historic day in Philadelphia with an emotional and unforgettable rendition of his favorite song and sentiment.

Nobody knew it, but Harry had less than six months to live. He'd suffered a silent heart attack sometime in 2008, but kept it hidden from all but his family and a few friends. Defying his doctors' warnings, Harry waited until February 2009 to undergo heart surgery. He delayed his procedure so that he could finish working the 2008 baseball and football seasons. He had made commitments to the Phillies, NFL Films and Westwood One radio, and intended to honor them.

Harry finally underwent heart surgery on February 11, and then started working Phillies spring training in mid-March. After returning home from Florida with the Phillies, he checked into a hospital for dehydration two days before the team's season opener. Instead of resting up, Harry left the hospital without his doctor's permission because he didn't want to miss a televised exhibition game the day before Opening Day. A week into the 2009 season, Harry Kalas, 73, died while preparing for a broadcast in the visiting television booth at Nationals Park in Washington, D.C.

Manager of broadcasting Rob Brooks and radio color man Larry Andersen tried to save Harry, but he was gone. Starting with a memorial service at Citizens Bank Park and continuing throughout the 2009 season, the Phillies and their fans celebrated Harry Kalas' life in a variety of ways.

Years before, above the door to his office in his Media, Pa., home, Harry had hung a sign reading, "It's a Wonderful Life." The 1946 movie by that name that starred Jimmy Stewart was Harry's favorite. Some would say that's fitting because Harry was one part George Bailey, the film's main character who put others ahead of himself, and one part Clarence, the guardian angel who earned his wings by helping save George. Despite some turmoil, eventually overcome, Harry did live a wonderful life.

"Harry lived and acted out his entire goal of life until he left this earth," said Glenn Wilson, an All-Star outfielder for the Phillies who thought so much of Harry that he named one of his sons Andrew Kalas Wilson. "All he wanted to do was be a broadcaster, and look at how many people he touched doing what he loved. Are you kidding? Yes, Harry lived a wonderful life. He went through trials and tribulations, but through it all he had high hopes, just like that song."

A VOICE OFF THE OLD BLOCK

Carol Oswald was on her way to class when she was stopped in the Naperville Community High School hallway. The 16-year-old junior with brown shoulder-length hair had caught the eyes of a classmate.

Harry Kalas, a blonde with a crew cut and new driver's license, wanted a date.

Carol was surprised. Harry had never shown interest before, but he seemed like a sweet guy. They'd known each other for a year, ever since Carol's family moved into the school district. Right away, Carol knew Harry wasn't her type. He was only 5-foot-4, her height. They had common friends, but Harry had a reputation for being a bit of a wild child. He was one of the guys who went outside during lunch to puff on cigarettes standing around his car.

But Carol always knew Harry to be a fun guy, and more importantly, a good guy. Plus, she had no weekend plans. Harry had his first date for the 1952-53 school year. He planned to borrow his father's car and take her to a drive-in movie in Aurora, Ill., which was just a short drive from his home in Naperville.

When Carol got home from school, she mentioned her date. Her mother wasn't thrilled. First, she wasn't happy that it wasn't a double date. And she wasn't happy that her date was with Harry Kalas.

"You better be careful," Carol recalled her mother warning her. "Harry's a preacher's son. They can be kind of aggressive."

Furthering his reputation, Harry picked up Carol in his father's black Packard, a vehicle his friends nicknamed "the pregnant elephant." At the drive-in, Harry was not well-behaved. Actually, he was rude. During their date, Harry watched the movie without saying a word to Carol. She wondered why he had bothered to ask her out, because it was obvious that he wasn't interested.

Eventually, Harry got bored with the movie, too. He started talking, but to himself. Out of the blue, Harry Kalas started announcing an imaginary baseball game involving his favorite baseball team, the Washington Senators. He had the pitcher winding up and throwing 2-2 fastballs that were driven into the gap for extra bases. This bizarre behavior went on and on.

"I know he's not asking me out again," Carol told herself. Another thought crossed her mind in the midst of the most wacky date that she'd ever have. Carol couldn't help but notice that Harry's broadcast skills were pretty good. When she got home, Carol went straight to her mother.

"Mom, you had nothing to worry about. There were no problems."

Carol rebounded from the strange night. Within a year, she was dating one of Harry's friends, a future attorney. In 2008, Gib and Carol Oswald Drendel celebrated their 50th wedding anniversary.

As for Harry, broadcasting baseball was his destiny.

Harry Norbert Kalas was born in Chicago at Grant Park Community Hospital on March 26, 1936, a Thursday. It was spring, the season Harry would most love as an adult. Spring for Harry always meant one thing: another baseball season was approaching.

Within a few months, a family move had little Harry living just three blocks from Wrigley Field, home of the Chicago Cubs. In March of 1936, there was plenty of optimism on the North Side of Chicago because the Cubs were the reigning National League champs. Maybe this would be the year they'd go all way for the first time since 1908. Then again, maybe not.

Although Reverend Harry H. Kalas, young Harry's father, was a baseball fan, his two biggest passions were serving God and providing for his family.

Born on an Iowa farm in 1903, Harry H., was serious enough about religion that he made it his livelihood, just like his father before him, Reverend Henry Kalas. When young Harry came into the world in 1936, his father was pastor of Trinity Evangelical Church in downtown Chicago. Little Harry was given his father's first name, but he wasn't a junior. Instead, he was given a middle name that belonged to an early 12th century saint, Norbert, a miracle worker and champion of the poor.

Later in life, Harry Norbert Kalas would joke about being named for a saint because, as he'd told his second wife, "I'm no angel." For years, he was a boozer and he'd left one wife to take another. Young Harry would opt for a different path in life than his father and grandfather, but ironically would do so much good that many people believed him to be saint-like. He certainly was given that sort of sendoff of one by his adopted hometown of Philadelphia when he died at age 73 in 2009.

Reverend Harry H. Kalas, young Harry's father, graduated from Westmar College in Iowa in 1925, then continued his education by receiving a Bachelor's Degree from Evangelical Theological Seminary in 1930. A month after his commencement, he married an Oxford, Mich., girl who was two years younger than he. Margaret Poole was a college graduate, too—a rare accomplishment for women in the 1920s.

The young couple found a home in Naperville when Reverend Kalas was hired to teach in the seminary affiliated with North Central College. On May 24, 1933, Margaret gave birth to the first of her two sons, John W. Kalas, who would be called Jim. The Kalas family moved to downtown Chicago in 1934 when Reverend Kalas took the pastor job at Trinity of Evangelical Church. They were still there when young Harry came along two years later to complete their family.

In so many ways, it was a different world in 1936. According to Nostalgia News Report, the average income for an American when Harry Kalas was born was $1,713. It cost $780 for a new car, $3,925 for a new house and 10 cents for a gallon of gas. Life expectancy was 59.7 years.

The world was at peace in 1936, but not for long. World War II would start in September 1939. In 1936, Hitler's Germany already was arresting Jews and Britain started manufacturing gas masks for all citizens. In America, President Franklin Delano Roosevelt was elected for a second term, the Oakland Bay

Bridge opened, and Bruno Hauptmann was put to death for the kidnapping and murder of the Lindbergh baby.

As an infant, Harry Kalas had a full head of thick blonde hair. He would be on the move a lot due to his father's ministry work. By the time he was 13, young Harry had lived in six homes and three states.

The merry-go-round began when Harry was just a few months old. The first relocation was from downtown Chicago to the North Side of the city—near Wrigley Field—when his father decided to further his education. Reverend Kalas left his pastoral position, landed a part-time job working for the Chicago Church Federation and enrolled in graduate school at Northwestern University. The family moved to Elgin, Ill., then back to Naperville, then to Des Moines, Iowa before returning to Naperville again, this time staying for eight years while Reverend Kalas worked for the World Council of Churches.

"My parents were well-liked wherever they went," Jim Kalas said. "My father was considered a bright young comer as a minister, and that's why we moved around so much. The church kept moving him to bigger jobs."

Naperville was just over a century old when the Kalas family settled there. Joseph Naper and his family were the first settlers to arrive at the wide banks of the DuPage River in July 1831. The founder named the area Naper's Settlement, which evolved into the Village of Naperville in 1857 and then into the city of Naperville in 1890.

When returning to Naperville in 1948, the Kalas' rented a two-story house on 153 North Julian Street, in a part of town that locals would call Old Naperville a half-century later. The red brick home had steps leading to a big front porch with a roof that was held up by thick pillars.

The Kalases were a middle-class family. They always had a roof over their heads, clothes on their backs and enough food in their stomachs. But they certainly didn't live lavishly. The family didn't have a television set until Harry was in middle school.

The family of four occasionally grew by one whenever Grandma Poole, Harry's maternal grandmother, would move in for several months at a time. She had become a widow and lost one of her five children as a fairly young woman. With her husband gone and surviving children grown, she decided to spend the rest of her life helping to raise her grandchildren, moving every few months from one of her children's homes to another.

Even after moving back to Naperville for a third time, Harry's father often was out of town for the World Council of Churches, so his boys didn't have as much father-son bonding time as they'd have liked. Reverend Kalas was all over the country for meetings to organize churches in cities such as Tulsa, Minneapolis and Detroit. Reverend Kalas was a workaholic, just as both of his boys would grow to become.

When home, Reverend Kalas was a good role model. Not only did he teach his boys right from wrong, he also instructed them to get along with people no matter their race, education, religion or economic status. Harry took these lessons to heart at a young age, then lived them his entire life. Reverend Kalas was a closet smoker and would have a few drinks on the road, but wouldn't dare do so in front of his boys or wife. He had a minister's reputation to live up to, even in his own home.

"My dad was always a people person," Harry said late in life. "I think I got some of that from him."

In time, Harry would get another gift from his father. When Reverend Kalas spoke, he did so with a deep baritone voice. As adults, both of his boys, especially Harry, would talk in a similar manner.

During the first of his two marriages, Harry filled out a child-rearing questionnaire that later was placed in a family scrapbook. It listed the few household rules he had to abide by during his childhood: pick up his clothes, and be home and in bed by a designated time. He said there wasn't much discipline. "Probably could have used more," he wrote. For inherited traits, he credited his father for his "voice and speaking ability" and "relationships with humans of all races."

But Harry's brother Jim says that Reverend Kalas could be strict about certain things. He said their father insisted his sons pray before every meal and attend every Sunday mass, whether or not Reverend Kalas was giving the sermon. The family would make two or three summer trips to Chicago for Cubs or White Sox games, but never on Sundays. In the Kalas household, Sunday was a day to worship God.

"Well, we sort of had to be religious," Jim Kalas said. "My dad was a minister. It was a matter of coercion. In those days, the church rules were you don't play around on Sunday. We could listen to the baseball games on the radio and do things around the house, but we couldn't go to the movies, we couldn't go to a baseball game. I never went to an NFL game until I was on my own."

A stay-at-home mom, Margaret Kalas enjoyed reading. Her kids loved her stew and banana bread. Margaret's passion was classical music. The record player in the Kalas living room played virtually nonstop. A lover of Beethoven, Margaret would pick up and head to the Chicago Symphony Orchestra every chance that she could. Often, she'd force one of her boys to tag along. Many of her friends were classical music lovers, too, and the women would gather at each other's homes to listen to records. Jim Kalas believed classical music was his mother's social outlet.

When Harry was disciplined, it usually came from his mother, who would take away privileges as punishment. But she wasn't that strict. Of course, she probably didn't know that by the time Harry reached high school he already was drinking and smoking.

Harry and Jim didn't revere their mother like they did their father, but they loved her. Margaret was more reserved than her husband and boys, but like the rest of her family, she was kind and giving. When her husband was on the road for work, which was often, Margaret stayed busy with church friends.

Harry's life began to change in grade school when his mother started to suffer from severe depression. Her personality changed from kind and friendly to moody and distant. Over the years, Harry speculated that his mother's illness may have been caused by loneliness due to his father's long absences.

Margaret Kalas' illness led to one of her youngest son's greatest childhood disappointments, the devastating loss of Harry's first pet. Harry was nine years old when his father brought home a fox terrier named Squiffy. Harry and his pet were inseparable for a year. When Harry walked four blocks to Ellsworth Elementary School, Squiffy often followed him there before turning around and finding his way home.

During her illness, for no apparent reason, Harry's mother decided Squiffy had to go. The dog was given away to a family that lived across a highway from his school, and Harry was furious. Once separated, the boy and his dog continued to meet up. When Harry walked out of school, Squiffy was there waiting. Harry would be followed all the way home, then his father would drive Squiffy back to its new owners. This went on for three weeks, then ended tragically. One day, Squiffy was hit by a car and killed crossing the highway that led to Harry's school.

"That broke my heart," Harry said.

This boy-and-his-dog relationship foreshadowed the social life of the adult Harry Kalas, who was a loving and loyal friend to so many. As for losing Squiffy, Harry never got over the hurt of having to give his pet away. Even late in life, he occasionally brought up Squiffy to his second wife, Eileen.

Forcing Harry to get rid of Squiffy may have been one indication that his mother needed professional help to treat her depression.

Eventually, Margaret Kalas was sent to Chicago for electroshock treatments. She routinely would go two or three times a month for treatment that was both painful and had serious side effects, such as short- and long-term memory loss. When home, Reverend Kalas took his wife to Chicago for her appointments, but he often was on the road for his church work. As a result, after turning 15, Jim Kalas received special permission to get a driver's license a year early so that he could chauffeur his mother to and from the hospital when his father couldn't.

Jim Kalas, who would go on to become a college professor, still has a hard time 60 years later talking about what his mother endured. He never got over the bitterness that came from doctors responding to his mother's depression in a manner that he believed was inhumane. His mother was "cured" in a year, but according to Jim Kalas, "her mind was never the same."

During his mother's illness, Harry was sent to Detroit at age 12 to live with his mother's sister and her husband, Florence and Hugh Sizemore. While this probably would be a traumatic move for many children, it was not for Harry. He adored his aunt and uncle, with whom he had spent family vacations in Detroit. Harry also got along great with his two cousins. For Harry, one of the best parts of living in Michigan was that his Uncle Hugh was a huge Detroit Tigers fan. That baseball season, Harry was a frequent visitor to Tiger Stadium.

After one year in Detroit, with his mother improving, Harry returned home to Naperville.

Back home, Harry tried focusing on another of his childhood loves, baseball. Most sports fans in and around Naperville pulled for just one of Chicago's two baseball teams, either the Cubs or the White Sox. Reverend Kalas and his oldest son, Jim, were in a minority and rooted for both teams.

Harry, on the other hand, was a fan of the Washington Senators—perennial losers from a time zone away to the East—because he'd never forgotten his first big-league game.

"Harry was crazy about baseball and talked about the Washington Senators all the time," childhood friend Gib Drendel said.

In 1946, shortly before the family moved from Naperville for a two-year stay in Des Moines, Iowa, Reverend Kalas took his boys to Comiskey Park for a White Sox–Senators game. A late-morning shower kept a lot of fans away from the ballpark, but benefited Harry. His father purchased seats next to the Senators' dugout. It was still drizzling when Reverend Kalas and his sons entered the ballpark. Batting practice was rained out, so they sat waiting for the weather to clear, as did the players in both dugouts.

That day, Harry developed a love for baseball when his heart was touched forever by Senators first baseman Mickey Vernon, a seven-time All-Star and two-time American League batting champion.

"Now, here's this wide-eyed kid sitting behind the Senators dugout with my dad, taking it all in, and some of the players came out into the dugout," Harry recalled. "Mickey Vernon was one of them. He popped his head out of the dugout and saw me sitting there. Well, he reached over and picked me up, and took me into the dugout. He gave me a ball and introduced me to some of the other players. I was just in heaven. I was there for about 10 minutes, then he put me back in my seat. That really started my love for the game of baseball and the Washington Senators. My classmates always teased me about being a Senators fan, but it was all because of Mickey Vernon."

Besides getting a new favorite player and team that day, Harry never forgot how someone famous could leave a lasting impression by doing a good deed. Later in life, after Harry had become a celebrity himself, he did the same time and again for his legions of fans in Philadelphia. Meeting Mickey Vernon was a lesson that he took to heart.

Throughout life, Harry told his Mickey Vernon story hundreds of times. Perhaps it was fate, but Harry and Mickey reconnected a quarter-century later and became close. Harry couldn't wait to thank Mickey for his greatest childhood thrill.

Incredibly, they'd spend the last four decades of their lives within a few miles of one another in Media, a suburb of Philadelphia. They kept in touch regularly, by phone and in person. Mickey drove to Cooperstown, N.Y., for

Harry's 2002 Baseball Hall of Fame induction. Harry attended Mickey's funeral in September 2008. Seven months after Mickey died, Harry was dead, too. As fate would have it, on the day of Harry's memorial at Citizens Bank Park, he was supposed to be in Marcus Hook, Pa., speaking at the dedication of Mickey Vernon Boulevard.

"Harry never forgot what Mickey had done," said Rich Westcott, a Phillies historian and author of a book on Vernon. "He told that story about every three days of his life. It was a very meaningful story to both Harry and Mickey."

After first meeting Vernon in 1946, Harry became obsessed with sports, baseball in particular. He played a lot of pickup games with his buddies and often played catch with himself by throwing a tennis ball off the side of the family home.

At age 10, Harry received a board game as a gift, one that would consume him through his early teenage years. In "All-Star Baseball," designed by former major league outfielder Ethan Allen, outcomes of plays are determined with a spinner and discs representing the hitting skills of real-life players. The discs are divided into pie slices numbered 1-to-14, with 1 being a homer. The better home run hitters had a bigger home run area on their discs.

Kalas considered All-Star Baseball the best toy he ever had. "Even as a kid, I'd announce games to myself with that baseball board game," he once said.

For sure, Harry was serious about his board baseball games. He made up teams, kept score with handmade scorecards, updated team standings and tallied players' statistics—at-bats, runs, hits, homers, RBI and batting averages.

"That's one vivid memory that I have," Jim Kalas said many years later. "He played on the carpet in the living room, and took up two-thirds of it. He'd be keeping records and announcing. He wanted to know the batting averages. Harry was like this his whole life. Even in his later years broadcasting Phillies games, Harry was very serious about preparation, details and statistics. That started very early with Harry."

In the last years of his life, Harry was brought to tears when he received as a Christmas gift a beautifully framed vintage 1944 version of All-Star Baseball. Eileen Kalas, Harry's second wife, had spread out the box, playing field, spinner and player discs in a large glass case.

"As soon as Harry saw that, he turned into a little boy," Eileen said. "He was explaining everything to me, saying, '1 is a home run, 2 is a walk.'"

Growing up, Harry usually played alone. He and his older brother got along, but there were age and personality differences. Harry, who was three years younger, sometimes would become frustrated trying to keep up with Jim, who was a better student and considered more disciplined.

"Jim was quite different from Harry," said Wally Baumgartner, Harry's Naperville classmate. "Jim was straight-laced and Harry was a man of the world. But, scholastically, Harry never had a problem in school. He was, I'd say, in the upper 10-15 percent in our class of 113."

Despite their differences, Harry and Jim always stayed in touch. Late in life, the brothers bonded better than they ever had.

"We weren't that close as kids," said Jim Kalas, a college professor who was still teaching education courses at SUNY Albany in 2009. "We sort of went our own directions. As years went on, we drew closer and closer. We talked every couple of weeks."

An A student, Jim Kalas was voted the president of his high school senior class in 1951. Harry was bright, but didn't work as hard as his brother. He still earned mostly Bs on his report cards.

"He could have been a better student," Jim said. "He was a bright guy, but didn't knock himself out."

Harry always was too busy having fun. After Friday night football games, Harry and his high school pals would meet up at one of their friends' farms to get drunk. One time after a night of heavy boozing, classmate Gib Drendel drove Harry home. Before Harry got out of the car, Gib joked that Harry would never make it from the car to his house without falling. Harry staggered his way to the front door, then fell flat on his face.

"Harry did a lot of things that his father didn't know about," Drendel said. "He liked to have a good time."

By high school, Harry was buying cigarettes for 25 cents a pack. Most of his crowd took up smoking as teenagers. Harry thought he was cool with a smoke in his hand and quickly became addicted.

When Harry started driving at age 16, he often was permitted to use his father's car. What Reverend Kalas didn't know was that Harry and his buddies often were cruising around Naperville and nearby towns downing six packs, which didn't hold the same stigma back then as it would in years to come.

Harry played a lot of sports as a kid—baseball, basketball and football, whatever was in season—but according to the people who knew him, he was drinking so much beer that he started putting on weight. He'd eventually grow to 5-foot-10, but was short in high school, maybe 5-foot-6 upon graduation. He was the second-shortest student in his junior-class play, only taller than one of the six girls among a cast of 19.

By his senior year, Harry had developed a bit of a "beer belly," causing his buddies to call him Potsie, or Pots for short.

Harry was very particular about how he dressed and the way he wore his hair. He rolled up his jeans to be cool and had a crew cut that he kept carefully combed.

"Back then, haircuts were whitewall sides, flattops, crew cuts, but Harry always had a crew cut where he'd comb his hair forward," childhood friend Charles "Whitey" Kilb said. "Harry always tried to get a flattop, but it never worked out. He'd comb it forward, then up in the front and it would turn into a ski jump. Every time he went to our barber, Earl would say, 'You're going to have to work on it.' Harry would say, 'Oh well, just make it a ski jump.'"

Harry began his freshman year at Naperville Community High in the fall of 1950. Naperville Community High opened in 1863, and would be renamed Naperville Central in 1970 when the city grew to the point that it needed a second high school, Naperville North. Nequa Valley became the city's third high school in 1997.

Besides Harry Kalas, his alma mater has quite a few famous alumni. The class of 1974 included ESPN anchor Gary Miller and CNN newscaster Paula Zahn. New Orleans Saints coach Sean Payton and *Sex and the City* actor David Eigenberg are 1982 graduates. Other notable grads include World Bank President Robert Zoellick (1971), Hootie & the Blowfish drummer Jim Sonefeld (1983), former NBA player Anthony Parker (1993), NFL tight end Owen Daniels (2003), WNBA star Candace Parker (2004) and former United States Army Major Sudip Bose (1992), the Iraq war physician who treated Saddam Hussein after his December 2003 capture.

Naperville teenagers didn't have many options for fun in the 1950s. Most activities were on the city's two main intersecting streets, Jefferson and Washington. Harry could walk there, as his house was just eight blocks away.

A few blocks away on West Jackson, Harry used to go to Centennial Pool, an old quarry made into a public swimming hole that everyone called "The Beach." It was open from June 1 until Labor Day and filled every sunny day with kids, many of whom got free season passes by showing their parents' electric bill as proof that they lived in Naperville. Surrounding the pool was a grassy park that was used for touch football games. Harry and his buddy Wally Baumgartner were at "The Beach" practically every summer day during their high school years.

On Thursday nights, the gang would stop at Dick's Popcorn Stand, then head to Centennial Park for the Naperville Municipal Band concerts. Harry also hung out at Prince Castle, a popular ice cream store on Washington. You could get a burger and fries there, too, and the popular soft drink was Green Rivers, a lime-like beverage. Teens would loiter at Prince Castle much in the way Richie Cunningham and the Fonz did at Arnold's in *Happy Days*, the popular 1970s television show. On Saturday afternoons, Harry and his pals would go to the Naper Theater, usually for a Western preceded by a 20-minute serial.

"There wasn't much to do hanging out in Naperville," Jim Kalas said. "Once we got our driver's licenses, we'd drive around this square in Naperville 25 times and go home. That's what you did on weekends. We were looking for action. There never was any. There wasn't much there."

To pass time, Harry amused himself by pretending he was a major league broadcaster. Sometimes he'd do it alone, other times while hanging out with buddies. In his high school World History class, Harry could get away with mischief because his teacher didn't hear well. He'd entertain everyone by cupping his hands around his mouth and doing play-by-play for a make-believe Washington Senators baseball game.

Mickey Vernon was Harry's favorite player, but he loved the way the name of Senators' pitcher Camilo Pascual rolled off his tongue—just as later in life when, as an announcer, he would relish saying the names of Philadelphia Phillies like Mickey Morandini, Ricky Bottalico, Michael Jack Schmidt and Juan Samuel.

"Indications of Harry's desire and dreams were evident early," classmate Charley "Whitey" Kilb said. "We used to congregate in a couple of basements where there was a poker table where we'd play Pitch, a Midwestern card game. My father had a table and we'd sit down there and play, and one night my father came down and asked each of us what we planned to do with our lives.

Harry said, 'I want to be another Jack Brickhouse.' At the time Jack was a great announcer for the Cubs. My father looked at Harry and said, 'That's great. I wish you luck. And I expect free tickets.'"

Nobody really believed Harry would make it big.

His friends brushed off Harry's broadcast talk and frequent fake baseball calls as Harry being Harry. But like Carol Oswald on her one date with Harry, they noticed that his words seemed to flow well from the strong pipes inherited from his father.

"Everybody always said he had an outstanding voice," classmate Wally Baumgartner said.

Fueling Harry's fire were the many afternoons and nights he had spent listening to baseball on the radio. The three closest major league teams to Naperville all had future Hall of Famers calling the action—Harry Caray and Jack Buck for the St. Louis Cardinals, Jack Brickhouse for the Chicago Cubs, and Bob Elson for the Chicago White Sox.

Harry wasn't thinking about baseball, however, when he talked classmate Whitey Kilb into going to a drive-in movie in 1954. Harry wanted to see *River of No Return* because he'd heard Marilyn Monroe had a topless scene.

Harry never had a steady girlfriend in high school. He didn't even do much dating, which surprised some friends he'd make later in life who saw the way Harry connected with women. As a teen, Harry was more into his buddies, sports and drinking beer. Another favorite pastime was after-school poker games. There were two Drendels in Harry's class—cousins Gene and Gib. Harry was closer to Gene, who hosted these poker games. Playing for nickels and dimes, big winners might take home a buck.

Harry's biggest high school crush was on his favorite teacher, Miss Anderson. Jeneinne Anderson Warnell—Miss Anderson at the time—graduated from Knox College in the spring of 1952 and started teaching sophomore English and ninth grade Social Studies at Naperville that fall. The next year, Harry was in her senior Communications class. Miss Anderson had short brown hair, an oval face, a big smile and a charming personality. She also was single, and at age 22, only five or six years older than her students. Harry absolutely adored her.

"He didn't flirt, but he would blush," said Jeneinne Anderson Warnell, who taught for 37 years before retiring in 1991.

After Harry's 2009 death, his former teacher got a kick out of hearing that Harry's wives even knew of his high school crush.

"I can't believe Harry told them," she said with a giggle.

During high school, Harry continued to think about his future. He loved sports, but realized he wasn't going to make a living as a player. "I thought of becoming a sports announcer, specifically a baseball announcer," Harry once said.

When Harry mentioned this to Miss Anderson, she was supportive, in part because she noticed her student's developing baritone voice and sincere ambition. "I think you can do it," she told Harry.

Harry gave some impressive speeches in his Communications class, but sometimes would struggle with his nerves.

"When Harry would give his speeches, I would be sitting at the desk and I could see how nervous he was," his teacher recalled many years later. "He was always twisting his hands. The audience never was aware of it, but he was nervous standing behind the speaker stand. He was very determined to be perfect, and he always had that beautiful voice."

Late in his senior year, Harry approached Miss Anderson after class.

"My parents would like to have you over for dinner," Harry told his teacher.

It was not uncommon in that era for students to invite their teachers home for dinner. Without hesitation, Miss Anderson accepted.

A year later, Harry was in college and Miss Anderson became Mrs. Warnell. But Harry never forgot his high school speech teacher, whom he called "a great lady." After he'd made it big as a broadcaster, he would send his former teacher a Christmas card and hand-written letter every year. When Harry was in Chicago with the Phillies, he frequently phoned her to catch up. And without exception, Harry always mentioned Jeneinne Anderson Warnell as one of the big influences on his career.

"I really didn't feel that I was, but he seemed to think so," his teacher recalled. "I always encouraged him, because I thought he was very talented. I knew he was going to be important someday."

Harry was a member of his high school drama club. As a junior, he wore a beret while acting in *Junior Miss*. During his senior year, Miss Anderson ran the club. For his senior play, Harry was coaxed into dressing in drag for the lead in *Charley's Aunt*, a three-act play performed April 2-3, 1954, at the Washington School Auditorium.

Anything for Miss Anderson.

Harry played Lord Fancourt Babberly, a young man who masqueraded as Charley's aunt, and he took his role seriously. "I can still see Harry in that long black dress and wig," Jeneinne Anderson Warnell remembered almost 55 years later. "He even changed his voice a little bit to try sounding like a woman. He was just marvelous in the part and so funny. He had a wonderful sense of humor. Harry's friend, Dave Hoods, was ad-libbing a lot and there were a couple teachers that were rather upset, but Harry always knew his lines."

Jim Kalas recalls his brother's performance. "I remember Harry being good. He had emotion in his voice, even then."

Besides joining the drama club, Harry was active in many high school activities. He wrote sports articles for the school's weekly newspaper and participated in several clubs—Student Council, Future Teachers of America, Science, Journalism and Spanish.

As a teen, Harry continued to make time for playing sports year round. Depending on the season, he spent a lot of time playing baseball, football and basketball. If a game broke out in someone's backyard, a neighborhood field or basketball court, Harry usually was there. He played to win and enjoyed the competition, but the camaraderie with his buddies was what he liked best.

Harry played three years of varsity football and two years of baseball, but didn't see much playing time. During Harry's senior year, Dick Haas was the school's star jock. He was the starting quarterback on the football team, the top pitcher on the baseball team and a starter in basketball. Haas also was a nephew to the town's biggest celebrity at the time, former big-leaguer Bert Haas, who played nine seasons in the majors and was an All-Star first baseman for the Cincinnati Reds in 1947. Anytime Bert was around, everybody was excited, especially baseball-crazy Harry Kalas.

Although cut by the varsity basketball team—Harry was short and lacked quickness—he would play intramural games at the high school on weeknights. Harry played a lot of basketball and had a pretty good two-handed set shot. Sometimes enough kids showed up to make four teams. Harry was known as a gunner, but he sometimes would put on showy displays.

"Harry was a very skilled basketball player, a very good shot," Gib Drendel said. "In intramurals, he was the best player in school."

"He stunk!" Wally Baumgartner joked. "Harry had a good shot, but his motto was 'Give me the ball and I'll shoot it.' And he wouldn't get underneath the hoop and rebound. He didn't want to get hurt."

On the varsity football team, Harry was an undersized, backup linebacker for coach Wes Spencer, but never shied away from contact when seeing action.

"I was a defensive end who played right in front of Harry, and if somebody came our way he would hit him," Baumgartner said. "He wasn't very good, but he played because Naperville was noted as a football town. Back when we were we young, Naperville was a town of 5,000 as opposed to 170,000 like it is now, and you played football."

Harry signed up because many of his buddies were on the team. Charles Kilb, Dick Haas, Gib Drendel and Wally Baumgartner played; Gene Drendel was the team manager. His senior year, Harry was one of 44 players and wore No. 28 for a squad that won six of its eight games. After victories, students would celebrate by driving through town honking their horns, usually with beer in the car.

A weak-hitting, decent-fielding third baseman, Harry didn't do much in baseball, either. It was obvious even then that Harry's best athletic skill was his voice.

"Harry wasn't obsessed with playing any sport," Wally Baumgartner noted. "He always wanted to be a baseball announcer."

On June 3, 1954, Harry Kalas graduated from Naperville Community High School. Reverend and Margaret Kalas were proud parents witnessing the commencement at the school's new auditorium, Barbara Pfeiffer Memorial Hall.

Harry Kalas didn't do everything by the book while growing up, but he always had a big-league dream, a God-given gift and as much determination to make something of his life as anyone in his class of 113.

In the 1954 Naperville High School yearbook, underneath his name, Harry Kalas predicted his career path in three words—"Future Sports Announcer."

THE EDUCATION OF HARRY

World War II had turned in America's favor. The Allied forces landed in Normandy on June 6, 1944, then pushed their way through northeastern France and headed for Germany. Hitler's troops were in retreat. His plan of taking over Europe was dying when German military leaders devised a last-ditch strategy to win the war: a massive counter-offensive against 500,000 American soldiers and 55,000 British troops who were stretched out for hundreds of miles across the forested, snow-covered Ardennes Mountains in Belgium, France and Luxembourg.

At 5 a.m., on December 16, 1944, the Germans launched a sneak attack in the middle of the Allies' line of advance, an offensive that would become known as the Battle of the Bulge. Nine months before officially winning World War II in September 1945, the Allies were victorious in the Battle of the Bulge, but not before suffering 80,987 casualties, most in the first three days. In the first month of the Battle of the Bulge, a missile from a German tank struck a tree. Branches and splinters flew in all directions. A 25-year-old U.S. soldier serving with the 87th Infantry Division near Bastogne, Belgium was struck in the eyes. The soldier, a radio technician who was afraid of the dark as a child, escaped with his life but lost his eyesight.

A decade later, Walt Stromer, the blinded soldier, would help steer a college freshman with a great voice into a career in broadcasting. After the war, Stromer became a speech professor at Cornell College, a small Methodist-run institution in Mt. Vernon, Iowa. Dr. Stromer was 34 years old when Harry Kalas walked into his Armstrong Hall classroom for the first time.

When Kalas spoke up, Dr. Stromer recognized right away that he was in the presence of a student with a gift.

"You have the kind of voice that can make it in radio and television," Dr. Stromer told Harry. "Son, you've got to become an announcer."

In the classroom, Dr. Stromer listened to Harry's speeches, working with him on tone, inflection and pronunciation. In the second semester of his freshman year, encouraged to gain radio experience, Harry landed his first job as a part-time disc jockey for WPIG in Cedar Rapids, Iowa, a small station that was an 18-mile drive from campus. Dr. Stromer often listened, so that he could critique Harry.

Dr. Stromer probably had more influence on Harry's career than even Miss Anderson, the high school speech teacher on whom he had a crush. Stromer knew exactly how to make a good voice sound even better. He couldn't see, but his hearing, instincts, intelligence and charming personality made him very popular with students.

"This blind man taught the rest of us how to see," Reverend Catherine Quehl-Engel, Cornell's chaplain, wrote two weeks after Stromer's 2005 death.

Harry's relationship with Dr. Stromer went well beyond the classroom. Having a great fondness for one another, they became friends.

"Harry used to say Dr. Stromer wasn't very good at gestures, but was wonderful with voice," said Jim Kalas, Harry's older brother. "He was the guy who really did develop Harry's voice. The quality of his voice at the end of that first year of college was remarkably different."

Dr. Stromer's influence was all accomplished in that one school year. Unfortunately, Harry had a little too much fun outside the classroom during his freshman year. And, since Cornell College had strict rules that apparently Harry didn't follow too well, he didn't return for his sophomore year at the suggestion of school officials.

Harry wasn't all that interested in attending Cornell College in the first place, but his father was an alumnus and the tuition was affordable, so off Harry went without much of a say. Reverend Kalas figured the discipline that Cornell required of its students would be good for Harry, too. But early on, it became apparent that Cornell College wasn't the best fit for Harry.

At Cornell, Harry spent a lot of time focusing on his social life. He hung out with his buddies, drank beer, wreaked some havoc and pretty much ignored his schoolwork. His grades were poor and his behavior, based on Cornell standards, was worse. Once around midnight, Harry was discovered on a third-floor fire escape in a girls' dormitory, more than three hours after curfew. He was suspended for two weeks. Later in the school year, Harry and a friend were caught setting off fireworks in a dorm room wastebasket.

Harry's conduct at Cornell disappointed his parents, but his work at the campus station and with Dr. Stromer convinced them that he deserved a second chance at college. The next year, they sent him to the University of Iowa, which was just 20 miles south of Cornell College in Iowa City. Known as one of the top broadcasting schools in the country, the University of Iowa turned out to be a much better fit for Harry.

"I wanted to call baseball games, so that was all the encouragement I needed," Harry said in a 2004 interview.

When Harry enrolled at Iowa, he already was on the "five-year plan" to get through college due to his poor grades at Cornell. While his official major was Speech & Dramatic Arts, many who knew him at the time suggest that it might as well have been "partying."

"By his senior year, they were ready to throw Harry out of Iowa, too," joked high school pal Gib Drendel, who also was with Harry at Cornell.

Although alcohol was banned on Iowa's campus, Harry purchased beer during his first year there from a buddy who sold six packs out of his dorm room. "Harry was one of my best customers," college friend John Bouma said.

Harry loved his University of Iowa years, and throughout life followed the Hawkeyes football team. In his later years, Harry frequently would pop into a baseball press box between innings to ask a sports writer for an Iowa football score. If the Hawkeyes were winning, he'd usually nod in approval, then break into a few bars of the "Iowa Fight Song"—"The word is fight, fight, fight for Iowa, let every loyal Iowan sing. The word is fight, fight, fight for Iowa, until the walls and rafters ring. Go Hawks!"

His first year at Iowa, Harry landed work at the campus radio station. WSUI aired some of the best college football and basketball in the country with the Hawkeyes competing in the Big Ten Conference. But before working his way up to the good assignments, Harry's frequent partying got in the way of his career path again. One morning after a night of drinking, he failed to make it out of bed in time for an early shift at WSUI. Harry was fired.

"Harry had trouble getting up in the morning, and one of the reasons is because he was spending so much time at The Airliner in the evening," Bouma said.

The Airliner is a food and drink establishment in Iowa City that has been a popular hangout for Iowa students since it opened in 1944. During school months, students day and night pack the place, which is located on South Clinton, right across the street from central campus. In the mid-50s, the drinking age in Iowa was 18, so most students were legal when starting college. Harry spent a lot of weekend and school nights at The Airliner. One year, he even worked there as a cook. He'd put in his hours, then after his shift head to the bar and blow his earnings on beer.

There never was a shortage of alcohol in Harry's final three years at Iowa, which he spent living in the Phi Delta Theta house.

"Have you ever seen the movie *Animal House*?" Harry's fraternity brother Phil Lainson said. "We had some wild times there."

Harry and Lainson were pledges together in the fall of 1955. Before being initiated on March 25, 1956, they endured hazing so humiliating that one of Harry's frat brothers had difficulty talking about it even 50 years later. The hazing, an initiation period for new fraternity recruits, is known as Hell Week. Phi Delts' hazing presently is less severe, but University of Iowa upperclassmen had free reign in the 1950s to deal out punishment that was painful and degrading. One Phi Delt ritual forced recruits to walk around campus and attend classes wearing a sign, held by string and tied around their privates, reading "I'm a Jerk-Off." Another demeaning act was forcing pledges to use their behinds to retrieve olives off the floor and then crawl across a room. The most common form of hazing involved severe paddling.

"Guys boarded you in the ass as hard as they could and as often as they wanted," said Randy Duncan, a frat brother of Harry's who also was the star quarterback on the Iowa football team. "Some guys had blood in their shorts."

The next year, the punished became the punishers. Harry received his share of hazing as a pledge, but always took it easy on recruits when he had the opportunity to deal out punishment. That's the way he was all through life. He never wanted to hurt anyone, even the few people in his life that weren't good to him.

The Phi Delt house, a mansion with an ivy-covered front, was built in 1923 and sits on the banks of the Iowa River. In 1956, Harry's first year with the fraternity, he was one of 74 Phi Delts, two-thirds of whom were housemates. Harry's frat brothers called him the White Rat. He was a blonde with a crew cut, and his face would turn pink when he was out in the sun too long. "He looked just like a rat," Duncan said.

One day, Harry received a surprise visit from his father. Welcomed at the front door by one of Harry's housemates, Reverend Harry H. Kalas was led to his son, who was in a room sitting next to a three-foot-high pyramid of empty beer cans. Reverend Kalas never uttered a word about it, but Harry was beyond embarrassed. Harry never wanted to let down his father, whom he revered.

During college, Harry found his first real girlfriend, who was, surprisingly, a divorced woman with two children. The relationship got serious enough that they discussed marriage. But everything changed when Harry told his father about her. Thinking that Harry dating a divorced woman with children would embarrass the family, Reverend Kalas expressed his disapproval, which in turn, led Harry to break up with the woman. Harry was in love, but he wasn't going to go forward with the relationship without his father's approval.

In his senior year at Iowa, Harry was chapter president of the Phi Delts, and after leaving school, Harry stayed active in the fraternity for the rest of his life. For years, he served on a committee that selected candidates for and voted on the prestigious Lou Gehrig Memorial Award, named for one of the most famous Phi Delts. In 1955, Grantland Rice, a famous sports writer and 1897 Vanderbilt University Phi Delt, helped create the award. It is annually given to the major leaguer who best exemplifies the character and integrity on and off the field of Gehrig, the New York Yankees Hall of Famer and 1922-23 Columbia University Phi Delt. Gehrig died at age 39 in 1941 of ALS, now commonly known as Lou Gehrig's disease.

During Harry's years at Iowa, the most recognizable faces on campus were two of the nation's best football players—defensive tackle Alex Karras and quarterback Randy Duncan, both Heisman Trophy runners-up a year apart.

Football was king at Iowa when Harry was on campus. In his last three years there, the Hawkeyes won 24 games, lost 3 and tied 2 while winning two Big Ten titles and their first two Rose Bowl appearances. Through 2009, the school's only two Rose Bowl victories had come with Harry Kalas on campus.

The 1958 Hawkeyes, with a tie against Air Force and a loss to Ohio State as their only blemishes, were voted national champions by the Football Writers Association of America. They finished second to LSU in the more prestigious AP and UPI polls, both of which had their final vote before the bowl games.

"In my opinion, the 1958 team was the best Iowa ever had," said retired *Des Moines Register* sports writer Ron Maly, a classmate of Harry's at Iowa who covered Hawkeyes football from 1965 to 1995.

Harry called many football games for the campus radio station. Bob Brooks, a legendary University of Iowa football and basketball broadcaster who called games for 54 seasons, became a fan of Harry's. With the campus station airing football games on tape delay, Brooks often would listen to part of the replay to get a feel for how the college broadcasters were doing. Along with Milo Hamilton, a 1949 Iowa graduate who also would became a Baseball Hall of Fame broadcaster, Brooks was most impressed with Harry Kalas.

"Harry was a young, energetic play-by-play guy," Brooks recalled in 2009. "He was pretty much a natural. The command of his voice and his enthusiasm were the things that stood out. You knew that he was in love with what he was doing and he had his goal in mind. His goal was the major leagues."

More of an expert on baseball at the time, Harry began to get a greater understanding of football while doing a project on the sport for a Television class. He'd played in high school, but his responsibility as a backup linebacker basically was limited to tackling. Getting his hands on some Hawkeyes game film, Harry sought out Randy Duncan for help with the class assignment. At the campus radio station, the quarterback meticulously dissected plays to give Harry a feel for what it was like to be an offensive coordinator.

"Okay, it's third-and-eight; what do you do?" Harry asked.

Duncan picked a play and went over why it would work against a particular defense.

"I got an A on the project, thanks to Randy Duncan," Harry proudly boasted years later.

Duncan was selected first overall in the 1959 NFL Draft by the Green Bay Packers, but he didn't like their contract offer and instead signed to play in the Canadian Football League with the British Columbia Lions. After two years in Canada, Duncan played his final pro season in 1961 with the American Football League's Dallas Texans—a franchise which became the Kansas City Chiefs—while attending law school at night at Southern Methodist University. He never had the same success in pro football that he had in college, but he became a successful lawyer.

During his second year at Iowa, Harry was back at WSUI. Over the next three years, he put in a lot of hours and eventually landed the best job at the station: doing play-by-play for Iowa football and basketball. He also gained valuable experience calling other Iowa sports such as wrestling and swimming. Broadcasting baseball, football and basketball was easy for Kalas, but he struggled with the others.

"We had a microphone at every event they had," said Harry, who was promoted to sports director at WSUI for his senior year. "It was great experience."

In addition to his campus radio duties and his school work, Harry was kept busy calling high school basketball games on weekends for a radio station in Quad Cities, Iowa.

Before his second year at Iowa, his parents moved from Naperville to Le Mars, Iowa, when Reverend Kalas became president of Westmar University in 1956. But Harry wasn't home much. He spent one summer working at KDSN radio in Denison, Iowa, reading news and doing deejay work. Another summer, he had similar duties working at KPIG radio in Cedar Rapids, Iowa.

Harry further honed his skills by continuing to broadcast pretend baseball games, just as he had done in high school. He did it a lot, sometimes in front of buddies at the frat house, sometimes in a tavern. Nobody believed him when he declared that he'd someday be calling real major league games. "Oh yeah, Harry, and I want to be a player!" responded one of his housemates with amusement.

Meantime, Harry continued to party. No matter how focused he was on his school work and setting up his career, Harry always found time to head to the bars for good conversation and a good buzz. "Harry had a great time at Iowa," Duncan said. "He loved to drink beer."

John Bouma, who graduated from Iowa in 1958 with high honors, was one of Harry's brightest and closest college friends. Like Harry, he also enjoyed baseball and beer, which was a good mix in their eyes.

When at school during baseball season, Harry and John would occasionally spend a night boozing together at The Airliner, then grab a couple six packs at last call and drive all night to Chicago to watch the Cubs or White Sox play an afternoon game the next day. This was before the freeway was built linking Iowa City to Chicago, so they'd reach their destination around dawn, sleep in the car for a few hours and down beers through nine innings of baseball.

"I can remember being very sleepy at those games," said Bouma, who went on to practice law and become chairman of a 450-person firm in Scottsdale, Ariz. "One game went 15 or 16 innings and we fell asleep. We woke up and the game was still going on."

Another time, Harry and John drove to Chicago for a game that was rained out. They ended up spending the day at a racetrack betting on horses and, as usual, drinking beer.

Harry and Phil Lainson would drive 270 miles to St. Louis for a Cardinals baseball game, then head to the Illinois state border after the game to hit a casino. Ever since he'd played poker with buddies during his high school years, Harry loved to gamble. Coming up with enough money to lay bets sometimes was an issue for Harry. Although usually holding a job and getting a few bucks sent each month from home, Harry was always low on cash. What little he had, he used on cigarettes, beer and baseball games.

"He was the only guy I knew who would write a check for 50 cents," Randy Duncan said. "I'd say 'Harry? Geez.' He'd say, 'I don't have any money and I want to cover it.' He was always busted."

Harry and his buddies would do anything to save what little money they had for beer. After a night of drinking in 1957, Harry and Phil Lainson drove to Iowa State Penitentiary in Fort Madison, Iowa, for a free meal. Phil's grandfather, the prison warden, escorted them onto the grounds, then hooked them up with the same chow that the convicts ate.

During one of Harry and John Bouma's baseball road trips to Chicago, on their way home they stopped in Naperville around suppertime. Harry phoned some of his high school buddies. The plan was for everyone to get a bite to eat, and then drink some beer. When they realized money was short, they improvised in order to save their cash for alcohol. For food, they crashed a Polish wedding reception in Lisle, a small town about a mile east of Naperville. Wearing Bermuda shorts and T-shirts, Harry and four pals pretended they were invited guests. They wolfed down a good meal, drank a lot of beer and didn't spend a penny. All the while, the young men told everyone there how beautiful the bride looked.

The boys escaped without being caught, but Harry's mischief with Bouma caught up with them during their wild summer of 1956 in Colorado Springs.

Harry set up the trip after telling a buddy he called "Boomer" that he'd found work for them as waiters at The Broadmoor, a spectacular 3,000-acre resort that sits below the Cheyenne Mountains. Neither of their parents approved of the idea, but Harry and John went anyway. With a few bucks in their wallets for gas and a few days' worth of food, they drove 855 miles from Iowa City through Nebraska and into Colorado in John's eye-catching 1953 yellow Buick Super 8 with a green hardtop.

Contrary to expectations, there were no waiter jobs for them at The Broadmoor. They ended up finding employment serving food at Antlers, another big hotel in Colorado Springs. But not for long; neither had experience waiting tables. When a family complained about Harry being slow, he and John both were fired after their first day on the job. They applied for construction work in Cripple Creek, Colo., but didn't get the jobs. With precious few dollars in their wallets, the boys discussed whether they should buy groceries.

"We decided on beer and popcorn," Bouma said.

Eventually, they landed jobs at The Broadmoor's golf course. Working with a group of Latinos, they spread fertilizer on the course, helped construct golf cart paths and did odd jobs. During breaks, they got their food and drink by sneaking bread out of the hotel kitchen and swiping ice bags. Harry was small enough that he could squeeze his arm into an ice machine and pull down a bag. Within a few days, they were out of work again when The Broadmoor gave their jobs to Air Force Academy athletes. At that point, Harry tried his hand at waiting tables again while John found work at a bridge supply company.

After work, they hit the bars. This led to more problems when Bonnie Lane, the girl John was dating and eventually would marry, drove to Colorado Springs with a friend for a visit. Harry, who had a nickname for most everyone, had one for Bonnie. He called her "Night Train," after NFL Hall of Famer Dick "Night Train" Lane.

With John and Bonnie out on a date one night, Harry was given permission to borrow his friend's car. Harry decided to take a joy ride through town in search of action. When spotting a pretty girl in short shorts walking on a sidewalk, Harry took a long look. Too long of a look. He took his eyes off the road and bumped into a parked 18-wheeler. Fortunately, he wasn't injured.

Damaging his friend's car had quite an effect on Harry; he started questioning the man he was becoming. His older brother, a better student and more straight-laced, never would have been in Colorado in the first place, let alone pull a stunt like this, Harry told himself.

"Harry was feeling awful and really unloaded one night," John Bouma recalled years later. "He started telling me how he was always considered the black sheep of his family, and this was just another incident. He felt bad for me. He wrecked my dad's car. It was insured and my dad paid the deductible, but it was a beautiful car. And we weren't supposed to be in Colorado anyway. My folks and his folks thought it was a bad idea."

Throughout life, Harry got more upset whenever he disappointed himself, his family and friends, than when he was wronged by others. He rarely found fault in anyone, even people who were disliked by his friends or co-workers.

There would be more self-blame for Harry in college. Another minor car accident led to Harry and a friend being detained in a Missouri police station for a few hours. With Harry in the passenger seat, Phil Lainson was driving his father's company car after a night of drinking. They were headed for St. Louis for a baseball game. Both were pretty drunk when Phil collided into a vehicle crossing an intersection. Like Harry's accident in Colorado, there were no injuries and minimal damage, but the man driving the other vehicle was upset about the small dent to his fender. Thinking the man was overreacting, Harry pulled out a quarter and stuck out his hand. Not amused, the man hustled to a phone booth to call the cops. Harry and Phil ended up being ushered to the police station because they were drunk. They stayed until Lainson's father, who lived in St. Louis, arrived to bail them out.

"We got hauled off to the can, then my father came shooting down and just gave us hell," said Lainson, who went on to become a dentist and the Head of Periodontics at the University of Iowa.

Eventually, Harry better learned how to mix business with pleasure. He started managing his time more wisely and kept up on his grades. Without giving up his late-night fun, Harry began focusing most of his daytime energy on setting up his broadcasting career. The reward was a Liberal Arts degree in Speech and Dramatic Arts.

Better yet, Harry now had experience and a marketable tool—a well-trained voice. Harry Norbert Kalas was going places.

He was going places, all right. On June 12, 1959, college graduation day, Harry proudly wore a cap and gown for the 9:30 a.m., commencement at the Field House in Iowa City. University of Connecticut president Albert Jorgensen delivered an address entitled, "Education and the World Community."

After the ceremony, Harry stopped by his frat house to say goodbye to his buddies. "I went over to check my mailbox and there was my welcome from Uncle Sam," Harry once told a reporter.

Harry's broadcasting career would have to wait. He'd been drafted into the Army.

Harry was furious at himself. In order to get around being drafted, Randy Duncan and some of Harry's other college buddies had signed up for the National Guard. Harry had planned to do the same, but kept putting it off.

"Harry always was going to do it the next day," John Bouma said. "He had to go home to Le Mars to do it, but he never found the time. He was going to do anything to avoid getting drafted. It was typical Harry."

In time, Harry would realize that being drafted wasn't such a bad thing. In fact, Phil Lainson said in retrospect, "it turned out to be the best thing that ever happened to Harry."

A-LOOOOO-HA

Harry Kalas was devastated having to go straight from college to the military. The Army would take the next two years of his life, which would put his pursuit of a broadcasting career on hold. He was angry with himself. Had he signed up for the National Guard like many of his high school and college buddies, he wouldn't have been drafted on June 12, 1959, his graduation day at University of Iowa.

Harry didn't want to be a soldier and wasn't looking forward to the discipline. Even with a minister for a father, Harry had always managed to skirt rules during his teen and college years. He knew he wouldn't be able to get away with breaking rules in the Army.

On July 22, 1959, barely a month after finishing college, Harry was inducted into the Army and sent to Fort Riley, Kan., for basic training. Harry arrived as a chunky, out-of-shape, free spirit, which made for two months of living hell. But he somehow managed to get through the mental, physical and emotional rigors of Army training. Harry Kalas, who had grown about four inches in college, was a fit and trim 5-foot-10, 155-pound soldier when he finished boot camp.

With the Army having more than 50 bases around the world at the time, Harry knew he could be stationed almost anywhere. As luck would have it, Harry was sent to Hawaii. He arrived on January 6, 1960, four days after Senator John F. Kennedy announced his candidacy for the Democratic presidential nomination and four-and-a-half months after Hawaii became the country's 50th state.

Suddenly, the Army didn't seem so bad. Harry had never been outside of the Midwest in his life, and now, at age 23, he would be serving his country on a tropical island in the middle of the Pacific. He couldn't wait to take his first ocean dip.

Harry was sent to the most popular part of Hawaii, the island of Oahu. He moved into Schofield Barracks in the town of Wahiawa, about a 30-minute drive from Honolulu. Schofield Barracks was named after Lieutenant General John Schofield, the Civil War veteran who served in Hawaii in 1872 and recommended that the United States build a naval base at Pearl Harbor. Built between two mountain ranges, Schofield Barracks was the setting for the 1953 Academy Award-winning movie *From Here to Eternity*, starring Frank Sinatra, Burt Lancaster, Deborah Kerr, Montgomery Clift and Ernest Borgnine. Coincidentally, Lyle Kimura, the brother of Harry's future first wife, had a bit part in the movie as a police officer, his real-life profession.

Harry's first job at Schofield was as a shell-firing mortarman and recoilless rifleman for the 27th Infantry Wolfhounds. When his master sergeant became aware of his broadcasting background, he encouraged Harry to apply for work as a broadcast specialist. Harry got the job, which had him taping interviews for hometown radio stations with soldiers who had been promoted.

During his time off, Harry performed in Army plays. He played the lead villain in *Stalag 17*, an adaptation of a popular 1953 World War II film. He acted and sang in a stage version of *A Hatful of Rain*, a 1957 picture about a soldier returning from the Korean War.

It turns out that the Army was really good for Harry. It seemed to help him get his priorities straight and focus on his career. While in the Army, Harry sharpened his broadcasting skills by doing play-by-play of high school football and basketball games for KGU radio. His first partner at KGU was Hawaii's best-known sportscaster, Chuck Leahey. Eighteen years Harry's senior, Leahey got his start in broadcasting not long after escaping death during Japan's December 7, 1941 attack on Pearl Harbor. The Navy shipman was 500 yards from the USS Arizona when the battleship was sunk, killing 1,177.

While Harry was in the Army in 1960, he and Leahey shared a radio booth calling high school and college football games at Honolulu Stadium. Harry would drive his convertible from Schofield Barracks into Honolulu for Friday and Saturday doubleheaders that often culminated with a University of Hawaii home game. Harry would do play-by-play in one game with Leahey providing the color, then they'd switch roles for the second game. Leahey became a mentor to Harry, who was working with a seasoned pro for the first time. Harry also got a lot of help pronouncing long Hawaiian names from Leahey, whose son, Chuck, and grandson, Kanoa, later went on to become popular Honolulu sportscasters.

As usual, Harry also managed to make time for fun. One of his favorite hangouts was South Pacific, a cocktail lounge considered one of the few hotspots in the rough Kalihi section of Honolulu. Bill Whaley, a minor-league pitcher from 1940 to 1942, was owner, bartender and Harry's future best man at his first wedding.

Harry was six months away from fulfilling his two-year Army commitment when he stopped into the South Pacific on a Sunday evening early in 1961.

"Stick around," Whaley told Harry. "There are a couple guys coming in that I think you'd like to meet."

After midnight, Harry was introduced to Buddy Blattner and Lefty O'Doul—two former major leaguers who made a stop in Hawaii after doing some offseason baseball work in Japan. Both gentlemen ended up being significant in Harry's life.

O'Doul had a short but great major-league career after converting from pitcher to outfielder at age 28. Although not a Hall of Famer, his .349 career batting average ranks as fourth-highest of all time, behind only Ty Cobb, Rogers Hornsby and Shoeless Joe Jackson. When he met Harry at South Pacific, O'Doul was 63 and running a joint in San Francisco, his hometown. Lefty O'Doul's Restaurant and Cocktail Lounge opened in 1958 and became a popular establishment for professional athletes and sports fans. In years to come, Harry would spend many a night singing at Lefty's piano bar.

Blattner was a journeyman big-league infielder who had retired at age 28 to start a second and more successful career broadcasting baseball for ABC and then CBS radio. It was at the South Pacific that Blattner, then 40, tipped off Harry that Hawaii would be getting minor-league baseball for the first time.

"A deal is in the works for the Sacramento Solons of the Pacific Coast League to move to Honolulu this year," Blattner told Harry. "They're going to need an announcer. You should go for the job."

Professional baseball took root in Hawaii in 1946 when the San Francisco Seals, managed by O'Doul, held spring training in Honolulu. By the late '50s, Hawaii became a realistic option for minor-league baseball because jet travel had become common.

The New York Giants relocating to San Francisco in 1958 paved the way for Hawaii getting a team. The Giants' move brought Major League Baseball to the Bay Area, but simultaneously led to the Seals' Pacific Coast League team moving to Phoenix and a major drop in attendance for Northern California's other PCL club, the Sacramento Solons. The top farm team for the Kansas City Athletics, the Solons were in deep financial trouble by 1960 when they were sold to Salt Lake City businessman Nick Morgan Jr., who promptly moved the franchise to Honolulu and renamed it the Hawaii Islanders.

Because the Islanders' closest opponent was 2,500 miles away, the PCL scheduled opponents for only two trips per season to Hawaii—once for a seven-game series, once for a four-game series.

When news of the franchise transfer broke, Kalas was one of the first candidates to apply for the Islanders announcing job. Along with his resume, he submitted a tape from a Minnesota-Iowa football game to KGU Radio, which had Islanders' broadcast rights. The Islanders empowered KGU station manager Pat Patterson to make the hire, and Patterson was impressed with Harry.

Harry rarely asked for favors. But he wanted the Islanders' job so badly that he called legendary University of Iowa sportscaster Bob Brooks, who happily made a phone call to recommend the young man who had impressed him a few years before working games at the campus station. Harry landed the job, which included the title of KGU Sports Director, in addition to duties as play-by-play announcer for Islanders games.

"Harry was a real surprise choice because he was a soldier at Schofield who didn't have baseball experience," said Lyle Nelson, a *Honolulu Star-Bulletin* reporter for three decades who served as Harry's radio color man in 1964. "I heard the owner had almost no input in the hiring of Harry."

Harry, at age 25, would be fulfilling a lifelong ambition. But before he could start his career in baseball, Harry had a big problem to solve: the

Islanders' inaugural season opened on April 20, 1961, four months before the finish of his military service commitment. Harry went to his Army superior, an officer named Willard Thompson who always liked him.

"Apply for an early release, and then hope for the best," Thompson said.

Harry, who had been promoted three times from Private E1 to Private E4, pleaded his case on December 5, 1960. To his relief, the Army ruled in his favor. His official Army discharge papers say he was discharged for "season employment" effective April 21, 1961. Harry was delegated into four years of inactive reserves, with his commitment to the Army officially ending on July 21, 1965.

The day before his Army hearing, Harry called the Hawaii Islanders' first-ever game, a 4-3 walk-off victory over the Vancouver Mounties that ended on a ninth-inning single by Chuck Harmon, a 36-year-old outfielder who had spent time in the majors from 1954 to 1957. A crowd of 6,041 showed up at Honolulu Stadium, an old city park that first opened in 1926, just three miles from Oahu Cemetery, the final resting place of Alexander Joy Cartwright, Jr., who is credited with inventing many of the rules of modern baseball in 1845. Nicknamed "Termite Palace," Honolulu Stadium was infamous for its swarms of bugs.

"On hot and muggy nights, they would be out in the millions swarming around the stadium lights," said Ferd Borsch, an Islanders beat writer for 27 years at the *Honolulu Advertiser*. "It was kind of difficult to write your story with all those termites flying around your head."

Harry Kalas didn't let the bugs bother him. He loved his job and appreciated Honolulu Stadium for its special charm and history. Babe Ruth, Joe DiMaggio, Mickey Mantle and many other big-league stars had played there in exhibitions over the years.

"The first time I saw Honolulu Stadium, I thought it was a little bit of Brooklyn in the tropics, with an old, ramshackle Ebbets Field kind of flavor," said legendary sportscaster Al Michaels, whose first job in the business was doing play-by-play for the Hawaii Islanders from 1968 to 1970. "The termites were having a field day. The grass was very, very green and the stadium looked like a jewel. It had that classic ballpark aroma—the smell of beer and cigarette smoke and old wood.

"Honolulu Stadium was like Wrigley Field in Chicago or Crosley Field in Cincinnati or Connie Mack Stadium in Philadelphia. Those places meant so much to people because they'd been around for half-a-century and generations had grown up attending games there. They were part of the tapestry of so many lives, and that's the way it was in Honolulu, too. The Stadium then was a great, great place. It was a time when construction cranes were lined up like soldiers on the Waikiki skyline. And here was this old wooden structure right at the edge of things."

One of Harry Kalas' most memorable nights at Honolulu Stadium found him locked inside after a game. He'd stayed late to do some work, lost track of time and had to climb a 10-foot wire fence beyond the right-field wall so that he could get to his car. But first, he had to outrun night watchman Johnny Kaahanui's big guard dog, which chased him to the fence to the tune of ferocious barking.

Honolulu Stadium's cozy dimensions led to a lot of home runs and helped Harry develop one of his key traits as a baseball broadcaster, signature home run calls. In Hawaii, Harry used a simple word that was perfect for the setting, "Aloha." The way Harry said it made it special: "A-looooo-ha!"

Calling Hawaii Islanders games in the 1960s provided valuable experience for Harry. But this job was different from what he'd encounter once he reached the major leagues.

During his 44 years working for the Houston Astros and Philadelphia Phillies, Harry actually was in the ballpark for every game. As the voice of the Hawaii Islanders, however, he attended home games only. When the ballclub was on the road, Harry sat in a Honolulu radio station calling games off simple phone reports, an art that was known in the business as "re-creation."

Harry had four different broadcast partners in Hawaii from 1961 to 1965. His partner would contribute to radio broadcasts as a color analyst for home contests, but was off the air during road games, tracking down and typing up game details for Harry's re-creations. Few minor-league clubs sent broadcasters on the road in the early 1960s, and the Islanders, who had to take longer road trips than any other club, stuck to that policy during and beyond the Kalas years.

In his first season, Harry called games on KGU with Carlos Rivas, a middle-aged man who was famous in Hawaii for re-creating major league games in the 1950s. The next season, Harry worked with Terry Braverman, a young Michigan State graduate who was a Honolulu sportscaster for a short time. In 1963, Islanders games moved across the radio dial from KGU to KGMB and Harry had another new partner, a 22-year-old *Honolulu Star-Bulletin* sports writer named Marty Chase.

Chase returned for the 1964 season, but missed the first two months for Army Reserve duty on the mainland. Lyle Nelson, another *Star-Bulletin* reporter, filled in for Chase during his absence.

Dubbed "Marty the Marlin" by Harry because he was forced to do a weekly fishing column by his sports editor, Chase worked for $10 per game. Harry received a bigger paycheck, but he certainly wasn't getting rich living in Hawaii on about $10,000 annually. Still, even when he was earning hundreds of thousands of dollars per year later in life, money never mattered much to Harry Kalas, according to his wives, colleagues and close friends.

Once discharged from the Army in 1961, Harry had moved from Schofield Barracks into a one-bedroom apartment in Honolulu, which was anything but lavish. After games, Harry hung out at the Green Turtle, the drinking establishment of choice for many sports fans in Honolulu. There, he'd toss back beer and munch on pupu, Hawaiian appetizers.

With Hawaii at least two time zones behind all of the other Pacific Coast League teams, night road contests aired at 7:30 p.m., the same time as home games. The two-hour delay meant Harry usually started his re-creations when the actual game was in the late innings, or even finished. Harry would sit in the studio behind a mike with his partner visible through a window in the next room, where he was preparing re-creation information. The color man would make a call to a ballpark in California, Texas or wherever the Islanders were playing. Usually, the partner would get information on the first five innings, then he'd type up what happened and pass it along to Harry so that he could start re-creating the game for his listeners. Later, he'd get information on the remainder of the game and repeat the process.

The information retrieved, often from a reporter, would only cover the basics (Islanders fourth: Carlos Bernier strikeout swinging, Irv Noren single to right, Stan Palys 5-4-3 double play). It was up to Harry to make up everything else. He could make a groundball to shortstop into a routine two-hopper or a sharply hit ball into the hole that required a diving stop and a long throw that had to be scooped out of the dirt by the first baseman. Harry decided how long at-bats lasted and if a pitcher threw an 0-and-2 hanging curve or a full-count changeup. It was his childhood fantasy games coming to life.

Harry bragged that he could get through an Islanders road game in an hour if he had a date that night or somewhere else to go. "Every batter would be first-ball swinging," Harry used to say with a laugh.

Even though a disclaimer was read before and after games alerting listeners that the broadcast was a re-creation, many were fooled. Sometimes, Harry would be recognized around Hawaii by befuddled Islanders fans when the team was on the road. "We would meet people on the street sometimes and they'd say, 'I thought you were in Vancouver last night. How did you get back so fast?" Marty Chase said. "To the sophisticated listener, it very much sounded like a re-created game. "But a lot of people out there didn't really pick up on the subtleties of the broadcast."

Retrieving game information wasn't always an easy task. When something went wrong, it was up to Harry to invent delays, such as downpours and bench-clearing brawls. One night, Harry had to take his ad-libbing skills to a new level when a *Dallas Times-Herald* reporter left the ballpark before passing along information on the final four innings of an Islanders-Dallas Rangers game. With Marty Chase frantically making calls to retrieve the missing information, Harry did his best to stretch out the first five innings. Every batter worked a full count and then fouled off 3-2 pitches. Managers had long conferences on the mound. There were injury delays. And the topper was a stoppage for dogs running onto the field. With Harry an hour into his stall tactics, Marty finally tracked down the wayward reporter at his newspaper office. The rest of the game was over in no time.

For sound effects during re-creations, Harry tapped a pencil on a wood block from a drum set to simulate the sound of the crack of a bat hitting a baseball. A radio technician, DJ George "Granny Goose" Groves at KGMB, pumped in a continuous loop of crowd noise.

"It seemed like there were 50,000 people at some of the road games," Kalas once recalled.

Harry quickly became popular with Islanders fans. It wasn't long before he was signing autographs for the first time. Flattered, he also took time to talk with fans.

"Harry was really liked," Marty Chase said. "He had an incredible ability to relate to other people, not just the big shots. He really had exceptional people skills and a genuine interest in whomever he was talking to. It didn't matter if it was the guy sweeping out the stadium, the engineer on the broadcast or really anybody he met. That's remarkable because there are very few people who do that."

Almost a half-century later, Islanders fans blogged fond memories of Harry after his 2009 death. One man wrote that he fell in love with baseball because of Harry, "who made the game alive to a nine year-old boy who really believed the re-created Islander road games were live."

After his second season, Harry was named 1962 Hawaii Sportscaster of the Year.

"Harry was eager," Lewis Matlin, the Islanders general manager from 1963-64, said when recalling a young Harry. "He wanted to jump three steps at a time. He wanted to get to the top as quickly as he could. He was a good broadcaster, but he got a lot better."

Early into his first year with the Islanders, Harry found his "better half" when introduced during a game to a single Hawaiian woman of Japanese descent. Jasmine Kimura, manager of Ming's Jewelry & Fine Arts, made a big sale to a group of Islanders players who visited her store looking for Easter gifts for their wives and girlfriends. The high-end jewelry was so well received that the girls wanted to meet Jasmine and invited her to a game. Many of her evenings were spent entertaining wealthy customers, but eventually Jasmine made time to get to Honolulu Stadium for her first baseball game. As she tells it, she enjoyed the atmosphere, loved the game and had a blast hanging out with the girls. Afterwards, Jasmine tagged along for post-game drinks at the South Pacific with Islanders players and their dates.

Never one to miss a night out with friends, Harry Kalas was there, too. But on this night, he was going with hopes of landing a date. He was intrigued by Jasmine when he had first met her that night at the ballpark. At the South Pacific, he hoped for the chance to get to know her better.

Right away, Harry showed his sense of humor. While parking his car, Harry noticed a beat-up decorated Japanese slipper on the ground. Knowing Jasmine was Japanese, Harry scooped it up and jokingly presented it to her as a gag gift.

"At least I'm bringing you something," Harry said.

Harry was fascinated with Jasmine, who was a beautiful woman with long, dark auburn hair and an easygoing personality. He also was impressed with her intelligence, drive and success in business. Jasmine really got good vibes around Harry, too. She was smitten with his well-cropped blonde hair, blue eyes and charming personality.

They were attracted to one another, but they also noticed differences right away. Harry was a good bit younger, smoked one cigarette after another and enjoyed his booze. Jasmine never smoked and barely drank alcohol, other than maybe sipping on a glass of wine.

"He's so nice," Jasmine told herself. "He's good-looking, personable and really funny."

That first night, Harry didn't get a hug, kiss or even a phone number. Jasmine was clearly no easy catch. She did agree to show up for another game and meet Harry again. After their second post-game date, Jasmine offered her phone number.

"You've never seen a more beautiful woman," said Bud Watkins, an Islanders pitcher in 1961. "Jasmine was absolutely stunning. All the ballplayers used to drool over her."

"She was a real lady in every sense of the word," Islanders general manager Lewis Matlin said.

Soon, they began dating regularly, but their dates usually consisted of just drinks after Islanders games because Harry worked almost every night during baseball season.

Harry called Jasmine "Kish," short for her middle name, Kishie. She became a regular at Islanders games and quickly grew to love baseball. After games, she'd drive Harry to restaurants and clubs in her company car, a blue Chrysler convertible. Harry would be the breadwinner in years to come, but starting early in their dating days, Jasmine often picked up bar tabs. To avoid embarrassing Harry, she routinely would slip him $20 under the table.

Regardless of their comparative economic circumstances at the time, whenever together Jasmine always had a blast with Harry.

In 1962, a year into their relationship, Harry proposed after picking up Jasmine for a lunch date. Harry had purchased a specially designed ring from Hildgund Bucky, Jasmine's top jewelry maker at Ming's. There was no hesitation from Jasmine. Very much wanting to be Mrs. Harry Kalas, she said "Yes" immediately.

Jasmine had an interesting background. She grew up in Kona, one of six districts on Hawai'i—the "Big Island." Her parents, father Mokichi and mother Fumi, owned four coffee farms and made a good living for their four children, three girls and a boy. Jasmine, the third born, always had nice things, but felt guilty because most of her school friends were poor. Their parents worked in the coffee fields that Jasmine's parents owned.

Jasmine wasn't one to flaunt her family's wealth. In fact, she sometimes pretended to be poor in an attempt to better fit in. When grade school teachers asked students how many bags of harvest coffee berries they had picked during vacations, Jasmine always made up a number so that her classmates wouldn't think that she was a stuffy rich kid. Her classmates also used to catch rats in the coffee fields and sell their tails for pennies. Jasmine, after confiding her elite status to a best friend, would purchase a few tails from her so that other classmates would see her cashing in. She came from money, but wanted to be treated just like the other little girls.

During high school, Jasmine lost her mother. After graduating from Konawaena High School in 1943, Jasmine moved to Oahu to attend classes at the University of Hawaii. During her freshman year, the Sociology major stopped into Ming's Jewelry & Fine Arts to look around. To her surprise, Jasmine's former grade school teacher was a salesman. While catching up, Jasmine confided that she was a lover of art and jewelry.

Within months, Jasmine was offered a full-time, well-paying job at Ming's. Thinking this was the field for her, Jasmine dropped out of college. At the time, Jasmine had no idea that her salesman job would lead to big promotions which eventually would make her the boss of her former teacher, or that it would be the reason that she'd someday meet her future husband, Harry Kalas.

At Ming's, which sold top-of-the-line jewelry and art pieces, Jasmine had some celebrity clients. She was managing Ming's when Frank Sinatra became a customer. Through married to Ava Gardner, Ol' Blue Eyes had stopped in to purchase jewelry for his ex-wife, Nancy, and their daughter. To get paid, Jasmine was told to meet with Frank at his hotel, the Royal Hawaiian. She had to go through three levels of personal security before reaching Frank in person.

From 1954 to 1959, Jasmine's work took her far from home. When Ming's opened three stores in South Florida, she was transferred to manage branches in Fort Lauderdale, Miami Beach and Coral Gables. In Miami Beach, Jasmine made a sale to Elizabeth Taylor and made a friend in Liberace.

Taylor entered Ming's one day in 1958 with her third husband, Mike Todd, and another famous Hollywood couple, Eddie Fisher and wife Debbie Reynolds. "Her blue eyes were just beautiful," Jasmine recalled. Within months, Todd died in a plane crash, then the next year Fisher left Reynolds to marry Taylor.

Liberace was in his 30s and performing for several weeks at the Eden Roc Hotel when he met Jasmine outside Ming's. They started taking daily morning walks together to make bank deposits. "Old ladies would come up to him and flatter him to bits, which he loved. He was a wonderful person, always cheerful to everyone who approached."

Jasmine felt the same way about her future husband.

A week into Harry's third season as voice of the Hawaii Islanders, wedding bells rang. On April 6, 1963, the Saturday before Easter, Harry and Jasmine married at St. Clement's Episcopal Church, which is two blocks from Punahou School, a K-12 prep school. In 1971, a 10-year-old fifth grader named Barry Obama started classes at Punahou. By the time he graduated in 1979, Barry was going by his birth name, Barack. In November 2008, Barack Obama was elected the 44th President of the United States.

St. Clement's was packed for Harry and Jasmine's wedding. A native Hawaiian, Jasmine had many friends and family members in attendance. A lot of Harry's buddies, including many of his Army and broadcasting friends, also were there. Reverend Paul Wheeler and Harry's father, Reverend Harry H. Kalas, conducted the ceremony jointly. Bill Whaley, the South Pacific bar owner, was Harry's best man. Harry's parents flew in from Iowa for the wedding, but his older brother, Jim, was attending graduate school and couldn't make it. The wedding reception took place in the church banquet room and the Delta Rhythm Boys, a popular Honolulu nightclub act, provided the entertainment.

During the reception, Reverend Kalas approached Jasmine. "You're now the daughter that I've never had," he told her.

Reverend Kalas and his wife posed for wedding pictures, and then headed for the airport to get back to Iowa so that he could preach at his church on Easter Sunday. Easter night, Reverend Kalas phoned Hawaii to say that he wore the same orchard lei for his Easter service that he had on for Harry and Jasmine's wedding.

With the Islanders' season not opening until April 13, Harry and Jasmine traveled to the island of Kauai for a short honeymoon—a wedding gift from KGMB radio.

Once back from his honeymoon, Harry moved out of his apartment and into Jasmine's place. Two months later, they purchased a three-bedroom home in Waialae Iki, a suburb of Honolulu. Their new home was a block from the ocean and provided a beautiful view when ships sailed by en route to Honolulu Harbor and Pearl Harbor.

Harry had a lot of fun in his four years of calling baseball in Hawaii. Besides loving his job, he greatly enjoyed getting to know Islanders' players and coaches. He made a lasting impression on them, too.

"Harry was one of the best guys you'll ever meet in your whole life," Islanders pitcher Bud Watkins said. "He had a very inquisitive mind and wanted to learn the game. For that, he should be commended. The manager loved Harry and the players loved Harry, who looked like he was 17 years old and smoked incessantly. There was nothing not to love."

With Kalas behind the microphone, the Islanders had two winning seasons and two losing seasons. He never came across as a big "homer" in the booth, but always rooted for his teams throughout his career. In Hawaii, Harry was an Islanders fan. While working the late innings of a re-created road loss one night, Lyle Nelson fed Harry the result of the opponent's game-winning homer. "Harry turned off the microphone and slammed his hand on his desk," Nelson recalled. "Then he clicked the microphone back on and says, 'Here's the pitch, it's a long drive. . . .'"

The 1961 Islanders, managed by Tommy Heath and Bill Werle, finished their first season with a 68-86 record, good enough to stay out of last place by one game in the eight-team Pacific Coast League. "We had a bad team," Islanders pitcher Bud Watkins said. "Heath would look down the bench when we'd be behind seven or eight runs and say, 'Hey, any of you bastards want to pitch?' I always wanted the ball. I would have done anything to stay in Hawaii."

The Islanders didn't have any future major league stars during the Harry Kalas years, although Hall of Fame pitcher Bob Lemon was their manager in 1964. Player-manager Irv Noren, a former major leaguer who skippered the Islanders to winning seasons in 1962 and 1963, kept the atmosphere business-like by fining players $50 for showing up to play with too much sunburn, which wasn't all that rare. It's a good thing broadcasters were exempt because Harry Kalas spent a lot of time sunbathing on Waikiki Beach during late mornings and early afternoons.

By his second year in Hawaii, Harry was a celebrity there. Although only broadcasting on radio, Islanders fans knew him. Occasionally, he'd get asked for an autograph. Often, he'd end up making a new friend or drinking buddy. This was a trait he would take with him to Houston and then Philadelphia. Early in his Islanders days, Harry became Hawaii's most famous sportscaster.

"If you have to do minor league baseball, I can't think of a better place than Hawaii," Harry said on many occasions. Harry loved living in Hawaii, but after four seasons with the Islanders he was ready to move on.

Mackay Yanagisawa, the part-owner of the Islanders who ran Honolulu Stadium, clashed with some of his employees, but adored the young Harry Kalas. "I can tell you, I was on the other side with Mackay during negotiations, and he could be very difficult if not prickly," Marty Chase recalled. "Harry and Mackay got along very well. Harry had the ability to get along with anyone."

On his own dime, Mackay invited Harry to accompany him to Houston in December 1964 for baseball's annual winter meetings.

"Mackay, I'm going to look for a major league job if you take me," Harry said.

"You belong in the major leagues," Mackay said.

The winter meetings are a three-day annual event where general managers discuss trades and make new hires. Day and night, reporters, scouts, general managers, managers, broadcasters, etc., talk in jammed hotel lobbies and bars. This was the perfect atmosphere for Harry to market himself. He loved talking baseball, especially with a lit cigarette in one hand and a drink in the other.

While in Houston, Harry campaigned incessantly for a major league broadcasting job. He finally caught a break when he met Dick Blue, the supervisor of broadcast operations for the Houston Colt .45s. Blue talked about his organization's exciting changes for the 1965 season. The franchise would be moving into the Astrodome, baseball's first domed stadium, and changing their Colt .45s nickname to Astros.

Harry really perked up when Dick Blue mentioned he would be adding a third member to his broadcast team. Blue wanted a radio host for the Astros' pre-game and post-game shows. His hire also would get one inning of play-by-play on a team that included lead announcer Gene Elston and color man Loel Passe. Dick wanted someone young with talent, someone who might eventually grow into a lead broadcaster. He wanted someone like Harry. Blue and Harry hit it off immediately in Houston. Better yet, he loved Harry's voice.

"Send me some tapes of your work when you get home and I'll get back to you," Blue instructed.

On the way home from the winter meetings, Harry got a good scare.

Somewhere between California and Hawaii, his plane had serious engine problems. Everyone braced for a death plunge into the Pacific. Fearing for their lives, passengers prayed for a safe landing. Harry pulled out a sheet of paper and wrote a love letter to Jasmine. To everyone's relief, the plane sputtered its way to a safe landing in Honolulu. When Harry met up with his new wife, he handed her the letter, joking that it was supposed to be a goodbye message.

Harry quickly gathered some tapes from his Islanders' broadcasts, sent them to Houston and prayed for a break. Harry didn't know that about 200 others had applied for the same job. Within a month, Dick Blue called back. He interviewed Harry over the phone, telling him that he was very impressed with the tapes. Before hanging up, Harry was offered the job with a $12,000 annual salary, which was more than the major-league minimum in 1965. Harry probably would have accepted for less. At age 29, Harry Kalas had a job that he'd dreamed about since his youth. He was now a big-league broadcaster.

Harry and Jasmine celebrated, and then began planning their big move from Hawaii to Texas. Jasmine put their home up for sale and began packing while Harry continued his normal winter routine of broadcasting high school and college basketball games.

One of his last assignments was on March 5, 1965. Harry and Marty Chase, his Islanders partner for two seasons, flew from Oahu to the Big Island to call the state basketball championships. While working two semifinal games on a Friday night, the broadcasters were informed that a nearby volcano had erupted.

After the games, Harry and Marty drove 20 miles to catch a glimpse. They parked and walked to a cliff in order to look down at spectacular fire-red lava fountains shooting out from Kilauea Volcano as it formed Makaopuhi Lava Lake. It eventually crusted over, but remains a spectacular site to this day. Amazed, they stayed until 4 a.m., before heading back to their hotel in Hilo.

A week later, Harry had to leave for Astros spring training, which was underway in Cocoa Beach, Fla.

Hawaii wasn't ready to lose Harry Kalas until it made one more special memory for him. Harry's friends threw him a big going-away bash, and then saw him off to the airport along with Jasmine, who would stay behind for a few weeks to close on the sale of their home. Boarding his plane, Harry was hardly recognizable. He had so many Hawaiian leis wrapped around his neck that you could barely see his face.

HOUSTON, WE HAVE A KALAS

A gentle breeze blew off the Atlantic Ocean on March 3, 1969 as Harry Kalas stood on a crowded central Florida beach waiting to be amazed. He had walked to Cocoa Beach with his wife Jasmine from his spring training home to watch the liftoff of Apollo 9, a Saturn V rocket that would spend 10 days in space. At 11 a.m., the young couple watched in awe as the giant rocket arched upward from a Kennedy Space Center tower in nearby Cape Canaveral.

"It's like a fireball," Jasmine called out in delight.

This would be the next-to-last rocket launch before NASA's biggest moment. A month later, on July 21, 1969, the world would watch in awe as Neil Armstrong became the first man to walk on the moon. America was captivated by space travel in the 1960s, and Harry Kalas was right in the middle of it, broadcasting Major League Baseball in Houston, home of Johnson Space Center, and attending spring training in Cocoa Beach, a 20-minute drive from Kennedy Space Center.

Four years earlier, Harry's 1965 arrival in Houston launched a new and exciting phase to his life. In March that year, while attending his first spring training with the Houston Astros in Cocoa, Harry received a momentous call from Jasmine, who was still in Hawaii working on the sale of their home. She had big news to share.

"Guess what? You're going to be a dad," Jasmine said.

Harry was absolutely thrilled. He used to have a blast playing with Jasmine's nephews during beach picnics in Hawaii. They were so fond of Harry that they used to fight to sit next to him. Harry adored them, too. He was as ready to be a father as he was to be a major league broadcaster.

When Harry arrived in Houston the following month for the regular season, he found out that baseball was the hottest thing in the region. All of Texas and much of the country was talking about the franchise's move into Harris County Domed Stadium, the world's first roofed stadium. The stadium, which came to be known as "The Astrodome," cost a record $37 million—$31 million for construction, plus $6 million for lavish decoration.

The Astrodome was still in the planning stages when Houston was awarded a major league franchise in 1961, so the club built a temporary 32,000-seat stadium next to the Astrodome construction site. Colt Stadium, which was completed in nine months for $2 million, was one of the worst places to watch a game in Major League Baseball history. During the franchise's inaugural season, extreme heat forced 78 fans and an umpire to seek medical attention during day games. Thousands of swarming mosquitoes made Colt .45 night games just as rough on fans, who could buy insect repellent at concession stands. A real dump, Colt Stadium was on the same site as what became Reliant Stadium, which opened in 2002 for the NFL's Houston Texans and hosted Super Bowl XXXVIII in February 2004.

There would be no sweating or bug bites inside the air-conditioned Astrodome, and baseball fans everywhere awaited its opening with great anticipation. This new climate-controlled palace seated 54,000 for baseball and 63,000 for football, was four stories high and had 54 luxury boxes. A weather station on the roof kept the temperature at a comfortable 72 degrees. Among its many other highlights was a 474-foot-long, $2 million scoreboard that launched into 45 seconds of fireworks-shooting, steer-snorting, cowboy-shooting animation dubbed Home Run Spectacular when an Astros player hit a home run. When the opposition homered, "TILT" appeared on the world's largest scoreboard, which needed four people to operate. Despite all the stadium's amenities,

Astros seats were affordable in 1965, with field box seats going for $3.50 and bleacher tickets for $1.50.

"The sooner people see something like this and realize you have some ideas, the easier it is to sell your products," Astros owner Roy Hofheinz, who dreamed up the huge indoor stadium and then made it happen when few thought he could, once said. Hofheinz smartly capitalized on Johnson Space Center being right down the road, changing his team's name from Colt .45s to Astros for the 1965 season.

"You'd walk into the Dome, and your mouth just hung open," said Gene Elston, a Baseball Hall of Famer who was the Houston franchise's lead play-by-play man from 1961 to 1985.

"This is in truth one of the great wonders of the world," a 1965 Astros advertisement boasted. Soon, the public agreed and the Astrodome was dubbed "Eighth Wonder of the World," a term that would stick for years.

Hofheinz was a tall, heavy man who smoked a box of cigars a day. Before getting into baseball, he served as mayor of Houston, a Harris County judge and President Lyndon B. Johnson's Congressional campaign manager. Known as "Judge," Hofheinz thought outside-the-box decades before it was a catchy cliché. He was an imposing man who probably believed he could sell sand in a desert, and he might have been able to, considering the way people gravitated toward him.

When the Colt .45s traveled during their expansion season in 1961, Judge Hofheinz insisted that all of his players, coaches and broadcasters dress in western-style outfits in team colors. It was embarrassing beyond words for the team to walk through airports and hotels with black cowboy hats, blue suits, white shirts with red baseball stitching, orange string ties and belts to which fake pistols were attached. The humiliation finally stopped in 1965 for the franchise's traveling party, but the Astros' game-day staff still was forced to wear costumes, with usherettes dressing in space outfits and the groundscrew wearing space helmets.

Judge Hofheinz, who turned 53 the day after his new palace opened, owned several homes. During baseball season, he often stayed in an extravagant apartment in the Astrodome's right-field rafters. He had an office, two bedrooms—one for his pal President Johnson—two bathrooms with velvet toilet seats, plus a barbershop, bowling alley, movie theatre and putting green. He also had an office with a spittoon that would rattle when Judge discharged his tobacco juice.

The Astros again captured the public's imagination in the Astrodome's second season by changing its playing surface from grass to artificial turf. Paint, added during the 1965 season to the stadium's glass-paneled roof in order to reduce glare and help players track fly balls, blocked sunlight needed to keep the field's Bermuda grass alive. As a solution, the Astros sought help from Chemstrand, a rug company that was a branch of St. Louis-based Monsanto. Since the early 1960s, the Ford Foundation, a non-profit organization founded by automobile giant Henry Ford, had been encouraging Chemstrand to develop a synthetic surface that could be used in urban schools. In 1964, two Chemstrand employees co-invented "Chemgrass," which was first installed that year at Morris Brown School, a prep school in Providence, R.I. In 1966, Chemgrass hit the big-time when it was added to the Astrodome and renamed AstroTurf. Within a decade, most newer sports stadiums across the country were using AstroTurf. Among them was Veterans Stadium, the multi-purpose venue in Philadelphia that Harry Kalas would help open when joining the Phillies broadcast team in 1971.

With the Astrodome inspiring so much newfound fan interest, the Astros' radio network expanded to more than 18.5 million homes. This was why the Astros decided to hire a third man for their 1965 broadcast team and why Harry Kalas, just 29 at the time, was swooped away from the Hawaii Islanders.

With President Johnson in attendance, the Astrodome opened for an exhibition game against the New York Yankees on April 9, 1965. Yankees great Mickey Mantle hit the first homer, but Houston won 2-1 in 12 innings on a walk-off hit by another future Hall of Famer, player/coach Nellie Fox.

Harry enlightened his listening audience that day, his very first day as a major-league broadcaster, with a barrage of inside information and statistics that in the 1960s was rarely provided. During one of Mantle's at-bats, Harry's words painted a description of the action and between-pitch happenings that was like listening to a talking encyclopedia.

"Mickey Mantle will lead off for the New York Yankees. He'll be followed by Bobby Richardson and Roger Maris. Mantle has one of the two hits off Turk Farrell. He singled to lead off the ballgame. Farrell winds, the pitch to Mantle. It's high and inside, ball one. One ball and no strikes to Mickey Mantle, who has hit 454 career home runs, more

than any other active player. Willie Mays is only one behind him. Mays has hit 453.

"High with the fastball, a ball, 2-0. Mantle is a switch-hitter batting left against the right-hander Farrell. Mickey's batting average is higher right-handed, but his home run frequency is higher left-handed. Mickey also leads all active players in career runs batted in.

"A high foul off on the left-hand side. That ball is out of play and a souvenir for a fan. A great grab up above us apparently as the fans down below look up and send out a round of applause for some fan who apparently made a nice play on the ball. Two balls and one strike to Mickey Mantle. Bobby Richardson on deck. No score, we're in the top of the third.

"Now the next pitch, swing and a bounding ball to second base, Joe Morgan, scoops, bobbles, recovers, throws to first. It's in time by a half-a-step. Mantle is out by a half-a-step. As Gene mentioned earlier, Mantle is still bothered by a pulled hamstring muscle and if he had not been affected by that, he would have beaten it out. But Joe Morgan recovered in time and Mickey is out of there and that'll bring up Bobby Richardson, the second baseman."

Throw in Harry's smooth as silk delivery and baritone voice, and the listening audience was privileged to witness not only the birth of a new ballpark, but also that of a historic major league broadcasting career.

Following four more exhibition games in two days against the Yankees and Baltimore Orioles, Harry sat in the broadcast booth on April 12th to call an inning of the inaugural regular-season game at the Astrodome, a 2-0 Astros loss to the Phillies that was covered by reporters from around the world.

Two weeks into the season, Harry finally was joined in Houston by his pregnant wife. On New Year's Eve 1965, Jasmine went into labor after going out for a birthday dinner for Harry's father. The birthday celebration was cut short by a birth—Todd Harry Kalas was born at St. Luke's Episcopal Hospital in Houston. Within two weeks, Harry was proudly showing off his new son at the Astros' offices.

Harry enjoyed only limited opportunities to show off his broadcast skills during his first year with the Astros. He hosted the pre-game and post-game shows, and called one inning of play-by-play each game on KPRC Radio. He subbed for Astros veteran lead broadcaster Gene Elston, a future Baseball Hall of Fame announcer, and sidekick Loel Passe.

Harry made a big impression during his one-inning stints. James Anderson, a lifelong Colt .45s/Astros fan and franchise historian, was a 19-year-old when Kalas arrived in Houston in 1965. Right away, he was captivated by Harry's voice. That first season, he and some buddies pulled out a tape recorder and imitated Harry's calls, then listened to see who sounded the most like him.

"I swear to God I did that," Anderson remembered. "What does that tell you? Harry was destined for greatness. He would draw you like a magnet with his sound. You knew he was going to be a great one. A lot of other Astros fans feel the same way. If you listen to some of his calls with Houston, the guy was great. Harry Kalas had charisma. We hated to see him leave."

As was the case in Hawaii, Harry came up with a catchy home run call. When an Islanders player hit a home run, Harry yelled, "A-looooo-ha!" After thinking it over, Harry decided to adopt one for the Astros that fit that franchise's image. When an Astros player went deep, Harry would call out, "That ball is in Astro orbit!"

Harry never bragged, but he knew he was good even back in 1965. He just didn't look the part. Before a 1966 game, Harry introduced himself to *Philadelphia Daily News* baseball writer Bill Conlin. "They must be having some kind of a contest where they're giving an inning to a high school kid who sends in tapes," Conlin told himself.

Pat Gillick, the Astros' assistant farm director when Harry Kalas arrived in Houston, was blessed with an uncanny ability to know a good baseball prospect when he saw one. Gillick, who went on to win three World Series as a general manager, two with the Toronto Blue Jays and another with the Phillies, was also pretty adept at identifying gifted young broadcasters.

"This guy is good," Gillick said when listening to Kalas call Astros games in 1965. "This guy is going to have a future."

Recognizing Harry as a special talent, the Astros expanded Harry's radio role from one inning of play-by-play to calling three innings for the 1966 season. For Astros television games—about half of their road games were aired—Harry worked all nine innings because Elston preferred radio.

Harry Kalas deserved his promotion in 1966, but it ignited a controversy because it took away airtime from Gene Elston, the Astros' top broadcaster since the franchise's debut. From the moment he arrived in Houston, Harry felt resentment from Elston, who was 14 years his senior. Extra airtime for Harry further cooled their icy relationship.

"I don't want to talk bad about anybody, but Gene Elston didn't treat me well," Harry once told his second wife, Eileen. "He did not want me in the booth and I got no help at all."

Elston was so upset about losing two innings that he vented to reporters during an offseason team function at a Houston hotel. Harry and Jasmine Kalas were there.

At one point, Elston's wife approached Jasmine and yelled, "This is terrible, Gene's quitting!"

Elston calmed down that night, but his relationship with Harry Kalas only grew worse.

"It was not a happy situation in the broadcast booth," Jasmine Kalas said. "Gene would come and give me a hug after I had my children and I'd think, 'Oh boy, after what he did to Harry.'"

Among Harry's best friends in Houston observing Elston's actions were Hall of Famer Joe Morgan, an Astros second baseman during the Kalas years, and Phillies chairman Bill Giles, Houston's VP of Marketing from 1962 to 1969.

"Gene Elston was an asshole," Morgan said. "He wasn't nice to Harry. I don't know what the deal was. I think maybe Gene thought of Harry as a threat because Bill Giles was his buddy."

Morgan wasn't protective of Harry only regarding Elston. During a golf outing one summer, Astros third baseman Doug Rader did some heavy-duty cursing after missing a putt in front of Harry, who rarely used bad language. "Calm down," Morgan angrily snapped. "Harry's father is a minister."

In reality, Harry wasn't bothered by swearing, but he was irritated by Elston's treatment. "Elston was a good announcer, but he did have a really big ego," Giles said. "When Harry started taking more of his innings from him, he was not happy."

Harry came home from one game and told his wife that Elston tore up tickertape so that he couldn't update listeners with out-of-town scores, part of his in-game duties.

"For Gene to do something like that would go completely against his character," Astros historian James Anderson said. "I've talked to Gene hundreds of times and he never made a negative or disparaging comment about Harry

Kalas, period."

Elston, who turned 87 in 2009, declined several interview requests, but he did agree to briefly discuss his stormy relationship with Kalas through a friend.

"I didn't like Harry Kalas," Elston told James Anderson. "Well, put it this way, it wasn't so much that I didn't like him. I preferred not to associate with him. We were different individuals. He was in a different age group than I was in, so we hung around with a different crowd."

Anderson noted that former Astros broadcasters Larry Dierker and Dewayne Staats were big suporters. Elston's detractors referred to him as "the Sergeant Joe Friday of baseball broadcasting," comparing him to the "just the facts" police detective in *Dragnet*, a popular radio and television series that aired from 1949-59 and 1967-70.

Elston also had an ally in the booth in Loel Passe, his broadcasting partner for 16 years. Passe, who died at age 80 in 1997, was known for his outlandish on-air sayings, such as "hot ziggedy dog," "ol' sassafras tea" and "peanut butter up and down, jam and jelly all around." Passe wasn't as mean to Harry as Elston was, but he wasn't particularly friendly, either. Giles called Passe "a real cornball guy who didn't know anything about baseball."

"Giles is right," Anderson said. "Loel Passe's shtick was being real hokey. He was hokey to the core, but he was a genuine person and there was not a man who loved baseball more. Baseball meant everything to Loel, just like it did to Harry Kalas."

Harry was bothered by the actions of his Astros broadcast partners, but he never complained. When mentioning an incident to his wife one night after a game, Harry finished his thought by saying, "Well, if they want to do it, let them do it." He never considered telling his boss. He wasn't that way. He did not like controversy. He was always a peacemaker. He just dealt with whatever mistreatment was thrown his way. Gene Elston's actions did inspire Harry to make a promise to himself. "If I ever work with a young broadcaster, I'm going to give him all the help I can," Harry told his first wife.

Harry lived up to his vow in Philadelphia. He nurtured Chris Wheeler and Andy Musser in the mid-1970s, Larry Andersen and Scott Graham in the 1990s, plus Tom McCarthy and Scott Franzke in the 2000s.

Harry and Gene Elston had differences in how they dealt with players, too. Harry regularly socialized with them, while Gene made it a point to be detached. "You get to know the players and become friendly with them, but I didn't want to be buddy-buddy and go golfing with them," Elston said in a 2006 *Baseball Digest* interview. "I was a reporter, not a homer."

While not known as an over-the-top "homer," Harry did have plenty of ballplayer friends. After road games, Harry often dined with the Astros' two black stars, Jimmy Wynn and Joe Morgan. Wynn had one of baseball's all-time great nicknames, "Toy Cannon." Harry and Morgan had nicknames for each other too. Joe was "Sweet Pea" to Harry. Mysteriously, Harry was "Vicious Thing" to Joe.

In 1967, Harry had some good times in Houston with Bo Belinsky, a left-handed pitcher who played for the Islanders during Harry's time announcing in Hawaii. Belinsky was one of the biggest playboy athletes of his era. He was romantically linked to one beautiful actress after another—Tina Louise, Ann-Margret, Connie Stevens and Mamie Van Doren, among others. For a time, he was married to Jo Collins, *Playboy*'s Playmate of the Year for 1965.

Harry used to joke that many of Belinsky's conquests were dumb blondes. In the spring of '67, Bo brought one to Harry's place for lunch. Jasmine made sandwiches for everyone. After their meal, Bo's date followed Jasmine from the dining room to the kitchen sink.

"Bo wants you to teach me how to wash dishes," the shapely blonde said.

"There's nothing to wash," Jasmine laughed. "We only had sandwiches."

During his time in Houston, Harry did a lot of post-game drinking, and it eventually showed up on his 5-foot-10 frame. Pudgy as a teen, he lost his gut in the Army. But in Houston it returned. His first season with the Astros, Harry gained 20 pounds, going from 155 to 175. The final weekend of the 1965 season, iconic St. Louis Cardinals announcer Jack Buck jokingly told Harry that he'd be up to 300 pounds in no time if he didn't start watching his weight. The young announcer took the message to heart. Harry didn't slow down on his drinking, but he started controlling his weight by playing more tennis.

Harry made time for his growing family, too. He enjoyed watching little Todd take his first steps and speak his first words. Seven weeks before his third birthday, Todd had a baby brother. On November 8, 1968, Brad Philip Kalas was born. At the last minute, Harry changed a flight for a football trip with the University of Houston so that he could witness the birth. Now a family of four, the Kalases were anything but rich, as Harry's annual salary was just $12,000. As in Hawaii, Jasmine's savings helped pay the bills.

Jasmine often took her boys to Astros games. Todd was still in diapers and too young to know what was going on, but managed to have fun flipping the stadium seats up and down, and waiting for the exploding scoreboard when the Astros hit a home run. In 1970, much to Harry's delight, Todd, 4, and Brad, 2, played in a Father/Son Game at the Astrodome.

Harry and Jasmine spent much of their free time with other families that had little ones. They hung out with Dr. Ray Morphew, the Kalas family physician, and his wife, Dee, who chose Harry and Jasmine to be godparents to their two children, Suzie and Lewis. Harry and Jasmine were even closer to Bill and Nancy Giles. Harry and Bill both had the gift of gab, infectious personalities and a love for talking baseball over beer.

Bill, who was 18 months older than Harry, was born into the game. His father, Warren Giles, is a Baseball Hall of Famer who served as National League president from 1951 to 1969. Before that, he was the president of the Cincinnati Reds from 1937 to 1951. Bill spent much of his childhood at old Crosley Field in Cincinnati. By his early 20s, Bill was working for the Reds at the start of a long professional life in baseball that eventually led to him serving as part-owner and president of the Philadelphia Phillies.

Giles left Cincinnati after Major League Baseball announced four expansion teams for the 1961 season—Houston and New York in the National League, plus Los Angeles and Washington in the American League. Giles was hired as part of the Colt .45s' five-man management team and moved to Houston in 1961 initially to serve as PR man for the Triple-A Houston Buffs. The next year, the Buffs moved and were replaced by Texas' first major league team, the Colt .45s, and it was Giles' job to help sell baseball to Houston folks.

One of Giles' first hires was Dan Rather, then a 30-year-old Texan working as news director for KHOU-TV. Giles paid the future network news superstar $10 a game to be the Colt .45s' first public address announcer. The next year, Rather was in Dallas on November 22, 1963 and is credited with being the first reporter to confirm President Kennedy's assassination to *CBS Evening News* anchor Walter Cronkite. When Cronkite retired in 1981, Rather took his spot, and for the next 24 years was considered to be one of the nation's most powerful and influential reporters.

Bill Giles saw talent early on in Harry Kalas, too. They mingled a lot in Houston. Jasmine soon became tight with Nancy. The ladies would talk on the phone, go shopping together and visit one another at the ballpark. The Kalas and Giles families started building their families around the same time, too. It was a bittersweet day for both when Bill's work took him to another city.

Known for his promotional gimmicks as much as for his family name, Bill Giles was hired in September 1969 by Phillies owner Bob Carpenter as the club's new Vice President of Business Operations. The Phillies wanted Giles, known as a marketing genius, to help improve attendance in Philadelphia.

With a string of bad teams and an old ballpark in a rough neighborhood, the Phillies had the second-lowest attendance in the National League in 1969, averaging just 7,316 per home date. The team was moving from Connie Mack Stadium to new Veterans Stadium in 1971, and Carpenter wanted Giles to help Philadelphia get excited about baseball again after a half-decade of declining interest. Making the job extra appealing was Carpenter's plan to retire in a few years and have his son, Ruly, and Giles take over running the club. When the Carpenter family sold the Phillies in 1981, Giles headed a group that purchased the club for $30 million.

A few days before Bill and Nancy Giles left Houston in October 1969, Harry and Jasmine gave them a going-away party at a Japanese tea house. Tears were shed. The couples had no idea that they'd be back together soon.

The Astros had five losing years and a .500 season during Harry's six years in Houston. Harry would have to wait awhile to call postseason baseball, but during his time in Houston he was around some great ballplayers, including Hall of Famers Joe Morgan, Nellie Fox and Eddie Mathews, plus All-Stars Jimmy Wynn, Rusty Staub and César Cedeno. The Astros' best pitcher in the Kalas era was Don Wilson, who treated Harry and Astros fans to a pair of no-hitters and an 18-strikeout game.

Harry's biggest Astros' highlight probably came on July 14, 1967 at San Francisco's Candlestick Park. Eddie Mathews, who played part of one season with Houston at the tail end of his Hall of Fame career, hit his 500th career homer that day. Harry called it on radio:

"Juan Marichal stretches. The pitch. Well-hit ball into deep right field. Way back [Ollie] *Brown. Number 500 for Eddie Mathews! Mathews has just hit the golden 500! Wynn and Staub cross in front of him, and this has got to be a tremendous thrill. The entire Astros bench is up. . . . It couldn't happen to a nicer guy, and it's poetic justice that it happened against one of the game's greatest pitchers, if not the greatest, Juan Marichal.*

And the Astros lead 6-4."

But halfway through his Houston years, Harry Kalas recognized that he was ready for a bigger challenge. A first opportunity came after the 1968 season when Harry interviewed with the Kansas City Royals, an expansion team in 1969. Harry flew to Kansas City for an interview. Jasmine, eight months pregnant with Brad, tagged along, with Harry's parents babysitting Todd in Houston. Harry was intrigued, but Jasmine was annoyed over being driven around town on a hot October day in a car with no air-conditioning.

"It was so hot," Jasmine recalled. "I hated Kansas City. Harry asked me what I thought and I told him the truth. We had a nice visit at Royals owner Ewing Kauffman's huge home, but that didn't make any difference to me. Harry let them know that he was not interested."

The Royals ended up hiring Denny Matthews, who would become Kansas City's version of Harry Kalas. Matthews was still with the Royals in 2009, his 41st year with a 41-year-old franchise. In 2007, he was inducted into the broadcaster's wing of the Baseball Hall of Fame, five years after Harry.

Another bite for a No. 1 play-by-play job didn't come for two years. After the 1970 season, Harry was sought out by the Cincinnati Reds during their search for a new lead broadcaster. Harry really was eager to move on. He'd been with the Astros for six years and still had not been accepted by Elston.

Harry packed for a two-city trip that would start with a University of Houston football game at Wake Forest and conclude with a job interview in Cincinnati. The football game was emotional because proceeds went to the families of the Marshall University football team, which had been killed in a plane crash following a game at East Carolina the previous weekend. The day of the Houston-Wake Forest game, Jasmine was in Houston when Bill Giles phoned from Philadelphia. The Phillies had an opening for their 1971 broadcast team and were very interested in hiring Harry, Giles told Jasmine.

"He's away on a football trip and going straight to Cincinnati to interview with the Reds," Jasmine told Bill.

"If Harry calls, tell him not to sign anything and call me immediately," Bill instructed.

Harry ended up scheduling a third leg to his trip. Now, he would fly from North Carolina to Cincinnati to Philadelphia.

The Reds and Phillies had the same two young talents in mind, Harry

Kalas and a fellow who was following in his footsteps as the lead broadcaster for the Hawaii Islanders, Al Michaels. Kalas began his broadcasting career as the first voice of the Islanders, who joined the Pacific Coast League in 1961. Three years after Kalas left for a big-league job in Houston in 1965, the Islanders hired Michaels.

In the coming years, Michaels would establish himself as one of the most prominent sportscasters ever. One of his claims to fame is his game-ending call in the "Miracle on Ice" hockey game between the United States and Soviet Union at the 1980 Olympics: *"Do you believe in miracles? Yes!"* A native of New York, Michaels got his start in television in 1965 when he worked for Chuck Barris Productions selecting contestants for two popular 1960s game shows, *The Dating Game* and *The Newlywed Game.*

"Right after I got married, I picked all the girls for *Dating Game*," Michaels said. "What a study of frustration that was."

In November 1970, Kalas was led to believe that he was the top choice for the Reds and Phillies. Harry wanted the job in Philadelphia, which offered a bigger market and the opportunity to work again with one of his best friends in baseball, Bill Giles.

"I liked Al Michaels and I liked Harry," Giles said. "They were kind of tied at the time in my mind. I knew Harry better than Michaels, so I decided to push the issue with Harry."

The Reds moved first by interviewing Harry and Al Michaels on Monday, November 23, 1969. During his talk, Harry told the Reds that he would be interviewing in Philadelphia the next day. The Reds made their decision and called a noon Tuesday news conference. *Cincinnati Enquirer* sports writer Steve Hoffman mentioned two candidates in a TV/Radio Column that appeared in Tuesday's paper: "former Cleveland Indians voice Johnny Dudley . . . and Houston Astros voice Harry K. Callis."

Hoffman got it all wrong. The next day, the Reds announced the hiring of Al Michaels, and Harry Norbert Kalas, after interviewing in Philadelphia, agreed to take the job with the Phillies.

PHILADELPHIA FREEDOM

Harry Kalas had a suitcase packed for a December 1970 flight from his home in Houston to Philadelphia so that the Phillies could officially sign their newest broadcaster and announce his hiring at a press conference. A day before Harry's trip, his phone rang. Bill Giles, one of his new Phillies bosses, was calling with news that was both disappointing and concerning.

"We think it's a good idea if you skip the press conference," Giles told Harry. "Bill Campbell isn't coming back, so Philadelphia might not take to you right away. I don't want you to go through the negativity."

His trip canceled, Harry was dumbfounded. Bill Campbell had been a popular Phillies broadcaster for years and Giles, going on an educated hunch, knew there could be a lot of public and media backlash when the change was announced. Until Giles' phone call, Harry had no idea that Campbell was being let go. During his interview and in subsequent phone calls, Harry had been led to believe that he'd be an addition to the Phillies' broadcasting team for the franchise's 1971 move to Veterans Stadium, just as he was when hired by the Houston Astros in 1965 for their inaugural season in the Astrodome.

Harry had been greatly excited about his new opportunity in Philadelphia. He was going to a bigger market for better money and more airtime. His annual salary would jump from $12,000 to $33,000, while his regular innings would increase from three per game to all nine. Plus, he didn't want to work anymore with Gene Elston, the Astros broadcast partner who had given him the cold shoulder for six years in Houston. A new life in Philadelphia also appealed to Harry because he knew from talking to cab drivers, waiters and bartenders during his trips there with the Astros that the city was sports crazy. But before he even officially joined the Phillies, there was controversy, which was something Harry always would go out of his way to avoid in any situation.

Learning that he was taking Bill Campbell's job was depressing for Harry. He knew and liked Campbell, who had been with the Phillies since 1963, sharing a booth with two legends who went on to become Baseball Hall of Famers, Byrum "By" Saam and Richie "Whitey" Ashburn. Campbell, nicknamed "Soupy" for obvious reasons, is short, stocky and wears glasses. As a senior citizen, he might pass for a George Burns or Harry Caray look-alike. He was blessed with an infectious raspy voice that, like Harry Kalas' baritone, was often imitated.

Born in Atlantic City in 1923, Campbell got his radio start in his hometown as a 17-year-old in 1940. The dean of Philadelphia sportscasters late in life, Campbell has had an amazing broadcasting career that has lasted seven-plus decades. Besides calling Phillies games, he was the voice of the NBA's Philadelphia Warriors (1946-62) and Philadelphia 76ers (1972-81) and the NFL's Philadelphia Eagles (1952-66). He also was a radio talk-show host for WIP and a sports commentator for KYW. First among Campbell's countless achievements is his broadcast of a basketball game in Hershey, Pa., on March 2, 1962. In Philadelphia's 169-147 win over the Knicks, legendary Warriors center Wilt Chamberlain became the first and still only player to score 100 points in an NBA game.

The more Harry Kalas thought about Bill Campbell being let go by the Phillies, the worse he felt. The last thing Kalas wanted or needed when starting in Philadelphia was the public turning on him because he wasn't Bill Campbell.

"It'll blow over," Bill Giles assured Harry.

On December 9, 1970—15 days after Harry agreed to a deal—four-dozen reporters showed up for the Phillies' monthly offseason press luncheon at a local Holiday Inn. The local media didn't know what was coming even though the *Philadelphia Inquirer* had reported a week earlier that Campbell would be fired in a two-paragraph article buried in the back of its sports section. Campbell found out about the *Inquirer*'s scoop when he returned home from running a morning errand to find his wife, Jo, sobbing.

"I picked up the paper and there it was," Campbell said.

A half-hour later, Campbell calmed down after taking a phone call from Bob Carpenter, the Phillies owner and president. "Sorry this was in the paper," Carpenter told Campbell. "It's erroneous. We have made no decisions."

Carpenter promised to get back to Campbell in a few days. Five days later, Campbell learned his fate in his next phone call from the Phillies.

"I hate to tell you this, you're through," Carpenter said.

"Why?" Campbell asked. "What's the reason?"

Carpenter said he was sorry, but offered no explanation.

Campbell, healthy and still working part-time at age 85 in 2009, was a relatively young man when he was dropped by the Phillies in 1970. He was upset, but not at Harry.

"There was never any resentment between Harry and I," Bill Campbell said almost four decades after his dismissal. "The Phillies made that decision. Harry didn't have anything to do with it. He didn't undercut me. I never felt that way."

The two remained cordial when seeing each other at sporting events and functions. In time, they became friends for life. Although Bill Campbell was considered to be a bit of a complainer, he and Harry were a lot alike. Both were considered great guys who loved having fun with anyone and everyone, especially colleagues and buddies.

"Harry made it a point to become friends with Bill Campbell," said Jasmine Kalas, Harry's first wife.

The hiring of Harry Kalas and firing of Bill Campbell remained a Phillies secret until it was announced at the club's December 1970 media luncheon. The timing provided cover for Kalas. The Phillies that day released some even bigger news. After a 21-year television relationship with WFIL, the Phils were switching to Channel 17. They were enticed by a five-year, $13.5 million contract—enormous money at the time. The new TV deal was announced with Bill Giles standing at a podium next to a man who was a stranger to the local media—Leonard Stevens, vice president of U.S. Communications Corp.

Giles informed everyone that the Phillies would be televising a club record 70 games in 1971, as well as adding a fourth camera, instant-replay and slow-motion. In addition, the club announced it had a new beer sponsor, C. Schmidt and Sons. That was noteworthy because beer sponsors were still footing the bill for broadcasters, and thus often had a big say in who was in the booth. Known for his creative and sometimes off-the-wall ideas, Giles also announced that the 1971 Phillies would play in red cleats. Eventually, Giles got around to revealing the news about Bill Campbell and Harry Kalas.

"Why?" a reporter called out from a lunch table.

"It's an unfair question to be answered at this forum," answered Leonard Stevens, who was speaking for Channel 17.

"You are aware the audience will want to know, aren't you?" another reporter said.

"Not necessarily," Stevens said. "It was hard-made, carefully considered with some pain-executed decisions. It was done with care and consideration given to the objectives of the total new baseball image on the air."

Seeing the local media upset, Bob Carpenter headed to the podium to chime in. "The ultimate decision in changing the broadcast team was my responsibility. I made the decision."

Later, Stevens tried to spin this controversial firing as a result of "experts" determining that a younger broadcaster would help attract younger viewers. Kalas was 35 in his first season with the Phillies, 13 years younger than Campbell.

"The demographics indicate that half the audience that watches baseball on television is over 50," Stevens said that day. "What is the average age of players? Twenty-six? If people playing are 26 and the people watching at home are 50, what builds the bridge? What interprets the action? The play-by-play team. The commercial world is from 18 to 29. Well, in an effort—rightly or wrongly—we've got to try and get a better marriage between the game and the audience. We want more young people watching. A survey was made of the broadcast team. It was a survey of viewer's attitudes. It was used as a guide to this decision. We heard tapes of Kalas, and he sounds sparkling as hell, and he looks even younger than he is."

Giles added his two cents. "The change wasn't made because of the survey. Channel 17 just felt we ought to have a new face and a younger face. With new sponsors and everything, somebody just had to go and Bill drew the black bean. People are going to put a rap on me because Kalas is from Houston, but it wasn't my decision. I will stand behind Kalas, though. He was my choice and he's a good announcer."

The news of Campbell's firing and Kalas' hiring had to compete with a lot of big news stories that week, including:

- With nearly 200,000 Americans still fighting in the Vietnam War, the United States and ally South Vietnam made a proposal for the release of all prisoners of war in peace talks with North Vietnam, which immediately rejected the offer.
- President Nixon held separate meetings with King Hussein of Jordan and Israeli Defense Minister Moshe Dayan in an attempt to initiate Middle East peace talks.
- Six months after the breakup of The Beatles, John Lennon released a solo album with a song containing a four-letter word that was the first to be banned for radio play by the British Broadcasting Corporation.
- Fort Lauderdale, Fla., civics teacher Leroy Bates, declaring that "there isn't liberty and justice for all," was suspended for refusing to say the Pledge of Allegiance with his students before class.
- Muhammad Ali stopped Ringo Bonavena by a 15th round technical knock-out at New York's Madison Square Garden to set up a heavyweight title fight with champion Joe Frazier.
- The Stanley Cup was stolen from the Hockey Hall of Fame.
- Stanford quarterback Jim Plunkett won college football's Heisman Trophy.

In Philadelphia, Bill Campbell was a much-debated story, but the Phillies strategy for low-keying change of announcers was successful. The day after the Phillies' press conference, the top story on page A-1 of all three Philadelphia newspapers was the nation's rail strike. In sports, the lead story was college basketball: Kenny Durrett, a future NBA player, exploded for 40 points and 15 rebounds at the Palestra to lead LaSalle, one of the city's Big Five schools, to a 97-77 victory over Miami.

The three Philadelphia dailies covered the Phillies luncheon with prominent columnists—Stan Hochman of the *Philadelphia Daily News*, Frank Dolson of the *Philadelphia Inquirer* and Jim Barniak of the *Philadelphia Bulletin*. Dolson and Hochman wrote pieces defending Campbell, while Barniak focused his column on the Phillies becoming the first team to wear red spikes full time. (The Cincinnati Reds wore them during the 1970 playoffs.)

"Static in Clumsy Ouster Widens Credibility Gap" headlined the piece by Hochman, who for years was considered one of the top sports columnists in the country. "The Phillies youth movement has claimed another victim," Hochman started. "Bill Campbell. Announcer-type fellow. Still has the tonsils. Can go from ho-hum to home run screech in 3.2 seconds. Can still snap open a can of beer with éclat. Also with cheese and crackers. Sings 'Fly Me to the Moon' better than anybody east of Andy Williams."

Hochman went on to compare Campbell's talents with those of his former partners in the Phillies broadcast booth, Byrum Saam and Richie Ashburn: "Saam is a tradition in Philadelphia. Like soft pretzels and hoagies. Been 'rolling along into the seventh inning' since Nellie Fox was knee-high to a fungo bat. Smooth voice, cheerful outlook. Is often stumped by the intricacies of the hit-and-run, and his pre-game interviews with Latin players are classics of that genre. Ashburn is Ashburn, blithe spirit out of Tilden, Neb. Knows the game, sounds like a rusty hay baler, but is witty and warm. Campbell might be the town's most professional announcer. Does his homework, talks to athletes, lets his emotion tumble through his descriptions. Maybe he gets too excited, but that is an excess to be cherished over the stifled yawn school of broadcasting."

Hochman quoted Campbell in his piece: "I don't know why the change was made," Campbell said in his first public comments on his dismissal. "They wouldn't tell me. I'm not angry or bitter, but I am disappointed."

Hochman ended his column with this line: "Oh by the way, the new man's name is pronounced Kal-us, as in callous."

Dolson's defense of Campbell, headlined "Firing of 'Voice' Strikes a Bad Chord," argued that Campbell's broadcasting demise was premature. "There have been times in those eight years when Bill had grown sick of the traveling, tired of trying to make a losing team sound exciting," Dolson wrote. "Times when he told the men traveling the baseball beat with him that he felt like quitting. But those were words. No more. . . . Bill Campbell enjoyed doing big-league baseball as much as his fans enjoyed hearing him do it. Which is why [his dismissal] came as such a shock."

In addition to Dolson's column, the *Inquirer* covered the Phillies' luncheon with a 12-paragraph news article, which had no byline and ran under the headline "70 Games in '71; Sign New Pact." The story read like a press release, opening with "A record 70 games will be broadcast in color in 1971, according to the terms of a $13.5 million contract signed Wednesday with WPHL-TV (Ch. 17) and its parent U.S. Communications, Inc." Nothing was mentioned on the broadcasting change until the eighth paragraph. "Harry Kalas, who broadcast the Houston Astros' games the last six seasons, will join Byrum Saam and Richie Ashburn on the Phillies' broadcasting crew. Bill Campbell will not return. Kalas, 34, a native of Chicago, covered Hawaii Islanders games before going to Houston."

Barniak, who would himself later become part of the Phillies' broadcast team, devoted only a few sentences to the Campbell-Kalas change in his column, which focused mostly on the Phillies' new shoes.

"Maybe Giles is hoping Larry Bowa will slip on his new tootsies and steal bases three at a time," Barniak wrote. "Maybe Deron Johnson will beat out infield hits the way he did 10 years ago with black shoes. It was Moira Shearer, the famous ballerina, who once said, 'Red Shoes made me what I am today.' And for all the Bill Campbell fans out there in radioland, there was a patch of blue. With a lump in his throat the size of a rosin bag, Carpenter announced that Campbell was being dropped from the broadcasting troika and will be replaced by Harry Kalas, who for the past six years has been humming along with the Houston Astros. Kalas, 34, is another in a series of changes geared at making the whole Phillies concept more appealing to youth. You may recall the team's jazzy new logo, a promise of mini-skirted usherettes, the all-Astroturf field, Philadelphia Phil and his girl, Phyllis, the home run spectacular and exploding scoreboard."

From there, Barniak returned to his footwear theme and gave Giles and Phillies GM John Quinn a forum to boast about red spikes.

"I'm always trying to think of something different," Giles said. "Even if they're nothing more than a conversational piece, how bad is that? I know the cynics are going to jump all over me. Like, 'What's this kook going to do next?' I like it to a certain extent. There's a little life around the Phillies and I like it."

"Anything that attracts attention, so long as it's in good taste, has to be good for the club," Quinn added. "Suppose we're the Game of the Week. Somebody in Keokuk, Iowa, who maybe doesn't know a thing about the Phillies, sees the game and remembers for the rest of the season that the Phillies are the ones with the red shoes. Something like that's bound to help the image."

The red shoes didn't help the 1971 Phillies' image. Harry Kalas did. In the years to come, his enormous popularity would make him not only the voice of the Phillies, but also a face of the franchise. Before that could happen, though, he had to ride out the public outcry over the Phillies' firing of Campbell.

Dan Stephenson, a 17-year-old Phillies fan in 1971, was bitter. Within a few years, he started his long career with the Phillies as a video production manager and would become a close friend to Harry Kalas. But from 1971 to 1973, Video Dan, as he is known, stopped watching the Phillies because his favorite broadcaster had been canned.

"I remember hearing the Phillies fired Bill Campbell and wondering, 'Who's this jerk they got?'" Stephenson said. "I hated Harry in 1971 because he took Bill Campbell's job, even though that's not what happened. Harry was a victim of all this and I remember saying, 'I'll never like this guy.' At the time, I sort of drifted away from baseball. I was annoyed. I said, 'That's it, I'm done with baseball. How can they get rid of Bill Campbell?' Bill Campbell was the star of the show."

Stephenson started paying attention again in 1974 when the improving Phillies contended for a playoff berth for the first time in a decade. "I got into it," he said. "And once you get into it, you fall in love with Harry because he makes you get into it. Soon, I became a huge Harry fan."

Mark "Frog" Carfagno, a Phillies groundskeeper from 1971 to 2004, was initially upset, too. "I was mad at Bill Giles for bringing Harry in."

The storm over Campbell's firing intensified two days after the luncheon when *Daily News* baseball writer Bill Conlin stuck up for Campbell in a column that was headlined: "Striking Out an Honest Voice." Conlin, a brilliant wordsmith who never was afraid to take on the powers that be, made an elegant case that Campbell deserved a better fate.

"Byrum Saam and Bill Campbell blended like white phosphorous and water," Conlin wrote. "They were the cobra and mongoose of broadcasting, their styles and approach to broadcasting as alien to one another as fire and ice. Saam learned very early in the broadcasting game that it is dangerous to rock the boat even a little bit. He learned that all that is expected is acquiescent mediocrity. Read the commercials on time and throw in a lot of plugs for the big four-game set coming up with the dashing young San Diego Padres, and if you're close to the ballpark, there still are plenty of seats. Saam is street smart. Byrum Saam never made enough waves to capsize a peanut shell. No man has ever lasted so many years broadcasting baseball games in one city for one sponsor.

"Now this Campbell had the potential to be a troublemaker," Conlin continued. "When he felt the advertising copy they mailed out for him to read insulted the intelligence of his listeners he usually told somebody about it. All

Bill Campbell ever wanted to do was call a good baseball game with some flair and integrity. That was two strikes against him. He is from a very small school of broadcasters who figure that to do a good job you have to do more than talk for five or six innings. When it comes to probing players for anecdotes and useful information, not even Vin Scully, the Dodgers' super-voice, is more thorough. While Saam would be wowing them with his back swing at some country club on the road, Campbell would often be sitting in the hotel coffee shop or lobby getting a kid pitcher to talk about himself. This falls under the heading of dedication and love for the job."

Conlin still recalled his Campbell column in an interview 39 years later. "I wrote a scathing denunciation of Soupy's firing. I had no problem with them bringing in a young announcer, but Saam was already starting to slip and was mailing it in. Campbell was still on top of his game and had established the same kind of rapport with Whitey that Harry later developed."

Four decades later, Giles claimed the "reason we fired Bill Campbell" was that the Phillies' new beer sponsor for 1971 ordered it. Schmidt's paid the Phillies $1 million for the broadcasting rights and wrote the broadcasters' paychecks, so it was their call, Giles maintains.

"The Schmidt's people didn't want Bill Campbell around because he'd done all the Ballantine beer commercials," Giles said in 2009.

Campbell doesn't buy that excuse. A 2006 biography on Campbell titled *The Voice of Philadelphia Sports* featured a picture of a poster showing the Phillies' entire 1970 broadcast team together in a Ballantine ad.

"Bill Giles blames it on a sponsor," Campbell said. "There wasn't any sponsor conflict. Bill wanted to bring Harry in, and the problem was the beer sponsor only wanted to pay three of us. Somebody had to go, and it wasn't going to be Richie Ashburn, that's for sure. And it wasn't going to be By Saam, who already had 25 years with the team. Somebody had to go and it was me. I drew the short straw."

"That's bullshit," Giles said when hearing Campbell's reflection. "I didn't want to embarrass the Schmidt's beer people so I put the onus on myself. When Schmidt's said Bill Campbell had to go, I knew the guy I wanted, so I called Harry."

Bill Campbell landed on his feet. The day he was let go, his duties doing the morning news at a local radio station were expanded to sports talk-show host. His station had big ads in the next day's papers: "Bill Campbell's Back!!!

on WCAU. Morning Newsbeat 6 a.m.-9 a.m."

Bill also landed a second job for the 1971 baseball season as a broadcaster for the Pittsburgh Pirates' 38 road television games on KDKA. After years of calling games for a lot of bad Phillies teams, Campbell joined a National League power. With future Hall of Famers Roberto Clemente and Willie Stargell leading the way, the Pirates won the 1971 World Series. Bill Campbell got a ring, but he wasn't happy working for the Pirates. A Philadelphia guy through and through, he left the club after one season.

A week after Campbell's December 1970 firing was announced, Harry and Jasmine Kalas traveled to Philadelphia in an unannounced visit. Harry was there to sign his contract and get to know Phillies management, while Jasmine came along to start looking for homes. Jasmine spent a few days looking at about a dozen homes in various upscale sections and suburbs of Philadelphia with her old friend from Houston, Nancy Giles, Bill's wife. Jasmine found a home she liked in the town of Radnor, about 20 miles west of downtown Philadelphia. When Harry stopped by for a visit, he approved. After returning to Houston, Harry made an offer on the house that was accepted. He had a new job and a new home in Philadelphia.

In February 1971, before the start of spring training, a moving truck loaded up Harry and Jasmine's belongings in Houston and headed east. With Harry busy broadcasting University of Houston college basketball games, Jasmine flew to Philadelphia with a friend to have their new home ready to live in by the start of baseball season. She even got Bill Giles to help hang curtain rods. Jasmine then flew back to Houston to do more packing. This time, she and Harry loaded up the family car and a trailer full of indoor plants for a 1,000-mile drive to Clearwater, Fla., for their first Phillies spring training. Harry and Jasmine took turns driving, with their boys, now 5 and 2, in the backseat with the family pet, a caged parakeet named Polo Manu between them.

Most Phillies employees in those days spent spring training at the Jack Tar Hotel in downtown Clearwater. But the Kalas family opted for Sun 'N' Fun, a beach hotel. Their first spring training with the Phillies convinced the Kalas' that they had made the right move. Springs with the Astros in Cocoa Beach were pleasant, but Harry and Jasmine considered Clearwater, located on Florida's Gulf of Mexico side, much more beautiful.

After a month in spring training, Harry Kalas made another long road trip, this time steering his car, trailer and family to their new life in Philadelphia.

THAT '70s SHOW

Harry Kalas began life as a Philadelphian in 1971, feeling lost and frustrated. After almost a full 24 hours of driving from Phillies' spring training in Florida, Harry, his wife and two boys arrived in the Philadelphia area on a cold early April night. Harry was exhausted and cranky. All he wanted to do was sleep as he drove through Delaware and finally into Pennsylvania. Eventually the Kalases arrived in Radnor, an upscale suburb outside Philadelphia that is part of the famed Main Line, one of the country's premier addresses.

With breathtaking rolling hills hidden by the darkness of the night, Harry steered through winding roads and into his neighborhood. Locating his home wasn't quite so simple. He drove around in circles, stopped to read his directions, and then drove around some more. Finally, he flagged down a vehicle and asked for help. The driver escorted him to 1198 Rossiter Lane, the Kalas' new three-bedroom, two-story blue house with white trim. The man had no idea who Harry Kalas was or would become. But his good deed set a tone for hundreds of good deeds that Harry went on to do in his adopted hometown.

It would take some time before Harry found smooth sailing in the broadcast booth. Phillies fans, many of whom were still upset about Bill Campbell's firing, would need some time to get used to Harry Kalas, who was being force-fed to Philadelphia. To the Phillies, he was a lot more than a new broadcaster. He was brought in to be the voice of the franchise's exciting transition from their old out-of-date Connie Mack Stadium to the new, high-tech Veterans Stadium.

Connie Mack Stadium, the Phillies' home from 1938 to 1970, opened in 1909 as Shibe Park, the second home of the Philadelphia Athletics, the city's American League franchise for a half-century. Located on 21st Street and Lehigh Avenue in North Philadelphia, it was state-of-the-art in its early days and the major leagues' first concrete-and-steel stadium.

Philadelphia became a two-team town in 1901 when the Athletics were born, 18 years after the Phillies' inaugural season as a National League franchise in 1883. Shibe Park was named after Ben Shibe, a former minority owner of the Phillies who founded the A's along with Connie Mack and two Philadelphia sports writers. Mack, the franchise's sole owner by 1936, famously managed the team for 50 years, from the beginning in 1901 through 1950, all the while wearing a suit and straw hat instead of a baseball uniform. Shibe Park took on a second tenant midway through the 1938 season when the Phillies abandoned their dilapidated Baker Bowl after 52 years. The ballpark, renamed Connie Mack Stadium in 1953, was down to one resident again by 1955, when the Athletics relocated to Kansas City.

Years before leaving Connie Mack Stadium, the Phillies began craving a new home. In 1964, Philadelphia taxpayers approved a $25 million bond referendum to finance a new all-purpose stadium for the Phillies and the NFL's Philadelphia Eagles. It would be located on Broad and Pattison Streets in a section of South Philadelphia that also featured JFK Stadium, an ancient football stadium that still hosted the Army-Navy game, and the Spectrum, home of the city's NHL and NBA franchises.

The city opted to stick with a growing trend around the country and build an oval-shaped venue with symmetrical dimensions for baseball that easily could be converted for football with rotating box seats. From 1964 to 1971, similar stadiums came up from the ground in Atlanta, Cincinnati, Houston, New York, Pittsburgh, San Diego, St. Louis and Washington, D.C. The venues all looked alike and in time would be disparagingly dubbed "cookie-cutter" stadiums, but they were popular in their early years.

The Phillies' new venue was named Veterans Stadium by the Philadelphia City Council in 1968, in honor of the veterans of all wars. It was scheduled for a May 1970 unveiling before weather and cost issues pushed its opening back until the Phillies' 1971 home opener. With a final cost of $50 million, Veterans Stadium seated 55,000 for baseball in its inaugural season and featured an AstroTurf surface, a giant scoreboard with computerized animation and a replica Liberty Bell hanging from the center-field roof.

For the Phillies, their move to Veterans Stadium was more than changing stadiums. This also was about changing their image. They were rebuilding on the field with young talents such as Larry Bowa, Willie Montanez and Roger Freed in the lineup, and wanted to attract younger fans after drawing just 700,000 for their final season at Connie Mack. With a new stadium and a rebuilding franchise, Harry Kalas was hired as a young voice to attract young fans. So when Veterans Stadium opened on April 10, 1971, Harry was picked to be the pre-game master of ceremonies instead of the Phillies' two popular returning broadcasters, By Saam and Richie Ashburn. Wearing a white trench coat and with his blonde hair blowing on a windy, 40-degree afternoon, Harry stood on the field and talked to Phillies fans for the first time with a microphone in his hand. He laid the groundwork that day for what would become a longtime, two-way love affair with Phillies fans:

"Ladies and gentlemen, good afternoon, welcome to new Veterans Stadium and Opening Day," Harry began. "And thank you, because above all the festivities, the response that you have shown in making this a sellout months in advance shows that Philadelphia has the best fans in the National League. On behalf of the Philadelphia Phillies, we thank you very much."

Behind future Hall of Fame pitcher Jim Bunning, the Phillies won the first of the 2,617 regular-season games they would play at Veterans Stadium, stopping the Montreal Expos 4-1.

Hearing Harry that first day, Phillies management knew they'd made the right decision in hiring him. Winning over fans wouldn't be so easy, but Harry went out of his way to make everyone he encountered feel special. He answered his mail with hand-written letters, signed autographs whenever asked and engaged in conversation during encounters before and after games at the ballpark, hotels, restaurants and bars.

"To see Harry was to know this guy was going to be pretty special," said David Montgomery, who sold tickets for the Phillies in 1971 and replaced Bill Giles as team president in 1997. "I was a Bill Campbell listener, and Harry worked in an environment that people questioned because of who he was replacing, but you could go on and on about the way Harry endeared himself to people in Philadelphia. Harry was so gracious and so giving of his time. Harry's gift was his people skills, and he fit in with everybody. Harry became part of Philadelphia. He didn't expect Philadelphia to adjust to him."

Harry's new broadcast partners took to him right away, helping smooth the transition. During his six seasons in Houston, Harry felt that he was treated like an outcast by the Astros top play-by-play man, Gene Elston. But in Philadelphia, Harry was accepted and befriended immediately by his new broadcast partners, By Saam and Richie Ashburn, both of whom already were legends in the City of Brotherly Love.

"Without Richie Ashburn and By Saam's help in taking me under their wings, I don't know if I would have made it," Harry Kalas said in 2002. "I think it took awhile before the Philadelphia public took me in and said, 'Yeah, he's our guy.' I think Richie Ashburn had a great deal to do with that because I think the public felt, 'If Whitey likes him, he must be all right.'"

Harry helped his image by participating in some of Bill Giles' zany pre-game entertainment, too. Harry and Whitey raced each other one year peddling tricycles built for six-year-olds. Another time, Harry wore an Eagles helmet while racing a small, battery-powered car. The topper in many fans' minds was Harry racing Ashburn in carts pulled by ostriches. When the race began, the ostriches panicked and ran around in circles. Frightened, Harry and Whitey jumped off their carts and watched the ostriches leap into the stands before being captured. No one was injured.

Harry saw a lot of bad baseball in 1971. The Phillies, coming off three consecutive losing seasons in their final years at Connie Mack Stadium, finished with a 67-95 record, dooming them to last place in the six-team National League East.

Aside from the home opener, the biggest highlight of the Phillies' 1971 season was provided in Cincinnati on June 23rd by 25-year-old right-hander Rick Wise, who made history by becoming the first pitcher to throw a no-hitter and hit two home runs in the same game.

The longest home run ever hit in Veterans Stadium also came in its inaugural season. On June 25, Pittsburgh Pirates slugger Willie Stargell blasted a towering drive to right field that touched down in an exit area of the 600 level, the second-highest deck of the stadium. A seat next to where the ball landed in Section 601 was permanently marked with a white circle surrounding a black 'S' for Stargell.

In the Pirates television booth that day was Bill Campbell, the man who was let go to make room in the Phillies booth for Harry Kalas. During his one season in Pittsburgh, Campbell worked with Hall of Fame broadcaster Bob Prince, the club's play-by-play man from 1948 to 1975. Nicknamed "the Gunner," Prince was famed for his screwball antics and numerous catchphrases. A double play was a "hoover," an extra-base hit "a bug on the rug." He quoted Jackie Gleason's "How sweet it is!" after each Pirates victory. And when a Pittsburgh player hit a home run, the Gunner would call out, "You can kiss it goodbye!"

Harry Kalas, who coined signature home run calls in Hawaii and Houston, came up with his famed "Outta here!" call early into his Philadelphia days.

The time and place has been lost in history, but legend has it that Larry Bowa, the Phillies shortstop from 1970 to 1981, was standing with Harry behind a batting cage when Phillies left fielder Greg "the Bull" Luzinski hit a towering batting-practice homer in the early 1970s.

"I remember standing behind the cage and Bull hitting one long one after another," Bowa said. "Watching, I'd go, 'Outta here . . . outta here . . . outta here.' Then Bull really hit one and I went, 'That ball's WAY outta here!'"

When Bowa said, "WAY outta here," Harry Kalas looked at him like he was onto something.

"That has a unique ring to it," Harry told himself. It sounded even better rolling off Harry's lips as "ahhh-ta-heeere" with excitement in his baritone voice. In time, Harry added a couple lines to make it even better, "Swing and a long drive, watch that baby, outta here!"

Bowa usually has Luzinski hitting the BP homer into the upper deck at Veterans Stadium, but he also has had it occurring at Jack Russell Stadium in Clearwater, Fla.

"I never said 'Outta here!' before, but for some reason I said it that day," Bowa recalled. "I didn't say it like Harry, but he looked at me and just ran with it. You can say the rest is history."

At first, Harry didn't use his home run call every time a player went yard. But within a few years, it became a trademark. Soon, kids were imitating the call in backyard Wiffle Ball games all over Philadelphia, southern New Jersey and northern Delaware.

"I imitated Harry," said Jamie Moyer, a suburban Philly kid who ended up pitching for his hometown team. "You always imitate broadcasters that you liked, and I liked Harry."

Harry always credited Bowa. "Until the day Harry died, he kept thanking me," Bowa said. "Obviously, that was his signature call. But if I hadn't said that, it wouldn't have mattered. Harry would have come up with some other home run call and still be in the Hall of Fame."

In 1972, the Phillies suffered through another terrible season, losing 97 games and finishing last in their division again. But that season marked the arrival of two future Hall of Fame players who would help the Phillies build themselves into regular World Series contenders.

Late into spring training, the Phillies traded Rick Wise to St. Louis for 26-year-old left-hander Steve Carlton, a 20-game winner in 1971 who was moved during a contract squabble with Cardinals ownership. Right away, Carlton was great, winning 27 games in 1972, accounting for almost half of the Phillies' victories that season. "Every time Steve Carlton was gonna pitch for the Phillies, I had an extra bounce in my step when I walked into the ballpark," Kalas recalled. "You knew you were going to see something special."

On September 12, 1972, Mike Schmidt, wearing injured outfielder Mike Anderson's No. 22 jersey, debuted for the Phillies in a game against the New York Mets. Just 20 at the time, the third baseman was 1-for-3 with a single, walk and two strikeouts in his first game. Switching to No. 20 in 1973, Schmidt had a rocky first full season before developing into an all-time great slugger and defensive whiz who was never fully appreciated by Phillies fans until late in his career. When listing his greatest thrills as a broadcaster, Harry Kalas answered: "Following Michael Jack Schmidt's entire career . . . from the get-go when he was booed by the fans, to the culmination where the fans finally realized, 'Wow, we're watching something very special, the best third baseman to ever play the game.'"

Harry Kalas became close to Schmidt and Carlton, but not because they were stars. Harry was friendly with everybody. Schmidt could be reclusive and

Carlton was regarded as quirky, but both gravitated to Harry, who was widely considered to be fun and trustworthy. To Harry, Carlton was "Lefty" and Schmidt was "Michael Jack," his full first and middle names. Soon, because of Harry Kalas, Lefty and Michael Jack became as recognizable names in and around Philadelphia as William Penn and Ben Franklin.

"As a kid, I thought one of the coolest things was the way Harry said 'Michael Jack Schmidt,'" said Ruben Amaro, Jr., a grade schooler in the early 1970s who would grow up to be a player and general manager for the Phillies.

With two young stars to go along with his great voice, terrific broadcast skills and catchy home run call, Harry started gaining acceptance.

"I loved listening to By Saam as a kid growing up, and when Harry first came here, I thought, 'Man oh man, Harry's got some big shoes to fill,'" Phillies longtime public address announcer Dan Baker said. "But he sure did."

Most everyone Harry met wanted to be his friend, and Harry wanted to be friends with most everyone he met. He hung out with ballplayers when he was on the road and with management after home games, but he also befriended everyone including media and radio technicians, food servers and bartenders, secretaries and clubhouse attendants.

"I liked Harry right away," said longtime Philadelphia radio man Skip "Memory Lane" Clayton. "I liked his voice on the air. I liked his enthusiasm. I liked everything about him. Most importantly, I liked him as a person. You couldn't help but like Harry Kalas."

Harry came up with the name "Memory Lane" for Clayton, who used to research statistics for the Phillies media guide and deliver baseball trivia questions for Harry and Richie Ashburn to use on the air. Harry made Memory Lane Clayton a household name in Philadelphia.

"My popularity really took off one day when a foul ball came my way," Clayton recalled. "The ball missed going in the press box by about a foot and hit a façade as it moved at a pretty good rate. I could have tried to catch it, but I wouldn't have had a hand. I looked over at Harry and he makes a hand signal that told me, 'Come on, you're supposed to catch that ball.' The next pitch, a foul ball goes over my head and I looked over to Harry again. This time, Harry stood up in the Phillies broadcast booth, looked my way and proceeded to give me two thumbs down, which in his mind was an error sign. From there, it took off every time a foul ball came anywhere near me. All the while, Harry was telling his listeners that Memory Lane Clayton had made another error. After awhile it was always, 'And you guessed it, another error on Memory Lane.'"

A young boy wrote a letter to Richie Ashburn wanting to know if Clayton was using a magnet to attract so many foul balls. Harry was sent a T-shirt from another fan that read, "And you guessed it, another error on Memory Lane." Memory Lane became so popular that he once was asked for an autograph at a funeral home.

After his first season with the Phillies, Harry had made enough of an impression on fans that a New Jersey travel agency, Haddon Travel, started an annual "Trip to Hawaii with Harry Kalas." Harry and Jasmine Kalas got a free vacation to their old home, and 100 or so couples signed up for Hawaiian vacations. Harry wasn't required to spend a lot of time with the guests, but he frequently did anyway.

The trip became an annual January event, usually lasting a week, and some of the same couples returned year after year. Occasionally, Phillies players would make the trip with their wives as well. Attendees included Mike and Donna Schmidt, Tug and Annie McGraw, Jay and Mary Jayne Johnstone, Greg and Jean Luzinski, Bob and Sue Boone.

Harry made close friends on these vacations with two of the regulars.

Joe Nunes recalls meeting Harry on the beach in Maui in 1972, the first year of the Hawaii vacations. "I just happened to sit next to Harry, and after awhile he says, 'Let's take a swim.' He lived in Hawaii, so I figure this guy knows what he's doing. We ended up on a coral reef and we come back with a million little cuts." A spunky 5-foot-9 real estate agent who had been mayor of Pine Hill, N.J., for eight years, Nunes loved to party as much as Harry did. When they returned to Philadelphia, they stayed in touch and became friends for life.

Bob Smith, who handled statistical data for a horse racing newspaper, was on the 1976 trip when a friendly gesture led to a lifelong friendship with Harry Kalas. "Harry and Mike Schmidt were doing an autograph session for the whole group, so I sent Harry a Mai Tai, not knowing that was his favorite Hawaiian drink," recalled Smith, who lives about 30 minutes from Philadelphia in Newtown, Pa. "I think that was what probably started the whole relationship. He was so overwhelmed that somebody sent him a drink. He signed a photo for myself and my wife. At that point, we got together one or two more times in Hawaii. I got home a week later and got a phone call from Jasmine, who invited my wife and I to join them in spring training for a week. We ended up going to Hawaii with Harry and Jasmine seven years in a row."

To celebrate Harry's return to Hawaii, the best man in his wedding to Jasmine hosted an annual luau, complete with a roasted pig. Bill Whaley, who lived on an oceanfront home, always encouraged Harry to bring along a few friends, folks like Bob Smith, Joe Nunes and their wives.

One year, the "Trip to Hawaii with Harry Kalas" shifted to Guadalupe Island, which is off the coast of Mexico. A highlight of this trip was when Harry, Jasmine and another couple talked their way into visiting a nudist colony of American vacationers. When one of the nudists recognized Harry, Kalas and his friends were invited to a buffet restaurant that was off-limits to outsiders. While filling their stomachs with food and wine, Harry's group noted that they were among the only people in the restaurant wearing clothes.

Of all Harry's travels, his favorite time of the year was going to spring training. He would do a lot of studying to prepare for regular-season games, but took it easy in spring training. There was a lot of family and fun time in addition to his time at the ballpark calling Grapefruit League games. He had enjoyed his February and March days in Cocoa Beach, Fla., during his six seasons with the Houston Astros, but spring training across the state with the Phillies was more fun. Harry thought the restaurants were better in Clearwater. His favorite was the Beachcomber. He also liked that there was more mingling in Phillies spring training.

"There are two ways to do spring training games," Harry Kalas used to say. "Either you work your fanny off because you don't know all the players, or you just kind of slide through it a little bit. I've chosen the latter."

This was Harry's way of saying spring training is a time to relax.

"It was probably the one time Harry ever slacked off in anything," said Andy Musser, a Phillies broadcaster from 1976 to 2001. "After he told me that, I started listening for it on the air and I never could detect it anyway. He still would get to the games early and prepare, but I guess somehow in his mind he didn't think he was doing as thorough a job as he could. The reason was, for Harry, Florida was vacation. There were day games, for the most part, and no one particularly cared if you won or lost. Everybody was in a good mood. The weather was good. It was family time for Harry, and he loved that time of the year."

During spring training nights, Harry would often go to Derby Lane, a dog track in St. Petersburg that attracted a nightly crowd of prominent baseball figures. The Phillies, Reds, Cardinals and—starting in 1977—the Blue Jays all trained in the area. Many of their players, managers, front-office people and broadcasters would congregate at the track for dinner and gambling.

"The last time I gave Harry meal money in spring training, I kidded him by saying, 'Do you want me to just take it over to Derby Lane and put it on your account?' said Frank Coppenbarger, the Phillies director of travel and club services. "Harry used to love going to Derby Lane. During its heyday, that was the spot for baseball. In the 1970s and '80s, that's where you saw the managers and coaches and players. The Derby Club had a prime rib that was about three inches thick and 15 inches long. You couldn't eat that thing."

Harry often was there betting on the "puppies," as he called them, while drinking gin and talking baseball with the likes of Pete Rose, Bill Giles and Reds scout Ray Shore, among others. FOX sportscaster Joe Buck said some of his earliest baseball memories are of nightly spring visits to Derby Lane with his father, the late St. Louis Cardinals Hall of Fame broadcaster Jack Buck.

"I knew Harry Kalas when I was five, six, seven, eight years old at Derby Lane," Joe Buck said. "Harry was the nicest guy in the world. I was a little kid hanging around, and my dad and Harry would be looking over dog-racing forms throwing money at the puppies. Nobody ever was jumping for joy or clicking their heels. There was a lot of ticket tearing back then."

Harry didn't win much money at Derby Lane, but he studied the dogs harder than he did the material for many of his school exams.

"Every day after the workout or game, we would sit by the pool and go over the track form for that night," said Ron Reed, a Phillies relief pitcher from 1976 to 1983.

One night while driving home with Bill and Nancy Giles, Jasmine said to Harry, "It's very embarrassing for you to lose $300."

"Jasmine, I didn't lose $300," he responded. "I lost $600."

In the mornings or early evenings, Harry played a lot of tennis with broadcast partner Richie Ashburn and *Philadelphia Daily News* baseball writer Bill Conlin.

Although not having much of a serve, Ashburn was terrific and rarely was beaten on the court. Harry and Conlin were closer in talent and usually would play at least a dozen three-set wars every spring in the 1970s. The tennis matches continued into the season during road trips.

"I learned a little about his self-discipline and competitive nature playing tennis with the guy," Conlin said. "Our styles were diametrically opposite. He was a human backboard. He would just block your serve back, block your big forehand back and hit short balls until you came charging up like a big weary water buffalo and hit the ball into the net or the back fence. Harry fought every point. He always gave you the benefit of the call. If it was an inch out, he gave it to you. He was that kind of sportsman. I learned a lot about the man's dogged nature and his iron will to succeed in everything he did playing those simple tennis matches."

Meanwhile, on the field, the Phillies started showing improvement in 1974. They finished with a losing record again, but their 80-82 record and third-place finish marked a big improvement after three consecutive last-place finishes. The 1975 Phillies took another leap, notching 86 victories for the franchise's first winning season since 1967.

Everything came together for the Phillies in 1976, America's bicentennial celebration of the signing of the Declaration of Independence in Philadelphia. The Phillies won the National League East to reach postseason play for the first time since 1950. For Harry Kalas, it felt great to finally be with a team that won something after not being associated with a playoff team during his first 15 seasons in professional baseball—four in Hawaii, six in Houston and five in Philadelphia.

The 1976 season, which ended with the Phillies being swept by the Cincinnati Reds in a best-of-five National League Championship Series, also included a big change in the Phillies broadcast booth. By Saam, the voice of the Philadelphia A's and Phillies for 38 seasons, retired.

Saam's pipes, like Harry's, had been perfect for baseball on radio. "By had a velvety voice that just put you at ease," Dan Baker said. "Like Harry Kalas, By had the ability to emote and raise his voice to show the excitement of a rally or a ball with a chance to be a home run. He was just a master of that."

Bob Kirk, a Phillies fan for more than 70 years and noted collector of baseball memorabilia, does not totally share Baker's feelings. "By was real good, but very plain," the retired supermarket employee from Quinton, N.J., said. "He was not at all flamboyant like Harry. As Harry described the game, he made it seem as if you were right there in the stands. Whether it was the steal of a base or especially a home run, Harry always made following the Phillies very exciting for listeners."

Unlike Harry Kalas, By Saam never became a beloved figure in Philadelphia. He was liked and respected, but never glorified. Late in his career, Saam made a lot of on-air mistakes. One day, he infamously began a broadcast saying, "Hi, By Saam, this is everybody" instead of "Hi, everybody, this is By Saam." Due to waning eyesight, Saam had all kinds of trouble tracking the flight of the ball by the 1970s. During a game in Pittsburgh, Saam called "long drive to left, that ball is. . . ." Richie Ashburn jumped in, "caught by the shortstop." Another time, By said on air, "There's a line drive to short . . . it's gone." Ashburn chimed in, "Yeah, By, solidly hit into the upper deck."

Saam's goofs became the stuff of comedy for some Phillies fans. One young man even kept a running total of Saam's errors in a college notebook. Mark Carfagno labeled his findings "By's Blunders."

"By Saam had a great voice and I liked him, but toward the end he began to lose it," said Mort Stein, a Phillies fan for more than 65 years who in 2009 was in his 16th season working security for the team during home games.

Still, By Saam was considered to be very good during his prime. That and his longevity eventually led to a big payoff. In 1990, Saam became a member of the Hall of Fame as a recipient of the Ford C. Frick Award for excellence in broadcasting.

Harry Kalas was ecstatic for By Saam. He never forgot how Saam helped him in 1971 in ways Gene Elston never did in Houston. Jasmine Kalas said By Saam was like a father to Harry. "He made my transition from Houston to Philadelphia an easy one," Harry Kalas once said of Saam. "He taught me a great deal about broadcasting and life."

The one major hole in By Saam's career had been never calling postseason baseball. Less than a year into retirement, By Saam was brought back in the booth for the Phillies' 1976 division clincher, a magnanimous gesture by management which was embraced by Harry and Whitey. "Thirty-eight years and no winner? Damn right he deserved a title," Ashburn said.

Andy Musser, a sportscaster at WCAU-TV in Philadelphia since 1971, was Saam's replacement.

Musser, known to all as a gentleman, was a veteran sportscaster who had done football and basketball play-by-play, but no baseball. He grew up a baseball fan, but learned quickly that he had a lot to learn, especially when flying solo on the radio while Harry and Whitey were together doing television games. That made radio-only games educational for Musser, who would sit next to Harry even when he wasn't on the air in order to study his style and routine.

"At the outset, Harry was very, very helpful," Musser recalled. "Having an opportunity to sit in the same booth as Harry, side-by-side, and hearing him do five or six innings most every night . . . believe me, that was beneficial. I didn't try to sound like Harry, but I think I quite naturally used some of his phraseology."

The next year, Harry was nurturing yet another newcomer when Chris Wheeler added radio duties to his public relations chores for the club in 1977, giving the Phillies a four-man broadcast team for the first time.

Kalas, Ashburn, Musser and Wheeler grew very close. Harry found an older brother in Whitey, a drinking buddy in Wheeler and a trusting friend in Musser. During an off day on Phillies road trips, they always dined together at a nice restaurant, taking turns picking up the tab.

"We all considered those the good years," Musser said. "Sometimes a player or someone from the front office would show up. Even Whitey showed up, and he always wanted to stay in his room, read a book, smoke his pipe and have room service. We all had very good camaraderie, and that kind of thing does carry over on the air."

After games, Harry and Wheels would go to the hotel bar and talk baseball with the players. "Harry was always drinking beers with the guys talking baseball until two in the morning," said Larry Bowa, the Phillies starting shortstop from 1970 to 1981. "Guys would migrate to him and listen to him. When we'd get there, there'd be two or three guys. When we'd leave, there would be 15. You'd argue about players. He'd say, 'This guy can't play' and I'd say. 'Yes he can.' If you ever said anything negative about somebody on our team, Harry would shoot back, 'He's a good utility player' or something like that ... no matter who he was. He loved the Phillies."

It was a two-way love affair, and within a few years Phillies veteran players broke with tradition by inviting Harry to sit in the back of the plane with them. Even such luminaries as Jack Buck, Vin Scully and Harry Caray sat in the front of their team plane with the other broadcasters and front office people. But Harry Kalas always was found in the back ... drinking, smoking, playing cards and telling stories with the players. Harry was one of the guys.

"In my mind, he was the Philadelphia Phillies," Greg Luzinski said.

Harry was a friend to the players, never betraying their trust. When necessary, he criticized their on-field mistakes, but in a gentle, dignified way. "When you're a broadcaster for a long time, you're going to say something where someone gets mad at you," Larry Bowa said. "I never saw anyone mad at Harry ... ever. If you want to call him a 'homer,' fine, but he genuinely wanted the Phillies and everyone on that team to do well."

While Harry always seemed to fit in when around Phillies players, he stood out everywhere he went ... and not just due to his infectious personality, top-notch broadcast skills and mesmerizing voice. Harry wasn't quite an Elton John of his time, but he'd wear white shoes, plaid pants and loud sports jackets—before, during and after they were in style. Harry's wife, Jasmine, purchased his first pair of white shoes during a shopping trip to New York City. Actually, she picked up several pair of Guccis—white, brown and black. Harry preferred the white ones and wore them until they needed to be resoled. Getting the hint, Jasmine bought all white Guccis the next time she went shoe shopping for Harry.

"I wouldn't say Harry was a wardrobe specialist," said Dallas Green, the Phillies' manager from 1979 to 1981. "He'd always dress pretty dapper, but he'd come up with some of the weirdest outfits I've ever seen. The signature white shoes and the off-color jackets ... not many of us had the guts to wear all that stuff, but they looked good on Harry."

The Phillies were looking good too. Their 1976 title was followed by division titles in 1977 and 1978, though both seasons ended with losses to the Los Angeles Dodgers in the NLCS. When Pete Rose, Harry's old spring training gambling buddy, arrived as a free agent in 1979, things really started looking up for the Phillies.

With Harry at the mike, the franchise would win its first championship in 1980 and return to the World Series in 1983. But later in the decade, Harry's wild side would cause him to experience an equally dramatic moment in his personal life. A new woman would change everything.

WIFE SWAP

The Alcatraz Lighthouse spotlight spun round steadily in the coal black sky, sending out a powerful beacon. Its red tint dented the ripples of the Oakland Bay down below the Golden Gate Bridge. The hilly downtown skyline was lit up, one building after another.

Patrons of the One Up lounge on the 36th floor of the San Francisco Union Square Hyatt marveled at the breathtaking view. Harry Kalas fixated on a different breathtaking view that night in the One Up. He couldn't take his eyes off the cocktail waitress.

The bar filled up with a big crowd on September 1, 1985, a Sunday night before Labor Day. Late into a baseball season that was going nowhere for them, the Phillies arrived in San Francisco by plane a few hours after they'd won an afternoon game in Los Angeles. The team would open a series in San Francisco the next afternoon, but its early evening arrival enticed some members in the traveling party to go out for a drink. The Phillies were staying in the Hyatt, so the One Up was just an elevator ride away.

Harry Kalas arrived at the One Up around 9 p.m. to meet up with a group of Phils players, including the team's two biggest stars—future Hall of Famers third baseman Mike Schmidt and pitcher Steve Carlton—along with catcher Darren Daulton, right fielder Glenn Wilson, pitcher Shane Rawley and a few others. Everyone took a seat at a table, and as usual, baseball emerged as a major topic of conversation. On this night, much of the talk also revolved around the 34-year-old, shapely blonde taking the drink orders. Wilson compared Eileen Vanwey to a young Marilyn Monroe. "Stunningly gorgeous," he mumbled under his breath.

Harry Kalas, a married man and father of two, was even more impressed. To him, Eileen looked like love at first sight. He was 49, a lot older than Eileen, but he couldn't stop sneaking peaks at her from his table. When she walked over with drinks, he went out of his way to flirt.

As the night wore on, the crowd thinned out, even though the next day was a holiday. Schmidt was one of the first Phillies to depart. Harry Kalas left his seat to take one at the bar, and Wilson followed to keep him company. Eileen had no idea who Harry or any of the ballplayers were. She knew of Joe Montana, who led the San Francisco 49ers to their second Super Bowl victory in 1984, but not much else about sports. The only celebrity she'd ever recognized in her establishment was a local who regularly stopped in for drinks and sometimes would break into song. Hearing Tony Bennett get coaxed into singing "I Left My Heart in San Francisco" from a barstool never got old.

Using his charm, Harry Kalas learned that Eileen was divorced with two children and on the outs with her boyfriend of three years, Leonard Crabassa. When the bartender, Jaime Arevalo, and Eileen momentarily stepped away from their work area, the telephone behind the bar rang. Harry reached over and picked it up just as Eileen was returning. Hearing a man's voice ask for the cocktail waitress, Harry thought maybe it was Eileen's soon-to-be ex. Actually, it was another hotel worker.

"She's not here," Harry said into the phone in an attempt to be funny. "She quit."

Eileen wasn't amused.

"What a jerk!" she told herself.

As the night went on, Eileen changed her mind as Harry sat in front of her drinking one gin and tonic after another. Behind the bar, there were mirrors. Without Harry knowing, Eileen was staring. "God, he's gorgeous," she mumbled under her breath. Hearing Harry's baritone voice, she could have listened to him talk all night, too.

"She was really hot and they just seemed to hit it off," Daulton recalled. "There was something there. You could feel the electricity. They were acting like little kids."

Deep into the evening, Harry popped a question. The Phillies had a day off between their final game in San Francisco and the coming weekend's series opener in San Diego. A group of players planned to fly to Las Vegas after Wednesday's game and stay until Friday morning.

"I'd love for you to go," Harry told Eileen. "I'll take care of everything and you can have your own room."

Eileen laughed off the invitation, but she was intrigued. There was something about Harry. In addition to finding him physically attractive, she thought he was charming, funny and intelligent. She asked the bartender to get the lowdown. He did. Eileen learned that Harry was a baseball broadcaster who also did voiceovers for NFL Films.

"Oh no," she said to herself with a chuckle. A year earlier, someone had tried and failed to set her up with a vacationing NFL Films employee. When Harry spoke again, a light bulb went off. Eileen knew his voice from narrating "You Make the Call" commercials on NFL Sundays, which she often had spent watching 49ers games with her boyfriend Leonard.

A few minutes later, Harry brought up Vegas again. This time, Eileen responded with an important question.

"Are you married?"

"I wouldn't lie to you," Harry said.

Disappointed, Eileen said, "I can't go to Vegas. You have a wife."

Deep inside, she really wanted to go. A free trip to Las Vegas with an interesting man, she figured, could be a lot of fun. Before leaving the bar that night, Harry brought up Las Vegas a third time. He told her to think it over and he'd stop in for a drink the next night.

Harry had a pretty good buzz going when the bar closed at 2 a.m. He and Glenn Wilson walked out together. Waiting for the elevator on the way back to their hotel rooms, Harry looked at his ballplayer friend and threw out an eye-popping statement.

"Willie, I'm going to marry that woman."

"You've had one too many tonight," Wilson said with a smile.

"No, Willie, I love her."

"No, Harry, that's called lust."

"I assure you, Willie, I will marry that woman."

Glenn Wilson let it go. He was sure the alcohol was talking for Harry. Besides, he was half-drunk himself and needed some sleep. The next day's early afternoon Phillies-Giants ballgame at Candlestick Park would come quickly.

The Phillies beat the Giants 4-3 in 10 innings on Labor Day 1985. That night, Eileen began her six-hour shift at 8 p.m., in a near-empty One Up lounge. One of the first patrons to arrive was Steve Carlton, who was there to campaign.

"Eileen, I'm a friend of Harry Kalas," the three-time Cy Young Award winner said. "A bunch of the Phillies are going to Las Vegas for a couple nights after Wednesday's game. Will you please go so Harry will shut up about you?"

"I don't date married men," Eileen said sternly.

Carlton was persistent. "Just go as friends."

Eileen waited a few seconds to respond. "Let me think about it," she said.

Torn on what to do, Eileen phoned her mother, who had been pleading with her daughter to break it off with Leonard. Eileen assumed her mother would tell her not to go to Vegas because Harry had a wife.

"Go and have fun," Eileen was told.

After thinking it over some more, she decided to accompany a married man to Sin City.

Following Wednesday's game, Harry headed to the airport with a group of Phillies players that included Daulton, Carlton, Rawley and Wilson. Eileen was driven to the airport by an attractive female friend, Linda Liotta, who was immediately invited to join the gang in Las Vegas. After initially rejecting the offer, Linda boarded a flight to Vegas later that night.

"Even though I knew he was a 'player,' I learned there was something shy and innocent about Harry," Eileen recalled years later. "It wasn't an act. He was such a gentleman."

Steve Carlton had a connection at the MGM Grand Hotel & Casino, so everyone's room was comped. The next night, a group from the Phillies and their guests, numbering about a dozen, met up in the hotel ballroom for a dinner that turned into a laugh-fest. With everyone dining at one big table, comedian Rich Little walked over and took a seat after recognizing Steve Carlton and Harry. At Glenn Wilson's urging, Little did dead-on impressions of John Wayne, George Burns and other Hollywood celebrities. He also did a pretty good Harry Kalas.

Harry and Eileen spent much of the next day together, away from the rest of the Phillies group. "It was a lot of getting to know each other," Eileen recalled. "We talked a lot about our families, our kids."

At Eileen's request, she and Harry went out that night for dinner and dancing. "Harry wasn't a good fast dancer, so I said, 'Let's slow dance.' He was terrible at that, too. I said, 'Let's not do this again.' He laughed. We ended up having drinks and talking. It was a lot of fun."

After another enjoyable day and night together, Harry and Eileen parted ways on Friday morning. Harry needed to fly to San Diego for baseball and Eileen returned home to San Francisco. Despite Harry's situation, they planned to talk regularly by phone and meet up again. Before saying goodbye, Harry talked Eileen into handing over a black-and-white photo of herself from her work ID card.

The youngest of four children, Eileen was born to Howard and Celia Blackman on July 9, 1951 outside Los Angeles. She grew up in a hurry. At age 15, she dropped out of high school to marry her 19-year-old boyfriend, Jerry Vanwey, who dropped out of college at Cal State Fullerton. Eileen wasn't pregnant, but both sets of parents approved. Celia and Jerry's mother worked together and were best friends. Eileen's father, a high school shop teacher, really liked Jerry.

They married on February 2, 1967. A month after turning 17, Eileen gave birth to daughter Julie in 1968. She delivered a son, Travis, in 1972. With not much money coming in from Jerry's job, the family of four rented a two-room house for $90 a month in the middle of an orange grove in Rowland Heights, Calif. Improvising, Eileen arranged furniture in one of the rooms to make a nursery for Travis and a bedroom for Julie.

"I swear to God, it was some of the happiest days that I remember," Eileen recalled.

When the good times ended, Eileen and Jerry split up in 1978 and divorced in 1982. Eileen rebounded by dating a SWAT officer, who promptly quit his job and moved to Idaho to work a farm that he had purchased. Eileen and her children went with him. A year later, Eileen was living in Gardnerville, Nev., with a new boyfriend, Leonard, and her children moved in with their father. Eileen ended up in San Francisco when Leonard decided to relocate there. By 1985, Eileen and Leonard's relationship was fizzling. She broke it off after returning from her 1985 Labor Day weekend in Las Vegas with Harry Kalas.

Two days after saying goodbye to Eileen in Las Vegas, Harry flew home with the Phillies from San Diego to Philadelphia. The Phillies got in late and Harry was met at the ballpark by Bob Smith, his buddy who worked for the *Daily Racing Forum*, a horse-racing newspaper. The Phillies had the next day off and Bob's wife, Linda, and Jasmine Kalas were waiting for their husbands at a beach hotel in Ocean City, N.J. Bob had picked up a couple six-packs for the 62-mile drive to the Jersey Shore in his Corvette. During the trip, Harry pulled out Eileen's work ID photo and showed it to his friend and talked about his Las Vegas adventure.

Bob Smith didn't know what to think. He adored Harry, but he'd been socializing for years with Jasmine and liked her, too. Besides, his wife and Jasmine were close. Hearing Harry talk about this new woman, Smith told his good friend, "I think you're crazy."

After meeting Eileen, Harry acted no differently than usual around his wife. He and Jasmine had always gotten along very well. But now, Harry was sneaking off to call Eileen every chance he got. Often, he would begin phone conversations by serenading her with a few bars of Lionel Richie's 1985 hit love song, "Say You, Say Me." Every few days, Eileen would receive a love letter in the mail, which she'd read again and again before placing in a drawer for safekeeping.

Jasmine had been suspicious of Harry in the past, but never had any real proof that he'd done anything wrong. She knew Harry had female flight attendant friends. During road trips that she'd made, she witnessed women throwing themselves at ballplayers. She called them "Baseball Bettys." Whenever Harry was out of town, Jasmine reminded herself how he was with the family at home. To her, he was a wonderful husband and fantastic father. She had no proof that Harry had ever done anything to betray her.

Within a month, Harry opened up about Eileen over dinner and drinks with Jeff McCabe, his police officer friend.

"You better step back and slow down, pal," McCabe responded. "This isn't

As a baby, Harry lived on the North Side of Chicago, three blocks from Wrigley Field.

Harry (middle) is given a free shot to the chin while boxing as a child.

Harry never got over losing childhood buddy Squiffy, who had been given away and then hit by a car.

Harry (right) with older brother Jim, who would become a college professor.

Reverend Harry H. Kalas (back) passed on his people skills and baritone voice to his two sons, Jim (middle) and Harry.

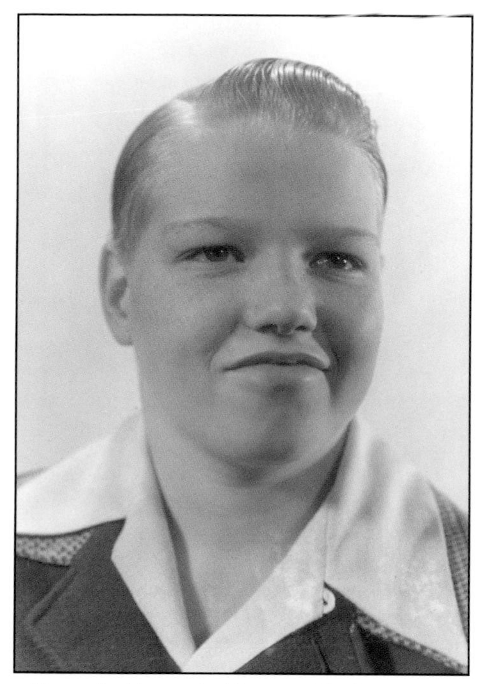

Harry, looking mischievous, liked dressing dapper even as a boy.

Harry, a backup linebacker on the Naperville Community High School football team, loved playing sports but didn't excel.

COURTESY OF JENEINNE WARNELL

One of Harry's first crushes was his high school Communications teacher. He would do anything for his favorite teacher, Jeneinne Anderson Warnell, even dress in drag for the school play.

CORNELL COLLEGE ARCHIVES, MOUNT VERNON, IOWA

Dr. Walter Stromer, a Cornell College professor who had been blinded in World War II, convinced Harry that his voice was something special.

COURTESY OF PHI DELTA THETA

This is University of Iowa's Phi Delta Theta house, a place in which Harry nearly partied his way out of a second college.

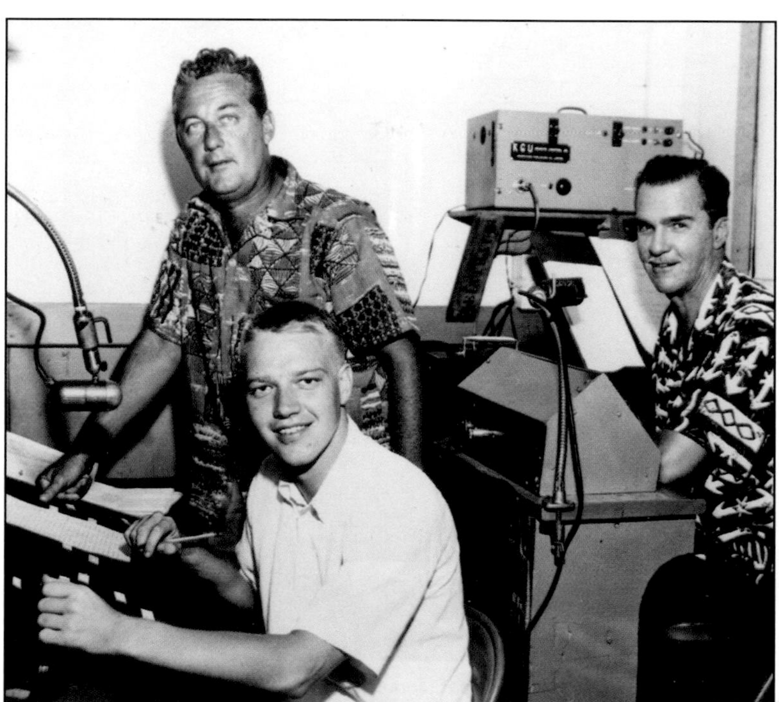

HONOLULU STAR-BULLETIN

The earliest known photo of Harry (front left) as a broadcaster, he's working a football game at Honolulu Stadium, circa 1960, with partner Chuck Leahey (top left) and a spotter.

Harry on his wedding day in 1963 with best man Bill Whaley, a bar owner and former minor-league baseball pitcher.

Harry and Jasmine Kimura were married at St. Clement's Episcopal Church in Honolulu, two blocks from where Barry "Barack" Obama went to high school.

COURTESY OF JASMINE KIMURA

Arriving in Houston from Hawaii at age 29, Cowboy Harry became a big-league broadcaster who helped open the Astrodome.

Harry (second from left) felt like an outsider in Houston while working with Astros' future Hall of Fame broadcaster Gene Elston (far right) and Loel Passe (left).

During their time in Houston, Harry and Jasmine became the proud parents of two sons, Todd (right) and Brad.

Close friends Harry and Michael Jack Schmidt, vacationing in Hawaii in 1976, deeply respected one another's different talents.

Harry relaxes in Hawaii with Joe Nunes (left), a drinking buddy since the 1970s and former small-town New Jersey mayor.

Close friends Jasmine Kalas (left) and Nancy Giles, Bill's wife, helped spearhead the Phillies' adoption of ALS as their official charity.

The night after his partner took a late-night visit to the Gateway Arch in St. Louis, Whitey Ashburn (right) made an on-air inside joke about Harry having "Faith" all summer long during a Phillies season that was going nowhere.

Harry always was considered a teammate by Phillies players, whether it was getting a shaving-cream pie to the face while interviewing reliever Steve Bedrosian (left) at Wrigley Field or being permitted to sit with veterans in the back of the team plane.

Harry would do anything to promote the Phillies, even riding a tricycle during a pre-game event at Veterans Stadium.

COURTESY OF NFL FILMS

Harry, known nationally for being the voice of NFL Films, went "ghost-hunting" while hosting a Halloween episode of a weekly highlights show with NFL Films President Steve Sabol (left) in the 1980s.

Baker Sound in Philadelphia is where Harry taped voiceovers and national commercials, such as Campbell's Chunky Soup and Coors Light.

Harry really struggled after the 1984 loss of his revered father, Reverend Harry H. Kalas, pictured late in life with wife Margaret.

Along with founding members Mike Schmidt, Steve Carlton and Larry Christenson, Harry was a member of the "Tough Luck Club," a group of mostly ballplayers who golfed and partied together every January in Florida during the 1980s.

Twenty-two years into his first marriage, Harry began a relationship in 1985 with San Francisco cocktail waitress Eileen Vanwey.

Harry moved in with Eileen in 1987, and two years later they were thrilled to welcome their son, Kane, into the world.

Harry absolutely loved being a middle-aged father to Kane Christopher Kalas, who may or may not have been named after Phillies longtime broadcaster Chris Wheeler.

PHILADELPHIA DAILY NEWS/SHERRIE BUSBY

During a feud that became downright ugly, Harry and Whitey (right) sought revenge against broadcast partner Chris Wheeler (middle), a former close friend whom they believed had betrayed them.

a good mix right now. You're a married man."

Harry went to a bar phone, called Eileen and put Jeff on the phone.

"Harry's a wonderful man, but he's married," Eileen told Jeff over the phone. "I don't know about this."

There were no cell phones in the 1980s, so Harry stayed in touch with Eileen by calling her from the ballpark, hotels and payphones. Chris Wheeler, Harry's broadcast partner and close friend at the time, often was the middleman. When Eileen wanted Harry to call her, she'd often phone Wheeler, sometimes well after midnight. Wheeler usually phoned Harry right away to pass along the message, unless it was so late that he'd have to wait until morning. After getting word that Eileen wanted to talk to him, Harry would make up an excuse to leave the house and go to a payphone. Usually, he'd say he was off to buy cigarettes at Colonial Village, a convenience store near his home in Radnor.

Within two months of their first meeting, Harry and Eileen got together again. Harry set up a second meeting during one of his weekend trips to South Bend, Ind., to broadcast a Notre Dame football game. The reunion went great.

By the winter, Harry confided to close friends that he was thinking of leaving Jasmine so that he could have a life with Eileen. But Harry felt guilty that he was hurting Jasmine. She had been very good to him for many years. He regarded her as a great mother and a very good woman. She cooked his favorite meals, ground round steaks and casseroles. She catered to his every need, spoiling him every chance she got. During their drives to spring training, Jasmine would call a friend to shop ahead to make sure Harry had fresh squeezed orange juice in the refrigerator when arriving.

"We talked and it was a huge struggle for Harry," Darren Daulton said. "Harry never had any intentions of hurting anyone in any facet of life. He didn't have a bad bone in his body."

Harry's friends were divided. Most everyone with the Phillies was close to Jasmine, who always was around and very involved in team charities.

"I felt sorry for Jasmine," Glenn Wilson said. "I worried for her."

Some of Harry's other friends thought he was more compatible with Eileen. Harry was a drinker and smoker, as was Eileen at the time. Jasmine never smoked and rarely drank.

"Filmmaker Howard Hawks makes movies where there's always women who could handle a gun, smoke a cigar and be just as tough as the men," NFL Films producer Dave Plaut said. "That's the type of woman Eileen is. Jasmine was your classic mom."

Early into 1986, Eileen became frustrated. She adored Harry and wanted to be with him, but being in a long-distance relationship with a married man hurt. Initially, she told Harry that she needed him to break it off with Jasmine and move in with her within a year. Then it changed to six months. When Harry couldn't make a decision, Eileen made it for him. She broke it off in a letter sent to him at NFL Films.

"It's over," she wrote. "I've moved on. Be faithful to your wife."

Harry begged Eileen to take him back and assured her that they would be together when the timing was right. He sent her a Richard Bach book, *The Bridge Across Forever: A Love Story*.

"Please read it," Harry told Eileen. "It's how I feel."

In an effort to convince Eileen that he was serious about her, Harry confessed his affair to Jasmine, who was given the news one day after returning home from a tennis match. She was very angry and hurt. At the same time, she wanted to fight to save her marriage. She loved Harry.

"I accepted certain things," Jasmine said years later. "Although it really hurt, I didn't make a big fuss about it. He was so nice to me when he was at home. We had a good life. We belonged to a country club. We had a lot of friends. We had a good life and I wasn't going to divorce him."

Hearing that Harry had come clean with Jasmine, Eileen agreed to continue the affair in hopes that he'd leave her sooner rather than later. During spring training in 1986, Jasmine was planning a 50th birthday party for Harry when he made up an excuse to fly to California to see Eileen. Harry said he had to shoot a blue jeans commercial for Levi's. When Jasmine caught on, Harry canceled his trip.

For most of 1986, Harry struggled to choose between the two women in his life. When pressed to make a decision one way or the other, Harry pleaded for more time.

"Please don't do this to me," Harry wrote in a letter to Eileen. "Give me time."

Looking back many years later, Eileen said her early days with Harry filled her with mixed emotions. She was excited about what might lie ahead, yet also felt guilty for dating a married man.

"I really felt bad for Jasmine," Eileen Kalas recalled. "I did have sympathy for her. I didn't want to break up a family. Harry was like a teenage boy when we started seeing each other, but I didn't think it was right from the beginning. It was a very hard decision for Harry to make. He went back on his decision once."

At home, he talked a lot about his decision with two of his closest friends, Jeff McCabe and Richie Ashburn.

"Harry loved his family, loved his boys," McCabe said. "He never said a bad word about Jasmine. He felt terrible about falling in love with someone else."

"Harry was so confused," Eileen said. "Whitey was pushing him to stay with Jasmine. He was a family man. He figured this was just an affair."

While working Notre Dame basketball games, Harry often talked about his situation with broadcast partner Jim Gibbons, a devout Catholic. Gibbons had Harry meet with Father Hesburgh, the longtime Notre Dame president who had counseled Harry two years earlier when his father died.

"Harry wasn't Catholic, but really respected Father Hesburgh," Eileen said. "Catholics don't believe in divorce, but he told Harry to 'go where your heart is.' "

Jasmine carried on hoping Harry would ultimately decide to stay with her. One day, Jasmine discovered two love letters and Eileen's work ID photo in Harry's briefcase. Furious, Jasmine took the picture and punched holes in Eileen's eyes with a pen. She placed the damaged photo where she found it. She assumed her actions would lead to a big argument once Harry discovered the photo. He never said a word.

Harry finally spoke up around Christmas 1986. He had decided to start a new life with Eileen. Harry, Jasmine and his boys, both in college, were in Hawaii for the holidays, as they'd done so often before. They stayed at Jasmine's sister's place in Honolulu. One night, Harry delivered the news.

"When we get home, I'm moving out," Harry told Jasmine.

Tears poured down Jasmine's face. She thought Harry's affair with Eileen just represented a midlife crisis and never believed that he would leave her. Seeing Jasmine so upset, Harry promised to think it over one more time.

Near the end of their vacation, Harry approached Jasmine again, this time telling her that he wanted to fix their marriage. Harry was headed to California the next day to work a college basketball game. He told Jasmine that he was going to make a stop in San Francisco to break off his relationship with Eileen in person. Jasmine urged Harry to do it by phone, but he insisted.

In San Francisco, Harry changed his mind once again.

"Quit your job. You're moving to Philadelphia," he told Eileen.

Harry flew home to Philadelphia, knowing there was no turning back this time. Harry broke the news to Jasmine in the kitchen of their home. She tried getting him to reconsider again, but it was too late.

A few days later, Eileen boarded a plane for a new life in Philadelphia. Eileen's arrival turned Jasmine's disappointment into anger.

Her first night on the East Coast, Eileen stayed with Harry in a hotel near the NFL Films offices in Mt. Laurel, N.J. They got into an argument.

"We'd both been drinking," Eileen recalled. "Harry went to a bar. We argued about something. I don't even know what about."

Harry told Eileen he was going home. When Harry left, Eileen took a stack of his $100 bills and tossed them in the toilet. Thirty minutes passed. An hour passed. Harry never returned to the hotel. Eileen phoned Harry's house. Jasmine answered.

"Where's Harry?" Eileen yelled.

"He's not here," Jasmine shouted back. "He's out with a redhead."

Jasmine hung up on Eileen, hoping that her instinctive lie that Harry was out with a redhead would put Eileen through the same kind of hurt that she'd lived through since Harry confessed he was having an affair with Eileen. In reality, Jasmine had no idea where Harry was. He hadn't been home or even called. Instead, he had met a friend from NFL Films for a drink. The friend advised Harry to get back to the hotel and patch things up with Eileen. Harry agreed. He returned to the room and apologized. Eileen, who had fetched his cash out of the toilet, did the same.

This night was a precursor of things to come for Harry and Eileen, who experienced some of their highest of emotional highs and lowest of lows in their years together.

"Harry made me feel alive," Eileen said. "He made me feel love, hate, sad, happy ... every emotion. He's the only person in the world that's ever done that to me."

The next week, Harry and Eileen moved to Sweetwater Farm Bed and Breakfast, a 50-acre estate in historic Brandywine Valley in Glen Mills, Pa., that was owned by the ex-wife of former Phillies pitcher Jim Kaat. They moved twice more in their first year together. First, they rented a house on Rose Tree

Valley Road in Media, Pa. Then they purchased a four-bedroom ranch home at 3308 Chatham Place in Media, next to Ridley Creek State Park. Harry loved the peace and quiet at their new home, as well as the views. Sitting on the deck, he would watch deer grazing in his backyard.

Meantime, Jasmine was still showing up for Phillies home games. She was using Harry's season tickets and visiting her many friends. When seeing Harry, she would make futile attempts to get him back. It took a few months, but eventually Jasmine realized Harry wasn't coming home and filed for divorce.

Nancy Giles, Bill's wife, found her old friend one of the area's leading divorce attorneys, Albert Momjian, who has been ranked one of the top family law attorneys in Pennsylvania three times by *Super Lawyers* magazine. Momjian had a reputation as a tough negotiator, making Harry realize that there would be no quick settlement. Harry's offers, deemed fair by his attorney, were laughed off by Momjian, who demanded a lifetime of security for his client. (Albert's son, Mark Momjian, now a partner with his father at Schnader Harrison Segal & Lewis, sat in on some of the Kalas divorce proceedings. In 2009, Mark Momjian took on an even bigger celebrity client in a divorce case, Kate Gosselin from television's *Jon & Kate Plus 8*.) Though they often found themselves in the same room during the divorce proceedings, Eileen and Jasmine never said a word to each other. Jasmine wouldn't even say Eileen's name to friends. It was always, "Harry's woman."

By late summer 1988, Eileen was pregnant. She was 37 and Harry was 53 when Kane Christopher Kalas was born on May 11, 1989. Holding his third son in his arms, Harry had tears rolling down his cheeks. The first visitors to the hospital were two of Harry's broadcast partners, Richie Ashburn and Andy Musser. Harry remained close with his older boys after his separation from their mother, but shielded them from Eileen for years. Harry usually spent a week with Todd and Brad each spring training without Eileen. Kane didn't even meet his older half-brothers until he was two.

"I love his kids," Eileen said. "Jasmine didn't want her kids to meet me, so for two years he invited them over for Christmas Eve and I'd go to the Rose Tree Inn for dinner alone. There were other times that I'd leave the house when I knew they were coming over."

At times, Harry's relationship with Eileen did cause problems with his children.

"When Todd was going to graduate from Syracuse, I made reservations for dinner after the graduation for Todd, Brad, Bob and Linda Smith, Harry and myself," Jasmine recalled. "Harry then informed me that 'she' did not want Harry to be standing or sitting with me at Todd's graduation or going to our dinner. He said, 'I'm going to be there, but I cannot be sitting with you.' Todd was so upset that we canceled everything—the hotel, the dinner party, everything. Todd refused to go to commencement."

Harry became close to Eileen's two children from her first marriage, Julie and Travis. Because their last name is Vanwey, Harry made up a nickname for Julie, calling her "Kiki" after former UCLA basketball and NBA star Kiki Vandeweghe. In years to come, both children would work for Harry—Kiki as a personal secretary and Travis as a limo driver.

"For years, Harry would call me his daughter-in-law, even though I was his stepdaughter," Julie Vanwey said. "He'd get mixed up. People would say, 'Are you married to Todd or Brad?' 'No, no, I'm single and Harry's stepdaughter.' Finally, he got it straightened out. But it took years. The last few years, when he'd buy me birthday cards, he'd say, 'See, it's a card for a stepdaughter. I got it right.' Then he'd say, 'You're really my daughter,' which made me feel great."

Years passed before Harry and Jasmine reached a final divorce settlement. Their old home in Radnor was sold to cover the expensive legal bills. Their spring condo was sold, too.

"Those were hateful times," Jasmine remembered.

On May 20, 1993, more than six years into their separation, the Kalas' divorce became final. The big winners were the lawyers. According to Eileen Kalas, Harry paid $347,000 in attorney fees and Jasmine was charged an estimated $500,000, a percentage of which Harry was required to pay.

During the early stages of their separation, Jasmine received $5,800 a month for alimony, but the figure dropped to $2,500 for the final settlement. Jasmine continued to live off the payments until Harry's death. On April 24, 2009, 11 days after Harry's passing, Jasmine received a letter from Terrance Kline, a Pennsylvania attorney who was handling the Estate. "I represent Mrs. Eileen Kalas," the letter read. "This is to formally notify you that there will be no further alimony payments to you."

Harry was a single man for just two months. On July 30, 1993, he and Eileen tied the knot at a Baptist church in Devon, Pa. Reverend James E. Bolin

Jr. performed the ceremony in front of one witness, Richie Ashburn. When the reverend got to "You may kiss the bride," Ashburn threw his arms around Harry's shoulders and planted a wet one on his cheek. Pretending as if he and Harry actually were the ones getting wed, Whitey looked at his best friend with a wry smile and said, "Oh God, Harry, we've waited so long for this." Eileen got a kick out of Whitey's act. She liked him right away even though he maintained a good friendship with Jasmine. Whatever Whitey may have thought about Harry's situation, he was always friendly to Eileen.

The newlyweds scheduled a honeymoon in Hawaii, but not for another seven months. The night of his wedding, Harry was in the broadcast booth at Veterans Stadium calling a 4-2 Phillies victory over Pittsburgh.

Jasmine and Harry never saw each other or even spoke again after their last court appearance. But they found ways to pass along messages to show that they still cared. Harry frequently asked his sons how Jasmine was doing and sometimes would drop a note to her when sending an alimony check. In turn, Jasmine would write letters to Harry addressed to the Phillies ballpark that provided updates on old friends.

In 2003, Jasmine left Philadelphia. It was time. One of her sons was in Florida, the other in California. She went home to Hawaii and rented a ninth-floor condo in Honolulu that overlooks four waterways that feed into the Pacific Ocean. From her balcony, she has a beautiful view of coconut trees and passing cruise ships.

Harry Kalas was married the last 16-and-a-half years of his life to Eileen, but maintained a special place in his heart for his first wife. "I will love Jasmine for the rest of my life," Harry told Richie Ashburn after his divorce.

Jasmine felt the same until the day Harry died.

"I still loved him," she said. "I remembered him for who he was. He was a great person, a great father and a great husband."

HIS WHITENESS

On April Fool's Day, 1987, the Philadelphia Phillies were two days from leaving spring training in Clearwater, Fla., and heading north to start a new baseball season. Harry Kalas wanted one more night out at his favorite spring hangout, Derby Lane. After working a Phillies-Toronto Blue Jays Grapefruit League matinee, Harry and his new live-in girlfriend, Eileen Vanwey, headed to the dog track for dinner and gambling with Richard and Lisa Ashburn, the son and daughter-in-law of Harry's broadcast partner Richie "Whitey" Ashburn. During the drive to the track, Harry boasted that he was an authority on picking winners.

A dog track novice, Richard kept following Harry's suggestions, losing every time. Twelve races in, he and Harry had nothing but losing tickets. Down to his last $10 and with only one race to go, Richard decided to go with his own instincts and put it all on a 50/1 long shot.

"You might as well throw that money in the bay," Harry said. "That dog has no chance."

Harry was wrong again. Richard's dog blew away the field, winning by

20 lengths. Richard won $500 and stuffed his winning ticket into his wallet as a keepsake.

On their way home, everyone was in a great mood. Their bellies were full, they'd had a few drinks and Richard had made some money. Harry was getting quite a ribbing about his so-called dog-picking expertise.

Harry dropped off Richard and Lisa at Whitey's Shipwatch Yacht and Tennis Club condo in Largo, then drove off with Eileen to their Indian Shores condo.

When Harry and Eileen reached the front door around midnight, their phone was ringing. Harry picked it up and heard Whitey on the other end, sobbing uncontrollably. Only minutes earlier, Whitey had received word that his 32-year-old daughter had been killed in a car accident. Jan Ashburn, the second oldest of Whitey's six children, crashed her 1987 Oldsmobile into a sign post in the Overbrook Park section of Philadelphia at 9:25 p.m., then was pronounced dead after being transported to Lankenau Hospital in Wynnewood, Pa.

Harry immediately rushed back to Whitey's place. Bill Conlin, a Phillies beat writer and longtime Ashburn friend who lived next door to Ashburn during spring trainings, was already on the scene. Conlin had tried his best to comfort his friend. But Whitey remained inconsolable until Harry walked in. Seeing Whitey slumped on a couch and weeping, Harry wrapped his arms around his best friend for a hug that lasted several minutes. Harry sat with Whitey on the couch for hours, trying to calm him down. The son of a minister, Harry did his best to support his shaken friend.

"It really became obvious how close they were," Conlin said. "Ashburn is crying like a baby and Harry just totally took charge of the situation. He sat Whitey down and soothed him. You could just see the way Whitey reacted to Harry."

The morning after Jan's fatal accident, Whitey and Richard flew to Philadelphia. Before making funeral arrangements, they made a horrifying trip to the hospital morgue to identify Jan's body. "By chance, I happened to look at the chart and the time of death was 11:18 p.m.," Richard Ashburn said. 11:18 p.m.—Richard Ashburn would remember that time forever.

Six months passed. Then one day while Richard was going through his wallet, he came across his winning ticket from Derby Lane. Looking it over, he became spooked. The race in which he won $500 had ended at 11:18 p.m. Richard called Harry Kalas.

"You're not going to believe this, Harry, but the dog won at the same time my sister was pronounced dead."

"I knew it, I knew it!" Harry responded. "Your sister had something to do with that dog winning."

Richard couldn't help but laugh at Harry.

After Jan's passing, Whitey Ashburn courageously recounted "the saddest day of my life" in his weekly *Philadelphia Daily News* column. "Harry Kalas shared our family's grief and helped us get through that night," Whitey wrote. "Harry's always there when you need him."

For 27 years, Harry and Whitey were the Phillies' version of Johnny Carson and Ed McMahon. Their *Tonight Show* was a daily dose of entertainment and comedy that remained fresh, fun and informative, baseball season after baseball season. Their amazing camaraderie in the announcing booth often revolved around straight man Harry setting up Whitey for one of his comic rants or humorous stories from his Hall of Fame playing days. Outside the booth, they became fast friends who played tennis, golf and cards together. Whitey was a Philadelphia Country Club member and sponsored Harry, who also became a member. When Harry married for the second time in 1993, Whitey was the only invited guest.

"Whitey was as good a friend as a man could have," Harry Kalas said on many occasions.

Richie Ashburn was called Whitey by his friends for most of his adult life because of his snow-white hair. Eventually, Harry boosted his friend to sainthood by referring to him as "His Whiteness."

"Harry and Dad really were two guys from the same cloth," Richard Ashburn said. "I'm not sure I know brothers who were as close as they were."

For several generations of Phillies baseball fans, Harry and Whitey were as much a reason to tune in for games as the games themselves. Harry did the play-by-play and Whitey provided the color commentary, while their banter led to a lot of laughs. Others served on the Phillies broadcast team during the Harry and Whitey era, including By Saam in the early years, and Andy Musser and Chris Wheeler starting in the mid-1970s. But no one else touched Phillies fans like Harry and Whitey. In addition to broadcasting the games and sharing stories from their lives, they always passed along birthday and anniversary greetings on the air, even after management asked them to stop.

"The relationship that the two of them shared on the air was unique,"

Musser said. "Harry had the ability to follow Whitey's sense of timing and integrate him into the broadcast much better than I ever did. With Whitey, you couldn't help but just let him go, and that was what Harry was very good at. He didn't really egg him on very much. He sat back and listened, letting Whitey be Whitey."

Both were easygoing Midwesterners. Whitey hailed from the plains of Nebraska; Harry came from Chicago. Both had infectious personalities, a wonderful sense of humor and the rare knack of finding the good in people from all walks of life.

But they also differed in many ways. Harry was nine years younger and never played baseball beyond high school. Whitey was one of the Phillies' all-time great outfielders, good enough to eventually get his ticket to immortality punched with a Baseball Hall of Fame plaque. Harry was a heavy smoker and spent post-game nights at bars boozing it up while talking baseball. Whitey sucked on a pipe stuffed with cherry tobacco, but rarely drank alcohol and spent many of his nights on the road alone, reading in his hotel room.

"Midwesterners are supposed to be laid-back people, but they certainly took over this town," said Larry Shenk, the head of the Phillies' Public Relations Department from 1964 to 2007. "Listening to Harry and Whitey call a game was like two uncles sitting in your living room talking baseball. There was some dead air, not a lot of overanalyzing and they just cracked you up. It was just pure entertainment in a very calm, relaxing, comforting way. There are changes in the world, changes in sports, but Harry and Whitey were a security blanket for people for a lot of years."

"I really think they were soul mates," said Ray Didinger, a one-time Philadelphia newspaperman who worked with Harry at NFL Films. "They had that same down-to-the-bone love for the game of baseball. It was their life. I think their bond came from the love and respect that they both had for the game. It was profound for the both of them."

Thanks to Whitey, Harry quickly became popular with Phillies players. Harry and Whitey were considered teammates to Phillies players, which is almost unheard of for announcers. The fact that Whitey was an ex-ballplayer helped get him accepted right away by ballplayers, but his easygoing ways and friendly demeanor played a role, too. Harry had the same personality, and his friendship with Whitey paved his way to becoming super friendly with ballplayers, as well.

"Ashburn was such a prince of a guy, so anybody that he says is a good guy is accepted," said Jim Bunning, the Hall of Fame pitcher and U.S. Senator who had played six seasons for the Phillies, including his final one in 1971.

The Phillies knew they were getting a talented young broadcaster when hiring Harry Kalas away from the Houston Astros for the 1971 season. But they had no idea that Harry and Whitey would form one of the great broadcast teams in all of sports.

"The relationship they had on the air was something I never planned," said Phillies chairman Bill Giles, who recruited Harry Kalas and campaigned for his hiring. "It just kind of happened."

It helped that Whitey already liked Harry before he was hired by the Phillies. They knew each other from Harry's six years in Houston and had shared some friendly ballpark chit-chats. Before the 1971 season, Whitey was introduced to Harry's wife at a dinner. "I really love your husband," he told Jasmine Kalas. "We're going to get along real well."

Whitey supported Harry during his transition to the Phillies broadcast team. He felt badly that Harry arrived amid controversy for replacing Bill Campbell, who was forced out after the 1970 season. Whitey's immediate acceptance of Harry helped Phillies fans get past Campbell's departure.

"My dad knew the situation with what went on with Bill Campbell and how popular he was," Richard Ashburn said. "He made Harry feel at home from Day One. He smoothed the trail for Harry quite a bit."

Worried about how Kalas would be received from the outset, Bill Giles had met with Ashburn before the '71 season.

"Make it fun," Giles told Whitey. "Show a sense of humor in the booth."

"Don't worry about it," Ashburn responded. "We'll take care of it."

Gene Kirby, the Phillies' television producer in 1971, had a talk with Harry about Ashburn. "I want you to work Richie in as much as possible. Get his inside baseball knowledge, get his expertise."

That wasn't always easy, because Whitey often had to be coaxed into talking more. "If I don't have anything pertinent to say, I'm not going to say it," Whitey told Harry before their first season.

Whitey was uncontrollable in the booth. Sometimes he wouldn't talk for minutes, but then other times he could be heard in conversation with someone in the background as Harry was doing play-by-play. He was a Phillies homer who would cheer, pout or vent depending on his mood. His dislike for pitchers and umpires was legendary.

"I never would want my daughter to marry a pitcher," Whitey said many times. "You can't trust 'em."

Whitey could do and say as he pleased because Phillies fans loved him so much. They loved him as a player, but they loved him even more as a broadcaster because he was so entertaining. Sometimes, Harry and Whitey made viewers laugh even when they weren't trying to be funny.

Harry: "It's a beautiful day here in Chicago."

Whitey: "Yeah, but it's going to rain tomorrow."

Harry: "Well, we won't be here, Whitey."

Whitey invented words in the booth. Players could look "hitterish" or "runnerish." He used a lot of clichés too. When Whitey made a prediction, it was a "lead-pipe cinch" to happen or you could "bet the house on it." One of Whitey's favorite lines became a classic: "Hard to believe, Harry." Often, it came spilling out in frustration.

Whitey's stories became legendary, especially the ones that revolved around inside jokes.

Chris Wheeler started working for the Phillies in 1971 in Public Relations. Before moving to the broadcast booth in 1977, Wheels constantly was razzed on the air by Ashburn, even though most Phillies fans didn't yet know him. During a road game, Whitey looked at the television monitor and saw a woman walking down a ramp. "That looks like the same dress that Chris Wheeler wore to the ballpark," Whitey said. Instead of explaining, Harry just let it go.

No one was safe from a Whitey jab. He used to tease radio producer Joe Gaines all the time. "A trained chimpanzee could do your job," Whitey would say again and again. One Sunday, they were together in the booth before a game at Veterans Stadium when Ashburn noticed a monkey act on the field. Without saying a word, Whitey looked at Gaines, then back to the monkey, then back to Gaines as if to say, "See, told you." Gaines called Whitey's silent attacks "Jack Benny moments."

Harry Kalas often found himself targeted on the air by Whitey, and soon realized that no jest was off limits. Whitey even poked fun of Harry's carousing with women during road trips. One summer, Harry had a female friend named Faith who traveled with him on some Phillies road trips. Late in the season when the Phillies were close to being eliminated from the playoff chase, Harry and Richie discussed the team's predicament during the opening segment of a telecast. With the camera on Harry and Whitey, Whitey told viewers, "In times like these, you've gotta have faith. And Harry, I for one know that you've had Faith all summer long." Harry swallowed hard, and then decided it was a good time for a commercial. "We'll be right back after this," Harry said. During the break, they laughed hysterically.

During a Phillies trip to St. Louis one summer, Harry took a late-night walk with a woman to the Gateway Arch, the famous 630-foot-high monument on the banks of the Mississippi River. At 6 a.m., Harry returned to the team hotel with grass stains on his white suit. He was spotted in the lobby by Whitey, who was up early and in search of coffee. That night, Whitey was up to his old tricks. During their opening, Harry and Whitey did a standup from the television booth in which the crest of the Arch could be seen over Busch Stadium. "Behind us is the famous Arch, the Gateway to the West," Whitey said on air. "Harry, they tell me you can get up to the top of that thing. Have you ever been up it? I know you've been under it." Once again, Harry immediately went to break, then cracked up.

On Labor Day 1996, during a Phillies home game with San Diego, Whitey was in the television booth with Wheels when telling viewers, "We want to send our best wishes along to former Phillies owner Ruly Carpenter, who was in a car accident today. His car was rammed by a pickup truck, but we understand that he's okay and we certainly hope that all is well."

Working in his office, Larry Shenk heard Whitey's television report. After the inning, the PR man darted to the television booth.

"Whitey, where did you hear Ruly was in a car accident?"

"I was having dinner in the press club and somebody told me."

"Whitey, you had dinner with me. I told you that my wife, Julie, was in a car accident."

The next inning, Whitey told viewers that he had received some misinformation and that Larry Shenk needed to work on his enunciation.

The next spring training, Whitey crossed paths with Julie Shenk, whose shoulder was still in a sling.

"What happened to you?" Whitey asked.

"I was in a car accident last September and needed surgery," Julie answered.

"You were in a car accident?" Whitey said. "Nobody told me! Nobody ever tells me anything!"

Many Phillies fans know of Whitey's most famous in-booth story. Harry told it time and again at banquets and functions. What most fans don't realize is that it actually was Ashburn and Wheeler in the booth for the biggest punch line of Whitey's Celebre's pizza routine, not Harry and Whitey.

The gag started in the 1980s. "Harry, it's time for a Celebre's," Whitey said. Thirty minutes later, four pies showed up in the booth.

Celebre's is a family-owned South Philadelphia restaurant specializing in pizza that opened in 1961 on Packer Avenue, just a couple blocks from where Veterans Stadium stood. If a Phillies home game was a long one or went into extra innings, Whitey would ask for pizza. This act went on and on, and usually Whitey didn't even eat the pizza. But he enjoyed knowing the folks at Celebre's were listening.

"We used to have the radio on," said Gloria Angelozzi, who started making pizzas at Celebre's in 1972 and celebrated her 37th anniversary there in September 2009. "As soon as we heard Richie, the bosses would yell, 'Fix some pies up for them.' We just thought it was great that Richie appreciated us and liked our pizza."

Eventually, the Phillies tried to put a stop to the routine because Celebre's was not a Phillies sponsor. Whitey was told in 1995 to cut it out by Dennis Mannion, the club's marketing VP. Ashburn responded by getting creative. While in the radio booth during a commercial break one night, Ashburn mentioned to Wheeler that he was starving for pizza. Whitey told Wheels his plan. Then they put it into action during the next half-inning.

"Whitey, we have a very special announcement to do tonight," Wheels said. "Some friends of ours had twins."

"Yes, they did," Ashburn said. "The Celebre's twins, plain and pepperoni."

Within a half-hour, Whitey and Wheels smelled the pizzas entering their booth.

"I was thinking, 'This guy's a genius,'" said Phillies manager of broadcasting Rob Brooks, who was a radio producer and engineer in 1995. "During a break, we let out a huge howl. After the game, we all went to the press club and howled some more."

Charlie O'Gara started working as a cameraman in the Phillies television booth at Veterans Stadium in 1971, the same year Kalas joined the club. In 2009, he was 68 years old and still there. During the Harry and Whitey years, he ate well between the innings of games.

"All they had to do was say something on the air about a food they liked, and the next thing you know it showed up in the booth," O'Gara said. "It wasn't just pizza. It could be cheesesteaks or fudge or whatever. Harry sometimes would say, 'I don't eat this crap,' then throw it to me." Fans seated directly above the booth in the 500 level would tie string to a basket, then lower it down to deliver homemade cookies and brownies.

Harry and Whitey also received numerous non-edible gifts, including ties and socks and shirts. Whitey always wore a hat during games, so fans frequently would send new ones to him, hoping they'd see Ashburn wear them on television.

Harry was shy about his growing fame, but Whitey ate it up. Whitey was humble on the inside, but enjoyed reminding his colleagues and Phillies executives how much power he had with fans. Harry had the same pull, but didn't flaunt it.

Together, Harry and Whitey made lasting impressions on hundreds of thousands of Phillies fans, including Philadelphia attorney Joe Hetrick, a Phillies fanatic since his childhood in the 1950s.

"For my generation, especially for kids in working-class neighborhoods like Port Richmond, the Phillies were a radio phenomenon," Hetrick said. "When young, it was By Saam and Bill Campbell, and while they were technically very good, their style was a very dry and factual commentary. For me, there was not really a personal connection. They didn't share their own life experiences, just the progression of the game. I finished college in 1970, the year that Connie Mack Stadium closed, and moved to Europe for three years.

"When I returned to Philadelphia in the fall of 1973, things had changed. During my absence, Rich Ashburn had been partnered with some foreigner from Houston, and they had a whole different approach to the game. The broadcasts were more conversational, much more warm and friendly, much better informed and infinitely more entertaining. Harry and Whitey became like extended family. They had come to know each other so well that there was a seamless conversation that ran through the play-by-play, the analysis and every other aspect of the broadcasts. Nothing was as soothing on a muggy Philly August day than tuning into Harry and Whitey, the two slightly eccentric and lovable uncles that I never had. Regardless of the outcome of the games, you always had a warm feeling from the two of them, always learned something, and above all really wished you could join them in that booth, as they seemed to be having such a damned good time."

Bill Giles, the man most responsible for pairing Harry and Whitey, played a role in assuring that they wouldn't be broken up after just two seasons together. It wasn't highly publicized, but Whitey was a finalist to become the Phillies manager for the 1973 season. Whitey always thought he'd be a standout field general. "Boys, if I ever managed, you wouldn't have enough fingers for your World Series rings," Ashburn used to tell players.

The 1972 Phillies were early into a terrible season when John Quinn retired as general manager and was replaced by Paul "Pope" Owens, who was bumped up from his position as the club's farm director. Wanting to get a better feel for his talent, Owens fired manager Frank Lucchesi and named himself interim manager. Then after a disastrous 97-loss campaign, Owens went looking for a new manager. His finalists included two outside candidates, Danny Ozark and Dave Bristol, and two inside candidates, Jim Bunning and Richie Ashburn. Phillies owner Bob Carpenter wanted to hire Ashburn, who had no coaching experience but was wildly popular with fans and probably would help sell tickets. Owens wanted Bristol, who had managed in Cincinnati and Milwaukee. Bunning, who went from the playing field in 1971 to managing the Class AA Reading Phillies in 1972, thought he was going to get the job after getting a second interview. But Paul Owens settled on Ozark, a coach for eight seasons with the Dodgers under Hall of Fame manager Walter Alston.

Bill Giles talked Owens into going with Ozark, who was brought in to implement the Dodgers' successful coaching techniques. Giles first had to convince Owens not to go with Carpenter's choice. "If you hire Whitey, he's going to get fired because he's taking over a bad team and it'll be a public relations disaster," Giles told Owens.

Whitey, who interviewed informally, didn't realize how serious a candidate he had been until attending a Christmas party after the 1973 season. "You can thank me for saving you from a miserable death," Giles said. Whitey was irked. He wanted the job. "Thanks a lot," Ashburn told Giles. "With friends like you, who needs enemies?"

The son of a machine shop owner, Richie Ashburn was unique from the very start of his life. After all, not many people have a twin sister with a different birthday. Richie, whose birth name was Donald Richard, was born in Tilden, Neb., just after midnight on March 19, 1927. A few minutes earlier, Donna Ruth had popped out, just before midnight on March 18. The twins were the youngest of Neil and Genevieve "Toots" Ashburn's four children. The Ashburns were poor. For years, the entire family slept in one bedroom.

Richie started playing baseball at age eight, but his twin was regarded as a better athlete during their childhoods. A fast runner, Donna routinely beat Richie in races until they were in high school. On the ballfield, Richie was a smallish catcher for most of his youth. Ashburn was first noticed by scouts when he played an American Legion All-Star Game at the Polo Grounds—then home to baseball's New York Giants—and signed with the Phillies in 1945 as an 18-year-old catcher. By 1948, Ashburn was in the majors playing center field, where as a rookie he hit .333 with 32 stolen bases. In 1950, he was a young gun for the Phillies' famed "Whiz Kids" club, the franchise's only pennant winner from 1916 to 1979.

For 15 seasons, Richie was one of the best pure hitters in a golden era of baseball featuring all-time great outfielders such as Willie Mays, Hank Aaron, Roberto Clemente, Mickey Mantle and Duke Snider. Whitey, who wore No. 1, was primarily a singles hitter who claimed two National League batting crowns, stole a lot of bases and covered acres of ground in center field. He led his league in putouts nine times, tying a record. All the while, "Putt Putt," Richie's nickname during his playing days, was loved by fans who embraced his friendly personality as much as they did his game.

Ashburn's Phillies career featured a number of amazing moments. In the 1950 regular-season finale, Ashburn prevented the Brooklyn Dodgers from winning the National League pennant with a ninth-inning throw to the plate that cut down Cal Abrams—a season-saving moment that made possible teammate Dick Sisler's three-run, pennant-winning homer in the 10th inning.

On August 17, 1957, Ashburn was involved in one of the craziest baseball incidents ever. During one wild at-bat, he hit a woman in the stands twice with foul balls—the first time in the face, then again while she was being carried away on a stretcher. The victim was Helen Roth, wife of *Philadelphia*

Bulletin sports editor Earl Roth. Ashburn visited her in the hospital after the game and apologized for breaking her nose. "You only apologized once," Roth said as she pulled up her nightgown to reveal a baseball-size bruise on the right cheek of her rear. Whitey's hospital visit became the start of a friendship.

With the Phillies in a down cycle, Ashburn was traded to the Chicago Cubs in 1960. Two years later, he ended his playing career with one of the worst teams in history, the 1962 New York Mets. An expansion team, the infamous '62 Mets lost a record 120 games. It wasn't Whitey's fault. He batted .306 and was named team MVP. "To be voted the most valuable player on the worst team in the history of Major League Baseball is a dubious honor, to be sure," Ashburn once said. "I was awarded a 24-foot boat equipped with a galley and sleeping facilities for six. After the season ended, I docked the boat in Ocean City, N.J., and it sank."

Despite building an impressive resume as a player, Whitey never came close to being voted into the Hall of Fame by the baseball writers. He was on the ballot from 1968 to 1983 and topped out with just 30.1 percent of the vote in 1980, far short of the 75 percent needed for election. His first five years on the ballot, he failed to receive even 4 percent of the vote. Ashburn, who registered over 2500 hits on his way to a lifetime batting average of .308, thought he'd put up Hall of Fame numbers. But the front door to Cooperstown stayed closed to him.

In due time, Ashburn would enter through the back door. Spearheading a move to elect Ashburn was a lifelong Phillies fan. During a Phillies-Reds game at Connie Mack Stadium in 1956, seven-year-old Jimmy Donahue became a fan for life after he obtained an autograph from Ashburn. Twenty-five years later, they met again at a November 1991 baseball card show. Donahue was angry that Ashburn's last shot at reaching the Hall had ended when the Veterans Committee changed its rules for electing players shunned by baseball writers. Donahue told Whitey that he'd like to start a grassroots campaign to pressure Major League Baseball into rethinking its position on the Veterans Committee. Whitey was flattered, but said, "You're flogging a dead horse." For the next two years, Donahue campaigned by collecting thousands of signatures that were sent to Major League Baseball. Meantime, he printed and distributed "Richie Ashburn: Why the Hall Not?" bumper stickers. With Donahue creating momentum, the Veterans Committee changed its rules in 1994 after another campaign began to get former New York Yankees shortstop Phil Rizzuto back on the Veterans Committee ballot. Rizzuto was elected by the Veterans Committee that year, then Ashburn became a Hall of Famer the next.

On July 30, 1995, with 25,000 Phillies fans in attendance, Whitey was inducted into the Baseball Hall of Fame in Cooperstown along with another Phillies great, Michael Jack Schmidt. Harry Kalas was absolutely thrilled for Whitey. "Do we have to treat you any differently now?" Harry asked his buddy. "Yeah, with respect—a lot of respect," Whitey answered in a deadpan tone with a sly grin.

As great a ballplayer as Ashburn had been, his broadcasting career took off slowly. In 1963, at age 35, Ashburn went straight from the playing field to the Phillies booth. Whitey got the job due to his popularity with fans, but was no natural. Some Phillies fans say he was pretty bad in his first few seasons. His first partners in the booth were future Hall of Famer By Saam and Bill Campbell.

"Campbell was the guy who took Ashburn under his wing, set him up for those good, dry lines," Bill Conlin wrote in a *Philadelphia Daily News* column two days after Campbell's January 1971 firing. "All the professional help that Ashburn got from Saam would not fill an earphone, even though the former Phillies star would bail By out of his frequent blunders."

Ashburn's popularity led to another brief television gig alongside Bill Campbell. A starting guard on his high school basketball team in the 1940s, Whitey provided color for Philadelphia's Big Five college basketball games for a year in the late 1960s. "Richie really enjoyed it and did a very good job," Campbell said. "He did it very much like he did baseball. He didn't talk your ear off."

In the Phillies' broadcast booth, Whitey eventually found himself playing peacemaker between Saam and Campbell on numerous occasions. "The amazing thing is Saam and Campbell co-existed for seven years," Conlin wrote. "You can thank Rich Ashburn for that. He saved the marriage more times than a neighborhood minister. He heard each broadcaster complain about the other so often he should have worn a striped shirt and a whistle."

Like Saam, Whitey wasn't flawless in the booth. Whitey would drive radio engineers crazy knocking off his clip-on microphone with his pipe. One time, he showed up for a television standup behind a green curtain wearing green pants and a green shirt, the only colors not permitted. When a technician complained, Whitey gave him hell.

For years, Whitey was in charge of taping radio interviews for the Phillies' pre-game show. They were a daily adventure. Whitey not only hated doing the interviews, he often struggled to work his tape recorder.

"Just hit the record button," producer Joe Gaines would say.

Whitey would then go off on his own in search of an interview. One time he didn't even make it out of the booth before dropping his recorder and breaking it. More than a few times, he'd return and brag, "Here is the greatest five minutes of radio you'll ever hear." Gaines would then turn on the tape and there'd be nothing. Sometimes Whitey would redo it. More times than not, he'd refuse. "My fans come to expect that from me," he would tell the producer with a shrug. "If I screw this up enough, maybe they'll take the show away from me."

Whitey didn't waste much time seeking out guests or preparing for interviews with the guests provided him. He'd simply ask his guest—often an opposing team's broadcaster—the first thing that came into his mind. His lack of preparation showed, but sometimes it led to hilarious bits, such as the time Whitey interviewed Cubs announcer Harry Caray before a 1992 game. Without being asked, Caray launched into a tirade about how the Cubs weren't going to spend the money to re-sign star pitcher Greg Maddux, who would be a free agent after the season. Not paying attention, Whitey followed the rant by asking, "So, do the Cubs have a chance to keep Greg Maddux?" Caray looked at Whitey strangely and said with annoyance, "Well, noooo!"

After a game one night, Whitey was enjoying a post-game drink with Harry Kalas in a New York hotel bar when a lady of the evening approached.

"Boys, I'll do anything you want for a hundred dollars," the blonde said.

"How about the pre-game show?" Whitey responded.

Some of Harry and Whitey's best times together came during drives to and from spring training, which became an annual event after Harry split up from his first wife. Most years, Whitey was pulled over for speeding. One winter, Whitey went out and purchased a radar detector, but their next trip to Florida led to bigger trouble. While driving through North Carolina, Whitey pulled off the side of the road for a nap. Before coming to a complete stop, Whitey and Harry heard a clinking sound. Within seconds, an officer who had been hiding in a patrol car behind bushes came charging out at them. Whitey had run over a speed-trap device.

Spring training was play time for Whitey, who usually had visitors. "There were lots of women," said Bill Conlin, who shared a condo with Whitey one spring and lived next to him for many other years

Whitey had an interesting 49 years of marriage to Herberta, who answers to "Herbie." They met as teens in Nebraska and married on November 6, 1949, after Richie's second season in the majors. The couple lived together for 28 years, and then separated for two decades with neither filing for divorce. They remained close friends the entire time.

After splitting up with Herbie in 1977, Whitey bought a home in Ardmore, Pa., from Phillies pitcher Larry Christenson, while Herbie and his children continued to live a few minutes away in Gladwyne. "I'm not staying here every day, but I'm still going to be here," Whitey told his children when he moved out.

Whitey lived up to his word. He regularly returned for family dinners and holidays. Before leaving, Herbie would make Whitey vacuum. He also supported his family financially.

"We're an extremely close family," Herbie said in 1995. "We're very much married. We just don't live in the same place. We don't seem to have too many disagreements. We have a great relationship."

All the while, Whitey had girlfriends. A woman named Andy Kaufman was a steady when he was home, but he had others around the country.

"The ladies liked Dad and my mom knew it," Richard Ashburn said. "She was seeing other people. Neither of them was ever serious. They always came back to each other. Even though they were separated, they still led as close a family life as you can. The way they lived was a little unnerving at first, but we all learned to live with it."

In his final days, Whitey wasn't healthy or happy. At 70 years old, he found himself a diabetic with declining eyesight and a bum elbow that forced him to give up tennis and squash. He also was upset with the Phillies because he'd been demoted. For years, he and Harry called the final innings on television. But in 1997, Whitey was ordered to work those innings on radio. Following the involuntary change in his role, Whitey talked nonstop to friends about being afraid that the Phillies would force him to retire after the 1997 season.

On September 8, 1997, Whitey worked a Phillies-Mets game at Shea Stadium. He was in the television booth for the first three innings, serving as Harry Kalas' color man, and then headed to the radio booth. He worked with

Chris Wheeler from the fourth through sixth innings, then did the final three with Andy Musser.

Everything seemed normal on the air. In a 13-4 Phillies victory, Whitey was sending out birthday wishes and harping on the plate umpire's strike zone. After the game, Whitey and Musser took the No. 7 train together from Shea to Grand Central Station in Manhattan, which was next door to the Grand Hyatt, the Phillies' hotel.

"Have a good night, see you tomorrow," Musser told Whitey when they parted ways in the lobby around 11:30 p.m.

Whitey went straight to Room 1502, where company was waiting. His guest was a woman named Izzy, an old friend.

The next morning, just before 5:30 a.m., Whitey woke up and made a trip to the bathroom. On his way back to bed, he suffered a massive heart attack. He slumped over, banged his head into an end table and fell to the floor. Whitey's guest frantically called the hotel operator and asked for Eddie Ferenz, the Phillies traveling secretary. Eddie phoned team trainer Jeff Cooper, who raced to Whitey's room.

It was too late. Richie Ashburn, age 70, was gone.

Harry Kalas, who was fast asleep three doors down the hallway in Room 1508, was awakened by Cooper around 5:45 a.m., and delivered the awful news that his closest friend was gone. Half asleep, Harry hung up the phone, and while lying in bed said to himself, "Did he tell me what I just thought he told me?" He phoned Cooper back to make sure he wasn't just having a bad dream. He wasn't. This was worse. Losing Whitey was a living nightmare for Harry.

Within a few hours, Phillies fans around the world woke up to news that one of their beloved all-time greats had died unexpectedly. All the news reports had Ashburn alone in his room and calling Ferenz. The Phillies planned it that way in an effort to avoid hurting Herbie Ashburn. But word spread throughout the Phillies family pretty quickly, and eventually it worked its way to the Ashburn family.

Richard Ashburn approached Harry one day asking for the truth about his father's death. Harry told him the truth. Years later, one of Richard's sisters told Herbie. Richard was angry with his sister until he found out his mother expressed happiness that Whitey didn't die alone.

Hours after Whitey's death, Harry Kalas phoned his wife, Eileen. "The press is coming to my room in 45 minutes and I have nothing to say," Harry told her. Eileen recommended that Harry quickly add a new final verse to a touching poem he'd written a few weeks earlier for Whitey's belated 70th birthday party. Eileen faxed the poem to the hotel and Harry went to work.

His new ending read:

Now the man all Phillyland loved
Has gone to join Jan in the heavens above
And Don Richie Ashburn by any measure
Was a man whose memory we will forever treasure

Later in the day, after he made it through the first round of interviews, Harry arrived at Shea Stadium for that night's Phillies-Mets game. By then, Phillies players already had black armbands with Ashburn's old No. 1 on a sleeve of their game jerseys.

With a heavy heart, Harry worked with Chris Wheeler on television and Kent Tekulve on radio. With his voice cracking, Harry read his poem on the air. "He was my best friend in life," Harry told listeners. "His dry Nebraska wit. His sense of humor. He was wonderful to be around."

The Phillies won their first game without Whitey by a fitting score, 1-0. After the game, Phillies players presented a game ball to Harry Kalas, who showed it off over beers and tears in the Grand Hyatt Hotel bar that night.

Back in Philadelphia, City Hall flags flew at half-mast and the crown of the PECO building was lit up with blinking lights that spelled out, "Goodbye Whitey, You'll Always Be No. 1." The next day, the *Philadelphia Daily News* devoted 34 pages to Ashburn. The front page headline read: "Whitey, We'll Miss Ya."

The Phillies played a twi-night doubleheader on the eve of Whitey's funeral. That day, the entire team, dressed in game uniforms, bussed to nearby Fairmont Park to join an eight-hour public viewing attended by many thousands of Phillies fans.

"There was a line of people probably a mile long waiting to go by Whitey's casket," said Frank Coppenbarger, the Phillies clubhouse manager in 1997. "They took us in through this side door and held the line up to let the team come through. There were all these people and the media, and then there's the body. It reminded me of seeing a President lying in state."

The Phillies bussed back to Veterans Stadium, and then split their double-header with Cincinnati. Harry Kalas went through his usual post-game routine for home games by heading to the press lounge for drinks and conversation. The party broke up quickly on this night, with Whitey's funeral to be held the next morning. But Harry stayed in the lounge by himself working on his eulogy.

Around midnight, Dan Stephenson, the Phillies video man, approached. "Harry, I just want to let you know I'm going to be there tomorrow with a camera, and I don't want you to be upset."

Harry kept writing for a few seconds, then looked up. "I have to give the eulogy for my best friend and I have no idea what I'm going to say," Harry mumbled in a voice that almost sounded like a cry. "I did my father's eulogy, and it was nowhere near as difficult. I've written it three times, and every time, it's wrong. I have 10 hours to do this."

Harry eventually drove home, and then continued writing in bed after receiving some encouragement from his wife. It took awhile, but Harry found all the right words. Harry expressed them the next morning in his typical unforgettable way at Whitey's private funeral.

"How many of us have said to ourselves, 'I wish I could have told him how much I love him. I wish I could have. I didn't get a chance to.' The suddenness has struck us all. But Whitey knew. He knew as surely as he knew a ball and a strike how we felt. He had such a wonderful life with love and friendship. He'd want us to carry on. As we leave here today, if we can make a difference in the life of just one person, make them love, bring them comfort, give them joy, as Whitey did for so many people. Then Whitey's memory will be fulfilled. If you loved Whitey, love one another. God bless you, pal."

Moved by the tribute, Stephenson remembered the late-night conversation that he had with Harry in the press club the night before. Stephenson wrote Harry a short note after the funeral. His message was, "I've never been as proud of another person as I was of you that morning because I saw the way you were Friday night."

Whitey was in Harry's thoughts continuously. "After Whitey died, Harry talked about Whitey every single day," said Scott Graham, a Phillies broadcaster from 1999 to 2006. "And I'm not exaggerating when I say every single day. Every single day it would be, 'As His Whiteness would say. . . .' It was Harry's way of keeping Whitey around."

The Phillies did their part, too, after moving across the street from Veterans Stadium to Citizens Bank Park in 2004. One of the highlights is Ashburn Alley, fittingly located in the center field concourse. Fans roaming this area can visit the Phillies Wall of Fame, buy a cheesesteak or admire the larger-than-life bronze statue of Whitey running the bases.

Right next to Ashburn Alley is Harry the K's, a two-story restaurant located below the left-field scoreboard. Visitors can watch the game from outside seats and order from a menu which includes Harry the K's Bratwurst or The Schmitter, a concoction of sliced steak, grilled salami, cheese, onions and tomato on a Kaiser roll.

These Citizens Bank Park tributes ensured that Harry and Whitey, even in death, would be together again.

Not long before Harry's passing, Dan Stephenson created a DVD of Whitey's life. Harry, of course, provided the narration.

"That was important to me because we knew Harry wasn't going to be around forever and wasn't in the best of health," Video Dan said. "I remember doing this Whitey thing and saying, 'It's important that we get Harry at the top of his game to do this.' And he was great. It was cool, because when you're writing stuff like that, you're writing for a narrator and I said, 'Wait a minute, it's Harry.' So it's not really going to be in the third person, it's going to be third and first. All of a sudden, it shifts and the second half becomes the story of the two of them. I didn't plan on that, but when the thing was done it turned out to be Harry's story, too."

When Richie Ashburn spoke at public banquets, he always referred to Harry Kalas as his best friend. Harry attended many of the same functions. He always called Whitey his special friend.

"Why don't you call him your best friend?" Eileen Kalas asked her husband in 1996. "Whitey says it every single time."

"I have so many friends," Harry responded. "I don't want to hurt people's feelings."

During one of their last functions together, Harry was at a podium, looked at his friend and said, "And there's my best friend Whitey."

Richie Ashburn's eyes lit up. Hearing that from Harry meant the world to him.

LIKE FATHER, LIKE SONS

When Harry Kalas left Houston in 1971, he moved to Philadelphia with his wife, two sons, Todd and Brad, and a blue parakeet named Polu Manu. The boys were Harry's pride and joy, but his bird wasn't far behind. He loved the little creature, who lived in a cage in the kitchen and often was let out to fly around the house. Jasmine Kalas, Harry's first wife, named the first family pet. A native Hawaiian, she kept it simple—Polu is the word for "blue" in the Hawaiian language and Manu translates to "bird." Thanks to Jasmine's training, Polu Manu was a talker, too. When Harry returned from home games, he usually would go straight to Polu Manu's cage and receive a cheerful greeting: "Hi, my name is Polu Manu Kalas. How was the game, Daddy?"

Polu Manu, a big part of the Kalas family for five years, even went to spring training. Harry was so fond of Polu Manu that he had to be talked into not having the bird sit in the passenger seat without a cage during a trip to the veterinarian. His boys were attached to the bird as much as Harry was. Polo was entertainment, a friend, and most certainly part of the family.

Everyone was devastated one morning in 1974 when Jasmine found Polu

Manu dead at the bottom of its cage. Harry, the son of a minister, took charge. He wrapped Polo Manu in a cloth and led a family funeral procession through the backyard to a vegetable garden. With his boys looking on in tears, Harry dug a hole and conducted a burial service for his little friend. He said a prayer for Polu and put a cross made of twigs on the dirt covering the grave.

Harry's religious training came from his father, Harry H. Kalas, a minister who was the son of another minister. Although a partier for most of his life, the Phillies' Harry Kalas passed down some of his father's best traits to his own three sons—Todd and Brad by his first wife Jasmine, and Kane by his second wife Eileen.

Harry inspired his children to befriend people of all races, religions and classes. Harry kept an even emotional keel and never lashed out in anger, and his children follow his example to this day. Harry always went out of his way to help strangers while expecting nothing in return. His children do the same. Harry admired his father. Harry's children revered their dad.

"It's very clear that when you talk to his sons that you see Harry's way, his style, his manner of dealing with people, that easy confidence," said Scott Graham, a close friend of Harry's from their days working together in the Phillies broadcast booth and at NFL Films. "I'm not denying these guys have mothers, but all that stuff comes from Harry. The fact that all of that got passed along in the limited time that he was around them is pretty impressive. A dad who works in baseball is a dad who isn't there a whole lot while you're growing up. His sons adapted to that and Harry adapted to that, and it made the time that they were together important."

Kane Kalas says his personality was shaped from observing his father in public. "Whenever we were out, I saw the way that he interacted with everybody, not just his colleagues or people who were rich and successful, but everybody. Some of his closest friends were people who weren't into baseball or not necessarily the most wealthy people in the world. Just watching that kind of taught me that this world is filled with people, all of whom are unique and all of whom deserve the time of day, regardless of their social economic status or if they're involved in the same line of work as you are."

Unlike his own father, Harry also sprinkled a lot of fun into his children's lives. As an adult, he was a kid at heart. Harry played a lot of backyard baseball and football with Todd and Brad. He went bowling, miniature golfing, threw baseballs and played board games with Kane.

"My father always wanted to have fun," Kane Kalas said. "I couldn't ask for a better dad. He was my inspiration, and he continues to be."

Harry became a father on New Year's Eve in 1965 when Jasmine gave birth to Todd. Almost three years later, Brad was born in November 1968. Kane came along in 1989 when Harry was involved with Eileen, whom he'd been living with since 1987 and would marry in 1993. After giving birth to Kane at age 37, Eileen Kalas had a hysterectomy. Harry was disappointed. "He wanted more kids," Eileen said. "Harry would have had five more."

Work travels kept Harry away from many of his sons' important childhood events, but he frequently talked to them on the phone. And every talk ended with "I love you, son."

"Some kids don't hear that until their father is on his death bed," Eileen Kalas said. "Harry's kids heard it a lot."

As a nine-year-old, Kane put his feelings into words by writing a touching Father's Day poem:

THE GREATEST DAD IN THE WORLD
I've got a dad, he's very kind. But sometimes he's hard to find.
He's always going to and fro. From Philadelphia to San Diego.
He does Phillies games day and night. He's so nice it's kind of a fright.
When he gets home, he's not that neat. But mom still thinks he's really sweet.
As for me, I think he's great. Isn't this some wonderful fate?

After finding Kane's poem on his desk and reading it, Harry was brought to tears. He framed the poem, then hung it in his home office.

All three Kalas boys had great times during spring training with the Phillies. Todd and Brad were home schooled by a tutor every March, but still enjoyed beach days and trips to the ballpark. Harry occasionally would treat his boys to a trip to Disney World or Busch Gardens.

When Harry was married to Jasmine, the family drove to spring training. They'd usually drive straight through from Philadelphia to Florida with Harry singing most of the way. These trips were painful at times for the boys because of Harry's smoking. Harry would crack his window, but it didn't help much. "It would be a smoke storm inside the car," Brad Kalas said. One winter, Brad offered to give up all of his Christmas gifts if his father quit smoking. Harry slowed down for a short time, but never quit. He loved his boys, but was addicted to cigarettes.

Spring trainings also included a birthday party for Harry, who was born in March. Every year, he'd break away from the adults at some point to play games with his boys and the other children.

"Harry always was the ringleader of post-dinner games," Bill Giles said. "He was so much fun back in those days. He was unbelievable playing games with his boys and my boys. He was a great father."

Like Harry, Todd and Brad grew up loving baseball. They spent a lot of time at the ballpark because their mother enjoyed going to Phillies games and made friends with a lot of players' wives and team executives. The Phillies gave Harry five season tickets behind home plate at Veterans Stadium—three for the family, and another pair for friends.

Jasmine kept her boys home on school nights, but they attended most every weekend and summer game together. When the games ended, the boys had to find ways to entertain themselves because Harry usually hung around at the ballpark for 60-90 minutes talking baseball and drinking beer in the press room with scouts, executives and media members. These gab sessions were where Harry would come to understand baseball strategies more complex than most fans realize, where he'd learn tendencies, strengths and weaknesses of players, where he'd get gossip and trade rumors.

"Every year, I learn more about the game," Harry Kalas said in 1981, his 17th year in the majors and 21st in professional baseball. "You never know all there is about this game. Every year in broadcasting, you come across situations and plays that you've never seen before. I learn from sitting around baseball people—scouts, managers and writers—after games. I like to imbibe for one thing, but you also hash over that night's game. Wherein did the Phillies or the other team fall? Did someone miss the cutoff man or fail to take an extra base or blow a sign? You learn as you go and never stop learning."

Jasmine Kalas passed the time by talking to wives of Phillies executives who also were in the press box. She understood her husband needed this time, and made her boys understand it as well.

"He'd have a few drinks and talk baseball," Brad Kalas said. "That's what he loved to do."

When Todd and Brad were still tots, everyone waited for Harry after games on a long sofa outside the family waiting room at Veterans Stadium. Little Brad often would fall asleep in his mother's arms and not awaken until the next morning, even though many people passed by, some talking loudly. As they grew older, Todd and Brad killed time playing Wall Ball, a form of handball that they played in the narrow runway leading from the Veterans Stadium home clubhouse to the batting cage.

Once Harry's post-game press-club gatherings broke up, there'd usually be another 30-minute wait. On most nights, dozens of Phillies fans would be waiting for autographs. Without exception, Harry signed for everyone every night. And when Harry signed for you, he often made the meeting extra special by talking to you a little.

"We didn't get upset," Jasmine Kalas said. "It was part of Harry's life, so we'd just go to the car and wait."

Even when leaving, Harry sometimes would volunteer to drive one of the scouts to a hotel. Often, the family didn't get home after summer night games until 1:30 in the morning.

"Dad always had that incredible ability to always have time for people," Todd Kalas said. "It's a very rare ability for someone to have that much passion for each person he meets and to have that much time to give to each person he meets. He was very, very consistent with that, and that made a huge impact on me as a kid."

By the time Todd and Brad were old enough to start school, they were spending a lot of their time at the ballpark playing with the children of Phillies players. Bret and Aaron Boone, Steve and Scott Carlton, Garry and Derrick Maddox, Ryan Luzinski and Pete Rose, Jr. were all around the same age. The boys roamed freely through a small basketball court outside the Phillies clubhouse, plus the batting cage, hallways and back rooms.

"That was basically our summer camp," Todd Kalas said.

"Those days at the Vet were so much fun," Brad Kalas said. "We'd get there two hours before the game and try to figure out what to do. You could make the batting cage and basketball court into anything you wanted to make it for stickball games or whatever."

The star of these games was Bret Boone, oldest son of Bob Boone, a Phillies catcher from 1972 to 1981. Bret amazed everyone with his athletic ability as a child. He was just eight years old when he started copying Phillies pitcher Tug McGraw by catching high fly balls behind his back during batting practice. Bret went on to become a three-time All-Star and four-time Gold Glove second baseman in the big leagues. Aaron Boone, his kid brother, would also enjoy a nice career in the majors. Garry Maddox, Jr., had a cup of coffee in the majors, while Ryan Luzinski and Derrick Maddox played in the minor leagues. Both decent athletes, Todd and Brad Kalas usually held their own with the ballplayers' kids.

All three Kalas boys played organized baseball, too. Harry took an interest in his boys' games, but couldn't attend many due to his long hours at the ballpark and frequent nights on the road. He did get to a lot of games in the summer of 1981 when major-league ballplayers were on strike for two months. That summer, Harry showed up to watch Brad play for Devon-Strafford, a travel team that almost made it to the Little League World Series.

During one Devon-Strafford game, Harry entered a small press box and gave some kids the thrill of a lifetime by playing PA announcer for a few innings. One of the starstruck kids playing against Brad that day was Mike Piazza, who would grow up to become one of the best catchers of all time. "Everyone went nuts saying, 'Harry Kalas is here,'" Piazza recalled. "I remember my friend saying, 'I didn't have anything for him to sign, so he signed my sneaker.' I don't even think I was playing in that game, but it was so cool that he came. That made him larger than life for me."

Kane Kalas played baseball until he was 14, but he never had the same passion for the game as his father and half brothers. Still, Harry and Kane had a lot in common. They both had a love for singing, gambling and poetry. Before he was talking in full sentences, Kane was bellowing out tunes with his father. Eileen pulled out a video tape recorder one night to record her two-year-old singing Reba McEntire's "For My Broken Heart" with Harry. In grade school, Harry and Kane would ride in the car together singing Frank Sinatra and Broadway tunes.

The spitting image of his father, Kane also was blessed with a close variation of Harry's adult voice. Harry used it to become a legendary sportscaster. By the time Kane was a teen, he was amazing people by singing opera and classical music at school, along with occasional renditions of the National Anthem before Phillies games.

Besides singing, Kane flashed talent in public speaking and acting during school plays, just like his father had done as a boy. His best sport was bowling. As a teen, he held a 212 average that was only about 10 pins below many pros' average, and once rolled a high game of 299. Like his father, Kane wasn't a bragger. "Lane conditions are a little bit tougher for the pros," he said. When Kane was in bowling leagues, Harry often was his ride. He'd always stay and watch in-between smoking breaks. A couple times a year, father and son would bowl together at Sproul Lanes in Springfield, Pa. Rolling a slow, straight ball, Harry usually averaged around 130.

It probably was harder on Kane when Harry was away than it was on his half brothers. At least Todd and Brad had each other. Kane was an only child in his house, unless his much-older half-brother Travis and half-sister Julie were around. Harry was Kane's favorite playmate.

"I think I witnessed Kane's first beer," said Jeff McCabe, Harry's longtime buddy. "We were playing a card game one night at Harry's house. Kane was four and sitting on the bar when Harry put a little beer in a shot glass. 'He's got to taste it sometime, pal,' Harry said. Kane loved it. I told Harry that Kane's got some good genes."

Kane did not become much of a drinker, but his gambling fervor was fueled by his father. For much of Harry's adult life, he habitually bet on horses all winter long. He'd drive to a convenience store first thing in the morning to get tip sheets, study them and then call in his bets. He even purchased a race-horse named Meandering in the 1980s, but it died within a year. This passion for betting, one of Harry's lifelong addictions, rubbed off on Kane. Before Kane was in school, he'd play children's board games with his dad for a dime. If Kane lost, he'd run to his room to get money from his piggy bank to pay Harry. By the time Kane was in college, he was a very skilled online poker player as well.

Harry's older boys also enjoyed gambling, but their childhood centered on sports. Todd and Brad played a lot of backyard Wiffle Ball games with neighborhood kids. When their dad was home, he'd join in. During nights, they'd play sponge ball in the basement. Harry would be the pitcher with Todd and Brad taking turns playing hitter and catcher. Harry would pretend to get a sign from the catcher, who would drop fingers down. During one of these games, Todd tried to copy what a Phillies player had done in a recent game and sneak a peak at Brad's sign. In the Phillies game, the opposing pitcher had knocked down the batter. In the Kalas family sponge-ball game, Harry playfully threw a lob at Todd's head, sending the boy flying out of the way, laughing.

During football season, Harry and the boys would head to the backyard during halftimes of Philadelphia Eagles games. Harry would play quarterback in a game of one-on-one between Todd and Brad that always stretched into the third quarter of the Eagles game. "Todd and I couldn't wait until halftime," Brad said. "There would be arguments, but we had so much fun."

In the winter, the boys played street hockey in front of their Rossiter Lane home, which was on a cul-de-sac, and ice skated on their oversized back porch, which was flooded purposely and turned into a mini-skating rink.

Jasmine was clearly the disciplinarian, but her boys usually were very well-behaved as children. But once in the mid-1970s, with Todd and Brad still in grade school, the brothers got into a screaming match while watching television in the basement. Harry was on the road, so it was up to Jasmine to calm the boys down.

"Cut it out," Jasmine yelled from upstairs. "Be normal boys."

When the boys kept it up, Jasmine became angry and uncharacteristically shouted some curse words. The fighting let up for awhile, then Jasmine heard more screaming. This time, she ran downstairs and cursed louder.

The next day, Harry returned home and was approached by the boys. They pulled out a tape recorder and pushed play so Harry could hear their recording of Jasmine yelling at them the night before. Turns out, the final fight was staged to catch mom swearing.

"Harry scolded them for upsetting me," Jasmine Kalas said. "They were normally good kids, but they really missed their dad when he first went on a road trip. They were so attached to their dad that the first day was always the worst."

Harry rarely got upset at his children. During his marriage to Jasmine, Harry sometimes got angry when his boys acted up during the long drives to spring training. Kane remembers his father being really mad at him just once. As a teen, Kane shouted "Fire!"—as in "fire the gun"—while rehearsing for his role of Enjolras for a school production of *Les Misérables*. Napping upstairs, Harry was awakened and hustled downstairs mistakenly thinking the house really was on fire.

Although Harry was the son of a minister, the Kalases weren't particularly religious, with the exception of observing a few yearly rituals. The family attended church services together every Christmas Eve and prayed before holiday meals with Harry always the one saying Grace.

When Harry was on the road during his first marriage, Phillies games were on television every night. Todd and Brad didn't pay attention to every inning of every game, but hearing their father helped take away the hurt of him being gone so much. "Part of the fabric of growing up was hearing Dad's voice around us," Todd Kalas said. "When he was gone for two weeks, those were the road trips that would get a little tough, especially in the summer time when you had a lot of free time."

Different yet alike, the Kalas boys ended up traveling their individual paths in life. Todd followed in his father's footsteps and became a Major League Baseball broadcaster. Brad moved to Los Angeles and did some acting, then found steadier work in the financial world. Kane began his sophomore year at the University of Miami in the fall of 2009, double-majoring in broadcast journalism and theatre arts.

Todd, who turned 44 in 2009, always showed more interest in his father's work than his brothers did. By middle school, Todd began an annual summer job that lasted a few years in which he'd sit in the Phillies radio booth during Sunday home games updating the out-of-town scoreboard off the tickertape. "Even though you were a kid, you felt like you were part of the broadcast," Todd said.

Brad had the same job for a day, but he became bored quickly and left the booth to wander around the stadium. Even as he grew older, broadcasting never was an option. "My dad had a really great life, but my thinking was, I already know that life," Brad said. "Why not try another career and see what that's like? Some of it was being naive. Where else can you go to baseball games for work and love what you do?"

Todd went through that stage, too. That's why he began college as a communications major at the University of Maryland following a 1983 graduation from Conestoga High School, which is regarded as one of the top academic high schools in Pennsylvania. During his freshman year at Maryland, Todd changed his major after one semester, switching to business management and accounting. To keep broadcasting as an option, he worked at the campus radio station.

When home for the summer after his freshman year, Todd decided that he would take a shot at broadcasting. He transferred to Syracuse University, a school with a top-rated broadcast journalism program and a tradition for churning out sportscasters, including the likes of Bob Costas and Marv Albert.

"I was very happy and very pleased when Todd decided to get into the business," Harry once said. "But the decision was all his. Todd was raised around the ballpark and the press box. I think it was a natural career choice."

At Syracuse, Todd stood out amongst hundreds of other young broadcast hopefuls. "Todd was so far ahead of everyone on the curve," said Howard Deneroff, a college friend of Todd's. "He had a base of knowledge coming in that none of us could come close to. He knew how to do a broadcast."

Deneroff abandoned his plans to be a broadcaster after observing Todd's advanced broadcast skills. After graduating from Syracuse, Deneroff instead became a producer for CBS Radio and Westwood One. Among his hires to work NFL games—Harry Kalas.

Todd gained a lot of valuable broadcasting experience at Syracuse doing football and basketball play-by-play for the campus station. His senior year was a dream year for the Orangemen. The football team went 11-0-1, capping off its undefeated season by tying Auburn in the Sugar Bowl, while the men's basketball team advanced to the 1987 NCAA Final Four before losing to Indiana in the championship game.

After college, Todd started his professional broadcasting career working minor-league baseball games, first for the Reading Phillies, then the Louisville Redbirds. He also worked in Clearwater as a sports director for Vision Cable. In 1992, at age 26, Todd Kalas became a second-generation "big leaguer," hosting the pre- and post-game shows on WFAN radio for the New York Mets. He was three years younger than his father had been when Harry landed his first job in the majors as a broadcaster for the Houston Astros in 1965. The Kalases were the latest in a string of father-and-son teams in the majors, joining the Bucks, Carays and Brennamans. "Nepotism definitely seems to be running wild," Todd Kalas joked after his hiring.

In 1994, the Phillies hired a second Kalas when Todd was brought in to be the play-by-play broadcaster for 40 cable games aired by the cable network PRISM. He didn't work directly with his father. Todd called innings 1-to-3 and 7-to-9 with Chris Wheeler as his color man, but was a part of the same Phillies broadcast team as his dad. Todd hoped that in due time he would share a booth with his father. But three years later, Todd's contract wasn't renewed for the 1997 season. Harry was very disappointed, and not just because Todd was his son. In his heart, he believed Todd was a talented broadcaster.

By 1998, Todd found a new baseball gig when he was hired to be part of the Tampa Bay Devil Rays' broadcast team. Eleven years later, he was still there hosting the pre-game and post-game shows on television, serving as the man in the stands during games and doing a little play-by-play.

Brad Kalas was an honors student at Conestoga High School, class of 1986, then earned a 3.5 grade-point average as a business major at Penn State University. After college, he had eight job offers and blew them all off to take his shot at fame. Although not interested in a broadcasting career, Brad was intrigued with show business. He packed his bags, moved to Los Angeles with a friend and enrolled in the two-year Meisner program. That acting school has launched the careers of movie stars such as Sandra Bullock, Tom Cruise, Kim Basinger, James Caan and James Gandolfini. Brad did well and was accepted into the actor's union, but never achieved fame. From 1997 to 2002, Brad built up a decent resume, appearing in episodes of well-known television shows such as *X-Files*, *Ally McBeal* and *Party of Five*. His best role was a bit part in *Wag the Dog*, a 1997 film starring Robert DeNiro and Dustin Hoffman. Although not a trained singer, Brad was selected to appear in the film as part of a group of 16 singers performing a song that was conducted by Willie Nelson. Brad still gets small residuals.

Brad gave up acting in 2003 to pursue a career that promised steady work and income. He landed full-time work in sales, then switched to the financial field. As of 2009, Brad was 41 and happily residing just outside Los Angeles with a steady girlfriend and a job he likes managing money for pension plans.

Kane Kalas struggled with reading during his youth, but was highly intelligent, articulate and street smart beyond his years. He began setting up his career during his sophomore year of high school when he moved to Hockessin, Del., and transferred to Sanford School, which offers an accelerated drama and music program. Harry purchased a home near the school for Kane, who was cared for there by his half-sister, Julie Vanwey, who is 20 years older.

After graduation from Sanford, Kane opted to go to the University of Miami, a decision that did not thrill his father. Harry preferred somewhere closer. In high school, Kane came home every weekend. His visits home from college would be much more infrequent.

Harry learned his parenting skills from his own parents, especially his father, even though Reverend Kalas had spent a lot of time on the road for work.

In his later years, Harry's father made up for lost time with his son. After retiring in 1974 following 19 years of running Westmar College, Reverend Kalas and his wife began making annual trips to Phillies spring training to visit with Harry, Jasmine and the boys. Reverend Kalas particularly enjoyed taking beach walks with his grandsons. "Harry's dad was a busy man, but tried to be with our children whenever he had time," Jasmine Kalas said.

Harry's parents spent their final years living at Otterbein Homes, a Methodist retirement community in Lebanon, Ohio. Reverend Kalas died in 1984 and his wife passed away 11 years later. Both donated their bodies to science.

"My grandpa and grandma were just great people," Brad Kalas said. "My grandfather was such a nice, genuine person. He really treated everybody the same. He was always encouraging and had good things to say. He was a big influence on my dad. My grandmother was more strict, but she was great, too. Like my dad, she loved the Phillies."

Harry adored his mother although he wasn't as close to her as he was to his father. A month before her 90th birthday, Margaret Kalas died of heart failure on October 5, 1995. Her two sons, Harry and Jim, were at her bedside.

A decade earlier, Reverend Kalas was hospitalized with a pancreatic tumor and chest pains. The day before leaving for a trip to cover an afternoon Notre Dame home basketball game, Harry had spoken with his father at the hospital and was encouraged. After checking into his South Bend, Ind., hotel, he phoned his father's hospital room. A nurse answered and passed along very sad news.

On February, 25, 1984, Reverend Harry H. Kalas, age 80, suffered a fatal heart attack.

Distraught, Harry told his mother that he wasn't going to broadcast the game, which had a tip-off scheduled in three hours time.

"Your dad would want you to do it," Margaret Kalas told Harry.

Harry listened to his mother. He worked the game, a 65-56 Notre Dame victory over Marquette, without mentioning his loss to anyone.

"My dad carried me through," Harry later recalled.

Harry stayed composed until the moment that he went off the air. "Then out of the clear blue, he dropped his head and bounced it off the table," said Jim Gibbons, Harry's Notre Dame basketball color man. "I panicked. I thought maybe he was having a heart attack and kind of put my arms around him saying, 'Harry, Harry, what's wrong?'"

Harry shared the news of his father's death, then sank into despair. A devout Catholic, Gibbons tried comforting Harry. Notre Dame coach Digger Phelps presented him with a medal of a Catholic saint. Nothing worked. Harry just sat there completely distraught. Even two private meetings with Father Hesburgh, Notre Dame's president, could not console Harry, so deep was his loss.

It took Harry a long time to recover from his father's passing, but something positive did come out of his grief. Following Reverend Kalas' death, Harry developed a newfound appreciation for the importance of family, especially his relationship with his sons.

"It really hit him and made him closer to the boys," Jasmine Kalas observed. "Harry became an even greater father after his own father died."

Harry gave touching eulogies at the funerals of both his parents. Years later, a moving public farewell was provided for Harry by his youngest son. The others did the same at their father's private graveside burial.

Indeed, Harry's fundamental goodness had rubbed off on each of his boys.

"What Harry gave his three sons," Scott Graham said, "more than anything else was his voice—not the baritone timber, but the way Harry carried himself, the way Harry felt with people, the easy smile, the way he made everybody feel important. Todd's got that in him. Brad's got that in him. Kane's got that in him."

A VOICE FOR ALL SEASONS

Harry Kalas planned a quiet Saturday evening on his night off in Buffalo. Back in the day, he would have been out on the town partying with friends at least until the bars closed. By the early 2000s, Harry was in his late 60s, and all he wanted to do was stay in his hotel room, call for room service and watch some college football before resting up to do radio play-by-play for Sunday's Buffalo Bills game.

This was Harry's late-in-life, night-before-the-game routine. But Howard Deneroff, vice president of Westwood One radio, decided to make his usual courtesy call with a dinner invitation anyway. To Deneroff's surprise, Harry accepted. The game Harry wanted to see wasn't available on his hotel room television, so he asked to dine in a sports bar carrying the game on satellite television. Broadcasting Phillies baseball had been Harry's full-time job for decades, but he enjoyed following other sports, especially college football. Harry and Howard headed to Tully's, which offered bar food and flat-screen televisions on every wall, including the Southeastern College game Harry had come to see.

When they arrived, Deneroff and Harry gave their name to the hostess, but a 15-minute wait led them to the bar for a quick drink.

"What can I get you fellows?" asked the man in his early 20s working the bar.

Just as Harry ordered a Coors Light, in perfect synchronicity one of his Coors Light voiceover commercials appeared on all of the television sets in the bar. "The NFL warrior has run out of Coors Light. Deep in his own territory, he unleashes a special teams masterpiece. . . ."

The bartender was dumbfounded. He looked at Harry, then to the TV, then back to Harry, who was oblivious to what was going on. Thinking the bartender was confused, Harry ordered again, this time with a hint of mock annoyance. "What will it take to get a Coors Light around here?"

Harry's voice wrapped up the commercial. "A fresh reserve of cold Coors Light. Now that's a Silver Bullet for the ages."

The bartender stood there staring at Harry for another second or two, then pointed to one of the televisions. Finally, Harry figured out what was going on.

"Yeah, I do the commercials," he said with some sarcasm. "Is that enough to get a Coors Light?"

"Yes, sir, I'm so sorry," the startled bartender said while hustling to grab Harry a cold brew that was on the house.

Harry took a big swig, then said, "Now that was worth waiting for."

The bartender approached Deneroff, leaned in and asked, "Who is that?"

"Harry Kalas, the voice of NFL Films," the Westwood One exec proudly answered.

Harry had one of the most recognizable voices in the country for more than three decades because of his Coors Light and Campbell's Chunky Soup commercial voiceovers, his Westwood One football broadcasts and, especially, his narrations for NFL Films. Although he was a beloved baseball broadcaster and a big celebrity in his adopted hometown of Philadelphia, Harry often could go on the road without being recognized. But his anonymity would end the moment he spoke in that familiar baritone.

Greg Dobbs, a standout pinch-hitter on the Phillies' 2008 World Series championship team, still chuckles when thinking back to the time that he met Harry Kalas. New to the Phillies during spring training 2007, the native Californian perked up when hearing Harry greet players during a stroll through the clubhouse.

"Oh my God, he's the voice from NFL Films," Dobbs said to a teammate. "What's he doing here?"

"He's our announcer," Chase Utley said.

Baseball consumed Harry's life and kept him on the road for more than 110 nights a year from March to October. For his entire adult life, he was a workaholic who took on many other adventures that kept him busy all year long—and often away from home. He loved everything about his line of work, which led to dozens of freelance opportunities coming along once he started working for NFL Films in 1975.

"Many times, I'd be in a football stadium on a Sunday and they'd be playing NFL Films on the Jumbotron at 10 in the morning," said Jack Ham, a Pro Football Hall of Fame linebacker who broadcasted NFL and college football games with Harry on Westwood One radio. "I'd hear Harry's voice there. Then I'd go in the radio booth and there would be a commercial for Campbell's Chunky Soup and I'd hear Harry's voice there. I would kid him that I'd hear his voice in my sleep sometimes."

In the 1980s, Harry Kalas served as the voice of Notre Dame football and basketball. He did commercials for the Arizona lottery and Kennywood Park, an amusement park outside of Pittsburgh. He was the voice of Animal Planet's *Puppy Bowl* for five years and did trailers for *Leatherheads*, a 2008 comedy film. Harry voiced a line of lyrics for a Snoop Dogg tune and commercials for NFL 2K2 video games. He narrated self-guided tours at the United States Mint in Philadelphia. And, during the weeks leading up to the Super Bowl for several years, Harry narrated profiles on Daffy Duck and Bugs Bunny for Cartoon Network's *The Big Game*. *"How many rabbits are self-made millionaires, live on a Beverly Hills estate and pal around with the likes of Hugh Hefner? Only one, Bugs Bunny."*

"I used to kid Harry, telling him that I hear him more in the winter than I do during baseball season," said Boston Red Sox manager Terry Francona, the Phillies' skipper from 1997 to 2000. "I'm watching TV and he's on everything."

It seems only natural that Jack Buck, the late Hall of Fame voice of St. Louis Cardinals baseball, would have been heard during inside walking tours of the city's landmark monument, the Gateway Arch. But from 1992 to 2007, it was Harry Kalas' voice you heard.

"I think it's a fascinating thing, actually," said Tom Etling, vice president of marketing for the Gateway Arch. "It's such a great voice that you hear when you go inside that you don't even think, 'Why isn't it Jack Buck?' Jack was the man, and so was Harry. They were both as good as it gets."

Mark Engler, formerly chief of museum services in St. Louis, was the one who chose Harry for the Gateway Arch narration. "I'd heard his voice with NFL Films and thought it commanded attention, commanded respect. I tried to find out who this was, and my search led me to Harry. I don't know if I should admit this, but I did not know Harry Kalas was associated with the Phillies. I didn't know the person who was behind his voice. I just thought his voice was awesome and I wanted to search him out."

The extra money coming from all of his side jobs came in handy, especially the paychecks from national commercials, which often brought in lucrative residuals. Harry never was one to brag about his career accomplishments, but if one of his commercials aired while he was in the presence of friends, he would proudly say, "ka-ching."

"You heard Harry all over the place—all over the place," former Phillies pitcher Randy Wolf said. "You're like, 'Oh, he's doing that too? Does he have a studio in his house?'"

"I'd be watching an NFL game at home and see a commercial and say, 'Oh, there's Harry,'" older brother Jim Kalas said. "That's how I found out these things."

From his early days as a professional broadcaster, Harry always did voice work on the side. While working his way up through the baseball ranks as a minor-league broadcaster in Hawaii, he called the high school basketball state championships in March 1965. After moving on to Texas to broadcast Houston Astros baseball from 1965 to 1970, he also announced University of Houston football and basketball. And, starting early into his long tenure in Philadelphia, he worked Big Five college basketball doubleheaders at the Palestra on Channel 17.

"As a kid, the Palestra seemed like a great place to watch a basketball game and Harry helped paint that picture," said Phillies pitcher Jamie Moyer, who grew up an hour's drive north of Philadelphia in Souderton, Pa.

In 1975, Harry became nationally known when NFL Films, headquartered 16 miles east of Philadelphia in Mt. Laurel, N.J., offered him voiceover work.

"I heard Harry doing some baseball—I'm not really a fan of the sport—but there was a quality to his voice, a resonance, a timbre that I thought might work for us," NFL Films President Steve Sabol said. "We started to mix our shows with more and more music. We would rather make people feel than make them think. We're dealing with emotion, and music is your most emotional element to filmmaking. We needed a voice that could cut through the music. I was intrigued by the sound of Harry's voice. At the time, I said, 'We ought to try this guy Harry Kalas.' That was met with some resistance because people said, 'Well, he does baseball.' I said, 'Yeah, but he's known in Philadelphia for baseball. If he does stuff for us, people in Denver, Dallas and San Francisco won't know who he is. It'll be a new voice, and maybe nationally he'll become known as the voice of NFL Films.'"

In time, that's exactly what happened. But initially, Harry served more as a regular contributor to the fast-growing company that already had a star narrator. To NFL fans, John Facenda was considered the "Voice of God."

"If the Last Supper ever had an after-dinner speaker, it would be John Facenda," Steve Sabol said.

NFL Films' roots trace to Steve Sabol's father, a New Jersey topcoat salesman. As a young man, Ed Sabol was a champion swimmer who was selected to represent the United States in the 1936 Summer Olympics in Berlin. Ed Sabol, who is Jewish, refused to compete in Nazi Germany. Instead, he fought in World War II. Sabol developed an interest in filmmaking after receiving an 8mm Bell and Howell camera as a wedding gift. By the late 1950s, he used his camera to shoot his son Steve's high school football games, and in 1962, he founded a small film company, Blair Motion Pictures.

Blair Motion Pictures already was on the map when Ed Sabol, a big fan of professional football, bid $3,000 to win the rights to film the 1962 NFL Championship Game, a Green Bay Packers 16-7 victory over the New York Giants at Yankee Stadium. Ed and Steve shot the footage, then composed a film that greatly impressed NFL Commissioner Pete Rozelle, who called it the best football film he had ever seen. By 1964, the NFL and Sabol struck a deal, and Blair Motion Pictures was renamed NFL Films. From then on, the company would shoot and preserve every NFL game.

From the outset, NFL Films showed a different side of football by producing *Game of the Week* segments for television, and season-in-review highlight films which were nothing like the typical game highlights that fans had grown accustomed to seeing. NFL Films included field-level camera angles, slow-motion footage, sounds from the sidelines—all set to music and punctuated by creative narration. As the popularity of NFL Films exploded, the popularity of the league did the same. Unable to compete with America's pastime prior to the late 1960s, the NFL eventually surpassed, then blew away Major League Baseball in television ratings. By 2009, NFL Films also had won its 96th and 97th Emmys.

"The single largest sports story of post-World War II America is football displacing baseball as big-game America," said Curt Smith, baseball author and former White House speech writer. "It was such an inversion of the old order where baseball had been almost synonymous with America. One sport probably knows how to utilize television and the other does not, and NFL Films is probably the best example of that."

"What we've done is take what every real football fan feels when he goes to a game—the excitement and passion—and through our filmmaking, we've amplified it and magnified it and intensified it," said Steve Sabol, who succeeded his father as president of NFL Films in 1995. "I think that's the core of our success."

Having one legendary narrator follow another didn't hurt, either.

"We have worked with two of the greatest voiceover talents in television history," Steve Sabol said. "John Facenda was the 'Voice of God' and Harry Kalas was the 'Voice of the People.'"

NFL Films has honored both Facenda and Kalas by hanging their portraits outside one of their studios.

John Thomas Ralph Augustine James Facenda was a popular Philadelphia radio and television newscaster for three decades when NFL Films went looking for a narrator in 1965. Ed Sabol recruited three well-known actors, but Orson Welles and Alexander Scourby weren't interested, and Richard Basehart asked for too much money. His fourth choice was Facenda, who in 1965 was in his 18th year as the news anchor for WCAU-TV, Philadelphia's CBS affiliate.

"My dad and I wanted to portray pro football the way Hollywood portrayed fiction, with a dramatic flair, and part of that drama would be a script," Steve Sabol said. "We wanted people to know when NFL Films came on, it wasn't just sports. This was a movie."

Before getting around to contacting Facenda, Sabol went out for a drink one night to the RDA Club, an after-hours joint within walking distance of

NFL Films' original office on North 13th Street in Philadelphia. Facenda was sitting at the bar when Sabol entered, and fortuitously, an NFL Films show was on the establishment's television.

"I started to rhapsodize about how beautiful it was," Facenda once said. "Ed Sabol came up to me and asked, 'If I give you a script, could you repeat what you just did?' I said I would try."

Facenda initially didn't think that he was right for the job because he was a newscaster and not a sportscaster. He didn't even follow football.

"My son will write it for you, and all you have to do is read it," Ed Sabol told Facenda.

Just 23 at the time, Steve Sabol developed the script for Facenda's first NFL Films documentary, *They Call It Pro Football*. "We went into a recording studio, and I'll never forget the first line Facenda read: 'It starts with a whistle and ends with a gun,'" Steve Sabol recalled. "I looked at my father and we knew right then this was going to work. But we found out that John couldn't read and watch football on a monitor. It confused him, so halfway through the recording I just said, 'John, don't even look at the picture. Just read the script.' And from then on, he never saw anything that he narrated. Harry Kalas was totally different. Harry wanted to see the picture."

Harry and John Facenda rarely crossed paths during their decade at NFL Films together. Harry usually came to the studio once a week during football season, while Facenda did most of his work there after the season.

"John did these big-event narrations and Harry would do the immediate stuff, the *Game of the Week* shows," said Dave Plaut, an NFL Films producer since 1976. "Don't forget, there was no ESPN back then, so you didn't get highlights except to see them on halftime of *Monday Night Football* or *Game of the Week*. Harry's voice lent itself more to that, where John did more of the poetic sweeping lines which could sound corny for other people to do. Over time, Harry was able to handle those in his own way, as well. We had plenty of work for both of them."

Harry looked up to Facenda. When Harry was starting out at NFL Films, Facenda would offer narration tips during their rare times together. Harry also paid close attention when listening to Facenda's work from afar. "John really became a mentor of mine," Harry once said. "He was the best narrator I'd ever heard and a wonderful man, so he was very influential to me."

To someone not in the business, narrating may seem like easy work, but it is so much more than simply reading lines. Harry Kalas was a natural reading from scripts, pacing himself and using voice inflection.

"Harry was real consistent in his reads," said Ray Didinger, an NFL Films senior producer from 1997 to 2008. "When you were writing his script, I wrote them at the pace that Harry's voice would read them. The pieces already had been cut, so you had the radio calls already in there, the sideline sound already in there, the cheering crowd already in place. Harry's lines had to fit the holes, and you had maybe 6 seconds to get that line read before the next radio call or next coach hollering from the sidelines. It was real specific. It couldn't be 5.8 seconds or 6.2 seconds. It had to be 6 seconds—or whatever. There was a hole, and he had to hit it. Harry was really good at that. He would hit that spot almost every single time. It was just uncanny. He just had a great feel for it.

"Technically with some narrators, you kind of have to direct them on the reads. You have to say, 'This line has to have some empathy here' or 'this is reflective, moody and warm' or 'this line is real powerful.' You never had to do that with Harry. He would read the script one time and say, 'I've got it.' Then you'd start rolling, and he would just nail it."

In 1997, Didinger took the job at NFL Films after working in newspapers for 27 years. The transition from being a newspaper man to writing scripts initially proved difficult, but Didinger always looked good when Harry spoke his lines.

"In writing for newspapers, my words were on a piece of paper," he said. "It's a whole different thing when Harry takes your words and reads them behind a microphone, and then they get mixed with music. Harry could take a line that you wrote, and the way that he read it, he'd find an emotion that you didn't even know was there. He'd bring something to it that I didn't even think of with an inflection or a pause. He would give it a texture that you, as the writer, didn't bring to it. He had a real gift. He would take the most mundane writing and just elevate it. And he did it all the time. He made our writing sound like poetry. Trust me, it wasn't poetry."

In his very first NFL Films assignment, Harry Kalas stood out just cutting a commercial for Red Devil, a caulking company that was the sponsor for the weekly *This Is the NFL* show. "Red Devil gave us a script that I bet was 175-

to-200 words, and it had to be read in 15 seconds," Steve Sabol said. "I gave it to Harry and said, 'I don't know whether you can get through this.' Not only did he get through it, but he did it in one take with no stumbles. Every word was pronounced. It was like an Evelyn Wood speed reading, and Harry Kalas did it in one take. And we never did it again. We used that same take over and over and over again. To us at NFL Films, that became part of his legend."

NFL Films lost a legend in September 1984 when John Facenda died at age 71. Without hesitation, Sabol made Harry Kalas the company's new No. 1 narrator.

"No one could replace John Facenda, but Harry Kalas came pretty darn close," Bob Costas said.

Harry was different, but became great in his own way.

"Harry was never like Facenda," Steve Sabol said. "Harry was a trained theatrical voice. Harry was a great sportscaster and an excellent reader. He could do things quicker, and the other thing about Harry is he could adjust to last-minute changes really well. John wasn't as good at that. Harry could be dramatic, poignant or funny. Whatever we asked him to do, he could do it on the spot."

"Over the years, we'd had a lot of narrators come in and try to be Facenda, and you couldn't," Ray Didinger said. "He was unique. But I think these guys had a sound in their mind of what NFL Films narration sounded like, and they tried to imitate that. Harry didn't even try that. Harry was just Harry. He didn't try to be Facenda. He has his own style, and his own way of doing it. And it worked. That's why he was better than the other guys, and that's why he lasted."

One of Harry's best-known NFL Films projects was narrating the weekly highlights for 32 years on *Inside the NFL*, which aired on HBO from 1977 to 2007, and then moved to Showtime in 2008. He also narrated *Game of the Week* for many years.

In his early years at NFL Films, Harry would drive to the office on Monday mornings to read scripts. In later years, Harry started his NFL Films work on Wednesday at 10 a.m., usually with a cup of Dunkin Donuts coffee and a pack of Parliament cigarettes next to him. When the company moved in 2002 to its current 200,000 square-foot building in Mt. Laurel, N.J., Harry would sit in Booth F reading from a sheet of papers with a monitor in front of him showing highlights that he was describing. His producer would be behind him and a director would be watching through a glass wall in the next room.

"When it was time for the narration, the picture would start and you'd tap Harry on the shoulder when you wanted him to begin his lines, which were numbered on a sheet of paper," Dave Plaut said. "He'd read the line, and then when the line was done, he'd stop and wait for you to tap him again for the next line. It helped to know Harry's cadence because he read at a different pace than some other narrators. They all have a different way of reading.

"Younger producers often would have a tendency to overwrite for Harry. He could read at a pretty good clip, but you didn't want him racing. You would lose a lot of the depth and texture of his voice if you did that. So inexperienced producers would have to learn to scale back, and they would sometimes rewrite it right there on the spot so Harry didn't have to race through it. The funny thing is you'd hear guys rehearsing, and sometimes they were doing their Kalas impressions. Most of them sucked. I happen to think mine is pretty good."

For the 1980 to 1987 football seasons, Harry Kalas and Steve Sabol were on-camera together hosting a syndicated weekly show of game highlights and player features that, due to sponsor changes, over time switched names from *NFL Review and Preview* to *Pro Magazine* to *NFL Films Presents* to *This is the NFL*. Both had a blast shooting these shows, which required some comedic acting. For Halloween and other special shows, the co-hosts routinely would dress up in costumes and act out scripts that led into NFL highlight packages. They were ghost hunters carrying rifles one time. Harry dressed as a giant purple grape another time. Steve once pretended to be a mad scientist working in a lab with Harry lying on a table as his patient.

"Harry always was willing to go along with a joke, and some of those skits were like junior high," Steve Sabol said. "But he had a lot of fun. He was very established in his career at this time, and I'm not sure a lot of people in his position would do the things that he did with us. But that was part of his personality. He was unassuming."

Harry made his usual positive impression on most NFL Films employees. He always made it a point to compliment his producers on their scripts, even if they needed polishing. He learned the first names of every secretary and intern, and became good friends to Steve Sabol and Dave Plaut, among others. For years, he hosted an NFL Films Christmas party at the Yankee Doodle Inn in Valley Forge, Pa., which according to Sabol, "was a highlight of our social calendar."

"There was a dance floor, food, open bar, DJ, and the party would go into the wee hours," Dave Plaut said. "Phillies would come by because they knew Harry was there holding court. It was just a lot of fun, and he did this for many, many years. When we started doing this, there were maybe 40-50 employees in the company. There are almost 300 now. Harry invited everybody—maintenance people, secretaries, people in video. And he picked up the whole tab."

Harry had a 34-year-run with NFL Films that probably would have lasted several more years had he lived longer. His last project, the 2008 NFC champion Arizona Cardinals' highlight film, was narrated a month before his April 2009 death.

Although Harry enjoyed narrating, he found broadcasting NFL games for Mutual and Westwood One more exciting. He thrived on being in the press box and, until he stopped drinking late in life, loved the nights on the road partying with broadcast partners such as Jack Ham and Rick Walker.

Starting in his college days, Harry spent many fall weekends calling football games. His first big-time college football gig was doing Notre Dame games for a stretch in the 1980s while working alongside color analyst George Connor. He also did a lot of college football for television networks such as Metro Sports—work that enabled him to call games such as Notre Dame's upset of Dan Marino and top-ranked Pitt in 1982 and unbeaten Penn State's win over Ohio State in 1995.

"They used to do the Notre Dame replays on Sundays when I was a little kid, and it was always Harry saying, "Touchdown, Allen Pinkett!" in that voice that you remember," former Phillies pitcher Ricky Bottalico said. "That voice was known around America."

For the last decade or so of his life, Harry worked an NFL game every Sunday after baseball season, but he never expected any special privileges. If he was scheduled to go to Seattle on Christmas, he went without saying a word.

"I wasn't going to put him on a Giants or Eagles game because the game was close to his home," Howard Deneroff said. "I always said, 'Harry, here's what I've got for you,' and he'd say 'fine.' One time he asked for an East Coast game because he had a wedding.

"He loved the stadium. He loved it in baseball and loved it in football. I don't want to say Harry was a rock star, but when he'd walk in, everybody would talk to Harry. He'd go on about the Phils. He'd probably spend an hour talking to anybody. I'd have to drag him away for voice check. He'd say, 'All right, my fans are calling. I gotta go.'"

Harry took his football assignments very seriously. He studied statistical packets and newspaper clippings. He also would write out detailed information and stats for each player on small white stickers, then attach them onto the front and back of a 16-by-18 inch homemade lineup board which he used for years.

"I knew that baseball was Harry's first love, but you wouldn't know it when he would broadcast football games," Jack Ham said. "You knew preparation was key to him. He knew his football, and all of us kidded him throughout the year about his Eagles. He was a Philadelphia guy, no matter what. I would pick his brain about baseball. 'How can you tell a cut fastball from a regular fastball?' I know nothing about baseball, and he would give me Baseball 101."

Rick Walker remembers Harry showing up for frigid games in the middle of the winter without a coat. "We had snow flurries in Minnesota and I've got on military gear and Harry's got a blazer with an open-collar blue shirt," Walker said. "I said, 'Harry, you must have embalming fluid going through your system.' He's carrying a Philadelphia Phillies traveling bag and his Bloomingdale shopping bag with his board made out of Formica that was chipped, and he had all his information on these stickers with his game notes. That was Harry all the time, always prepared."

"In football, it is bang-bang, you've got to know the players and you've got to have good vision, although we do have a spotter," Howard Deneroff said. "He had it written down and he'd memorize it. And he'd have to memorize it, because in the heat of a play, if LaDainian Tomlinson is breaking off left tackle and cutting to the sideline, spins away, then goes back to the right hash and has one man to beat—you better know who that one man is. Then to say, 'Touchdown, LaDainian Tomlinson, it's his 20th of the season' without looking at a chart. You can't fake it.

"Harry was great at that. Harry was an excellent football play-by-play guy made better by the voice, although sometimes I think that was lost because people would go, 'Oh my God, listen to those pipes.' They wouldn't hear Harry say, Brett Favre 'rifled in the pass' instead of 'threw it,' or 'he tip-toed out of bounds at the 22-yard-line'—great stuff for radio. Not everybody does it. He did it. But I don't think he always got the credit because everybody remembers his voice, which was his calling card, fair or unfair."

Harry's loyalty to his football commitments never faltered. Two days after the Phillies' 2008 World Series championship parade, Harry was in East Rutherford, N.J., working a Giants-Cowboys game. Also in 2008, he delayed having minor heart surgery—not only until the end of baseball season, but until after the 2009 Super Bowl so that he could fulfill his NFL Films and Westwood One commitments.

"It used to bother Harry that he wouldn't do the first four weeks of football for us. And understand this, when I hire people I hire them for a full-season package," Howard Deneroff said. "But to have Harry for 12 weeks versus someone else for 16, I'd rather have Harry. Before the 2008 football season when his wife called to tell me that he was having an eye procedure and would be fine, I said, 'Look, this is Harry's job. It's Harry's seat until he tells me it's not his seat.'

"I watched the Ernie Harwell debacle in Detroit when the Tigers pushed him out of the booth. Was Harry as good as he was five years ago? No. Ten years ago? No. But there are certain guys that deserve the right to be there. He called and said, 'Those Fightin' Phils are going to the playoffs. I might have to miss another couple weeks.' I'd tell him, 'Whenever you get there, buddy.' Everybody on the crew loved him. It didn't matter if you were a spotter or an executive producer, in the first five sentences of a broadcast Harry gave you credit. He'd come on the air saying, 'Along with Jack Ham, I'm Harry Kalas with our producer, our spotter, our gopher, our gopher's girlfriend. . . .'"

Harry also was proficient at broadcasting hoops, which he'd done regularly since his college days through the 1980s. During his time calling Notre Dame basketball games, he made a great friend in broadcast partner Jim Gibbons. Plus, he also became friends with Fighting Irish head coach Digger Phelps, who had been an assistant at the University of Pennsylvania from 1966-69, before Harry's Big Five days.

"Harry knew the game," Jim Gibbons said. "He knew when to say something and when not to say something. I listen with a fine-tuned ear on everything I watch—whether it's football, basketball, baseball or tennis—and when he was working with me or working with someone else, he knew when to stop and let the people who were getting paid to explain the game do it. I worked with a lot of people in basketball and some of them didn't like it at all that I was doing my thing. He never ever did that."

Harry's workload expanded even more in the mid-1990s when he started landing national commercials for some of the NFL's top sponsors. The opportunities came when Harry, at the urging of his second wife, Eileen Kalas, hired a talent agent for the first time. Until then, for years Harry had been doing a lot of commercials and speaking engagements for little or no money, often donating his time as a favor to friends. For instance, he typically received no compensation for emceeing the annual Philadelphia Sports Writers banquet. Plus, according to Eileen, he did projects for free such as narrating a 2004 PBS college football documentary titled *The Lehigh-Lafayette Legacy*.

"Harry would get calls—'Can you host this?'" said Jeff McCabe, a longtime close friend. "There was no money. Eileen used to go to a lot of them. I used to go to a lot of them. It might be an American Heart Association or United Way dinner. Whatever it was, he never said no. That's the way Harry was."

Eileen was often criticized for encouraging her husband to aggressively attempt to increase his income. Her critics called her money hungry, but she says that she simply was stopping people from taking advantage of Harry.

Seeing Eileen at work, Jim Gibbons nicknamed her "Relentless."

"If somebody would do anybody in her family wrong, Eileen would jump in," Jeff McCabe said. "That's why they call her 'Relentless.'"

In the mid-1990s, Eileen handpicked Marc Guss, a young agent then with the prestigious William Morris Agency, to seek out freelance opportunities. "When I first started working for Harry, he would say 'yes' to everything," said Guss, who also has represented the likes of actress Lauren Bacall, boxer Floyd Mayweather and comedian Gilbert Gottfried.

"Then Eileen and I had to make sure that when he did get a phone call, that he'd politely say, 'Speak to my agent.' Because he's such a nice guy, it took a while for that transition to happen. But it was worth it in the long run because we did a lot of great deals for him."

Guss brokered well-paying commercials for Campbell's Soup and General Motors.

"There was a whole lot more national exposure after very many years of limited national exposure," said Bob Smith, a Kalas friend. "His new agent definitely was a positive, and I think Eileen pushed it. Harry was the kind of guy who would just sit back and let the world go around. Eileen was more motivated toward using his resources, and I have to give her credit for that."

While married to his first wife, Harry had done commercials for Chrysler in 1971. Harry received little money, but landed sweet deals on new cars. Harry also had done ads for a clothing company in which his monetary compensation was low, but they'd outfit him with new suits. His freelance finances increased dramatically with Guss calling the shots.

"At the end, Harry was making more money from the commercials than he ever made with us," Steve Sabol said.

One of Harry's perks from doing General Motors commercials was a big discount on a black Cadillac STS for his son Kane's 16th birthday in 1995.

"My friends were envious," Kane said.

From 2001 to 2007, Harry did 77 radio and television spots for Campbell's Soup, which is headquartered 10 minutes from Philadelphia in Camden, N.J. Harry did voiceovers for Campbell's Chunky Soup's "Mama's Boys" campaign, which starred NFL players such as Donovan McNabb, Jerome Bettis and Michael Strahan in spots with their mothers.

"It was a pretty nice array of NFL stars, and then the guy who brought the continuity in that was Harry and his voice," said John Faulkner, director of brand communications for Campbell's Soup Company. "As the voice of NFL Films, and certainly with the type of delivery that Harry had, he was a great signoff at the end of the spot. There were a lot of components to help the brand grow the way it did, but during that time frame the sales of Chunky doubled. That was really the great growth spurt for the Chunky brand."

Marty Stock, who oversees Coors ads as executive vice president, wanted Harry to narrate Coors Light commercials when the beer company became partners with the NFL.

"Because Coors is the official beer of the NFL, we like to share icons with them—everything from the NFL shield and other trademarks that the NFL has," Stock said. "We thought that extended to an announcer, and if we were going to hire somebody, let's hire the icon of the NFL. We all knew Harry Kalas from NFL Films, and we knew that he obviously was a big voice of Philadelphia. We love to use authentic things where we can, and if you could get an icon like Harry Kalas, whose voice brings back memories of NFL highlights, it just increases the authenticity of the engagement with the listener. So it was a very simple decision for us. Voices are so critical in commercials, and in our corner of the world—the beer business—getting somebody of Harry's stature is a huge deal. You get a huge amount of credibility and authenticity."

Other than his narrating work for NFL Films, which was done in New Jersey since the 1970s, Harry did most of his voiceover freelance work and Phillies narration projects at Baker Sound in Philadelphia.

"When Harry came in, he was so low-key," said Rick DiDonato, Baker Sound's president and chief engineer since 1987. "He would get his coffee, sit down and wait for his session to start. He would always give everybody an 'Outta here!' call.' I always wondered if he'd ever get tired of saying that, but I guess he never did."

On March 12, 2009, Harry did the narration and acted in a 30-second commercial for Super Pretzel, a brand of J & J Snack Foods in Pennsauken, N.J. Before the commercial was scheduled to start airing the next month, Harry passed away. Instead of scrapping the ad, it ran in the Philadelphia region with a tribute message at the end: "Harry, we will miss you."

ONE OF THE GUYS

Philadelphia policemen on horseback lined the Veterans Stadium outfield foul lines waiting to go on crowd-control duty. Phillies pitcher Tug McGraw stood on the mound with 65,838 roaring fans praying for one more strike. Kansas City Royals outfielder Willie Wilson dug in from the right side of the batter's box with two outs in the ninth inning, the bases loaded and the Phillies up two runs in Game 6 of the 1980 World Series. Before looking in for a sign from catcher Bob Boone, McGraw noticed one of the horses dropping a dark brown pie.

"If I don't get out of this inning, that's what I'm going to be in this city—nothing but a pile of horseshit," Tug told himself. After almost a century of disappointment, the Phillies found themselves one strike from their first World Series title.

With nervous excitement and some disappointment, Harry Kalas took it all in from a press-level booth, but not from the broadcasting booth itself. Harry wanted this championship for the organization, their players and the city of Philadelphia as much as anyone. But he could only silently watch it all play out because there was no microphone in front of him.

As McGraw looked to finish off the Royals, Joe Garagiola set the scene in the NBC television booth: "Bases loaded. Two outs. Two strikes on Willie Wilson. The crowd will tell you what happens."

When Wilson swung and missed at 11:29 p.m.—McGraw called his pitch "the slowest fastball ever thrown in Philadelphia; it took 97 years to get there"—Garagiola lived up to his promise and let the ecstatic roar of the long-suffering Phillies crowd tell the story.

"The Philadelphia Phillies are the champions of the world," Vin Scully, working the game for CBS Radio, told listeners with his typical elegance.

October 21, 1980, a great day for the Phillies, was one that for Harry Kalas was extremely bittersweet. The Phillies finally had their world championship, but their longtime play-by-play man was robbed of fulfilling his dream of making the championship call. Major League Baseball rules didn't allow it. Harry and the rest of the Phillies broadcasters—Richie Ashburn, Tim McCarver, Andy Musser and Chris Wheeler—couldn't do the games on television or radio because MLB gave networks exclusive rights for World Series coverage.

"It's depressing, frustrating and disappointing that after working the Phillies through the entire season and playoffs, we can't work the Series," Harry said after the '80 World Series. "It's like being in reach of the plum and not being able to grab it. But that's the nature of the beast, I guess."

For three decades, networks had one of their broadcasters working the World Series together with the top play-by-play men from the participating teams. For instance, in the 1969 World Series, NBC broadcaster Curt Gowdy worked on television with Mets broadcaster Lindsey Nelson in New York and with Orioles broadcaster Chuck Thompson in Baltimore. Meantime, Jim Simpson called the games on CBS Radio, partnering with Thompson in New York and Nelson in Baltimore. This format remained in effect while NBC held television rights from 1948 to 1976, and radio rights from 1957 to 1976. But ABC decided not to use local broadcasters from participating teams when the network gained television rights for the 1977 and 1979 World Series, and NBC stuck with its rival's revised format when it regained Series' broadcast rights for 1978 and 1980. CBS won radio World Series rights in 1976 and continued the practice of using participating teams' announcers for one year, but then in 1978 decided to start using just its own announcers.

Current *Sunday Night Baseball* broadcaster Jon Miller, who worked as an announcer for the Boston Red Sox in 1980, blames ABC's longtime news and sports division chief Roone Arledge for ending what many baseball fans considered a wonderful tradition. "When ABC got involved, Roone Arledge had a policy that nobody who worked for the organization could broadcast a game involving their team on that network," Miller said. "That's saying I'm not professional enough to do a game geared toward a national audience. That's just ridiculous. But that was the rationale behind the local announcers not doing the World Series."

Not calling the World Series had left a void in Harry's career. But he loved the 1980 Phillies, who were led by future Hall of Famers Mike Schmidt and Steve Carlton, plus eventual career hit leader Pete Rose. Harry at the time was only a few years older than most of the players, and many were his drinking buddies.

Founded in 1883, the Phillies won just two National League pennants in their first 97 seasons. The 1915 Phillies won Game 1 of the World Series, but then lost four in a row to a Red Sox ballclub that didn't even need its 20-year-old pitching star Babe Ruth, who was limited to one pinch-hit at-bat in the Series. Loaded with young standouts like Richie Ashburn, Del Ennis and Robin Roberts, the 1950 Phillies—The Whiz Kids—were and still are one of the most beloved teams in franchise history. They won the National League, but ran into Joe DiMaggio and the New York Yankees in the World Series, where they were swept in four games. After 1950, the Phillies didn't play another postseason game for a quarter-century. They won the National League East three years in a row from 1976 to 1978, but each time lost their best-of-five National League Championship Series for the pennant and a berth in the World Series.

In 1980, the Phillies won their division again, then played for the pennant in an epic five-game series with the Houston Astros, the last four of which went into extra innings. The Phillies won Game 1, but dropped the next two, leaving Houston with two chances to win the pennant in its building. In Game 4, the Phillies trailed at the Astrodome 2-0 after seven innings, but rallied to win 5-3 in 10 innings to push the series to a fifth and decisive game. In his Game 5 intro for WPHL-17, Harry told partner Richie Ashburn, "I've never been to a World Series or involved in games like this in my years of broadcasting."

Harry hadn't seen anything yet. Houston had the Phillies in deep trouble in Game 5, leading 5-2 after seven innings with future Hall of Famer Nolan

Ryan pitching. Their season down to six outs, the Phillies exploded for five in the eighth to pull ahead, but Houston came right back to score two in the bottom of the eighth and tie the game. After nine innings, nothing was decided once again.

When the Phillies finally took the lead for good in the 10th, Harry struggled to control his emotions. "A base-hit, I believe ... Maddox! Yes it is! Garry Maddox! A hit! Phillies take an 8-7 lead. Maddox at second base. Phils lead 8-7 in the 10th inning!" The passion in Harry's voice was palpable. When the Phillies hung on to win, Harry scooted to the ecstatic visiting clubhouse to do post-game interviews and take a champagne shower.

Up to this point, the 1980 National League Championship Series was the highlight of Harry's career, and even decades later, this Phillies-Astros showdown is still regarded as one of baseball's best postseason series ever. For Harry, it had extra-special meaning because his first major-league job was broadcasting Astros games from 1965 to 1970.

A couple of hours after Game 5, Harry returned to the Phillies' hotel in Houston, the Shamrock Hilton, arriving at the same time as *Philadelphia Daily News* sports writer Ray Didinger.

"Raymond, do you believe that they pay us to do this?" Harry asked.

Didinger learned that night just how much baseball meant to the voice of the Phillies. "That line—'Do you believe they pay us'—that said it all," Didinger said. "Baseball was Harry's game and his life. He loved it that much. It never was a gig to him."

Harry's enthusiasm that night made missing out on broadcasting the 1980 World Series even more difficult. Phillies President David Montgomery served as director of sales for the club in 1980. His duties included finding World Series seats for the club's broadcasters. "It just didn't seem right," Montgomery said. "One of the decisions was, 'Where do we ask these guys to sit? Are we going to put them in the stands?'"

Harry, Richie and the crew had good seats, though not the seats they wanted, for some good baseball. The Phillies' first World Series in 30 years began with two come-from-behind victories at home, then Kansas City took the next two in its building. The Royals were home again for Game 5 and had a lead in the ninth inning, but the Phillies scored two runs off star closer Dan Quisenberry to pull out a 3-2 victory.

One of American sports' least successful franchises headed home needing just one win in two games to claim its first world championship. For the biggest game in team history, the Phillies broadcasters sat together in a booth next to the Veterans Stadium press box.

"To me, it was just one of those things, and you deal with it," Chris Wheeler said. "It wasn't like the policy hadn't been in place and they took it away from us. But Philly made a big stink."

Many Phillies fans were furious. They felt cheated not hearing their hometown broadcasters, especially Harry Kalas and Richie Ashburn, call the World Series. Major League Baseball discovered the wrath of Phillies fans even before the World Series began. Late into the 1980 regular season, Harry's first wife helped start a movement to change the MLB policy. Sitting in a seat behind home plate at Veterans Stadium, Jasmine Kalas was approached by a teenage Phillies fan named Kim Sparks. Her family had front-row season tickets in the same section, and she had met Jasmine earlier.

"There was a story in the newspaper about the broadcasters not being able to do the World Series if the Phillies got there," Jasmine recalled. "This young girl, maybe 18 years old, was upset and said, 'Mrs. Kalas, we need Harry and Whitey doing the World Series games. What should we do?' I said, 'Let's get signatures!'"

Jasmine and Kim ended up walking around the Vet that night convincing hundreds of Phillies fans to sign a petition. The following two days, Kim and a friend continued to get signatures, and from there the mission really took off. "We let the Phillies know that their fans wanted their broadcasters to announce the World Series," Jasmine said.

Others joined the fight during and after the World Series. According to baseball author/former Presidential speech writer Curt Smith, 600,000 Phillies fans signed their name to the cause. "I had several sources for that number, and it was a stunning example of what Harry meant to the Tri-State area," Smith said. "And it was very spontaneous. It showed just how personal we do take our broadcasters."

Hundreds of irate fans wrote letters and phoned the Phillies, television networks and Major League Baseball. At the time, baseball wanted to preserve exclusivity for the networks.

"Everybody was outraged," said *Philadelphia Daily News* columnist Bill Conlin, a Phillies beat writer from 1966 to 1986. "Whitey was really pissed off.

We didn't have emails cascading into our mailbox the way we do today, so it was a little harder to get a finger on the pulse. But there were call-in shows on radio, and a major topic of conversation was 'How come we didn't get our own broadcasters?'"

Bill Giles, an executive VP for the 1980 Phillies, took up the fans' fight by contacting MLB commissioner Bowie Kuhn and the networks. "I was the head of the television committee back in 1980, and when we got all the static from the fans about how they wanted to hear Harry and Richie, I went to NBC, ABC and the commissioner and said, 'We gotta change this. We've got to allow the local guys to do something.'"

Phillies fans were heard. About seven weeks after the World Series, the rule was changed during the 1980 Baseball Winter Meetings. Starting in 1981, participating teams could use their local radio stations for World Series games.

"The fans just inundated the radio and TV stations and the Commissioner's office, so now the local broadcasters will be able to work the Series games," Harry said in 1981. "It was a result of the outcry of the fans, the Phillies fans in particular. It's gratifying to know that the voice of the fans could be heard and that it was us they wanted to hear."

Harry was absolutely delighted. "The Philadelphia fans changing that rule meant more to Harry than him calling those games," Eileen Kalas said.

Eventually, Harry did put his spin on the 1980 World Series. On a record album the club made that winter, besides doing the narration for "The Fantastic Phillies," Harry re-created all of the big moments in a recording studio. He also did a redo of his emotional, if uncharacteristically choppy call of the winning hit in Game 5 of the NLCS, this time saying, "Maddox swings. Line drive to center field. Puhl can't get it. Unser scores and the Phillies lead it 8-7."

Harry also got to re-create the final out of the 1980 World Series:

"Sixty-five thousand plus on their feet at Veterans Stadium. The Tugger needs one more. One more out. One-two pitch. Yes! He struck him out! The Phillies are the World Champions, World Champions of baseball! Tug McGraw being mobbed by his teammates. Who better than Tugger to finish the 1980 World Series? The Phillies are World Champs. This city knows it, this city loves it!"

Harry's powerful pipes made his words sing, but to those who knew he hadn't done it live, the call lacked real emotion and sounded staged.

"It sounds like all re-creation," Chris Wheeler said. "You could tell. No matter how good you are—and Harry was as good as anybody at that stuff—it came off that way. It sounded great, and Harry did the best you could with it. But it wasn't the same."

Re-creation wasn't necessary for the 1983 World Series. By then, the Phillies and their fans had forced Major League Baseball to change its broadcast rules, allowing Harry, Whitey and the rest of the Philadelphia baseball announcing crew to call the games on the radio for the Phils' October showdown with the Baltimore Orioles. The change helped another future star broadcaster, the Orioles' Jon Miller, get to call his first Fall Classic. "We wouldn't have been able to do that if Phillies fans weren't so vehement phoning into stations and talk shows—'How come we can't hear Harry?'" Miller said.

The Phillies fell to the Orioles in five games in 1983, depriving Harry of the chance to call the final out of a winning World Series for his Phils. Harry would have to wait another quarter-century to enjoy that moment, which only arrived six months before his April 2009 death.

After his 1980 World Series disappointment, later in the decade Harry the K was in the booth for his most famous call. On April 18, 1987, Michael Jack Schmidt hit his 500th home run.

"I was taking my kid to a Little League game and stayed in the car because Schmidt was coming up for that at-bat," said Howard Eskin, a longtime Philadelphia sports-talk host on WIP radio and Schmidt friend. "I remember the spot where I waited in the car. I didn't want to miss it."

Mike Schmidt, maybe the greatest Phillies player ever, by then had become very tight with Harry Kalas. For years, Schmidt toiled as an underappreciated superstar in Philadelphia. The game came so easily to Schmidt that it seemed to some fans like he wasn't giving his all—even though Schmidt won three National League Most Valuable Player awards, eight home run crowns, 10 Gold Gloves and a spot in 12 All-Star games while establishing himself as perhaps the top third baseman to ever play the game. Yet despite his amazing talents and achievements, Schmidt was booed a lot in Philadelphia. Early on, Harry became a confidant and close friend to Schmidt. They talked during flights and after games in hotel bars and took offseason vacations together—once going to Hawaii with their wives and often heading to Florida for a week of golf.

"He and we players had a special relationship," Schmidt said while eulogizing Harry Kalas in 2009. "It was built on respect. We shared serious inside baseball discussions. But we also had our Harry sayings, facial expressions and gestures, like a bunch of young kids. We loved when he made us look good, as he always did during a game. Often he'd stop in the clubhouse before a game to take a team's temperature, to pump us up, as they say. It always seemed like he knew what was going on with each one of us. He'd reference a hot streak, a great play, someone's history against a pitcher, anything to lift our spirits and our confidence. He did this for 40 years with a natural sense of timing. It was never about Harry, always about us."

Kalas was around for Schmidt's entire Hall of Fame career, all of it spent in a Phillies uniform. Harry was in the booth to call "Outta here!" for every one of Schmidt's 548 homers. Harry announced Schmidt's first homer (off Montreal left-hander Balor Moore in September 1972), his four-homer game at Wrigley Field in 1976, the round tripper that won an unforgettable 23-22 slugfest at Wrigley Field in 1979 and his final home run in 1989.

By the 1980s, Schmidt was climbing the all-time home run list. He hit No. 300 at Shea Stadium on August 14, 1981 and belted No. 400 on May 15, 1984 at Dodger Stadium. In 1986, a season in which Schmidt won the last of his three NL MVPs, he cracked 37 homers, leaving him five shy of 500 for his career. The next season, he went deep four times in the Phillies' first 10 games, blasting No. 499 at Pittsburgh's Three Rivers Stadium. The next day, April 18, 1987, Schmidt and Kalas made history together. Michael Jack hit No. 500 off Pirates righty Don Robinson, Harry called it and most every Phillies fan has heard it dozens of times since:

"Schmidt has four career home runs off Don Robinson. Samuel at third, Hayes at first. Two outs, ninth inning. Phillies trail 6-5. Here's the stretch by Robinson, the 3-0 pitch. Swing and a long drive! There it is, No. 500! The career 500th home run for Michael Jack Schmidt, and the Phillies have regained the lead in Pittsburgh 8-6! And the Phillies dugout comes pouring out to home plate!"

That Mike Schmidt and Harry Kalas dual highlight became an instant classic moment in Phillies history, one that hasn't lost its zest decades later.

Usually stoic on the field, Schmidt did a little dance with his arms leaving the batter's box after blasting his 500th. "I was on third base and I never saw Schmidt so excited before," teammate Juan Samuel said. "He never did anything when he hit a home run. Seeing Schmidt doing that, I thought, 'He's human.' Then I heard Harry's call on the news. I knew Mike's middle name because of Harry. For him to call him Michael Jack, you have to be close."

"That was my favorite call ever," Harry Kalas said in 2004 as the 25th anniversary of Schmidt's milestone homer approached. "I always say 'Outta here!,' and for Schmidty's 500th, I just said, 'There it is, the 500th career homer for Michael Jack Schmidt.'"

"Harry had a way of expressing pure joy and excitement that wasn't phony, and I think that came out in Schmidt's 500th home run call more than any I've ever heard," said Dallas Green, a longtime Phillies executive who also managed the club's 1980 World Championship team.

Harry's call was replayed so many times over the years that generations of Phillies fans still often refer to the great slugger as "Michael Jack" instead of Mike—usually while trying to imitate the Hall of Fame broadcaster's baritone voice.

"My 500th always has been a benchmark of my career, and I've heard Harry's call thousands of times. That helped make it special because Harry tagged me with the Michael Jack nickname," Schmidt said. "What Harry meant for my career is something I'll never forget."

In addition to Schmidt, over the years Harry became close friends with dozens of Phillies players, including Steve Carlton, Larry Christenson, Glenn Wilson, Darren Daulton, John Kruk, Larry Andersen and Ricky Bottalico. During his 39 years with the club, Harry became friendly with almost all of the Phillies players, whatever their race, nationality, religion or batting average.

"I know Harry didn't speak a whole lot of Spanish, but all the Latino players knew he was a very important part of our club," said Juan Samuel, a star second baseman for the Phillies from 1983 to 1989.

According to Christenson, in 1977, Harry started sitting in the back of Phillies charters with veteran players, which represented an unusual show of mutual affection and trust. Broadcasters socializing in the back of planes with players was—and is—almost unheard of in the sports world.

"It's funny how that all evolved," Christenson recalled. "It had to do with Jeff Cooper, our trainer. The manager, all the coaches and the press were up front, then the players had the rest of the plane. Cooper ended up going to the very back because he thought if a plane ever crashed, that's the safest place, in the tail. Then Tug McGraw got talked into it. Richie Hebner used to hang back there, mostly to drink a little bit more. It became pretty much the libation section with Hebner and the Tugger.

"Harry not only thought Cooper's theory was correct, but it also was a lot of fun back there. That's how Harry ended up in the back of the plane. And by then, Harry was a guy who could walk into our locker room more than anybody else out of uniform and be accepted to no end. We all liked Whitey coming in, but when Harry walked in, we all lit up. We all wanted to be in his presence because he was delightful."

For approximately his first 25 years with the Phillies, Harry was considered a "teammate" by many players. They regarded Harry as a trustworthy friend and drinking buddy—a guy more famous than most of them, yet incredibly humble.

"I was with the Cardinals before the Phillies, and their longtime broadcasters Mike Shannon and Jack Buck were up in front during our flights," said Frank Coppenbarger, the Phillies director of team travel and clubhouse services. "I couldn't sit back there and I've been with the Phillies for 21 years. They'd run me out in five minutes if I went back there. Harry was absolutely one of the boys. I go through the plane passing out the meal money, and Harry was always the last guy that I came to in the last row."

As part of a traveling baseball team, everyone is fair game for pranks, and Harry wasn't spared. When a Phillies player shoved a shaving-cream pie into the face of the star of a Phillies victory during an on-field post-game interview, Harry would sometimes get one, too. One night during a charter, Harry had cigarettes stuck in his nose and hung from his eyelids—courtesy of pitcher Steve Bedrosian, who pulled out a Polaroid instant camera to snap a picture as evidence.

When returning from road trips, Harry used to bum rides from players. For a time, he caught lifts home from Von Hayes. Later, John Kruk became his driver.

"I talked to Yankees broadcaster Michael Kay about it, and he said that he would never dare ask Derek Jeter or Alex Rodriguez for a ride home," Kruk said. "I drove Harry home quite a bit. After trips, 'Kruker, I need a ride.' 'No problem, Harry, I'll take you.' We drove to New York together. We had a driver, Nick. Harry would say, 'Nick's out in the parking lot. The gear's in the car. Let's go Kruker.' The gear meant cigarettes and beer. I remember him sitting in the back, pretending to play a ukulele and singing 'On the Way to Cape May.' He strummed with his eyes closed. He was off in his own place, and I used to sit there and just marvel at it. You didn't need the radio.

"When you talk to other announcers about the relationship that we had with Harry, they're in awe. You have to look at it from our standpoint. We were in awe of him. This was Harry Kalas. This wasn't Joe Schleppi they pulled off the street to come to a game. Let's put it this way: I've turned down many an interview. When Harry Kalas asked me, I did it, no questions asked. If Harry's going to honor you by talking to you, you're going to do a dang interview with him. We loved him. We absolutely loved him."

With Glenn Wilson, an All-Star right fielder for the Phillies in 1985, Harry attained the status of a second father. Wilson was five when his real father died. Shortly after being traded to the Phillies in 1984, he began leaning on Harry for advice.

"It seems like my whole life I was in search of a father figure," said Wilson, who with the Phillies for four seasons. "When I came to Philadelphia and met Harry for the first time, it was as if I'd found my earthly father. He was like my dad for four years. Then after those years, we would talk every winter. He was the greatest man I've ever been around."

On July 10, 1991, the youngest of Wilson's three boys was born. His name: Andrew Kalas Wilson. Glenn preferred Kalas for a first name, but his wife vetoed it, fearing other children would make fun of him. Harry was so touched that he wrote his namesake a letter:

Dear Andrew,

Welcome to the wonderful world of life. You've got a beautiful mommy and daddy, a wonderful grandma and two great brothers, Glenn and Lance. Hundreds of years ago, a man named Shakespeare penned the words, 'This above all, to thine own self be true. And it must follow, as the night the day. Thou canst not then be false to any man.' Those words are as true today as when they were written, and the wisdom of the words will always apply. When you're honest with yourself, Andrew, you're then able to give up yourself and have human compassion for your fellow man and woman. I'm anxious to meet you. If there is ever anything that you need, and I am able, I will always be there for you. God bless and be well.

Harry Kalas

PS—I am both proud and humbled that my name will be a part of your legacy.

The letter was framed and placed on a wall beside Andrew's bed. Eighteen years later, it was still there. "When I read the letter, it gave me chills," Glenn Wilson said. "If you did something small like name a kid after Harry, he was going to make sure that he went out of his way to do something better for you."

Andrew Wilson, who finally met Harry as a teenager, was finishing his junior year at Klein Oak High in suburban Houston when his namesake passed in April 2009. A Division 1-A baseball prospect, Andrew then started signing his full name on school work in tribute to Harry. "It's an honor to be named after a Hall of Famer," he said. "I wish I would have gotten a chance to sit down with him and hear some of his aspects on life because my dad told me that Harry Kalas was an awesome man."

As much as Harry loved all of the Phillies teams he was around, the 1993 ballclub was his favorite in all of his years in the broadcast booth. This wild bunch finished two victories shy of a world championship, but won a division and a pennant. In the process, they won over not just Philadelphians, but baseball fans around the country.

The 1993 club included a lot of guys who enjoyed smoking and drinking, just like Harry. John Kruk, with his scraggly beard and bulging belly, served as the team's poster boy. And the roster included plenty of other hard-living, fun-loving guys, like Lenny Dykstra, Dave Hollins, Darren Daulton, Pete Incaviglia and Larry Andersen, among others. Harry affectionately called this team "throwbacks."

"They were kind of one-year-wonder renegades," Chris Wheeler said. "They had that 'screw you' personality to everybody—to the media, to the fans on the road. They'd come into a town with their beards and bellies, smokin' and drinkin'. I'll say one thing for them: they talked baseball. They'd be in the trainer's room and talked the game. They came to the park early and they stayed late. Was that good for their personal lives? Probably not."

Harry absolutely fell in love with this team, and they absolutely loved him back. Harry called a lot of the guys by nicknames like Dude, Dutch, LA, Inky, Kruker and Mitchy-poo.

"The fact that he called me Mitchy-poo on the air . . . I didn't want anyone to know about that nickname, but somehow with Harry it was okay," said former Phillies closer Mitch Williams, who was given the name in 1993 as Harry described Williams' famous, 4:41 a.m., Game 2 doubleheader walk-off single—the last of his three career hits.

Coming off a 70-92 season, the 1993 Phillies won their first three games and were in first place for good by the second week of the season. After living through some really down Phillies years, Harry relished being around a winning team again. But the players, his kind of guys, made it extraordinary.

"We epitomized his life—the hard-charging, go-for-broke, no-matter-who-we-hurt-we're-going-to-do-it kind of thing," John Kruk said. "I think if you look at that team, so many guys ended up divorced. A lot of us had the same qualities that Harry had . . . drinking a lot. I think that's why he liked us so much. We weren't looking for next year. We were living for that day."

The 1993 Phillies lived for late nights at the bars, too, just like Harry did for many years.

"If Harry wasn't there with us after a game, we went and searched him out," said Larry Andersen, a Phillies reliever in 1993 and future broadcasting partner to Harry. "We expected him to be in the hotel bar. We wanted him to be there. He was just one of the guys."

For many of the 1993 Phillies, one of the best memories of the season came the night they won the National League East division title in Pittsburgh. When their celebration was winding down, everyone went into a small trainer's room for a beer. Harry then walked in and led the group through a rousing rendition of his theme song, "High Hopes."

"We felt like it wasn't an official National League East championship until Harry sang," John Kruk said. "We were in that little trainer's room at Three Rivers Stadium, and here's 25 players with coaches, the manager and the staff in there. As soon as Harry walked in, it got quiet. LA said, 'HK, let's go.' We tried to sing along, but it just wasn't right. It was like Elvis coming in and singing 'Blue Suede Shoes' and someone grabbing a mike and joining in."

"Everybody in there was smoking cigarettes and drinking beer, and Harry was just in all his glory," Frank Coppenbarger said. "That was as happy as I've ever seen him. He loved the '93 Phillies. He always wore his 1993 World Series ring, not his 1980 World Series ring. And the '80 team won. That says a lot. I think Harry deeply cared about the '80 team, but he had a special appreciation for Daulton and the '93 gang."

The 1993 Phillies' season ended in disappointment, a World Series loss to Toronto, the clincher coming on a Game 6, three-run, walk-off homer by Joe

Carter off Mitch Williams in a ninth inning that began with the Blue Jays down a run. It took the Phillies and their fans years to get over that loss, in part because injuries and aging of star players led to a down cycle, starting in 1994 and stretching to the franchise's next winning season in 2001.

Harry's favorite season led into his saddest. In August 1994, players went on strike and didn't return for 233 days, until Major League Baseball was close to starting 1995 with replacement players. Along the way, baseball went without a World Series and lost a lot of fans. To Harry, this was tragic. Scott Graham, the Phillies' post-game radio host in 1994, still remembers his colleague's on-air signoff after the final game before the work stoppage.

"I'm sitting next to Harry and on the air he starts telling the story about watching *Eight Men Out*," Graham recalled. "He was talking about Shoeless Joe Jackson coming down the steps and this little kid with big eyes saying to him, 'Say it ain't so, Joe.' And at this point, Harry choked up and he starts to cry. And he just said, 'No more baseball in 1994, say it ain't so, Joe.' He's freely crying and says, 'This is the Phillies radio network.'

"It was touching and something totally unexpected, and I don't know how many people caught it because it was the radio show of a midseason game before a strike, but the emotion that he carried with him showed his love for the game. It was true emotion in a spot where you wouldn't expect it."

There would be more heartache. The 1994 season led to bad times for the Phillies, and hopes for better days suffered a big blow a few years later when the franchise couldn't sign heralded outfielder prospect J.D. Drew, the second overall pick of baseball's 1997 draft. Drew rejected the Phillies' signing bonus offer of $2.8 million, then the most lucrative offer ever made to an unsigned draft pick. Drew opted to go back into the 1998 draft, and was later selected by the St. Louis Cardinals. The finality of the saga became apparent when Scott Boras, Drew's hard-line agent, held a fruitless negotiating session with the Phillies while the club was in New York in April 1998. The night of the negotiations, a group of Phillies beat writers was having drinks at the Grand Hyatt Hotel bar when Harry walked in.

"We'd spent the whole night chasing down Boras and Harry walked in liquored up," said Martin Frank, a *Wilmington News-Journal* sports writer. "He asked what was going on and we told him about the Drew stuff. He looks at us, and says slowly with anger in his voice, 'F--k J.D. Drew.'"

Since Harry rarely used obscenities, it was clear that he was offended.

An even greater disappointment in Harry's 39 years with the Phillies came on May 31, 2001 when he and broadcast partner Larry Andersen were ordered out of the back of the plane for a charter flight. Harry had no idea what he'd done, and he was hurt and upset.

"Harry's comment to me with tears in his eyes was, 'LA, I don't know if I can ever root for this team again,'" Andersen said. "For Harry to say that, I realized how devastated he was. That speaks volumes."

The parties responsible for Harry's exile never came forward. But the brunt of the blame fell on three short-time Phillies players—pitcher Chris Brock and outfielders Brian L. Hunter and Rob Ducey, although manager Larry Bowa reluctantly signed off on the controversial decision. Mark "Frog" Carfagno, a Phillies groundskeeper from 1971 to 2004 who left his job on bad terms, said he witnessed the decision getting set in motion. Carfagno recalled watching a portion of a Phillies game on television in the video room at Veterans Stadium with Brock, pitcher Randy Wolf, and one of the team videographers, either Dan Stephenson or Kevin Camiscioli. Neither videographer remembers being there, but Stephenson admitted that starting pitchers sometime did visit his office during games when it wasn't their day to throw.

"We're in the video room," Carfagno recalled. "Brock and Wolf were there—I guarantee it—and Harry and Larry Andersen were on the air going on about how much fun they had in the back of the plane. Brock jumped out of his chair. He was upset. He says, 'What's Harry talking about the back of the plane for? He shouldn't even be back there. It's a privilege for him to be there. He should be up front with the rest of the non-players. I'm going to tell somebody about it.'"

From there, the Phillies held multiple players-only meetings concerning Harry and Larry Andersen's presence in the back of the plane.

"There was probably four or five guys involved," Andersen said. "The only thing I know for a fact is Ricky Bottalico stood up for us."

"I was the one sitting next to him all the time and I never had a problem with Harry back there," Bottalico said. "I loved it. I would sit there when we got on the plane and we'd talk about what happened in the game that day. Then that would end 15 or 20 minutes later, then we'd have a couple beers and BS about whatever. To me, he never should get kicked out of the back of that plane. I was angered by it. It wasn't half the team. I think it was a very limited number of people that didn't want him back there. They didn't know. They came from teams where the announcers did not sit back there. But to me, I never had a problem with it.

"I played on the Cardinals and if Jack Buck wanted to sit back there, he could have. You have to understand that not all ballplayers are prima donnas, and to me, Harry was bigger than anybody there. This guy was going to be there longer than I was in Philadelphia, and he was there before I was there, so he had every right to sit where he wants."

Doug Glanville, a center fielder on the 2002 Phillies who was crazy about Harry, wrote in a *New York Times* column he penned after Harry's death that the issue was a hot topic in the clubhouse for a few days:

"After an alleged back-of-the-plane incident had violated the rule that states 'what happens in the back of the plane, stays in the back of the plane,' the team became divided. The jury of Phillies debated whether all non-players should be banished from the back of the plane. But that would lump Harry into the realm of the guilty, which he was not. Day in and day out we discussed the implications: could we really remove a legend, and virtual teammate, who had been grandfathered into the players' zone out of sheer respect? The debate went painfully on, even though under normal circumstances the transgression would have almost certainly ended in harsh baseball justice. But Harry's immunity was so powerful that our manager had to step in and end the dialogue on the issue, which was rapidly becoming more of a topic of discussion than the team we were about to play. I think we had more Harry meetings than we had defensive meetings that week. Because whichever side of the matter a player came down on, no one wanted to offend or hurt Harry in any way."

Bottalico decided to go to Bowa for help. He figured Bowa surely would intercede. After all, Kalas had been around Bowa for years. They'd always gotten along great.

"I told Bo that Harry deserves to be back there," Bottalico said.

Bowa agreed. But the first-year manager was also trying to fight a reputation for being too tough on his players. Wrongly thinking a majority of veteran players wanted Kalas and Andersen out of the back of the plane, he made a tough call to go along with their wishes.

"I don't even know who the players were, to be honest, but they all came to me and said, 'We need our privacy back there.'" Bowa said. "I was shocked. The whole thing was to make sure the players were happy and all that bullshit. I would have never done that. I was trying to make a smooth transition. It turned out to be a bad thing."

Wolf, who is alleged to have witnessed Brock's outburst, refused to name names while claiming his innocence.

"I remember somebody told me LA was mad at me," Wolf said. "I said, 'Why is LA mad at me?' He said I voted against Harry being back there. I said, 'What?' First of all, I would never tell him to get out. Second of all, I never had an opinion. That upset me. I went to Harry and told him, 'Hey, Harry, I had nothing to do with this. There's no way I would ever have anything to do with this.'

"I was young and just trying to get my feet wet in the big leagues. I only had one full year in and I remember a few of the new players came in and didn't like media in the back of the plane . . . no other team did it. I remember being asked when we had a team meeting in the clubhouse, and I said, 'I don't even have an opinion on it.'"

Bowa recalls the ban lasting only a road trip or two, but it actually continued for the remainder of the 2001 season. After awhile, Harry put up a good front and pretended he was adjusting. "The Coors Light is just as cold in the front as it is in the back," he joked. In reality, the thought of being an outcast crushed him. He'd been considered a ballplayer pretty much since joining the Phillies in 1971, as he had been during his time as an announcer in Hawaii and Houston.

"When they first told Harry, he was heartbroken," Eileen Kalas said. "He couldn't imagine what he'd done because he loved to sit with those players."

The Phillies began 2001 with a 35-18 record that had them first in the NL East. After Harry and Andersen were booted from the back of the plane, the Phillies went into a 7-18 tailspin—a slump caused by angry baseball gods, joked some team insiders. The Phillies never really recovered and missed the playoffs, losing the division to Atlanta.

"A few of the guys were like, 'If our plane crashes, we know why,'" Wolf said. "There's not many metaphysical things that I believe in, but sometimes I believe in karma."

Neither Brock, Hunter nor Ducey was with the Phillies after the 2001 season. The next spring, after Harry's ban was reported in Philadelphia newspapers, Bowa lifted it.

"Some people have said since then that Harry whined and went to the media and got himself back there, and that's not really how it happened," said longtime *Philadelphia Daily News* baseball writer Paul Hagen, who broke the story. "I heard about it from a third party and approached Harry. He was very reluctant to even talk about it."

When Harry's old buddies on the 1993 Phillies heard the news, they were furious.

"I highly doubt that would have happened when I was there," Darren Daulton said.

"It absolutely pissed me off," John Kruk said. "What bothers me is you had two or three guys who aren't true Phillies trying to get guys to change the way the system goes. The fact that the Phillies would actually listen to them was very disappointing. That's when you tell them, 'You need to know your place. Harry goes where he wants, does what he wants and if you don't like it, tough.'"

At least Harry's back-of-the-plane ban turned out to be temporary. Late in his great career, he ran into a problem that never got resolved—a behind-the-scenes feud with a fellow Phillies broadcaster, Chris Wheeler.

THE WHEELS COME OFF

The screaming from the back of the Phillies' broadcast booth at Dodger Stadium was one-sided. On August 9, 2002, 12 days after Harry Kalas was inducted into the broadcaster's wing of the Baseball Hall of Fame, Chris Wheeler was in his longtime partner's face.

"If you don't shut your wife up, I'm going to throw your ass out of the booth!" Wheeler yelled a few inches from Harry's face only 10 minutes before the start of a Phillies-Dodgers game on a Friday night in Los Angeles. Recounted by Harry Kalas to numerous friends and colleagues and confirmed by Wheeler himself, the incident stemmed from a phone call Wheeler had taken a few minutes earlier during which his live-in girlfriend, Renee Gosik, accused Eileen Kalas, Harry's wife, of making a call to their home to spout insults and accusations.

The demise of the longtime, close friendship between Harry Kalas and Chris "Wheels" Wheeler was a complicated and often ugly matter. According to Harry's camp, it started after the 1996 season when Wheeler replaced Harry's close friend and colleague Richie "Whitey" Ashburn as color man for the final three innings of Phillies games on television, with Whitey demoted to doing them on radio. Ashburn believed Wheeler had set the change in motion by continuously gossiping about Ashburn's so-called struggles in the booth due to his declining eyesight from diabetes.

"I'm going to get that Wheeler if it's the last thing I do," Harry said Ashburn told him after his demotion.

Wheeler vehemently denies ever being disloyal to Ashburn and blames Eileen Kalas for destroying his decades-long close friendship with Harry. During the worst of times, Harry attempted to avoid working in the same booth as Wheeler and even filed two official written complaints to the Phillies against his one-time drinking buddy. In their final years together, their professional relationship improved, but Harry wanted no part of Wheeler outside of the broadcast booth—and Wheeler wanted no part of Kalas as long as Eileen Kalas remained Harry's wife.

During spring training 2008, Eileen was at a store buying juice when Wheeler walked in. Eileen said, "Hi, Chris," but Wheeler didn't respond.

"I was cracking up so bad," Eileen said. "I thought, 'You hate me. Now you know how Whitey felt.'"

"What was I going to say?" Wheeler said. "I don't want any contact with her. I ignored her."

Eileen took the feud public in 2003, revealing it first to reporters covering the Phillies, then to *Philadelphia* magazine, which published an inflammatory report in their April 2004 issue that made Wheeler look bad and triggered plenty of juicy material for local sports columnists and radio talk-show hosts.

Retired Phillies pitcher Larry Christenson attempted to end the feud. "I told Wheels and Harry, 'This is bullshit. What can I do to help patch this up? Can I bring you two together?' But it is what it is. I know there's bitterness, grudges and all that."

From 1996 until Kalas' death in 2009, Harry and Wheeler often went out of their way to avoid each other at the ballpark.

"It was awkward when you were around the two of them," said ESPN baseball analyst John Kruk, a former Phillies star first baseman and broadcaster who was close with Kalas and is friendly with Wheeler. "Any time they were in close proximity, you kind of felt bad talking to one when you weren't talking to the other. But that's the way they wanted it. That's the way it had to be.

And it stinks. Two guys who worked together for that long and that closely, and over words . . . it just comes to the point where they couldn't get along anymore. And the thing with Wheels, no matter how great Wheels is, he's never going to be accepted because this is Harry's town. That's Harry's booth."

But Wheeler remained in the broadcast booth and enjoyed the support of Phillies management, which did its best not to take sides in the feud. While most Phillies employees revered Harry Kalas, Wheeler had a lot of close friends at the club, too. Harry was warm, friendly, generous, loyal and a lot of fun. Wheeler has a charming personality as well. To this day, during a stroll through the press box, Wheeler greets everyone. And like Harry, he comes off as humble and likable to his friends, colleagues and many others who know him well.

According to all sides, Harry and Wheeler engaged in only a handful of arguments, most of which consisted of Wheeler losing his temper with Harry in response to what he deemed personal attacks on him by Eileen.

"I believe it was the relationship between Eileen and Wheels that deteriorated," Phillies President David Montgomery said when summarizing the entire mess during the summer of 2009.

Up until their feud began, Wheeler had been one of Harry's closest buddies and confidants for years. When Harry was on the road with the Phillies from 1971 until the 1990s, Wheeler was out with him after games almost every night. When Harry was living a double life—romancing Eileen while still married to Jasmine—Wheeler even helped him conceal the deception.

"Harry was very close to Whitey in the broadcast booth, but outside the booth he was very close to Wheels," said Jasmine Kalas, Harry's wife from 1963 to 1993. "Harry and Wheels would go out to eat after games when Whitey would stay in his hotel room a lot. Wheels came to our place several times with whomever he was seeing in spring training."

The eldest of Christopher and Terry Wheeler's two boys, Christopher Charles Wheeler was born on August 9, 1945, just outside of Philadelphia in Darby, Pa. He then grew up in Newtown Square, a 20-mile drive from Connie Mack Stadium, the Phillies' home during his youth. Just like Harry Kalas, Wheeler started loving the game of baseball and dreaming of becoming a broadcaster as a small boy. Wheeler followed the Phillies religiously for as long as he can remember. He attended a lot of games, often taking a subway to the ballpark with friends by the time he was in grade school. His baseball hero was

Richie Ashburn, his future broadcast partner.

At age 15, Wheeler met his first girlfriend, Susan Harvey, during a summer job at a swim club. Susan's father was Ed Harvey, a popular host at Philadelphia's WCAU radio who became famous for originating the country's first talk show featuring callers on the air. Wheeler and Susan Harvey's relationship developed into a close friendship, and Ed Harvey became a father-like figure after Wheeler lost his dad to a heart attack while in college at Penn State University.

While in college, Wheeler gained his first broadcasting experience doing play-by-play for Nittany Lions baseball and men's basketball games on the campus radio station. In the fall of 1966, his senior year, Wheeler hosted a Friday night radio show that included a taped interview with Penn State's new football coach, Joe Paterno.

During his college years, Wheeler also played American Legion baseball, where he was a solid shortstop who got recruited to play slow-pitch softball for WCAU. Ed Harvey wanted to line up a summer job at WCAU for Wheeler, which included a plan to impress program director Jack Downey—a man who sometimes seemed to care as much about his company softball team as running the station.

"Here's how we're going to do it," Harvey told Wheeler. "I want you to work out with us before a game and Jack Downey will like you because you're young and can play."

Excited about the potential radio opportunity, Wheeler drove 200 miles each way from Penn State to Bala Cynwyd, Pa., to take batting practice and field groundballs in view of Downey. With Downey quite impressed by his play, Wheeler was given a part-time summer job in the WCAU newsroom, making him a colleague of television news anchor John Facenda, who later became famous throughout the country for his NFL Films narrations. Wheeler also befriended WCAU sportscaster Andy Musser, another future Phillies broadcast partner. Musser allowed Wheeler to tag along to Phillies games—a great thrill for the baseball-crazed college student.

All the while, Wheeler was treated like royalty due to his star status in the Philly-area media softball league, which was filled with guys twice his age. Downey even occasionally ordered the WCAU air traffic plane to fly to Penn State to pick up Wheeler for softball games, then fly him back in time for classes the next morning.

"My college buddies couldn't believe it," Wheeler recalled.

Wheeler returned to WCAU for a second summer during college He was promoted to doing morning and afternoon aerial traffic reports from a single-engine Cessna—the same plane that transported him to and from softball games.

After college, Wheeler was drafted into the Army and served six months of active duty. While stationed in San Antonio in 1968, he was first introduced to the broadcast skills of a young Harry Kalas while listening to Houston Astros games on a transistor radio. After serving his time in the military, Wheeler found off-the-air work with CBS-affiliated radio stations in Chicago and New York. In Chicago, he started dating a co-worker, Joanne Rosati, and in November 1970, while Wheeler was working in New York, the couple married.

A layoff sent Wheeler and his bride back to his roots in Philadelphia, and early in 1971, he found a job writing news releases for General Electric's space program. He hated it. This wasn't what he wanted to do with his life. He wanted to be a sportscaster, but he'd settle for doing anything in sports.

As luck would have it, Phillies Public Relations Director Larry Shenk was looking to hire an assistant for the 1971 season. Thanks to Musser putting in a good word, Wheeler was offered a job. It paid 30 percent less than his General Electric job, but Wheeler gladly took it and started that July after fulfilling his summer Army commitment.

"That was the beginning of the end with my wife," Wheeler said. "I went home and told her I was going to make $5,000 less and never be home."

Wheeler began as Shenk's assistant, a job that kept him on the road and away from home a lot. By 1974, four years into their marriage, Joanne Wheeler filed for divorce. Chris Wheeler was represented by future Pennsylvania Governor Ed Rendell, then a 30-year-old family law attorney. The divorce was finalized in 1976, the same year Wheeler did his first Phillies broadcast.

Over the years, Wheeler remained friendly with his ex-wife. In the mid-1980s while driving to an eye doctor's appointment, Wheeler was passing through the East Falls section of Philadelphia, near Grace Kelly's old home, when he spotted two vehicles that had just been in a bad crash. "It was a taxi and a car head-on, and I remember vividly looking at it and thinking, 'Oh, that's not good,'" Wheeler recalled. That afternoon, Wheeler learned in a phone call from Larry Shenk that his ex-wife had been killed in that head-on crash involving the car and taxi. "Spooky," Wheeler said years later.

For his first six seasons with the Phillies, Wheeler was content in his public relations role. During home games, he was part of a small crew working the Veterans Stadium scoreboard. During road games, he prepared game notes and patrolled interactions between Phillies players and the press.

"I didn't know where I was going with the Phillies, and I didn't really care," Wheeler said. "I was just happy to be there."

During his PR days, Wheeler became close with the Phillies broadcasters, especially Harry Kalas, who had become a drinking buddy. He also became friendly with his boyhood idol, Richie Ashburn, and in turn Ashburn, in his special way, showed affection by teasing Wheeler relentlessly on the air with constant references to fictitious mistakes. "Richie Ashburn used to make fun of me when anything ever went wrong," Wheeler said. "It was my mistake. . . . 'Chris Wheeler gave us an inaccurate release.'"

Late in the 1976 season, Wheeler got his big break, making an unplanned Major League Baseball broadcasting debut. On September 26, the Phillies clinched their first playoff berth since 1950 by winning the opening game of a doubleheader on a Sunday afternoon at Montreal's old Jarry Park. This led to a bizarre clubhouse champagne celebration that was 26 years in the making, but had to be closed out after about 15 minutes because the Phillies still had the second game of the their doubleheader to play. Manager Danny Ozark rested all but one of his regulars, but the Phillies' broadcasting crew had to towel off and head back to the booth in order to call the second game.

Harry and Whitey were on the air in the visiting television booth when Wheeler walked in to pass along some information. Whitey had a brainstorm. "Here's this Chris Wheeler I've been talking about," Ashburn said on air. "Wheels, I know you've always wanted to do this, so I'm going to take off and leave you here to work with Harry." Wheeler assumed Ashburn was joking. He wasn't. Whitey removed his headset, handed it to Wheeler and exited the booth.

"I didn't have time to get scared," Wheeler said. "Right from the beginning, Harry made a point that I see things that nobody else sees. He said, 'Talk about what you see out there. Do your job.'"

Wheeler wasn't bashful providing color. He knew both teams well and tipped off viewers with fresh insights such as Expos pitcher Dennis Blair being inept at holding baserunners. Wheeler figured this opportunity was a one-time deal, and it might have turned out that way had Expos television carried the doubleheader. Since it didn't, the Phillies telecast was piped into the box where Montreal general manager John McHale sat. By chance, Phillies Vice President Bill Giles watched the second game with McHale, who was impressed.

"Who's that announcer?" McHale asked Giles. "He's pretty good. He knows our players better than we do."

"He's one of our PR guys," Giles responded. "I don't know what the hell he's doing in there."

What was to be a one-time opportunity ended up leading to a new career for Wheeler, whose duties in 1977 expanded to include radio commentating for Phillies games when Harry and Richie worked the television broadcast. By Saam had retired before the 1976 season and Andy Musser, Wheeler's old WCAU colleague, had been hired to fill the vacancy to do radio play-by-play. Musser worked the 1976 season alone, except for Sunday home games when Hall of Fame pitcher and former Phillies Whiz Kid Robin Roberts sat in to provide color.

Ironically, the day Wheeler's broadcasting career began with his impromptu performance in Montreal, Saam had been invited back to call the game on radio—an honor extended to him by the club to give the legendary broadcaster the chance to call his first playoff-clinching game. Starting in 1977, Wheeler began a run in the Phillies broadcast booth that had reached 33 seasons in 2009.

"I think we've been well-served by a lot of broadcasters," David Montgomery said. "Harry would certainly be at the top of the list, Whitey would be right there, and I think Wheels deserves to be on that list as well."

Wheeler boasts a reputation among baseball people for knowing the sport inside and out. He never played professionally, but spent thousands of hours learning the game by talking about it at hotel bars, press clubs, clubhouses and on charter flights with some of the top baseball minds on the Phillies payroll—Tim McCarver, Larry Bowa, Paul Owens, John Vukovich, Jim Fregosi and Hugh Alexander, among others.

"To me, baseball is the No. 1 game to talk about because every game is so unique," Wheeler said. "Part of my education came from going out after games with players when we were the same age. The hotel bar was one of those places where you'd congregate. Sometimes the manager and coaches would be there. Harry was always there, too."

Harry and Wheeler first became close in the early 1970s when both began working for the Phillies. It wasn't the same kind of friendship that Harry enjoyed with Whitey, who was like a revered older brother to Harry. When Harry did something he wasn't proud of, he was embarrassed to tell Whitey, whom he respected as much as any man he had ever met.

Harry's friendship with Wheeler was different. Wheeler knew all of Harry's dirt. In fact, he was right there to witness a lot of it. When Harry began an affair with Eileen in 1985 while still married to Jasmine, Wheeler served as their secret go-between. If Eileen wanted Harry to call, she phoned Wheeler to pass along a message. He always did, claiming it was out of his friendship to Harry. After Harry left Jasmine for Eileen, the two often went out with Wheeler and Kary Kates, Wheels' girlfriend at the time. During baseball season, they ate together before games, worked together in the booth and drank together in bars. In the winter, they went on golf trips together, attended the same Christmas and New Year's Eve parties and frequently talked on the phone.

"Kary and Eileen were together all the time," Wheeler said. "Eileen used to call Kary her daughter. All of us were together. I helped them find their home in Media. I'm the one who talked him into living in Delaware County. Eileen wanted to live up in New Hope. When Eileen and Harry first got together, she would call me at three or four in the morning from California telling me to have Harry call her. I would just deliver the messages, dumbass that I was."

In May 1991, Eileen gave birth to Kane Christopher Kalas, a baby boy who was given a middle name the same as Wheeler's first name. Shortly after Kane was taken home from the hospital, Wheeler was invited to the Kalas home and held Kane for pictures that remain in a family photo album to this day.

"They told me they were going to name their son after me," Wheeler said years after his relationship with Harry and Eileen had soured. "The first time I saw Kane, he was a little wee baby with a great big head. I said, 'You named that kid after me?'"

Eileen Kalas laughed off Wheeler's claim. "Kane is named after my godchild, Kristopher. Harry was going to spell Kristopher with a 'K,' but we didn't want him to have the initials KKK. If Chris wants to think Kane was named after him, that's fine. . . . Maybe Harry did ask Chris. Who knows?"

Wheeler blames Eileen for destroying his friendship with Harry. Eileen claims Wheeler ruined it by trying to undermine Harry and Whitey in attempts to further his own broadcasting career—an accusation that Wheeler dismisses as preposterous. Everyone familiar with the situation seems to have a different take on what triggered the fallout. One thing is for sure—it involved Richie Ashburn.

Shortly before the start of spring training in 1997, an outraged Whitey showed up unexpectedly at Harry's home. He vented to Harry and Eileen about learning that his broadcast role would be changing for the upcoming baseball season. Instead of working the final innings on television with Harry, his role for many years, Whitey would be in the radio booth with Andy Musser. Replacing Whitey in the television booth would be none other than Chris Wheeler. Ashburn blamed Wheeler for his demotion, believing Wheeler had complained to David Montgomery, the Phillies' executive vice president at the time, about Ashburn making frequent on-air mistakes.

"Harry, you cannot trust Wheeler," Ashburn said that day during an encounter Ashburn and Harry recounted to many friends and family members.

Hearing the story in the summer of 2009, Montgomery let out a chuckle. "None of that is accurate," he said. Montgomery insists television executives recommended moving Ashburn from television to radio, which he approved only after various warnings to Ashburn were ignored.

"I was hearing from Sam Schroeder, who was at PRISM and Sports Channel Philadelphia, and Randy Smith, who was at Channel 17, that there was concern about Whitey's lack of dialogue late in games, particularly games we were losing," Montgomery said.

"And my conversations with Whitey went along the same lines: 'Whitey, we gotta hear more from you.'

'David, you're not going to like what I have to say the way we're playing.'

'Whitey, the problem is they want to hear you. You are popular.' "

Eventually, Montgomery signed off on Whitey and Wheeler switching roles. "The decision was made for us," Montgomery said. "That's why Wheels shouldn't be pulled into this forum. It's a shame."

Wheeler's problem, according to many in the know, is that he didn't protect Ashburn and his declining eyesight when having conversations at the ballpark with Phillies employees and friends in the media. Several journalists recalled Wheeler approaching them to point out errors Whitey was making on the air and to elaborate on Ashburn's health problems.

"Anything ever said about Whitey's eyesight was kidding around," Wheeler said. "We all kidded him. It wasn't just me. Harry said the same thing. It wasn't malicious. Everybody knew he was struggling. Fans were coming up to me about it. It was no big deal. Nobody was ever going to take him out of that booth."

"It *was* a big deal," Eileen Kalas insisted. "Whitey said to me and Harry, 'People are saying I'm losing it. I'm not losing it.'"

The day Whitey showed up at his house, Harry tried convincing his friend that Wheeler was innocent. But when Eileen heard the story, she became as angry as Whitey, whom she adored. She didn't know for sure what had happened, but she bought Whitey's version of it. She decided Whitey needed to write down his account of what happened then sign and date it for evidence. She figured the letter might come in handy some day. Over the next few years, every time that Harry had an issue with Wheeler or the Phillies, she similarly had him write down the details, then sign and date it.

"I have a whole stack of letters in Harry's handwriting," she says.

As this controversy brewed, Whitey didn't have long to live. He died in August of 1997, less than six months after he'd shown up distraught at the Kalas home to complain about Wheeler. But he criticized Wheeler every chance he got for the short remainder of his life. Even Richard Ashburn knew of his father's belief that Wheeler was behind Whitey's demotion.

"My dad did warn Harry to be wary of Chris," Richard Ashburn said. "Dad wouldn't trust him toward the end of his career. I know that. For my dad not to trust you, that's saying something. I heard that Chris was sort of involved in it. I can't say it happened, but there were a lot of people who told me it did. Harry didn't believe it. He didn't think Chris could be that ruthless. He didn't think Chris had it in him to be that way to my father and him, but Harry found out through his own sources, not just Eileen, that there were problems."

In March 1997, Harry Kalas received a spring training visit from one of his old friends. Joe Nunes is a short but feisty former two-term Republican mayor of the Borough of Pine Hill, N.J., who had been a Kalas drinking buddy since the early 1970s. Nunes, who turned 78 in 2009, idolized Harry Kalas. When hearing from Harry that Ashburn had been demoted and blamed Wheeler, Nunes became livid at Wheeler. That spring, Nunes went out for a post-game dinner in Clearwater, Fla., with a group that included Kalas and Wheeler.

Merely being in Wheeler's presence upset Nunes.

"I kept saying, 'Harry, let me punch that bastard,'" Nunes said. "Harry said, 'No, please don't hit him.' I said, 'I want to punch him. I don't like him.'"

That same spring, Ashburn had a long talk one night with veteran *Philadelphia Daily News* baseball writer Bill Conlin, who owned a condo next to Ashburn's condo at Shipwatch Yacht & Tennis Club in Indian Rocks, Florida. Whitey started off blaming Montgomery.

"Somebody's always going to be out to get you, pal, and I can live with that," Ashburn told Conlin. "I thought David Montgomery and I had enough of a relationship that he would have stopped this from happening. Apparently, he just did what the broadcast people wanted him to do, and that's replace me. They say I'm getting forgetful. Well, hell, I was always forgetful."

As Ashburn continued, he turned his ire on Wheeler. "Whitey said Wheels would go and blow the whistle on him," Conlin recalled. "He said he knew that Wheels was telling people, 'Whitey didn't remember this, Whitey forgot that.' I have no idea whether these allegations have any substance. I'm just recounting what Whitey told me. I have no axe to grind with Chris Wheeler. All I know is somebody decided that Whitey was losing his skills, and he probably was. You have to come down to a hard decision for what's best for the broadcast. Do you want a guy who no longer can follow the ball and makes frequent factual errors on who's in the game? And Whitey never, ever did the homework the other guys did as far as keeping an update on who's hurt or not."

Late into the 1997 season, Conlin interviewed Ashburn for a column that ran on August 20 under the headline, "Surely Comcast Can Find Room for Whitey." Conlin's piece, which was printed 20 days before Ashburn's death, served as a warning to Comcast SportsNet, a new 24-hour sports channel in Philadelphia that would replace WB 17 as the cable television home of the Phillies beginning in 1998.

"There is rampant speculation Ashburn will be pastured," Conlin wrote. "Whoever dumps His Whiteness is going to have some splainin' to do." In Conlin's column, Ashburn issued a threat of his own: "Boys, when I retire from this job, I'm probably going to write a book about my years with the Phillies. There won't be an ocean liner big enough to hold all the people who are going to have to leave the country. If I'm going down, I'm taking everybody with me." In the same column, Ashburn defended his broadcasting skills. "I get screwed up with the stats sometimes, but I never get screwed up with what's going on in the game," he said.

Throughout the final months of his life, Ashburn confided to friends about fearing for his job security. "It was worrying him terribly what was going to happen to him the next year," said Bill Campbell, a Phillies broadcaster from 1963 to 1970. "It was bothering him a great deal because he didn't know what he would do if he didn't have the Phillies."

After Whitey's death, Wheeler made an attempt to clear his name to Richard Ashburn, whom he'd known for years. "Chris called me when all the Harry and Chris stuff was going on a few years ago," Richard Ashburn said. "He said he heard something about the Ashburn family being upset with him . . . blah, blah, blah. I said, 'Chris, I'm going to ask you up front because I've heard these rumors for years and you've always been good to me, kind of like an uncle.' He said, 'Well, ask whatever you want to ask.' I said, 'I've heard rumors that you were trying to kind of kick Dad out and then Harry.' He said, 'Richard, I loved your father. I probably played more golf with him than anybody on the planet. Sure, we've had our moments, but we always made up and went to dinner. We always talked things out. There were definitely problems between all of us, but I always felt like I worked well with your father.'"

Wheeler remembers the conversation differently. "I asked Richard if the Ashburn family had any problems with the relationship between Whitey and me," Wheeler said. "He said, 'No.' He never asked me a question. I asked the question."

Wheeler went on to say that Whitey reached out to him the weekend before his 1997 death when a news story reported that their favorite college football teams would be meeting in 2002 and 2003. "On Saturday night in Montreal, prior to our game with the Expos, Whitey came into our radio booth," Wheeler recalled. "He said, 'Pal, Penn State and Nebraska are going to be playing a home-and-home series. I want to take you to Lincoln and I want you to take me to State College.' True story. Really sounds like a guy who hated my guts."

After Whitey's death, Eileen sought to get even with Wheeler, especially when the Phillies' 1998 broadcast pairings were released, and Harry wasn't scheduled to be on the air with Larry Andersen, a good friend who was hired in February to fill Ashburn's position. Andersen was a veteran reliever and clubhouse prankster on the 1993 Phillies, Harry's favorite team ever, and had been a minor-league pitching coach in 1996 with the organization's Class AA affiliate, the Reading Phillies.

No one could ever fill Whitey's shoes, but Andersen was the perfect replacement in Harry's eyes. Like Whitey, Andersen always made Harry laugh with his sarcastic wit. Unlike Whitey, Andersen was a drinking buddy. Harry never got over losing Whitey, but very much was looking forward to working with Andersen.

"Harry was so glad that he'd have Larry," Eileen Kalas said. "They always loved each other. He was one of his best buddies to go out with when Larry was a player."

Sam Schroeder, VP of programming and production for Comcast SportsNet, had released a preliminary television schedule that didn't have Harry and Andersen working together. Harry was shocked, according to Eileen, because he'd been promised that he and Andersen would be calling games together.

"Harry was upset, really upset," Anderson recalled "He wanted to know why we weren't working together. I was just starting. I didn't say I wanted to work with Harry. I didn't say I didn't want to work with Wheels."

According to Eileen, Harry went to the Phillies office, argued his case and ended up getting his way. "Harry went in and complained," Eileen said. The broadcasting team of Kalas and Andersen was, to Harry's delight, a reality.

Andersen got TV time with Harry for the next nine years before moving to radio full time in 2006 to work with Scott Franzke. But the 1997 schedule still paired Kalas and Wheeler for the final innings on telecasts. Harry complained about that, too, but the Phillies and television executives stood their ground.

As a result of their bitter feud, in 1997 Harry and Wheeler went from being close friends to co-workers who rarely spoke off the air. Then in 2002, their feud escalated, compelling Harry to act in ways that belied his decades of unfailing courtesy and professionalism. Harry, at Eileen's urging, started calling Wheeler "Chris" on the air to annoy him. For years, he always had been called only by his nickname, "Wheels."

"He's going to hate it," Harry told Eileen.

"Just try it," Eileen said. "You're not calling him 'asshole.' You're just calling him 'Chris.' 'Wheels' is endearing and you don't really like Chris. He's not good to you, so why call him Wheels?"

Just as Eileen suspected, Wheeler became annoyed when Harry began referring to him as "Chris" during broadcasts. Wheeler politely asked Harry several times to stop it. When Harry referred to his partner as "Chris" again during the opening of a 2003 spring training telecast in Dunedin, Fla., Wheeler lost his cool.

"Don't be calling me Chris on the air," Wheeler shouted. "I'm 'Wheels.' I know what you're doing."

"I was right there when everything came down, but I didn't know what it was about," Larry Andersen recalled years later. "The one thing about Harry, through their differences . . . Harry just didn't badmouth anybody. He didn't talk bad about people. When your mom says, 'If you don't have anything good to say about somebody, don't say anything at all'—Harry lived by it. He really did."

On the air, Harry and Wheeler didn't kid around like they had in the past, but viewers initially had no idea that they were at war.

"I think Wheeler's whole desire in life was to replace Harry, and however he had to go about doing it, he was going to do it," said Bob Smith, a long-time Kalas friend. "It's sad to see what happened with those guys. Harry and Wheels were very good friends."

There has been a lot of speculation through the years among many people about why and how the feud escalated to the point it did, especially knowing Harry's gentle and non-confrontational nature. Many who were close to the situation and apparently neutral believe Wheeler initially was being loyal to his friendship with Harry instead of Harry's relationship with Eileen. While some of Harry's buddies believed Wheeler was out to get Harry, others who were friendly to both broadcasters disagreed. Some suggested Wheeler simply was an easy target because he had vented his anger to too many people when he should have kept quiet, and his words eventually spread. Eileen, who is known to be a passionate and loyal person, readily admits that Wheeler's alleged treatment of Ashburn and Harry infuriated her. While the real reason for the feud may never be known, there was clearly something much deeper at play.

As time passed, Eileen Kalas definitely suspected the Phillies were mistreating her husband due to his issues with Chris Wheeler. She'd also come to believe that Harry had been underpaid for years.

Interestingly, Harry never was officially a Phillies employee. He was an independent contractor who was paid from 1971 to 1997 by the club's over-the-air television station, and from 1998 on by the Phillies themselves. The checks were written to Tobra, Inc.—a one-man corporation. Jasmine Kalas, Harry's first wife, came up with the name Tobra by using the first few letters of their two boys' first names, Todd and Brad.

"My job for years was to be in the middle of that sandwich," David Montgomery said. "Because when it came to a compensation situation, Richie and Harry would encourage me to ask the station to be generous on their behalf, and the station would be encouraging me on their behalf to ask the talent to be reasonable."

Harry went to spring training in 1998 without a contract, after being told during negotiations that the Phillies were having financial problems and the broadcast team would have to take a salary cut. "I'm not going to take a pay cut," Harry told Eileen. "I think I'm doing a good job. I don't deserve a pay cut." Harry eventually got a new contract with a small raise.

These contractual issues with the Phillies continued over the years, including when Harry's contract expired following the 2003 season.

In December 2003, at Eileen's urging, Harry replaced his longtime advisor, Bucks County attorney Bill Eastburn. He hired a big-time sports and entertainment lawyer out of Beverly Hills to serve as his agent. Ed Hookstratten represented famous newscasters Tom Brokaw and Bryant Gumbel, as well as the Los Angeles Dodgers' Vin Scully, baseball's highest-paid broadcaster with an annual salary of $5 million.

According to one of Harry's friends, he was making about $400,000 from the Phillies, less than one-tenth of what Scully was getting from the Dodgers. "Harry has been grossly underpaid for years," Hookstratten said at the time.

During contract negotiations, Hookstratten made threatening demands on Harry's behalf. The agent insisted on big money and no more on-air time for Kalas with Wheeler. "I put in a complaint last year that I didn't want to work with Wheels," Harry said in December 2003. "It's not that I refuse to work with [Wheeler]. I never said that. I wouldn't. That's up to the Phillies. What I said was that Whitey and I worked so well together as partners, and that I would like to have that same relationship with Larry Andersen, who was supposed to replace Whitey for as long as I'm doing this. I just feel more comfortable with LA. But again, that's the Phillies call."

If Harry didn't get his way, Hookstratten said his client would leave the Phillies to pursue other options.

"I know Harry got a new agent and threatened to quit," said John Kruk, who had signed on to join the Phillies' broadcast team for the 2004 season. "That caused a big stir."

In reality, Harry never would have quit his job. He loved the Phillies way too much. According to Eileen Kalas, Harry heard rumors in the late 1980s that New York Yankees owner George Steinbrenner wanted to hire him. One of his friends said he also had an opportunity to broadcast games for the Chicago Cubs. Out of loyalty and love for the Phillies, Eileen said her husband never made inquiries.

"Harry heard that Steinbrenner was interested," Eileen said. "He had other chances to go national, too, but he wanted to stay in Philly. He absolutely adored the fans and people in Philadelphia."

But after the 2003 season, Harry still wasn't totally happy with the Phillies due to his contract and issues with Wheeler.

Eileen Kalas decided to clue in a handful of Philadelphia reporters. The result was juicy stories that shocked the region about Harry's feud and desire to land a new contract that assured that he would no longer be working alongside Wheeler.

The Philadelphia newspaper accounts of this soap opera included a Wheeler ally stepping forward. "Chris Wheeler is one of the finest guys I've ever met," Tim McCarver, a former Phillies catcher and broadcaster, said at the time. "To have his name sullied in this way upsets me."

Carefully weighing his words, Wheeler gave a brief diplomatic response. "I consider it a privilege and an honor to be part of the Phillies broadcast team. Who I work with and what innings I work are not my decision."

The Phillies were angry about the new agent and Wheeler allegations being made public. Harry told friends that David Montgomery "yelled at him," but Montgomery denied ever having a confrontation. Fearful that he might have overplayed his hand, Harry decided to cut a deal with the Phillies. Not taking Hookstratten's advice, Harry negotiated a new three-year contract on his own and ended up with another small raise and $1,000 annually for lending his name to Harry the K's restaurant in Citizens Bank Park, which was scheduled to open in 2004.

Harry and the Phillies compromised on the Wheeler situation. For the 2004 season, Harry would work with John Kruk during home games and Wheeler only on the road. "We'll work the innings that we're doing together, and we'll do it as professionally as possible," Harry said after signing his contract on February 24, 2004. "I think we can do it."

This wouldn't be easy because another bombshell was about to drop.

In the spring of 2004, Eileen Kalas granted an interview to *Philadelphia* magazine, which in turn printed a story that hit the newsstands that April. The article broke news of Ashburn's late-in-life outrage with Wheeler, Kalas calling his partner "Chris" instead of "Wheels" on the air and marital problems between Harry and Eileen, none of which was public knowledge.

Reported in the story:

- Eileen Kalas said, "Chris took a lot of calls from women who wanted to talk to Harry." She went on to say that Kalas had confessed to cheating in 1998 but that the couple had resolved their problems through counseling. "The party was over and Chris didn't like that," Eileen said.
- Harry and Wheeler no longer were speaking outside of the booth.
- Richie Ashburn, according to Eileen Kalas, believed David Montgomery and Wheeler were "joined at the hip."
- Ashburn warned Kalas that Wheeler couldn't be trusted.
- Ashburn feared he may be ousted after Montgomery replaced Bill Giles as team president in 1997. "You know, Wheels is Monty's boy," Ashburn was quoted in a story that ran 6½ years after his death. "Maybe I'll just retire after this season. I've done this too long to get low-bridged by the likes of Wheeler."
- Harry believed he was being criticized on the air by Wheeler enough that a formal complaint was made to the Phillies. "What Chris does on the air is very subliminal, explaining the game to Harry and interrupting him." Eileen said.
- Eileen believed "Chris used Whitey in life and uses him in death" by talking about him during telecasts.

Naturally, the Phillies were upset by the article. Years later, David Montgomery responded this way: "I've been in this business for 39 years. There's a lot of stuff that gets written and you just live with it."

Eileen Kalas has no regrets about going to *Philadelphia* magazine. The final straw, she has said, was Wheeler commenting sarcastically during a Phillies telecast when a camera caught Harry with a lit cigarette in a radio booth that had a no smoking sign posted. Eileen retrieved a tape of the game and saved a 10-second clip as evidence.

Harry wasn't thrilled that Eileen spoke up, but he couldn't stop her. "Harry called me and said, 'Eileen is talking to the media,'" said Jeff McCabe, a close friend of Harry's for decades. "He said. 'I don't want her to talk to them. She feels she has to so I don't look bad.'"

Explaining her actions, Eileen Kalas said, "At the end of the article, I said, 'Chris used Whitey in life and he uses him in death every time he mentions his name.' The same thing now holds true with Harry Kalas."

When Harry went into counseling in 1998 to work on problems in his marriage to Eileen, he discussed his feud with Wheeler during sessions with a Wynnewood, Pa., practicing licensed psychologist for psychotherapy.

"Harry found the situation very, very difficult," said Dr. Jack Porter, who was given permission from Eileen Kalas to speak about his many years of counseling the two of them. "Anything dealing with anger or negativity was difficult for Harry. When he experienced what he perceived was disloyalty from Wheeler, he severed. Disloyalty was an anathema to Harry."

When the *Philadelphia* magazine article came out, most everyone took Harry's side. Harry Kalas, after all, was a living legend in Philadelphia and friend to the fans.

"When the fans call me, they can't stand Wheeler," said Howard Eskin, a long-time talk-show host on Philadelphia all-sports radio station 610 WIP. "So when it gets out there that Harry and Wheeler aren't getting along, you know who they're going to side with even if Harry was at fault . . . which he clearly is not and was not. Make that clear. I'm telling you, Wheeler's got to have pictures."

Eskin has had a long-standing feud with Wheeler, too. According to Eskin, they haven't spoken since Wheeler became upset with his criticism of Jim Fregosi, the Phillies manager from 1991 to 1996. In Eskin's eyes, Wheeler is pro-Phillies to a fault. He's not a fan of Wheeler's broadcasting, either, saying he talks down to viewers. Eskin also alleges that Wheeler had correctly predicted many Phillies hit-and-runs and steals over the years only because he had been given signs by two close friends who had been longtime third-base coaches for the club, Larry Bowa and John Vukovich.

"Bo and Vuk volunteered the signs to me because we were so close and they trusted me," Wheeler said. "They thought it would make it more interesting for me because they knew how much I enjoyed the inside part of the game. But not one time in my whole career did I ever see a sign and predict it was going to happen. If we put a squeeze on and I saw it, did I ever say we were going to squeeze? Of course not. If those two guys ever thought I did that on the air, that would have been the end of me knowing the signs."

Eskin is just one of Wheeler's detractors. Another is Richard Ashburn, who received feedback from Phillies fans while running batting cages at Walt's Golf Farm in Limerick, Pa.

"I talk to a lot of people and they can't stand Wheeler," Ashburn said. "Dad and Harry didn't bullshit the fans and I think Wheeler does bullshit the fans in his own way. He's just not as likable as Dad and Harry."

The Kalas-Wheeler feud has become legendary. Joe Conklin, a popular Philadelphia comedian who does dead-on Harry impressions, has even incorporated Harry and Wheeler's feud into his act and regular spots on WIP's morning show. He also takes Kalas' side.

"I used to do a bit, right up until Harry died," Conklin said. "I trust my own instincts with that kind of stuff. Of course, fans are going to root for Harry over Wheels. Wheels is a doormat. He's annoying. He's a PR guy that sneaked into the booth and acts likes he's a baseball expert now teaching everybody the game that they played since they were a kid. As far as the shtick and the act, it was easy making Wheels the villain. When it all came out, I'd have Wheels pimping for Harry in hotel bars, then I used to have Harry say, 'We're out here in Pittsburgh and you know what kind of slim pickings there are in that Steel Town. Wheels, you gotta help me out. I'll give you the bottom of the third and the top of the fifth.' A lot of people kill Wheels, including myself . . . but he's been nice as hell with me. Whenever he sees me, he comes right up and says, 'Hey, how you doing?'"

There are others who feel badly for Wheeler.

For years during spring training, Wheeler has been a regular patron at Villa Gallace, a popular Italian restaurant in Indian Rocks Beach, Fla. Luigi Gallace, the owner, has golfed with Wheeler on several occasions and his dispute with Kalas never came up in conversation. "I heard stories from people, but never from Wheels," Gallace said. "I've never heard him speak a bad word about Harry, and I feel he's had many opportunities in my presence."

Dan Schwartzman, a 31-year-old sports talk-show host for 97.5 FM and

950 AM in Philadelphia, says Wheeler has been a mentor. "Wheels is one of the most kind and gentlemanly people I've ever met in the media world," Schwartzman said. "In a business that does not promote young talent, Wheels has never been afraid to offer support to help the young media members improve. And I honestly can't remember him ever saying a negative thing about Harry Kalas in the four years that I've known him. I tried to avoid the subject."

When told that his feud with Wheels was being debated over the airwaves, Harry was embarrassed. "Harry called me and said, 'Gosh, I'm hearing that there was a lot of media attention on WIP about me and Wheels,'" Jeff McCabe said. "He said, 'I don't want to be involved in this.'"

Harry's three boys felt the same.

Todd and Brad have liked Wheeler since they were small boys hanging out at Veterans Stadium. Their feelings never changed. In their eyes, whatever happened between their father and Wheeler was between them, which was fine with Harry. Even after Harry's death, Todd and Brad spent time catching up with Wheels.

"It wasn't like a forced yield for me that I had to avoid the issue or choose a side," Todd Kalas said. "I understand what I've read and I understand how Wheels was with me, and I've always had no problem with Chris Wheeler. I've heard stuff through the grapevine, but it wasn't like Dad ever said, 'You need to change your relationship with Chris because of this or this.' Dad knew that I was fine with Wheels, and I don't think that he ever had a problem with it."

Even Kane Kalas, Harry's son with Eileen, took the high road when asked about Wheeler. "It's something that I'd heard about, but it's never been something that's been ultra significant to me," he said. "Certainly it was to my father and mother, especially when it was in the media, but it's not something that I'm sitting here twisting my mustache about."

Wheeler is reluctant to talk on the record about his issues with Harry and Eileen—he says the Phillies won't allow it—but he did stick up for himself in an April 2008 interview with the *Allentown Morning Call*.

"It was a personal thing that was really no one's concern," Wheeler said. "Someone said some things and decided to call someone in the media and told some lies. Unfortunately, the media ran with it without getting my side of the story. I'm not allowed to talk about it, but it was something between the two of us and it didn't need [publicity]. It has never affected anything on the air.

We work fine together."

In his 2009 book, *View from the Booth,* Wheeler surprisingly doesn't tell many Kalas stories and never mentions their feud. "I told Harry there would be nothing in there," Wheeler said.

Eventually, the air was cleared somewhat after the Phillies and television executives pleaded for Harry and Wheels to improve their on-air banter.

"Unfortunately, I also was around when Harry and Chris Wheeler, great friends for many years, had some problems," said Jon Slobotkin, who produced Phillies telecasts for Comcast SportsNet from 1998 to 2005. "I tried to mend fences wherever I could. There was the personal side, which they dealt with between them. But professionally, even when they personally were not good, they worked good together. They never refused to talk to each other on the air. They never ignored what the other was saying. I give them credit for never allowing whatever feelings had been between them to get in the way of the telecast and I did my best to speak to them. I talked to them individually and told them, 'Just be professional about your job.'"

Harry and Wheels never were friends after 1997, but did get to the point where they made small talk when around one another. Occasionally, they even sat at the same table in press clubs while eating pre-game meals.

David Montgomery noted that Wheeler was "big-time" helpful when Kalas occasionally would become confused or make on-air errors in his final years.

"I don't think Harry was making a lot of mistakes, to be honest," Wheeler said. "When he had trouble seeing the ball, every once in awhile he might have had the wrong guy in the game and I would point to his scorecard and show him the name. Nobody would even know it."

Phillies television producers agreed that Kalas often was aided by Wheeler. Montgomery even thinks that deep down inside they never stopped caring for each other.

"The stuff that happened wasn't for reasons in the booth," Montgomery said. "Some people grow together and some people grow apart. As Harry's circumstances changed . . . his life took a different direction at times and his relationship with his broadcast partners did as well. Harry and Wheels had a very, very close friendship and then circumstances prevented them from being as close, but I still think there was affinity for one another. I know there was. I'm going to leave it at that."

Eileen Kalas disagrees, and points to Harry's continuing mistrust for Wheeler surfacing again as part of contract negotiations with the Phillies after the 2006 season. After 2004, John Kruk had left the Phillies booth to join ESPN as a baseball analyst. Harry again was stuck working with Wheeler full-time for the next two seasons.

In the winter of 2006, Harry hired an aggressive new agent from the prestigious Beasley Firm in Philadelphia. Dion Rassias, 44 at the time and a fan of his client, asked for a three-year contract that included a clause to "address" Wheeler allegedly putting down Harry during telecasts. The Phillies countered with a two-year offer and insisted that Wheeler was a non-issue.

Right away, Rassias wanted to play hard ball with the Phillies, but that was difficult because of Harry's affection for the organization and his job.

"When you walk through the Phillies offices with him, every single person walks up and hugs and kisses him, without exception," Rassias said. "Whenever we talked about how we're going to approach it, Harry would always say, 'You know, Dion, I love the Phillies.' When a guy basically tells you that he'll work for free, your elbow room is somewhat limited."

When three meetings over three months led to no progress—the Phillies kept insisting on a two-year deal—Rassias decided he had no choice but to use Harry's issues with Wheeler to get his way.

Rassias concocted a sneaky plan that worried Harry.

"Dion, I'm not comfortable with this," Harry told his agent.

"Come on, give me a little something," the agent shot back. "You want me to go down and get your raise and get a third year, you gotta give me an inch to maneuver. I'm really good in the corners."

Rassias put his plan into action during an early December 2006 meeting with Kalas and Montgomery.

"I hate to do this, but really the problem is Chris Wheeler keeps running Harry down, and Harry is preoccupied by it at times in the booth," Rassias said in the meeting. "We need to address this in the contract."

Montgomery disagreed, saying, "We don't need to address that. They're grown men."

Rassias responded that Harry still didn't want to work with Wheeler.

"Our sponsors really like Wheeler," Montgomery said,

"Which sponsors?" Rassias asked.

Montgomery didn't answer.

Knowing what Rassias was about to spring, Harry excused himself from the meeting to smoke.

"Look, this thing with Wheeler is getting out of hand," Rassias said after Harry left the room. "We need to address this, and one of the things we're going to do is give Harry the security for the third season."

Montgomery again said no.

"Well, I want you to look at this," Rassias said as he pulled out six CDs in clear plastic cases and flipped them onto the negotiating table like a deck of cards, the corners of one overlapping the others. The CDs, painted to look like official baseballs, were titled "Wheeler Speaks" and numbered 1-to-6.

Looking nervous, Montgomery at first didn't touch the CDs.

"I'm asking you to listen to these and tell me whether or not this is worth the third year," Rassias said.

"All right, we'll get back to you," Montgomery said.

Montgomery left the room, then returned almost immediately and handed Rassias the CDs. It was clear to Rassias that the Phillies had never listened to any of them.

"We'll get back to you tomorrow," Montgomery said.

The next day, Kalas received a three-year contract offer that was signed on December 4, 2006.

So what was really on the CDs?

That 10-second clip of Wheeler commenting about Harry's smoking that Eileen Kalas had saved had been copied onto all six, and that was all.

The Phillies had been suckered and never did find out. "They will when they read about it in this book," Rassias said with a laugh.

What if Montgomery had listened to the CDs?

"I'd have told them my secretary made a mistake copying them," Rassias said.

Rassias has no problem admitting that he tricked the Phillies, but he believes it wouldn't have worked unless the organization had known that the CDs could have had hours worth of "Wheeler Speaks" evidence that may have been offensive to Kalas.

"They knew Eileen was a little neurotic and could be home working a VCR trying to tape everything," Rassias said. "In my mind, I'm happy with the fact that I hold this belief that Wheeler's effort to subvert Harry helped us get Harry a vested third year. I think Wheeler was the guy who was always chasing Harry in terms of what he's done, what he stands for and how the people feel about him."

The day of Harry's memorial service at Citizens Bank Park in April 2009, Rassias received what he believed was further confirmation that he was right to make Wheeler an issue in contract negotiations. Before the service, Harry's family, friends and co-workers were invited to a gathering in the ballpark's Diamond Club. While at the bar getting a drink, Rassias overheard a Kalas friend saying, "Everybody loved Harry . . . except Chris Wheeler." A few minutes later, he heard someone else say the same line, then another.

"It started to catch fire in that room and became a little running joke," Rassias said. "Somebody would say Harry was such a nice guy and everybody loved him . . . then you'd wait for somebody to say . . . 'except for Chris Wheeler.'"

Told about Rassias' Diamond Club story, Wheeler simply shook his head in disbelief.

"I cared a great deal about Harry," Wheeler said. "We shared a lot of fun times that I'll always remember. And those memories belong to me and nobody can take them away."

PRINCE HARRY

The tough reputation of Philadelphia sports fans became a topic of discussion in August 2008 while the Phillies were in Los Angeles. The day before a night game at Dodger Stadium, two star players were in Beverly Hills for a television appearance on *The Best Damn Sports Show Period*.

"It isn't that bad is it?" *Best Damn* co-host Chris Roberts asked Jimmy Rollins and Ryan Howard. After Howard responded, "In Philly? Ummm. . . ." Rollins quickly chimed in to offer an honest assessment of what he'd noticed over his first nine seasons in the big leagues. "It's one of those cities—I might catch some flak for this—but they're front-runners. When you're doing good, they're on your side. When you're doing bad, they're completely against you."

Rollins' comments immediately set off a firestorm of controversy in Philadelphia, and when the Phillies returned home, the reigning National League Most Valuable Player was greeted by some boos at Citizens Bank Park. Rollins said he wasn't bothered by the fan treatment that night and that he stood by his unpopular comments.

What did hurt Rollins was a surprise pre-game visit from Harry Kalas, who approached Rollins as he sat at his locker. "J-Roll, why did you say that?" Harry asked.

Rollins was shocked that Harry came to ask that question. Harry wasn't one to get involved in situations like this. "Harry, I'm just telling the truth," Rollins said. "I'm not calling anybody out. I'm just calling an apple an apple."

Harry listened to Rollins' answer, then turned and walked away. The voice of the Phillies had made his point.

"I was like 'Wow, Harry came down and said something about that,'" Rollins recalled a year later. "It kind of just blew me away. I didn't think I made a mistake, but I felt bad for Harry because he'd been with the Phillies longer than anybody.

"When I saw how what I said affected Harry, I thought, 'Wow, he's part of the fans.' When you're an insider, you think Harry's on this side of the fence. You don't really consider him being on the other side of the fence, but broadcasters are because they have to talk to the fans, too."

The Phillies were Harry's team from the time they hired him in 1971 until his 2009 death, but his legions of fans had a big piece of his heart, too.

"Harry really didn't like the word 'fans,'" Eileen Kalas said. "He'd say, 'those people are my friends.'"

Harry Kalas made it a point to be extraordinarily friendly and accessible to fans all the way through his wildly successful 49-year professional career. He maintained that policy even after he became a living legend in Philadelphia as the beloved voice of the Phillies and famous nationally for his NFL Films narrations. Harry's autograph policy was to sign any time and anywhere for anyone. "I parked next to Harry for 32 years at Veterans Stadium," Phillies President David Montgomery said. "We'd leave together a lot of times. I was amazed. He would just stay there at his car and sign and sign and sign. He'd do this every game and the same people would show up."

"It was just unbelievable how people swarmed to Harry—young and old, black and white, men and women, Hispanics," said Jim Gibbons, Harry's Notre Dame basketball broadcast partner in the 1980s. "He always thanked them for asking for the autograph."

Harry was interrupted frequently while dining at the Dilworthtown Inn in West Chester, Pa. He had no problem putting down his fork to meet a fan. "I know a lot of athletes have this ill-founded sense of entitlements, but I never found Harry to have that whatsoever," restaurant owner Jim Barnes said. "In a public environment, some celebrities or athletes just don't want to be bothered. Harry was quite the opposite."

Even when he was working, Harry found it hard to say no to a fan request.

"We would do games in spring training when I needed Harry on headset between innings, and I would be told by the stage manager that he can't be with me because he's signing an autograph," said Jon Slobotkin, a former Comcast SportsNet producer. "I would say, 'Can you tell him that we're in the middle of doing a game and that's a little more important?'"

Harry's broadcast partners often became amazed watching him interact with the public. They couldn't believe how much time he devoted to fans.

"Off the air, it was a real inspiration for a young broadcaster to watch the way he connected," Phillies radio broadcaster Scott Franzke said. "He never said no to an autograph or a photo with somebody. He never turned down doing somebody's voicemail message. And he didn't have to do any of that at this stage. He was already 'Harry the K.'"

"How do you do it?" Franzke asked Harry while they drove together to a 2008 spring training game. "Don't you ever want to just walk away? You've got things to do, places to be."

"The fans are why I do what I do," Harry responded. "That's why we're here. We wouldn't have jobs if it weren't for the fans."

According to Harry, fans around the country took an even greater interest in him after his 2002 induction into the broadcaster's wing of the Baseball Hall of Fame. "It's very humbling to be recognized and meet people who want your autograph or a picture," Harry said in March 2009. "Being inducted into Cooperstown made a big difference. I remember Bob Murphy, the longtime Mets announcer, said, 'Harry, it's going to change everything.'"

Yet it never changed Harry. Late in life, he was treated like a rock star. He was mobbed everywhere he went. Yet Harry remained incredibly humble. He had no ego to feed.

"I'd go, 'Harry, this is unbelievable,'" Phillies broadcaster Tom McCarthy said. "He'd just look at me and smile. You could see he was appreciative. But he would never talk about it. Never. I know that he tried to show them every way he could how appreciative he was. To me, just being on the air was a way to show it, but he'd go out of his way."

Billy Atkinson runs the Citizens Bank Park press elevator during Phillies games. He'll never forget seeing Harry, a few days before his death, humbled and gracious over being recognized by a fan. Harry was headed to the basement for a quick smoke during his inning off when the elevator door unexpectedly opened on the first-floor concourse.

"A woman noticed Harry and called out to him," Atkinson said. "Harry waved back and the woman inquired if she could shake his hand. He stepped over, reached for her hand and thanked her for taking the time to notice him. When we proceeded to head towards the basement, Harry turned to me and asked, 'How sweet was that woman I didn't even know taking the time to notice me?'"

Harry always went the extra mile to make someone happy, whether it was for a close friend or a casual fan. "You could meet the guy taking out the trash in the lobby, and the next day they'd be in the booth," Whitey Ashburn once said.

If Harry met a child at the ballpark, he usually initiated a conversation. "I introduced Harry to my friend's son," Phillies videographer Dan Stephenson said, "and Harry looked him right in the eye and asked 'How old are you? What grade are you in? Do you play baseball? What position?' The kid never forgot it because Harry was interested in him. Harry made a fan for life in the dad and the kid."

If a friend or charity or anyone in need came to Harry with a request, Harry felt it was his duty to try to fulfill it without asking for anything in return. Harry worked a busy schedule, but his rare nights off didn't become nights off until someone didn't need him for something.

"We got Harry to do a safety video for state troopers," former Phillies pitcher Larry Christenson said. "Harry didn't want any money. He said, 'Let me know when you need me again.' Harry went out of his way all the time. He always had a soft spot in his heart and would do anything you asked."

And then some. Without the press finding out, Harry occasionally would sneak into St. Christopher's Hospital for Children in Philadelphia to visit sick kids. He also volunteered his time to emcee events for the American Heart Association, United Way and other groups free of charge. He'd tell friends, "It's the best feeling in the world doing these types of things."

"I always saw Harry throwing hundreds in charity buckets," said Dion Rassias, an attorney who negotiated Harry's last contract with the Phillies. "He didn't get paid and was putting his own money in."

Only months before his death, on December 22, 2008, Harry Kalas was fully in the Christmas spirit. At age 72, his offseason had remained as hectic as ever. He'd just flown back to Philadelphia after working an NFL game the previous day in Minnesota for Westwood One radio. The week ahead would include voiceover work for NFL Films and other projects. But first on Harry's to-do list was his annual trip to the Fair Acres Geriatric Center, a full-care nursing home in Lima, Pa., near his home in Media.

John Brazer, the Phillies director of publicity, picked up Harry at the Kalas home. Decked out in a Santa hat, Harry was ready to spread some holiday cheer by singing Christmas carols, posing for pictures, signing autographs, answering baseball questions and doing anything else asked of him. The Phillie Phanatic and Phillies ball girls also would be showing up to entertain about 60 people in a packed main lounge of the Fair Acres' high-rise building. During the drive over, Harry surprised Blazer with a rare request.

"I don't want to be singing 'Jingle Bells,'" he said.

Although Harry wasn't a regular churchgoer as an adult, he was the son of a minister and a traditionalist who felt deeply about the true meaning of Christmas. Handed a microphone, Harry started out by leading everyone in "Silent Night" as a pianist played next to him. When finished, he broke into "O Come All Ye Faithful." The group, made up mostly of senior citizens, grew more and more excited seeing the famous voice of the Phillies in person, crooning one Christmas tune after another. Harry was enjoying himself, too.

Then, five songs into his set, a woman called out loudly, "Jingle Bells. Do Jingle Bells." Harry gulped, then looked over to Brazer and rolled his eyes. Harry didn't want to do it, but he couldn't bear disappointing anyone.

"Dashing through the snow, in a one horse open sleigh. . . ."

A senior citizen himself by that point, Harry ended up performing for over two hours. "Harry coming in was something the residents anticipated all through the Christmas season," said Noreen Tully, a Fair Acres employee. "He came every year and lifted spirits."

Some celebrities do charitable work to improve their public images and bolster their careers. Some do it because it makes them feel good. Harry did it to make others feel good.

"Harry was part of that old guard, the same group that my dad was a part of," said FOX baseball and football broadcaster Joe Buck, son of legendary St. Louis Cardinals broadcaster Jack Buck. "Not just guys who had great voices and really sounded like baseball, but dedicated basically their adult lives to one organization in one city. Those guys are unfortunately dwindling. Where those guys take the next step is with charitable stuff and what they do in the community. It's not just balls and strikes, not just home runs. It's having a voice and making a difference, and I know that's what my dad tried to do and what Harry tried to do."

In the early 1970s, Harry did his part when ALS first became the Phillies' official charity. Amyotrophic lateral sclerosis, a neuromuscular disorder that causes progressive paralysis and leads to death, is called Lou Gehrig's Disease after its most famous victim, Baseball Hall of Famer Lou Gehrig.

When Harry was hired as a Phillies broadcaster in 1971, first wife Jasmine became heavily involved in the Phillies charity work which at the time was spearheaded by Nancy Giles, wife of Phillies executive Bill Giles, and Sheena Bowa, whose husband Larry was the team's starting shortstop. To raise money for charities, Phillies wives held bake sales, dinners and fashion shows, and Harry always made himself available to promote and emcee their events.

The Phillies' charitable efforts really took off after Malvina Charlestein, the mother-in-law of a dying young man, convinced the Phillies to build a relationship with the local ALS chapter. Alan Phillips was 34 when first diagnosed with ALS in 1982. "My mom believed that ALS belonged in baseball because of Lou Gehrig," said Ellyn Phillips, Alan's wife and president of the Greater Philadelphia ALS Chapter since 1984.

In the winter of 1983, after Charlestein set up a meeting with Nancy Giles, ALS became the official charity for the Phillies' wives. In 1984, Alan Phillips and family accepted an invitation to a Phillies game. Severely disabled, Alan was carried down steps into a club box that was next to the Phillies radio booth and in plain view of Harry Kalas, who watched with great sadness.

"Do you know this is what Lou Gehrig went through?" Charlestein said after approaching Harry.

"No matter what I can do, please let me know," Harry said softly with tears rolling down his cheeks. "I want to help."

Later that year, Alan Phillips was gone at age 34.

By 1989, the wives' charity was elevated to the status of official charity of the Phillies organization. Today, the club holds an annual auction and autograph show at Citizens Bank Park, during an off day for the team, which is attended by every Phillies player and coach.

The Phillies' wives raised $28,000 for ALS the first year. The 2009 Phillies Phestival brought in $867,000. All told, the Phillies have raised more than $11 million for ALS since 1984.

"Harry was involved every year and had a lot to do with it," Ellyn Phillips said. "People would come to our luncheons just to hear him."

Harry gave to individuals, as well as organizations. For years, Phillies press box attendants would receive personalized Christmas cards from Harry with a check, often for $100. "I thought, 'What did I do to deserve it?'" said Art Cassidy, who has worked in the Phillies press box since 1963. "I just tried to be nice to him."

For many years, Harry served as master of ceremonies, for no compensation, at the Philadelphia Sports Writers Association's annual award banquet.

"For the job that he did, Harry could have commanded $5,000," longtime Phillies public address announcer Dan Baker said. "But he loved Philadelphia and loved the sports writers. Initially, we paid him something, which he'd give back to the organization."

NFL Films President Steve Sabol personally witnessed Harry's generosity in 2008 when HBO dropped *Inside the NFL*, a show that Harry had narrated during football seasons for a quarter-century. Before Showtime picked up the series, Sabol phoned Kalas.

"Harry, we're off the air," Sabol said. "I think we'll be back on, but we're not going to get the same amount of money."

"I'll take a pay cut," Harry shot back.

Everyone but Harry ended up making less.

"We did take a pay cut, but because Harry said that, I said, 'Harry Kalas is going to get paid the same.'"

Harry's love for people was exhibited in so many different settings. One spring training game, Harry wandered into the stands and invited three fellows who were sitting alone in different parts of the ballpark to his beach place for dinner. He thought that they looked lonely, but they showed up with their families, which led to Jasmine having to cook a bigger pot of spaghetti than had been anticipated. On another occasion in Florida, Harry was dining out with an old friend when he noticed an older gentleman eating alone. Harry invited the man to sit at his table. In the 1980s, Harry was out to eat at a bar with a Phillies player when a fan approached asking for autographs. The player shooed the intruder away, saying, "Can't you see we're dining?" Upset that the autograph seeker had been let down, Harry left the table to apologize.

It is doubtful that Harry ever fully understood how important he was to fans and how far that relationship spanned. While fighting for his country all over the world, Ret. U.S. Army Colonel William Davis, a 60-year-old former Green Beret, greatly appreciated the break which he got from living in a war zone when he could pick up Phillies games on Armed Forces Radio.

"I listened to Harry, and when a soldier or sailor is serving overseas, especially in wartime, it's a piece of home again," said Davis, a former Phillies bat boy. "Because of the work I did, I was in some real rat holes. You're not being shot at every moment, but you can go crazy. When you heard that voice of Harry's, it goes back to red, white and blue America."

As a former soldier himself, Harry went out of his way to honor veterans. When he received fan mail from a vet, he'd often send an autograph and free tickets to a baseball game. Late in life, Harry even wrote a poem about veterans that he titled "America's Heroes."

One night, Harry went out for drinks on Veterans Day with pal Jeff McCabe, who had shown up at the bar a few minutes early and was, by chance, sitting next to a wounded Vietnam Vet when Harry arrived. The fellow asked for an autograph.

"There's a condition on that," Harry said. "You have to give me *your* autograph."

While exchanging signatures, both men began to tear up. "It was so sincere that I'm thinking this is something that should be videotaped," McCabe said. "The fellow writes his autograph on a napkin and Harry saved it. A couple years later, Harry still had that autograph at home in a top drawer."

For Dan Stephenson's wedding reception in 1990, Harry agreed to announce the bridal party's entrance. After finishing the introductions, Harry spontaneously asked everyone to stand up, then said, "Let's all hold hands as one and sing 'God Bless America' in honor of the American troops fighting in Operation Desert Shield."

Like most Americans, Harry was deeply affected by 9/11. "I remember speaking to my father about it, and he said, 'Son, this makes no sense to me,'" recalled Kane Kalas, Harry's youngest son, who was only 12 at the time. "It was incomprehensible to him and upset him."

Before the Phillies played their first game after the terrorist attacks, Harry helped Philadelphians heal by delivering an emotional pre-game speech.

"From the cradle of liberty, Philadelphia, Pennsylvania, do we have closure? No," Harry said that night. "No, the heinous acts of terrorism last Tuesday will be with us for as long as we all shall live. Here at Veterans Stadium we have various displays of nationalism and patriotism. Yes, baseball will go on. It won't be the same. It will be a long time before it's the same. But sports has always been a diversion from our everyday problems, and in this case, from a national tragedy."

Most everyone in the house had wet eyes listening to Harry. "Gee whiz, the comments Harry made after 9/11 were unbelievable," Phillies longtime PR director Larry Shenk said. "That was all him. Somebody didn't write that for him."

After the Phillies game that night, a 5-2 victory over Atlanta, Harry went to the press club to have drinks with friends. A couple beers in, Harry said, "All right, boys, stand up. We're gonna sing 'God Bless America.'" Everyone made a circle around the table, then grown men held hands and sang together.

"It was a real emotional night, and Harry was a wonderful shepherd through moments like that," said Scott Graham, a Phillies broadcaster in 2001. "That's a big part of his brilliance."

When Harry was doing his NFL Films narrations, his kindness towards others showed in how he showered the young producers' work with compliments.

"I always noticed when Harry worked with one of the kids or a rookie," former NFL Films producer Ray Didinger said. "They would go into the booth with their script and it was a little intimidating. You're wondering if it's good enough, and almost without exception, Harry would read it and say, 'Ah, this is good. That's a good line.' When he'd finish, he'd say, 'Rory, that was a pleasure.' You could just see the kids gain a little more confidence in their work, and I'm sure Harry did it consciously. I saw it enough that I know it wasn't an accident."

Almost every day, someone would stop Harry to request that he record a phone answering machine message for them. He never said no. The messages always were similar: So and so "can't come to the phone because he's on a long drive . . . he's outta here!"

"Harry almost got as big a kick out of people enjoying his voice as the people did listening to him," said Rob Brooks, the Phillies' manager of broadcasting. "To him, there was this degree of wonderment like, 'Why are these people so elated to hear me?'"

Eventually, the requests got a little out of hand. Late in life, he received hundreds of letters from fans asking him to read off the names of wedding parties for their receptions.

"I was the guy who recorded them," Brooks said, "and some of them would be strictly names. But some people would write these elaborate scripts. 'I'm glad you could all come out to today's ballgame here at the Valley Forge Military Academy. Let's get to our starting lineups. . . .' Harry would roll through it, and, of course, at the end he'd say, 'I wish them well, because soon they'll be on a honeymoon. Like a 3-2 pitch to Michael Jack Schmidt, they'll be outta here!' I ended charging people a donation to Phillies Charities, but Harry didn't make any money for it, and he didn't care."

NFL Films producer Dave Plaut was thrilled when Harry agreed to cue up his famous voice in order to broadcast a few video highlights of his daughter Rebecca pitching a youth softball game for her Bat Mitzvah DVD. "Harry didn't just do that for me," he said. "It was everybody."

When Harry attended his agent's Christmas parties, he showed up with six-dozen new baseballs to autograph for kids. "Harry walked around singing Christmas carols and passing out signed baseballs," Dion Rassias said. "My son plays Little League Baseball and Harry said, 'Send me the roster.' They all got a signed baseball—every player and coach. Everybody wanted to play on my son's team because Harry did that every year. Those are things that Harry did, because that's the way God made him."

On the surface, it seemed like Harry Kalas and Rick Walker didn't have much in common. Walker is a 6-foot-4 black man who was an NFL tight end for nine seasons, six with the Washington Redskins. He also was 19 years younger than Harry. But when they were put in the same broadcast booth to do football games together for Westwood One, they got along great and became close friends.

"I'll tell you what, I loved Harry like a brother and I feel blessed that I was a small part of his life," Walker said. "If you didn't love Harry, it was only because you didn't get to know him. I just hate that he didn't get to see his Eagles win a Super Bowl. If the Eagles won a game that we didn't do together, the moment it was over I'd get a call. 'Hey pal, how about those Birds?' He'd sing the Eagles fight song. It was like clockwork. If the Skins won, I'd call and sing 'Hail to the Redskins.'"

Harry's infectious personality even enticed big-name athletes that he never was around much and celebrities that he didn't know well to gravitate towards him. Guys like Charles Barkley, Donovan McNabb and Joe Frazier found Harry to be a delight. "We were on our way to Hawaii one year and walking in the United private club and Ed McMahon goes, 'Harry . . . Harry Kalas!'" Eileen recalled. "Harry goes, 'Ed.' They sat down together."

No matter who Harry was around, he had a special knack for finding a way to make him or her feel special.

"Harry had a great recall of names," Westwood One executive producer Howard Deneroff said. "I had an intern come with me to a Giants game, and Harry gave the kid credit on air when he was doing nothing. He did get him tea once. At the end of the broadcast, before he left, Harry said, 'Hey E.J., hope you enjoyed it. Good luck.' The kid was on Cloud 9. Then Harry calls me four days later and E.J. happens to answer the phone. Harry says, 'Is this E.J?' I think E.J. talked about it for four weeks. He couldn't believe Harry remembered his name."

Most of Harry's friends can tell many similar stories.

"When I co-authored *50 Phabulous Phillies*, Harry wrote the foreword for no pay," Skip "Memory Lane" Clayton said. "Not only that, he did a book signing with us. We went to a Barnes & Nobles in Plymouth Meeting. Because Harry was coming, when we arrived there were a lot of people waiting. Harry said, 'Let's do a Q & A,' then afterward we signed the books. Later, another group came in and Harry said, 'Let's do another Q & A.' He stayed for two hours. Tug McGraw had a book signing at the same store years earlier and a worker there told me we had outsold Tug by one book. I told her, 'Harry Kalas outsold Tug McGraw by one book.'"

When at home, Harry used to spend hours in his office going through fan mail. He received more than most players but answered every letter.

"Dad always did love the Philadelphia fans," said Todd Kalas, Harry's oldest son. "He made sure they were the last part of his acceptance in Cooperstown. I think with the way that he connected with everybody, whether he met them in person or strictly was their friend through the airwaves, was a very special relationship. It's an overwhelming feeling to know that your dad had a positive impact on so many people."

In 1999, Harry showed how far he'd go for a fan after he received a touching letter from a 13-year-old boy. The young Phillies fan wrote to say that he had recently lost his grandfather, who had been a big fan of Harry's. In his letter, the boy also invited Harry to his upcoming Bar Mitzvah. A few weeks later, Harry made a surprise appearance at the Bar Mitzvah with his wife Eileen in tow. They stayed for two hours, with Harry sitting at a table signing autographs, not even stopping to eat.

"Harry was a Hall of Fame announcer and a Hall of Fame human being," Larry Shenk said.

In the late 1990s, Harry used to give Phillies players a thrill by emceeing the first round of their annual Fantasy Football League draft. One year, it was held in a hotel boardroom during an off night in Montreal. With Phillies players sitting at tables with draft sheets, pizza and beer, Harry was up front at a podium making like NFL commissioner Roger Goodell.

"You sit there and make your pick and Harry gets up there and says, "the Northeasters select Marshall Faulk from the Rams,'" former Phillies pitcher Ricky Bottalico said. "It gave you goose bumps and made the draft exciting."

"I remember just cracking up," said Terry Francona, the Phillies manager from 1997 to 2000. "It sounded like it should have been on national TV."

Many Phillies players believed that Harry was more popular than they were. "He absolutely was," John Kruk said. "You have to remember how many homes that Harry went into for all these generations of Philadelphia sports fans. Yeah, we noticed it in hotel lobbies, going out in towns. Hey, he's not a bad guy to take a second fiddle to. And the thing about it is, he was so gracious to everybody that approached him."

One way Harry gave back to fans was going against his bosses' wishes by announcing birthdays and anniversaries on the air during games. "Harry and I clashed about personal messages that he used to give on the air," former Comcast SportsNet producer Jon Slobotkin said. "I just didn't think it was really appropriate to use such a specific forum as Phillies baseball to give people birthday and anniversary wishes. Harry called them 'shout-outs.' We would go back and forth. Ultimately, I understood it was important to him, because

Harry had such a strong connection to his fan base. He knew there were objections, but he also knew that it was part of what he felt that he needed to do to stay connected to his public."

Harry was so popular in Philadelphia that he once unintentionally upstaged a famous singer during a concert. When Harry and Eileen had front-row seats to a Kenny Rogers show, the singer called three audience members up on stage to sing with him. Not knowing who Harry was, Rogers chose the Phillies broadcaster first. "People were yelling, 'Harry, Harry, Harry,'" Eileen Kalas recalled. "Kenny Rogers says, 'Who is this guy?'"

Celebrities were fans of Harry, too. Even U.S. Presidents. In the 1980s, Harry was dining with buddy Joe Nunes near Washington, D.C., when approached by a stranger.

"The President recognizes your voice, but can't put a name to it," a Secret Service agent said. Harry looked to a nearby table and realized that President Ronald Reagan and First Lady Nancy Reagan were having dinner with six others. Harry identified himself to the Secret Service agent as the Phillies announcer and voice of NFL Films. Before he knew it, Harry was chatting with the President.

During the All-Star break in 2008, President George W. Bush held a "Salute to Baseball—America's Pastime" dinner at the White House. Hall of Famers Frank Robinson, Jim Bunning and Harry Kalas were on a list of about 60 guests. With Eileen out of town, Harry took his friend Jeff McCabe.

"When we get there, there was a reception line for George and Laura Bush," McCabe recalled. "George puts his hand out and says, 'Harry, it is my honor to meet you after all these years. You have the greatest voice. You are a legend of baseball broadcasting.'"

Harry was a legend, but he also took a great interest in the young up-and-coming talent in his broadcasting field. He'd never forgotten how he felt during his first Major League Baseball job when he was made to feel like an outcast by Houston Astros veteran broadcaster Gene Elston. Every time the Phillies hired an inexperienced broadcaster, Harry always went out of his way to help him, as he did when John Kruk became a rookie broadcaster for the Phillies in 2003.

"I don't know what I'm doing," Kruk told Harry before the season.

"There are two things you have to remember," Harry responded. "I do the play-by-play, so when the pitcher is getting ready to pitch, shut up. The other thing is, you've played the game. React to the people in your own sense of style and humor. There's a certain line that you can't cross because you're a Phillies broadcaster and you're being paid by the team, but as long as you don't get personal. . . . If a guy doesn't hustle and you 'call him out,' the player is probably going to get mad at you. But the thing you have to remember is not to treat the fans of Philadelphia like they're dummies. Don't forget that you're talking to a pretty intelligent group of people that know if a guy is dogging it or not."

In 2001, Comcast SportsNet hired Glenn Wilson, who had no broadcast experience, to work as an analyst for the Phillies' post-game show. "Harry would say, 'You're doing great,' even though I was stinkin' it up," Wilson said. "I was there just one year."

Harry did the same thing on December 1, 1996 when a renowned football coach made his broadcasting debut as a one-game fill-in. Just 11 days after resigning as Notre Dame's football coach and at the start of what became only a two-year retirement, Lou Holtz flew into Philadelphia on a Sunday morning to work an Eagles-New York Giants game for Westwood One with Harry Kalas.

Harry picked up Holtz at the airport. Jeff McCabe was there, too, because he was the play-by-play spotter for the game. During their short ride to Veterans Stadium, Holtz seemed concerned. He'd been a great college football coach since the early 1970s and his Notre Dame teams were 100-30-1 in 11 seasons. But now he was going to have on-the-job training in broadcasting an NFL game with a national audience listening.

"All right, Harry, how does this go?" Holtz asked when jumping in the car.

"Coach, there is nobody that knows the game better than you," Harry said. "When you want to say something, jump in."

"Are you going to give me a hand signal?" Holtz asked.

"No, you talk when you want to talk," Harry said again.

With Harry going out of his way to help, Holtz got through that day, and down the road he found a new career as a college football television analyst, first for CBS and later for ESPN.

"I was right there next to Harry, and he made Lou really feel comfortable that day," Jeff McCabe said.

One of the things that impressed Philadelphia radio host Howard Eskin most about Harry was how he responded to the Phillies being criticized. "When the Phillies were bad, people in the organization didn't like the things that I said and they resented it," Eskin said. "Harry never, ever, ever held that against me. The organization did. Ashburn would kid me about it. Harry showed me something when he wasn't like a lot of other people."

Phillies outfielder Jayson Werth experienced Harry's great respect for others firsthand. Harry made an emotional plea for forgiveness from Werth after Harry felt he had disrespected him on the air the night before. On April 10, 2008, the Phillies lost a 12-inning game to the Mets in New York. When describing Angel Pagan's walk-off hit on television, Harry announced that the game was over as soon as the line-drive single to center field touched the ground. But after watching the replay, Harry realized that Werth nearly threw out speedy Mets baserunner Jose Reyes at home plate. Harry was angry at himself for discounting Werth's strong throwing arm.

"The next day, HK came up to me at my locker with tears in his eyes," Werth said. "He was apologetic that he messed up the call. He was upset about it. I think he lost sleep over the fact that he knew that he didn't give me a chance to throw the guy out at home in his call. Who am I to even deserve an apology from this guy? And I didn't even know. I went back and listened to the call and I didn't think I needed an apology. That's so Harry. It just gave me more of an idea what a great guy he was. It took stones for someone to come up and say that to me, let alone HK."

In the winter of 1984, Scott Graham was a college sophomore at the University of Pennsylvania who worked at the campus radio station. He was responsible for doing the halftime shows for the men's basketball games and decided to take a crack at interviewing Harry Kalas. Harry called back the next day.

"It freaked me out," Graham said. "I could not believe he'd take time in the middle of the winter to call back a college kid. He had no idea who I was. I told Harry what I wanted. He told me he'd be happy to do it."

Harry and Scott met at a coffee shop on the Penn campus and talked for 90 minutes. The experience provided Graham with one of the best lessons he learned during his Ivy League education.

"You have a list of questions," Harry told Graham. "That's great. It's good that you're prepared. But you can't just go off that list because if I say something in the middle of the interview that you want to react to, you'll straight-jacket yourself into what it is that you're asking. Go with the flow of the conversation."

Graham took it all in. "Not only was Harry helping me out by giving me an interview, now he was teaching me. Yeah, I remember my first meeting with him pretty well."

And, vice versa. A year later, Graham entered a Harry Kalas sound-a-like contest at a bar. He made the cut, and then headed to a Phillies game for Harry to judge the five finalists and pick a winner on the field between games of a doubleheader.

"I made it to the finals against a sportscaster from Texas," Graham recalled. "Then we go out on the field and Harry came out and said good luck to everybody. It was 'Hi, how are you?' Then he got to me and it was like, 'Hi, Scott, how are you doing?' Everybody else went, 'Oh God.'"

Graham was declared the winner. His prizes included a Phillies season-ticket package and, best of all, a visit upstairs to broadcast an inning with Harry and Whitey. Five years later, Graham became part of the Phillies broadcast team in 1991, working the post-game show. In 1999, he started a seven-year run doing play-by-play. Later, he worked with Harry again at NFL Films. Along the way, Harry and Graham became close friends.

Harry helped nurture numerous young colleagues. When baseball season was over, Harry often would spend winter nights listening to a local college basketball game if one of his friends happened to be working the game.

"When you'd talk to Harry in the offseason, the first thing out of his mouth was, 'Tough game last night for those Dragons, Brooksie,'" said Phillies manager of broadcasting Rob Brooks, who also worked as a radio color man for Drexel basketball. "There was no reason in the world for him to be listening to that, but he knew that I was doing it, so he'd go out of his way to listen."

Phillies broadcaster Tom McCarthy said, "I would always get a phone call from Harry after I did a St. Joe's basketball game. Always. And he would watch the whole game. 'Way to bring those Hawks to victory.' That to me was great."

Jeff McCabe, a friend to Harry for 33 years, took his family to a Phillies game in September 2008 to celebrate his daughter's 10th birthday. With seats near the field, McCabe brought a new baseball just in case Katie got a chance to get an autograph from her favorite player, Chase Utley.

During a phone talk with Harry the day before, McCabe said, "I'm getting there early. We're going to be down by the Phillies dugout. Do you know if Utley comes out?"

"Just come up to the press box," Harry responded.

"Don't go out of your way to do anything," McCabe said.

Harry did, of course. When the McCabes arrived at the booth about 15 minutes before the first pitch, Harry said, "Let's take a walk." They headed down to a door that led to the Phillies clubhouse. Harry went inside, then a minute later he returned with Chase, who handed Katie an autographed baseball and posed for a picture.

Normally, Utley would have been unavailable to meet a fan so close to game time. He has a pre-game routine that he follows religiously.

For Harry, he made exceptions.

"A few times during a year, Harry would catch me during that time and ask me to come out in a hallway and meet some kids," Utley said. "I could never say no to him. It shows how much respect we all had for him and the kind of person he was. I never wanted to let him down. Honestly, he was a great guy. He was a very caring guy. He was the face of the Phillies for so long and made a lot of people's lives better."

LIFE OF THE PARTY

A travel day for the Phillies was winding down. After having the first part of Monday, June 18, 2001 to relax at home, the ballclub had caught a late-afternoon flight from Philadelphia to Pittsburgh for a three-game series with the Pirates that would begin the next night. At the Westin Convention Center in Pittsburgh, a group of Phillies spent the last part of their night having drinks at the hotel bar, Fish Company Restaurant. Harry Kalas was there, as were two of his broadcasting partners—Larry Andersen and Scott Graham. Others in the crowd included Phillies third baseman Scott Rolen and his fiancée.

The bartender announced last call around 1 a.m.—an hour before the mandatory closing time for Pennsylvania bars. Graham told his buddies that he was going to bed to get some rest for his early morning golf game, but Harry and the others weren't ready to shut it down quite yet. The bartender directed them to open establishments just outside the hotel on the 900 block of Liberty Avenue—a section of town that has been cleaned up in recent years, but which was still part of Pittsburgh's red-light district at the time.

The Phillies' contingent stopped into the first bar they found, Images.

Walking in on karaoke night, they could tell from a quick scan of the all-male crowd that Images was a gay bar, not the type of place they usually frequented. But Images served cold beer and would allow them to hang out together for another hour before calling it a night, so Harry's group headed to a big table in the back near the pool tables.

Soon after, Larry Andersen made a trip to the restroom. Standing at a urinal, Andersen heard two men walk in. From behind, one of them called out to him, "Nice ass!" Although secure in his sexuality and not one to judge, Andersen was a bit startled. Not knowing what to say or do, he surmised that he shouldn't ignore the comment. Still doing his business, he turned his head back towards the men and responded in a low voice, "Thank you."

When returning to the table with his friends, Andersen announced, "Drink up, we're leaving. I just got hit on in the bathroom. I don't feel comfortable here."

Everyone laughed, but Andersen was serious. Harry suggested that they head to the bar directly across the street—Chez Kimberly, a bar that no longer exists. Walking in, Kalas and his friends noticed that although there were women there, they weren't exactly lookers. They then took a longer gaze and noticed dancing girls on three stages. It turned out that they had left a gay bar only to wander into a go-go dive bar. Harry and friends had decided to stay . . . that is until an unattractive waitress covered with purple bruises and Band-Aids showed up.

"It was the sleaziest, dirtiest place I'd ever seen," Andersen recalled.

Harry Kalas, usually never one to complain, felt out of place. After ordering a beer, he spoke up with obvious exasperation. "Can we go back to the gay bar?"

And so they did.

The next day, Graham approached Harry in the Phillies' television booth. "So you went out last night, huh? How was it?"

"Yeah, I went out," Harry said. "Scott Graham, when a gay bar is the best place to go in Pittsburgh, it's not a good night."

That was the rare instance when Harry Kalas didn't find a bar to his liking. From the time he developed a taste for beer as a teenager until he gave up drinking late in life, Harry's idea of great fun was heading out to an establishment, any establishment, where he could drink, smoke, hang out with friends, and maybe even do some singing.

"Give Harry a bar with a piano, a cigarette and a drink, and he was in heaven," said Larry Christenson, a Phillies pitcher and regular Kalas road drinking buddy from 1973 to 1983. "He wanted to be singing, listening to music and around people. That was Harry the K at his best."

Friends who drank with Harry had their vocabularies expanded. Gin and tonic, Harry's favorite drink, was a "see-through" because it looked like water and you could see right through it. When Harry had one in his hand, he'd often hold up his glass and yell "see-through, see-through!" That was his way of bragging that he was drinking hard stuff instead of beer. Harry called his smokes "schmags." Christenson said, "When he lit up, Harry would say, 'I got a schmag, LC.'"

Another unusual word associated with Harry was "bounceability." This term was coined by the late beloved Phillies executive Paul "the Pope" Owens, who used it for people like himself and Harry who didn't wake up feeling sick after a night of drinking. "Harry never had a hangover, and I would have one for two days and not get out of bed," said Eileen Kalas, Harry's second wife. "I thought, 'How in the world can he do this?'"

For decades, Harry enjoyed working his dream job broadcasting baseball games and then having cocktails afterward. This pretty much summed up his life from 1965, his first year doing minor-league baseball in Hawaii, until the early 2000s, when he gave up alcohol in order to save his marriage to Eileen.

"I remember the good, the bad and the ugly," Christenson said of his many nights out with Harry.

Chicago ranked as one of Harry's favorite cities. He often visited The Lodge, a cozy hangout on West Division Street with peanut shells covering its floor. Popular with the media and ballplayers, The Lodge features a jukebox of oldies that includes "High Hopes." When Larry Andersen hangs out at The Lodge until it closes at 4 a.m., he tells friends the next day that he "saw the lights come on." Over the years, Harry and LA saw the lights come on a lot at The Lodge.

Once after a long night of partying in Chicago, Harry returned to his hotel room and called for a 6:30 wakeup call.

Confused, the woman working the front desk asked, "a.m. or p.m.?"

"A.M.," Harry responded.

"Well, it's 6:20 now," the woman said.

"It's 6:20 a.m.?" Harry asked.

Ten minutes later, he received his wakeup call.

Harry rarely drank at home. He just loved being around people in a drinking atmosphere. He consumed a lot of alcohol in his lifetime, certainly more than his share. But the conversation, whether it was with friends or strangers, apparently gave him an even bigger buzz.

"When Harry was younger, he was pretty active off the field," said Dallas Green, the manager of the Phillies' 1980 championship team. "He fit right in with the players. He also fit right in with that gang that would stay up a little late at night. I wasn't one for going home early, either, so I got to see him in action a lot of times."

One drinking story Harry really was proud of occurred in the early 1980s during a vacation in Los Angeles with his buddy Joe Nunes. One day, Harry and Joe dressed up in suits and went out for a fancy dinner that was to be concluded with a night of gambling at a horse track. While driving through Beverly Hills on the way to the track, Harry noticed a gatekeeper at a mansion directing cars where to park. Assuming the owners were hosting a bash, Harry had a mischievous brainstorm.

"It's a party," Harry said. "Let's crash it!"

Harry steered his rental to the driveway gate and was approached by the gatekeeper. When Harry gave his name, he was pointed to a parking spot.

"The guy didn't know who Harry was, but he let us in," Nunes said.

When inside, Harry and Joe realized that they were in the home of noted Hollywood actress Jane Powell. Among the party guests were Bob Hope and Charlton Heston.

"We stayed for four hours . . . until we had enough to eat and drink," Nunes said.

Harry especially enjoyed his offseason vacations with friends. He attended five Super Bowls as a fan in the 1970s and '80s with Joe Nunes, including one in New Orleans that was a party from start to finish. "We were down on Bourbon Street," Nunes said. "We drank all day, then Harry would go to his room for two hours, take a little nap and start all over again like he hadn't had a drink."

In January 1981, Harry also took a mini-vacation to New Orleans for Super Bowl XV in which his Eagles lost to the Oakland Raiders. "We're at the airport, sitting at the bar and Harry was pretty sloshed when an Eagles fan approached him," said NFL Films president Steve Sabol, Harry's traveling partner during the trip. "Harry tells the guy, 'I think you've had a little too much to drink. I can tell because you're a little blurry.'"

Even before his Super Bowl vacation, 1981 had started as a bit of a blur for Harry, who went to Florida on New Year's Day to play golf with the newly formed "Tough Luck Club." The previous winter, Mike Schmidt invited Phillies teammates Steve Carlton and Larry Christenson, and another friend, John Dickinson, to his place at the Innisbrook Resort and Golf Club in Tampa for a week of serious golf and serious partying.

"How it started," Christenson said, "was I missed a birdie putt and Schmidt is leaning on his putter and goes, 'Tough luck, LC.' I got pissed. On the next hole, Schmidt hit one in the water, so I leaned on my club and went, 'Hey, Schmidty, tough luck.' Then Carlton was on the tee and shanked one into the woods. We went, 'Hey Lefty, tough luck.' It became 'tough luck' and laughing for three days straight."

On their plane ride back to Philadelphia, they decided that they would hold an annual winter golf trip, and invitees would be dubbed "Tough Luck Club" members. Three months after the Phillies were crowned 1980 World Series champions, Harry Kalas and Richie Ashburn were among the eight charter members of the "Tough Luck Club" in January 1981. The next year, 12 people participated. Over the decade, "the TLC," as its members came to call it, grew to 24 members, including newcomers such as Bob Boone, Garry Maddox, Darren Daulton, Tim McCarver, Jim Kaat and Chris Wheeler.

"I think that 'Tough Luck Club' really brought us close together, especially with Harry and Whitey," Christenson said. "We talked about it all year long."

Instead of just playing daily rounds of golf, the TLC divided into teams for various tournaments played under a number of different formats—better ball, scramble, etc. The annual trip highlight was an awards banquet on the trip's final night, which players attended dressed in custom-made blue blazers with lapels bearing TLC patches. "It was a lot of fun, but after awhile I was like, 'I ain't wearing this jacket,'" Darren Daulton said with a laugh.

Harry had no problem with the blazers. He'd been wearing colorful jackets all through his four decades as a Philadelphian. Besides, he'd do just about anything in the name of fun.

In addition to the TLC getaway, Harry looked forward to another annual party in Philadelphia. After the final regular-season home game every year from the early 1970s until the Phillies left Veterans Stadium following the 2003 season, two nurse sisters, Rita Lyons and Joan Rosney, who worked in the stadium's first-aid room, hosted a big bash outside their working area. Guests included stadium employees, EMTs, and the police officers who had worked Phillies games during the season. The party usually featured a performance by more than three-dozen members of the Quaker Valley String Band, a regular at Philadelphia's annual New Year's Day Mummers Parade.

Harry Kalas didn't just make an appearance at this event. After two or three hours, Harry would motion for everyone to get in line. Harry would then lead a march from the first-aid room to the playing field. From there, the revelers would strut around the infield and outfield while the string band played oldies such as "Happy Days Are Here Again," and "Alabama Jubilee." They closed, of course, with a sing-along to "High Hopes."

"Watching Harry leading the way doing that Mummers strut was comical," said Henry Clay, who works in the Philadelphia media.

Harry just loved being part of this tradition. He always enjoyed taking part in any group activity, and Harry always seemed to fit in. The group activity Harry participated in most frequently, of course, was going out for drinks after games with Phillies players, writers and fellow announcers, plus just about anyone else who wanted to tag along.

Philadelphia Daily News baseball writer Bill Conlin, a frequent tennis opponent and road trip drinking buddy of Harry's in the 1970s and '80s, believed Kalas' immense capacity to handle his liquor made him a freak of nature. Conlin many times witnessed ballplayers having bad games due to too much drinking the night before, but he never once saw Harry let alcohol affect his broadcast of a ballgame.

"We're talking probably 30 years where he drank heavily, and I'm not talking garden variety social drinking here," Conlin said. "I'm talking about big-time, heavy-duty drinking—gin and tonics, martinis, vodka—from the minute he walked into the press room after a game until it closed, then he always went someplace else.

"However, Harry had incredible discipline. Never once in all the years that we were around each other did I ever see Harry walk into that announcing booth appearing to have so much as a drop of alcohol in his system. To me, this defined his ability to be the successful man and broadcaster that he was because he had this terrible affliction which has dragged so many people into the gutter. Harry not only had this iron will to only do it where it did not interfere with his work, but evolved into just about as good as anybody who's ever done that kind of work."

Despite his uncanny ability to handle his liquor, Harry's drinking did land him in trouble outside of work on more than one occasion. When Harry was a young man, it contributed to Cornell College suggesting he not return after a troubled freshman year and temporarily caused him to lose a job at the University of Iowa campus radio station following his transfer. Far more serious drinking-related issues came up later in his life. In the 1980s, he was on his way back from the Jersey shore and just a few blocks from his Radnor home when he totaled his car. Police officers cut him a break that night. But a few years later, he was charged with a DUI after getting pulled over for a minor traffic violation. His drinking also led to marital problems with both of his wives.

Harry's close friends always stood by him. "The reason you can't say anything bad about Harry is because he gave so much to others," former Phillies outfielder Glenn Wilson said. "If he had a car wreck because he drank too much, we were like, 'We've got to protect him better.' Everybody wanted to help him because he had given so much forgiveness and love to everyone."

Even with all his drinking and nights out, Harry engaged in just one bar fight—a first-round, one-punch TKO of Harry delivered by none other than Bill Conlin. On May 10, 1980, two future Hall of Fame pitchers in their primes—the Phillies' Steve Carlton and Tom Seaver of the Reds—dueled in a Saturday matinee at Cincinnati's Riverfront Stadium. The Phillies led 2-0 after their at-bat in the fifth inning, but the Reds Dan Driessen then launched a Carlton fastball into the seats for a two-out, game-tying homer. The Reds went on to win 5-3.

Conlin normally would have had the day off because the *Philadelphia Daily News* doesn't publish on Sundays, but he was there working on a freelance assignment for another publication. After the game, Harry was having a drink in the press room when Conlin walked in and blamed the Phillies loss on Carlton.

"Why in the hell would Carlton throw a cock-eyed fastball when Driessen couldn't hit his slider if you told him it was coming?" Conlin asked.

Harry knew that Conlin had a checkered history with Lefty, who was eight seasons into his "no-interviews" policy. Carlton had a 27-10 record for a 59-victory, last-place Phillies team in 1972, then slipped to 13-20 for a 71-win team the next season. In 1973, Carlton stopped talking to the press after a column by

Conlin in which he speculated that the pitcher wasn't taking care of himself and had been spending too much time in hotel bars. Since that column appeared, Carlton had spoken to Conlin just once. During spring training one year, Conlin and Tug McGraw were talking and smoking at Tug's locker. Carlton walked over and screamed, "Get that damn cigarette out of here!" Conlin joked that the Surgeon General never issued a smoking warning so harsh.

Whether or not Harry Kalas thought Conlin had an agenda after that 1980 game, he certainly went out of his way to stick up for Carlton, a good friend.

"You know Lefty's a Hall of Famer," Harry shot back at Conlin in the press club that day. "He's entitled to a mistake like anybody else. Accept him for the great pitcher that he is."

The argument over Carlton was over for the time being. Conlin returned to his hotel room to write, and Harry went out with Reds scout Ray "Snacksie" Shore, who had previously scouted for the Phillies and become good friends with Harry, his spring training neighbor. Harry spent most of the evening drinking at Shore's house, then Harry went for a nightcap at the Phillies hotel bar. Conlin, who—unlike many nights on the road in those days—had not been drinking, eventually walked into the bar. Harry walked up to Conlin to continue his afternoon defense of Carlton.

"Well, I guess you spent the whole night ripping Lefty?" Kalas said. "You're always looking for an excuse to rip him. That's what you do. That's the one thing that I don't like about you. You get on somebody's case and never get off. Now I know why he never wants to talk to you again."

Harry rarely initiated arguments, but on this night he seemed to be intent on picking a fight with Conlin.

"Harry, it looks like you've had a few too many," Conlin said.

"You don't know what I had," Harry shouted back.

Harry moved closer to go nose-to-nose with Conlin, a much bigger man.

"I need you to get out of my face," Conlin said.

At that point, Conlin says Harry reached out with his left hand and grabbed him by the shirt collar up around the throat. "He started to pull me toward him," Conlin recalled. "Somebody grabbed him and somebody grabbed me. I broke away and threw a right hand that smacked Harry in the left eye."

Conlin's punch opened a wound on Harry's face that took 12 stitches to close. While Harry was at the hospital, a police officer showed up at the hotel bar to question Conlin, but decided not to charge him after hearing eyewitness accounts of the incident. The next day, Harry showed up to the ballpark wearing dark sunglasses. After he spotted Conlin, Harry approached and growled, "That's it, no more tennis! No more me and you!"

When Harry's wife Jasmine found out about the fight, she became angry with Conlin. Jasmine and Harry had socialized with Bill and his wife Irma during many spring trainings. Their sons were spring pals as well. "I called Irma," Jasmine said, "and when Bill came home she gave him hell. She was on my side. I had to put makeup on Harry's face when he went to work for awhile."

Over the next 18 months, Harry avoided Bill Conlin. But by 1982, their fight was forgotten and they became friends again. "The fight was never spoken about at any time," Conlin said.

While it was an uncharacteristic case of Harry losing control under the influence of alcohol, the incident with Conlin also showed how far he would go to defend a friend.

Harry's loyalty to a Phillies pitcher nearly brought him to blows on another occasion. The Phillies had hosted the 1996 All-Star Game at Veterans Stadium, but Harry was off for the three-day break and spent one night in Atlantic City, drinking and playing blackjack with his police officer friend Jeff McCabe. They were watching the All-Star Game in a bar characterized by McCabe as a "private high-rollers" area. In the fifth inning, Ricky Bottalico, the Phillies' lone All-Star that season, entered the game to pitch for the National League. Although only 25 years old and in just his second full big-league season, the outgoing Bottalico already had become close to Harry. So the announcer jumped to the young hurler's defense when a drunk seated a few bar stools away started badmouthing Bottalico, even though the pitcher had worked one perfect inning in the game.

"This guy says something rude and Harry looked over and says, "You know, pal, that is a horrible comment. That is a nice young man and he's a great pitcher."

"That's bullshit," the drunk said. "He stinks."

The drunk, who didn't even recognize Harry Kalas or his famous voice, obviously wasn't a Phillies fan. He continued berating Bottalico. Eventually, Harry jumped off his barstool to go after the guy, but Jeff McCabe stepped in between them. While being held back, Harry yelled, "You don't talk about guys like that when you don't know them. He's a good young man."

Hearing the shouting, a maitre d' came running over. When McCabe and others explained that Harry was provoked, the drunk was asked to leave. The fight with Conlin and the near fight in Atlantic City were aberrations for Harry. Most of his longtime friends say they never ever saw Harry get upset, let alone angry enough to fight.

During a Phillies visit to San Francisco in July 1994, Harry actually prevented a potentially ugly bar fight between rival World Cup soccer fans. Richard Ashburn, Whitey's son, was on the trip and out for drinks with Harry. Not surprisingly, they patronized one of Harry's favorite bars, Lefty O'Doul's. Harry was having a blast singing away at the piano bar with Ashburn and a small group of strangers when everyone heard a commotion. Only hours after World Cup semifinal matches that day in Florida and New Jersey, Lefty's had become a melting pot of soccer fans from around the world. Eventually, a group of Italians, Spaniards and Irishmen started arguing to the point that people suspected a fight would break out.

Thinking quickly, Harry got up from his seat with a plan. "I'll handle this," he said.

"Things were getting testy and Harry goes over to the piano, takes the mike and starts singing the Italian national anthem," Ashburn recalled. "I thought, 'How does Harry know this anthem?' Then the Italian guys come over and they're patting him on the back. And then Harry waves everybody over and he starts singing the Spanish national anthem, then the Irish national anthem. Before you know it, the place is one big happy bar. Harry took a situation that may have gotten out of hand and made it a whole lot better. Thanks to Harry, everybody was singing and happy. It was just something to see."

The piano was the main attraction at Lefty's for Harry, who had regular spots where he could sing in most cities that the Phillies visited. "Harry would be in his glory at any piano bar," Larry Andersen said. "He wanted to sing. He didn't care if he sounded good."

If a bar didn't have a piano, Harry often would sing along to the jukebox or bellow out a tune *a cappella*, as he did the night he befriended a sailor at the Phillies' hotel in Chicago. "This bar was on the mezzanine level, and down below was the lobby with this huge fountain," recalled Frank Coppenbarger, the Phillies' director of team travel and clubhouse services. "Well, by the time the night was over, the poor sailor's hat was a Frisbee tossed over the balcony and into the pond to the tune of 'Anchor's Away.' Thanks to Harry, it became a big sing-along. We were singing every college fight song we could think of."

One time Harry turned into a lounge singer after wandering into a piano bar in Montreal. Although most of the crowd's first language was French, Harry felt the need to put on a show in English. "He would have the mike and start walking around the restaurant singing 'High Hopes' and 'Take Me Out to the Ballgame,'" Larry Andersen said. "The people were oblivious to who he was, but Harry worked the crowd like he was singing with Dean Martin or Sammy Davis, Jr."

Harry also did a lot of singing at parties. "High Hopes" evolved into his theme song after he began singing it at the annual spring training birthday party held in his honor. He also loved the Christmas parties that the Phillies held for their front office staff in the Veterans Stadium executive dining room. Harry would lead everyone in Christmas carols.

"He'd say, 'Let's all hold hands and sing the greatest song ever written about Christmas, 'Silent Night,'" Phillies video coordinator Dan Stephenson said. "We're all singing it and nobody knows the second verse but Harry. So Harry's singing away and we're all humming and laughing." His Christmas party routine always included a special version of "Twelve Days of Christmas." Harry would assign parts to everyone. For instance, he'd point to somebody and say, "Six Geese a Laying," and that became his or her part for the song.

During one of these Christmas parties, Harry was sitting at a table when he overheard someone mention the movie *Field of Dreams*. Harry got quiet, then started tearing up. "The greatest movie ever about the game of baseball," Harry said while sobbing. "He built the thing for his father." Eventually, the entire table had wet eyes. "Only Harry could get us crying at a Christmas party over *Field of Dreams*," Stephenson said.

Probably the biggest problem friends faced when going out with Harry was that they sometimes didn't get much of a chance to talk to him. If fans approached, Harry usually struck up a conversation. That happened one night when he was out with a group that included Charlie O'Gara, a cameraman who has worked in the Phillies television booth since 1971.

"We were having a few beers and talking," O'Gara said, "then all of a sudden we heard a scream, 'Harry Kalas!!!' And that was the end of it. Everyone in the bar came over to shake hands and talk to Harry, and just moved us out of the way. We never saw Harry the rest of the evening. We finally just finished our beers and left. We couldn't get near him. That's how he would attract people. I told everyone, 'He's the one guy, if you see him on the street, don't be afraid to walk up and introduce yourself because he will be a gentleman and talk to you. He talks to everyone.'"

After Harry moved in with Eileen in 1987, one of his favorite hangouts became the Towne House Restaurant, which was only a few minutes from his home in Media. Harry often would go there for dinner and stay for drinks. One time Harry was sitting at the Towne House bar when a couple of fellows from a wedding party in the dining room stopped in to find out the score of a ballgame. "They saw Harry, started talking to him and an hour later almost the entire wedding party was in the bar talking baseball with Harry, including the groom," bar manager Jerry Donahue said. "Every 20 minutes, one or two of the girls would come upstairs and say, 'Hey guys, we're having a wedding downstairs.' They'd say, 'Just a minute, just a minute.'"

When Harry was on the road working NFL games for Westwood One radio, he sometimes would spend hours in a bar waiting for his broadcast partner Rick Walker to show up. Harry routinely would fly into town on a Saturday afternoon, but Walker usually wouldn't get there until late that night because he'd be calling an afternoon college game in another city.

"By the time I'd get to the bar, everybody knows Harry, no matter what city we're in," Walker said. "I'd get there around midnight and he'd have three or four drinks lined up for me. You'd be looking at him like he wasn't conscious and he'd give you something on the next day's game like 'Thurman Thomas is two catches away from becoming the Bills' all-time leading receiver.' He'd blow me away in the state of mind that he was in. He had all this stuff locked in this incredible brain of his."

After last call, Walker often tried to get Harry sobered up by offering to take him out for breakfast. Harry always refused. Instead, he usually headed to his hotel room around 2:30 a.m., to catch a few hours sleep. "He'd say, 'I'll meet you in the lobby at 8 a.m., pal,'" Walker said. "I'm thinking he's not going to be able to do the game. I get down there at 8 and he's sitting there looking and feeling better than I do. I had maybe one or two drinks, and I'm in my late 40s, and this guy is in his 60s and he'd been there all day at the bar."

All this partying did catch up with Harry a few times. One night in the 1980s, Harry was pulled over in Philadelphia for swerving his car at three in the morning. A big Phillies fan, the officer let Harry off under two conditions: One, the officer was going to follow him home to make sure he arrived safely; and, two, Harry owed him a beer.

Two years later, that same policeman was out to dinner one night and noticed Harry at the bar. The officer walked over and said, "How about that beer you owe me, Harry?" Recognizing the face right away, Harry smiled and said, "Anything you want, Officer."

A couple of years later, Harry had a long night of drinking during a fundraiser event in Atlantic City with Whitey Ashburn. Harry drove down to the Jersey shore with Whitey, then decided to make the 80-mile drive home to Radnor that night. He was fine until he dropped Whitey off, but had trouble staying awake while driving alone. "Richie told him to sleep at his place, but Harry said he could make it home," said Jasmine Kalas, Harry's wife at the time.

Only a few blocks from his house, Harry dozed off. A couple of seconds later, he woke up to a thundering boom. He had crashed his Chrysler through a yard fence next to a home in his neighborhood. His windshield broke, sending glass everywhere, and there was so much damage that the car had to be sent to the wrecking yard. But Harry survived without a scratch.

"God was watching over him," Jasmine Kalas said.

So were the local police officers, who were Harry Kalas fans. The officers didn't question Harry about his drinking even though it was obvious that he'd had a few. Harry never asked to be cut a break, but was let off with only a warning. Harry was beyond thankful. When the officers drove him home, Harry wouldn't let them leave until he gave them tickets to a Phillies game.

Years later, Harry's luck ran out. On August 3, 1996, less than a month after his near-incident with the drunk in Atlantic City, Harry stopped into the Towne House with Eileen and a few friends following a Saturday matinee at Veterans Stadium, a 7-6 Phillies victory over Pittsburgh. Harry spent a good portion of the night talking, having drinks and enjoying the piano tunes of Bobby DiMuzio, a blind man who had worked for years at the Towne House. Bobby usually would get a ride to work from his mother and a lift home from a police officer. Harry took Bobby home once in a while, too, and sometimes they'd make a stop along the way to have a drink together. Harry's running joke was, "Bobby, I had a couple of beers, you better drive."

Bobby asked for a ride that night from Harry, who couldn't say no. Eileen ended up catching a ride home with a friend while Harry hung around at the Towne House until Bobby had finished his shift. Leaving the bar after midnight, Harry seemed fine to drive despite having had a few drinks.

"Harry was what I called a three-beer guy," bar manager Jerry Donahue said. "Once he had three beers, he stayed in that condition all night. You could tell he was drinking, but it was no big deal."

Harry was in no hurry on the way to Bobby DiMuzio's house. It was past 1 a.m., when Harry came to a stoplight. He slowed down, but didn't come to a complete stop before making a legal right on red. His timing was bad. A police officer was right there and pulled Harry over. He asked Harry if he'd been drinking.

"I've had a few," he told the officer.

The officer recognized Harry, but went by the book. Harry was ordered out of his car, handcuffed behind his back and led to the back seat of the police car. After another officer showed up to drive Harry's blind passenger home, Harry was taken to a local hospital for a blood test. Harry felt humiliated walking in and out of the hospital in handcuffs.

At one point, he said, "You know I'm not going to go anywhere, officer. You know who I am."

The cop responded, "I know who you are, but that doesn't mean that you get any special treatment."

When Harry's test results came back with a blood-alcohol level just above .10 percent, the legal limit at the time, he was arrested for Driving Under the Influence. Once Harry was processed at the police station, he was free to go home. However, when he phoned his wife for a ride, Eileen was so angry that her husband had been drinking and driving that she refused. "When he told me where he was, I said, 'Good for you. You can just stay there. I've had enough.' I didn't pick him up."

Courtesy of an officer, Harry arrived home around 2 a.m. The first thing he did was phone Jeff McCabe, his close friend who at the time was a police officer in a neighboring county. Harry wasn't phoning for help. He just needed to understand how much trouble he was in, and he didn't want to wait until morning to find out. Besides, he figured McCabe still would be up. Harry was right.

Richie Ashburn (right), the only invited guest at Harry's 1993 wedding to Eileen Vanwey, planted a wet one on his partner when the minister said, "You may kiss the bride."

During one of his first Christmases, Kane met his half-brothers Todd and Brad for the first time.

Pitcher Larry Andersen (bottom) signals "We're No. 2!" when Harry and the 1993 Phillies exit the plane in Philadelphia following their World Series loss to Toronto.

New Hall of Famer Whitey Ashburn gets a man-hug from best friend Harry while being honored before a 1995 Phillies game.

CHARLES FOX/PHILADELPHIA INQUIRER

Harry pauses as he enters the broadcast booth at Veterans Stadium to touch a Rich Ashburn plaque honoring Harry's longtime broadcast partner. This is a ritual Harry did every time he entered the booth which was named after Ashburn.

Harry, honored by the Phillies for making it to Cooperstown, takes a victory lap in front of 58,000 adoring fans on Harry Kalas Day at Veterans Stadium.

At his home in Media, Pa., Harry spotted deer from his back porch and amused neighbors by retrieving the newspaper while dressed in pajamas.

After seeing his Hall of Fame plaque for the first time, Harry posed for a family picture. From left to right: sister-in-law Mary Kalas, brother Jim, Eileen, Harry, sons Kane and Brad, and stepdaughter Julie.

After partying for years with Harry, former small-town New Jersey mayor Joe Nunes was in Cooperstown to help honor his friend.

Taking his place in Cooperstown among baseball's greats, Harry ended his Hall of Fame speech by reading a touching poem that he wrote especially for Phillies fans.

PHILADELPHIA DAILY NEWS

In the front row of a massive crowd that included thousands of Phillies fans, Eileen Kalas and son Kane lead the applause for Harry.

During Harry's 30th anniversary celebration in 2000, the co-emcees dressed the part—Glenn Wilson (right) played Harry and Darren Daulton impersonated Whitey.

Three days before being inducted into the Baseball Hall of Fame in July 2002, Phillies players came out of the dugout and tipped their hats before Harry sang "Take Me Out to the Ball Game" during the seventh-inning stretch at Chicago's Wrigley Field.

Many Phillies greats were on hand, but it was Harry given the honor of changing the "countdown clock" for the final game at Veterans Stadium in 2003.

Harry relaxing in his home office in Media, PA.

Harry belted out “High Hopes,” his theme song since the 1970s, while getting doused by Ryan Howard after the Phillies won the 2007 NL East title.

With confidant Jeff McCabe (right) along as his guest, Harry attended a 2008 White House party which included a meeting with President George W. Bush and First Lady Laura Bush.

In his 38th year with the Phillies and 44th year in the majors, Harry finally got to make a championship call in the 2008 World Series, won by his Fightins.

Harry is all smiles during the Phillies 2008 World Series championship parade, but was in pain that day due to health issues that weren't public knowledge.

Harry posing with his beloved Phillies' 2008 World Series championship trophy.

©AL TIELEMANS/SPORTS ILLUSTRATED/GETTY IMAGES

Wearing his son's jacket because he'd lost so much weight, Harry threw out the first pitch before what would become his final Phillies home game only days after leaving a hospital bed against medical advice.

Four days after their father's passing, Harry's three sons—Kane, Brad and Todd (left to right)—wait to throw out the ceremonial first pitches during a Citizens Bank Park pre-game tribute.

Before Harry's coffin was closed, his body was wrapped in a special blanket that funeral director Mark McCafferty had custom designed with a baseball motif that included the Hall of Famer's famous home run call.

As 9,000 Phillies fans listen to "Bridge Over Troubled Water" with teary eyes, Phillies manager Charlie Manuel (front left) helps guide Harry's coffin into the hearse near the conclusion of the ballpark memorial.

Had Harry lived to see President Obama (right) accept a Phillies jersey from the 2008 World Champions at the White House, the legendary broadcaster would have been there without stepdaughter Julie since he was not permitted to bring a guest.

© RANDY MILLER

Amidst the final resting places of Civil War generals at historic Laurel Hill Cemetery in Philadelphia, Harry's gravesite includes four Veterans Stadium seats and eventually will be highlighted by a massive microphone headstone.

COURTESY OF LAWRENCE NOWLAN

Sculptor Lawrence Nowlan works on a 24-inch prototype of a seven-foot-high bronze statue of Harry that is being funded by public donations and will be presented to the Phillies as a gift.

McCabe wasn't even home yet when Harry reached him on his cell phone.

"Hey, Pal, I got into a little jam and I want to tell you right off the bat, I'm not calling you for any help," Harry told his friend. After hearing about what happened, McCabe told Harry, "You're not going to jail. It's your first offense and there was no car accident. You're going to lose your license and probably going to have to go to a driving school, and if I know you, you'll be at the head of the class."

Harry laughed at McCabe's attempt at humor, then followed with an important question. "I know this will get out in the media. What are your thoughts?"

"Harry, how do you want to respond?"

"I just want to take responsibility for what I did because I was wrong. I learned a lesson."

The Philadelphia newspapers reported on Harry's DUI, but didn't make a big deal of it. "Harry accepts full responsibility for his actions and his behavior," William H. Eastburn, Harry's longtime lawyer, told the *Philadelphia Daily News* the day after the arrest. "He's going to resolve it as promptly and appropriately as humanly possible and will accept any of the necessary consequences. This is a very responsible citizen."

McCabe, who had worried Harry's arrest would become a major story, felt the Philadelphia media responded sympathetically. "There was a blurb and I told Harry, 'See that, you're too good of a man to throw stones at.'"

McCabe's initial prediction was correct. Harry lost his license for three months and had to attend driver's education school. "I would have liked to have helped Harry," McCabe said. "I couldn't. But even if I could, with his integrity he wouldn't have taken the help. I guarantee it."

After losing his driver's license, Harry often had to rely on a family friend for rides, an arrangement Eileen Kalas insisted continue even after Harry regained his driver's license. She always worried when Harry was driving home after a few drinks even though he often wasn't legally drunk.

Driver or no driver, Whitey Ashburn was worried about Harry, too. Two months after the DUI, McCabe went to a Phillies game at Veterans Stadium and stopped in the television booth to see Harry. During his visit, McCabe was approached by Ashburn.

"Jeff, I know Harry's hurting over that DUI," Whitey said. "Do me a favor.

Take care of that man. I love that man."

Touched by Ashburn's show of affection for Harry, McCabe got teary-eyed. "He's fine," he told Whitey. "He's embarrassed and it's over."

But Whitey wanted Harry to slow down on his drinking. He didn't want to lose his best friend.

"Dad got on Harry about his drinking like nobody else," Richard Ashburn said. "He really would bust on Harry . . . in a brotherly fashion, not in a scolding fashion. Harry listened. Did he listen that well? No. But I think Harry respected my dad for not being one of the people who just said 'Yes' to him all the time. Dad flat-out told Harry, 'You're going to kill yourself, and that can't happen.'"

In addition to alcohol, Harry had another issue to deal with on the road—temptation. Both of his wives believe that Harry's extramarital behavior was fueled by his desire to live the stereotypical ballplayer life, even though many of his married friends in the game were able to stay faithful. When Harry strayed sexually, he often confessed his transgression to a close friend, usually with tears in his eyes. Harry's missteps caused him a lot of personal shame, guilt and pain, which some of his pals traced back to his religious upbringing. His late father, after all, was a minister. During his confessions to Jeff McCabe, Harry was encouraged to move on and try to avoid making the same mistake again. When Harry ended up succumbing to the same enticements, he'd get even more disappointed in himself.

Former major leaguer Dickie Noles understands as well as anyone the temptations that Harry faced.

In the early 1980s, Noles emerged as one of the best young arms in baseball as a hard-throwing, right-handed pitcher for the Phillies and Chicago Cubs. He had his good moments over 11 years in the majors, but his alcoholism undermined his career. "Alcohol, no matter what people want to say, can be the greatest social drug in the world," Noles said.

Dickie had a dark side as a young man. The more he drank, the tougher he got. The tougher he got, the more fights he got into. While with the Cubs, he was sentenced to 13 days in jail after a bar fight in Cincinnati that ended with him kicking at police officers. That was April 8, 1983. He hasn't had a drop of alcohol since. He was 26 when he stopped drinking and he turned 53 in 2009, so he's been sober now more than half his life. Today, Noles is a dedicated born-again Christian and a longtime Phillies employee who counsels players at all levels in the organization through personal problems.

Noles never worked with Harry Kalas, but he believes that he understands what Harry went through.

"Being on the road is a difficult thing, especially for the married guys," Noles said. "You get done with a game, you call your wife—now do I lay in bed and watch TV? There's nothing wrong with that, and many of the athletes have found out that that's okay, but you also really want to fit in. You start throwing this macho-ism that we have and you start doing things that you probably wouldn't have done. A lot of men battle with that sexual stuff. Who wouldn't? You see a beautiful girl and you have things that go through your mind. When you throw booze in there. . . ."

In August 1998, Eileen Kalas made a Phillies road trip to Denver. One night after a game, Harry was out in a bar with Eileen when she asked, "Harry, have you ever gone out on me?" Harry paused for a second, then started confessing.

"Well . . . once," he said.

"Really?" Eileen said with a shocked look on her face.

"Well, maybe it was more than once," Harry said.

Looking back on that night, Eileen says, "The bartender heard the conversation and ducked. It was like, 'Oh my god, if she has a gun, she's going to kill him.' But I was so interested. I wasn't angry at the time. I got angry later."

A friend of Harry's asked him why he confessed to his wife. Harry responded with one of his favorite Shakespearian quotes—"To thine own self be true. . . ."

Eileen knew Harry had fooled around on his first wife, Jasmine—that's how Eileen and Harry had gotten together—but she never thought that he'd cheat on her. She thought about leaving him, but she still loved Harry. On top of that, they had a young son. Kane was just nine.

"I think if I was younger, I would have packed up, taken Kane and just gone," said Eileen, who was 47 at the time. "But I was older and curious. Why? Was it because I had quit drinking?"

Eileen gave up booze in the early 1990s after she and Harry had a bad, alcohol-related argument. "When we'd drink, we'd fight," she said.

Once she stopped drinking, Eileen still went out to bars with Harry, but she feared her husband thought that she wasn't as much fun anymore. She wondered if that's what led him into the arms of other women.

"I think there was some animosity there because Harry no longer had a drinking buddy," said Bob Smith, a longtime Kalas friend. "Harry was a party man."

Once Harry had admitted in Denver that he'd been unfaithful, Eileen started snooping. In his briefcase, she found a picture with Harry and five airline stewardesses. Harry insisted that they were just fans, but Eileen was fed up. At this point, she said they were either going to go to counseling or split up. Harry chose counseling. And that's where this often troubled chapter of Harry's life found a happy ending.

"Harry really loved Eileen," Rick Walker said. "He always had a lot of options. The guy was smooth as silk, but he tightened up his belt buckle. He called me and said, 'Hey pal, it's the end of an era. Eileen got into my briefcase. I gotta go get some help. I can't afford to screw this relationship up. I love her. I love Kane. I can't lose her.' And he was dead serious. And I'm telling you what, from that moment on, he was a different guy on the road. Completely different guy. He made up his mind. He wasn't bullshitting."

Eileen Kalas recruited a local practicing licensed psychologist for psychotherapy sessions. Dr. Jack Porter, whose office in Wynnewood was just 11 miles from the Kalas home, became more than a therapist to the family. In time, he also was a trusted friend. During his sessions, Dr. Porter met with Harry and Eileen alone and together, and also met with their son, Kane, who was nine when his parents began working to save their marriage.

"Eileen was a major motivator for professional intervention on the basis of family values," said Dr. Porter, who received written permission from Eileen to discuss his sessions with her and Harry. "Out of that, she had exerted a strong desire for the family to be reinforced in a positive, strengthening way. When Harry had divulged to Eileen some of his behavior, he agreed to evolve into self-understanding. They were learning experiences for him that there's a better way for having a lifestyle of doing what he did. He proved it by still being happy in other ways. And don't forget that Harry was a product of the baseball world, where their code is very different."

By all accounts, the psychotherapy sessions conducted over a number of years—sometimes on a regular basis, sometimes less frequently—helped Harry a great deal.

"Dr. Porter was wonderful with Harry," Eileen said. "Harry never thought that deep in his life. While going through the counseling, Harry said one day that he had a 'deep thought' and he was real proud of himself. I wrote it on the calendar to be a smartass, but I asked him if it felt good. He said, 'It really did.' He was thinking deeper instead of shallow—baseball, drinking, women. Psychology is great. Harry could take things and put them in slots, then put that away. When he was home, that was a slot. For me, everything touches each other. You can't have an affair and not have it affect your home life. Harry could compartmentalize. How can somebody's brain work so differently?"

Eileen says the therapy helped her move on, too. In the end, it made her understand herself and Harry. She credits Dr. Porter for strengthening their marriage and making their final years together some of their best.

"I forgave Harry, but I didn't forget," Eileen said. "I had to figure this out. What is it about me that I'm picking these types of men? I'd done it before. Where does this come from? Why is he doing this? When he's home, he's so sweet, so in love, so kind, so good to his son. What is it? I thought, 'Well, I can leave and pull Kane away from a wonderful father, or I can figure this thing out.'"

She chose the second option, and never regretted it because Harry was so receptive to changing and strengthening his behavior and values.

"His honesty was superb," Dr. Porter said. "There was nothing he would deny when confronted. He worked very, very hard, and it's not easy for a man like that to recall childhood matters, very sensitive family matters. He knew it was necessary. He repaired very well before he passed away."

Dr. Porter, who also is a university professor, considered Harry a unique patient because of his fascinating ability to find the good in all people.

"You have to understand Harry's concept to change," the doctor said. "He's probably the most authentic person I ever met. The man was consistent to who he was. He had a strong conviction—'I like you who you are. Don't change me and I won't change you.'—His acceptance of people was amazing.

"He had two facets to his personality, one in the booth where he was an exciting broadcaster who was adored by the players and respected by everybody. In everyday life, on the other hand, he was very subdued. He kept his emotions inwardly. He was very much in control of his feelings, his love. All of that was very self-contained. And his two-faceted personality type of struggle, the broadcast booth and everyday life, was based on 'live and let live,' and 'I love you as you are.' His voice resonated with a message of authenticity, caring, love, dignity, and that's where people who knew him and didn't even know him responded. He led his own life and followed the philosophy to be 'who you are.' When he did change, he did it on his own because of family values, not because of guilt. He was convinced that it was the right thing to do."

Harry and Eileen's young son, Kane Kalas, also got help from by Dr. Porter through what proved to be the most trying period of his childhood. "It was difficult for me because I wasn't really as accustomed to bad times," Kane said. "For me, there weren't too many problems until I was in fourth or fifth grade. It was difficult for awhile, but I told myself that there are certain things that I want to do and I'm not going to let this get in the way. I think I was able to overcome that, but it was a tough time for me."

Although Harry stopped seeing other women, he did continue drinking for a time. In 2003, Harry didn't use his driver friend one night and returned home drunk. Eileen threw a fit.

"That's it, I've had it," Eileen yelled. "I'm not going to be in this house and have you kill a family drinking and driving."

Eileen hurled three glass ashtrays in Harry's direction. She missed on purpose, but made her point. "I told him, 'You better duck.' I didn't try to hit him. I tried to scare him, and I did. After I scared him, there was glass everywhere. I said, 'You can clean it up.'"

Eileen told Harry that he had to stop drinking or she would leave him. "The affairs we were working on," she said. "It was the drinking and driving. He knew better. I took the pictures off the wall and said, 'I'm moving. You have a great life. I'm not going to be there when you kill somebody.' He quit drinking within a few weeks. He just quit."

After giving up alcohol, Harry became even more romantic with Eileen, like he'd been during their early years together. For Valentine's Day and other special occasions, he'd leave a note for his wife on the refrigerator telling her to go to a different part of the house, where there'd be another note with instructions. He'd send her on a wild goose chase all over their home before ending it with a jewelry box containing diamond earrings or a ring or necklace. "Harry was like a 17-year-old kid putting these notes all over the house," Eileen said. "It was cute."

In their final years together, Eileen saw only the best of Harry. They stopped arguing and had mostly good times. "To see somebody grow was so beautiful, and I was growing, too," Eileen said.

Some of Harry's friends felt differently. They missed the old Harry, who always had been the life of the party. They wondered if Harry was content being clean and sober.

"The last couple years, he didn't seem to be the same happy person as he once was," friend Bob Smith said. "You could just see it."

Larry Andersen agreed. "To me, when he stopped drinking, that was a part of Harry. I don't know if that's the right thing to say, but Harry and a beer or Harry and a see-through was like soup and a sandwich, a horse and carrots. It's like when he gave up half of that, he gave up half of his life. I'm not trying to make him sound like he was a crazy drunken alcoholic. He liked sitting around having a beer and talking about baseball."

On the other hand, Kane Kalas saw a transformation for the better. "I noticed a physical change. He lost a little bit of weight after he quit drinking. But I guess the more important change is I would say that he was more family-oriented. He'd always been close to me. I'd say he was more close after he stopped drinking."

A month before his death, Harry told a reporter that he was content with his life since giving up alcohol. "I'm not so much of a night owl anymore," he said.

A skilled poet, Harry further showed his late-in-life contentment by composing a Mother's Day ode for his wife:

MY EILEEN
As beautiful as a rainbow painted on the graying sky
As precious as a star sapphire on an endless dessert lie
Strong as the pounding surf
Yet gentle as Blue Grass turf
Her children were her passion
And they received all that she could fashion
But her children were more than three
She extended her caring to so many
If ever a soul could make a world right
Eileen would try with all her might
Her spirituality sent out a glow

So those of us blessed to love her would know
That Eileen was by our side
If we need her, she would guide
With affection, caring and love
Her spirit was a gift from above
A lady of such beauty could always win
But the true beauty of Eileen is within
From the day that our eyes met, I will never forget
This is the lady that will give the most beautiful gift
A reason to give, to care and to share
And she was always there
And so, I thank the Lord above
For the only woman I have ever loved

This loving tribute to Eileen, while obviously heartfelt and sincere, ignored Harry's earlier loves. While there is no question that Harry was deeply in love with Eileen, he previously mentioned to close friends about the love that he once felt for his first wife, Jasmine, as well as for the college girlfriend whom he gave up to appease his father.

In his last year, Harry expressed his happiness with life in general to Jeff McCabe, a longtime confidant.

"I love my life," Harry told his friend. "I'm a homebody now. I love being home with my wife. I still love my job. I love the Phillies. I love the fans. I just don't have the desire to do what I used to do."

Remembering their talk, Jeff McCabe said, "I was just trying to make sure he's still happy. I was trying to find out how he was really feeling. He was still positive about life. He felt totally blessed. As for Harry's drinking and the other things . . . all people have weaknesses. Harry's was to overdo it when he was out. Once he stopped drinking, Harry would just go to his room and read a book when he was on the road. He was happy doing that. When he was home, he was happy spending more time with his family. He loved life."

Despite all the alcohol and marital problems he had faced, Harry Kalas enjoyed more than his share of fun in life. After he was gone, a caller to a Philadelphia sports talk-radio show said enviously, "I'd rather live 73 Harry Kalas years than 100 of anyone else's."

CALL TO THE HALL

Harry Kalas stopped for a beer at Yankee Doodle Inn on his ride home from a late 1970s Phillies game at Veterans Stadium. Jeff McCabe, a police officer and new drinking buddy at the time, was waiting for him.

"Harry, you called a good game tonight," McCabe said after they took a seat at the bar.

"It's God-given, pal . . . God-given," Harry responded in his familiar baritone. "And I thank God for that every day. Every day."

Harry was blessed with special genes. His father had a similarly low-pitched and compelling voice. Reverend Harry H. Kalas utilized his vocal cords to preach and further his work as a highly respected clergyman. His son Harry used that voice to celebrate what has become a sort of cultural religion to many Americans—Major League Baseball. Working as a professional baseball announcer became young Harry's dream before he reached adolescence. Once his voice changed and took on his father's rich, resonant tone, it became his destiny.

"How many guys have a voice like that?" asked Jerry Coleman, the Hall of Fame voice of the San Diego Padres. "I told Harry, he's a lucky turkey."

The second-deepest male vocal designation, baritones like Harry sound manly and authoritative to most Americans.

"In the American culture, the people who sell the trucks and beer are those that have this lower, more sustained voice quality—not so strong in its consonants, but more the vowels and that booming kind of quality with a little raspiness with it, which seems to be macho in our society," said Ingo Titze, Director for the National Center for Voice and Speech. "Probably in Europe or Japan or other places, they wouldn't think of that as a macho voice. The Samurais and Nazis were people of power, but they didn't speak with low voices at all. They spoke with very elevated-pitch voices."

Harry Kalas owned one of the most recognizable voices in America during his lifetime, but not just due to the low, distinctive tone which he inherited from his father. Harry's voice may have sounded like a gift from God, but it was also a well-trained work of art.

"It wasn't just the quality, but the pace in which Harry Kalas spoke and how he timed himself and what syllables that he stressed," Ingo Titze said. "He was more than voice quality. To me, it's in the delivery. When I hear the NFL Films, he paces himself quite smoothly. When you talk about football and the action that goes with it, most people scream and get excited. Harry's voice was very well-paced and measured. That with the low voice quality gave it its appeal. It had a certain intelligence with it."

To keep the tool of his trade healthy, Harry would suck on Halls throat lozenges. His other helpful medicine of choice was his nicotine habit, or at least so he thought.

"Harry kept telling me that smoking kept his voice the way it was," high school buddy Wally Baumgartner said in 2009. "I told him he was full of crap."

Nearly 60 years of heavy smoking did change Harry's voice. The Harry Kalas who arrived in Philadelphia in 1971 and the Harry Kalas at the turn of the 21st century didn't sound all that much alike. Harry had a baritone his whole adult life, but his two-pack-a-day Parliament cigarettes habit had made the voice noticeably deeper over time.

"It was one of the few times in which Harry Kalas was dead wrong," said Dr. Robert Sataloff, a senior associate dean of Drexel University and head of the school's Otolaryngology department, who also works as a voice coach and opera singer. "Smoking is fundamentally unhealthy for the voice, and it can lead to cancer, which can cost somebody the voice altogether.

"However, in the process of causing voice problems, it causes irritation and swelling that give the voice a certain grittiness, so Harry's not the only person who used that unhealthy method to his advantage. There are other sportscasters, blues singers, nightclub entertainers and movie actors who have distinctive voices created either through smoking or sometimes yelling and intentionally ruining their voices. Most of these people have shortened vocal lives and sometimes shortened lives. Some people can get away with that."

Harry got away with it. But like many longtime smokers, his voice deepened over time from a disorder known as Reinke's edema, which is a swelling on the edges of the vocal folds.

"It lowers the voice," said Dr. Sataloff, who has written more than three-dozen books and published over 600 articles on vocal issues. "Usually when people get that from smoking and then they stop smoking, that swelling does not go away. The damage is done unless you remove the swelling surgically. Harry could have stopped smoking long ago and he still would have had that low voice that he liked without putting his larynx, his lungs and life at risk. I would have recommended that he stop smoking, and if he didn't like the changes in his voice from when the swelling and irritation from the smoking went down, that he take a few sessions with a voice coach who would be able to show him how to access whatever sound that he wanted without the cigarettes. Actors do it all the time."

Healthy or not, there's no debating that Harry's methods took him far in life, even if they did shorten it by a few years. He was beloved in Philadelphia as the voice of the Phillies for 39 years, known by sports fans across the country for his NFL Films narrations and recognized by most everyone else for his voiceovers for Campbell's Chunky Soup and Coors Light commercials.

"Harry managed to go through a long career with essentially no vocal health issues, which is not all that common in people who have to talk as much as he did, especially over noise and with as much passion as he was able to express in his voice," Dr. Sataloff said. "I thought it was a great voice. It was distinctive. It was expressive. He was able to use it over a wide range of pitch, emotion and loudness for long periods of time. As soon as you turned on the radio, you knew exactly who it was, and it was the identity of the Phillies and, in many ways, the identity of the city. From all aspects, I consider it an outstanding and singular voice that will remain one of the sounds of the century."

KDKA in Pittsburgh aired the first Major League Baseball game on radio on August 21, 1921. Harold Arlin, a writer for the *Pittsburgh Post-Gazette* and grandfather to former major league pitcher Steve Arlin, called the Pirates 8-5 victory over the Phillies from a box seat near the first-base dugout. Before too long, baseball and radio would go together like apple pie and ice cream. For decades, radio became the primary link to generations of fans and their teams, and the guys in the booth emerged as the leading storytellers in their era. Even after television debuted in 1939 and found its way into millions of American homes by the 1950s and '60s, most fans experienced baseball primarily through the radio until the 1970s when Major League Baseball began airing more games on TV. Like the early broadcasting greats Red Barber and Mel Allen, Harry Kalas honed his skills doing play-by-play for a radio audience.

"I think broadcasting baseball on radio is the toughest sport of all to do," Cincinnati Reds Hall of Fame broadcaster Marty Brennaman said. "I did 13 years of television, and I don't like TV. You simply cannot broadcast baseball unless you can ad-lib intelligently, because we all know nothing happens until the pitch is thrown."

During his early days announcing baseball in Iowa and Hawaii, Harry worked only on radio. He did some television work during his six seasons in Houston, but just about all the games he announced for the Astros aired exclusively on radio. For the second half of his career, especially from the 1990s on, Harry spent most of his games in a television booth. Calling baseball for radio and TV audiences presents different challenges, but Harry became a master of both mediums. He expertly painted word pictures on radio and filled in the blanks with a lot less talking on television.

"Harry Kalas was one of those great announcers who could transcend TV and radio," said Atlanta Braves announcer Chip Caray, a third-generation baseball broadcaster who is the son of Skip Caray and grandson of Harry Caray. "On radio you've got to talk. On TV, you don't have to say a word. You can let the viewer hear the sound of bat hitting ball, the crowd roaring. Those are the kinds of things Harry was excellent at, and he also had that voice, which was an unbelievable gift."

"He didn't give you too much chatter in the middle of the game," said Scott Graham, Harry's partner in the Phillies booth from 1999 to 2006. "And then there's that dramatic moment and the hair stands up on your arms because of the way he brings it to you. Harry was consistent every single day."

The Phillies have boasted their share of standout broadcasters over the years. Chuck Thompson (1946-48), Herb Carneal (1954) and By Saam (1939-49, 1955-75) all preceded Harry Kalas into the Baseball Hall of Fame. Saam was regarded as a legend in Philadelphia, although many believe that it is more for his longevity than broadcast brilliance. "The Phillies have a great history in broadcasting and Harry's at the summit," said Rich Westcott, a Phillies historian and author.

Starting in 1961, Harry began his climb when calling Hawaii Islanders' Pacific Coast League games.

"When you listened to Harry early on and with the Phillies, the basic patterns are the same," said Marty Chase, one of Harry's broadcast partners in Hawaii. "What really made him extraordinary in my mind was he always had an accurate and measured call of the game. And he almost never made a mistake. Having done some play-by-play, I know how tough that is. People often said Harry had no sense of humor when he was in Hawaii, but I think he had a very dry and very sharp sense of humor that he slipped into his broadcasts at the right time."

Listening to Harry on the air offered fans so much more than the chance to follow a baseball game. For Philadelphia attorney Howard K. Goldstein, it took him back to a time when he was a rabid New York Yankees fan while growing up in Brooklyn during the 1950s and '60s.

"A highlight of my childhood days was listening to the voices of Mel Allen and Red Barber broadcast Yankees games," Goldstein said. "While Red had become more neutral in his announcing by that time in his Hall of Fame career, Mel remained an irrepressible and unapologetic Yankees fan. As a result of Mel's over-the-top enthusiasm, I developed a particular fondness listening to his portion of the broadcasts. When the Yankees canned Mel after the 1964 season, for reasons that have never been adequately explained, I thought that I would never again hear the likes of him.

"After moving to Philadelphia in 1978, I slowly but surely began to develop a fan relationship with my new hometown team, the Phillies. One of the main things that I initially liked about the Phillies was Harry. Kalas' all-knowing voice and unwaveringly optimistic spirit drew me into its welcoming embrace. While Phillies fans were died-in-the-wool pessimists, their beloved lead announcer appeared to be the all-time optimist. The disconnect between the two never made sense to me, but it really didn't matter. What did matter was that listening to Harry broadcast Phillies games brought me back to the Brooklyn of my youth. Harry was Mel Allen reincarnated."

Players came and went, but Harry Kalas served as a mainstay of baseball in Philadelphia for almost four decades. His excellence not only won over the fans, but also many players, some of whom originally came to know him during their youths.

"I truly didn't consider myself a major leaguer until I heard him do his first call for me," said Mike Piazza, a 12-time All-Star catcher for the Los Angeles Dodgers and New York Mets who grew up outside of Philadelphia. "I remember when I was a kid watching him on TV. That inspired me and was a big key in my desire to want to become a major leaguer because Harry was so passionate and did his job so well."

"It was a highlight for me when he called my first major league home run," said Ruben Amaro, Jr., a Philadelphia native who went on to play for his hometown team and later become its general manager. "He brought a tape of it to me in the locker room right afterwards. I still have it."

"I made a play on Tony Perez in the hole in 1975," said Larry Bowa, the Phillies' shortstop from 1970 to 1981. "Harry said on air, "That's the greatest play I've ever seen in my life.' He went on and on and on. Somebody said, 'You gotta hear this call.' I got goose bumps when I heard it."

Phillies alumni Mickey Morandini and Ricky Bottalico each played in an All-Star Game during their time with the franchise. But both may be known in Philadelphia as much for how Harry ingeniously pronounced their names as for what they did on the field.

"People still come up to me when I'm in Philadelphia and say my name the way Harry said it," said Morandini, who ended his playing career in 2000. Harry would draw out and linger over the syllables of Mickey's name, pronouncing it 'Mic-key Mor-an-di-ni', as if it was some fabulous Italian dessert.

"I know Harry loved saying my name and Mickey's name," Bottalico said. "We had the right amount of syllables and it just rolled off his tongue. I'm proud to say that I was one of the names that he liked to say."

Before even meeting Harry, Phillies manager Charlie Manuel says he used to listen to him on HBO's *Inside the NFL* just to hear his voice. "It wasn't because I needed to know the scores," laughed Manuel.

In addition to vocal talent, homework played a key role in Harry's excellence as an announcer. "I was always amazed at how prepared he was," Phillies radio broadcaster Scott Franzke said. "Harry would look a couple days ahead on starting pitchers. He never was on the Internet, but he would have the PR notes and the media guides that he'd look through. He'd say something every night about a guy and, nine times out of 10, I didn't know those numbers yet."

The National Association of Sportscasters and Sports writers honored Harry for his efforts by naming him Pennsylvania Sportscaster of the Year 17 times from 1978 to 1996. Harry also earned Mid-Atlantic and national Emmy Awards.

"Here was a guy who was a giant in the business," Hall of Fame broadcaster Ernie Harwell said. "I think everybody that ever heard that great voice of Harry Kalas felt that he was a very close friend of theirs. That's the epitome, I think, and the goal that every announcer likes to reach.

"I think it's a great responsibility because you are amazed that people care that much about you. But I believe that if a man comes into a region and begins to broadcast . . . people have to listen to him and they take him wherever they go. He goes on the picnics and to the mountains and the beaches and the cars, and places like that, and he really becomes part of the family. They spend more time with him in the summer than their brothers and sisters, wives and husbands. Because of that, it's a great responsibility on the part of the announcer. I think of the thing that's a thread through all the announcers' careers is that they all deeply appreciate the want and affection that they get back from their listening audience."

Harry loved his fans as much as they loved him, and he showed it. Many of his fans can still picture Harry waving to them with tears streaming down his face on July 29, 2000—Harry Kalas Night at Veterans Stadium. Honored for his 30 years with the Phillies, Harry was overwhelmed that evening during a touching pre-game ceremony in which two of his favorite alumni served as co-emcees—Glenn Wilson posed as Harry in a white jacket, white shoes and black pants; and Darren Daulton masqueraded as Richie Ashburn in a newsboy hat. Wilson also did his imitation of Harry singing "High Hopes," a rendition self-described as "awful."

Deep into what would become a seventh consecutive losing season, the

Phillies drew 35,189 that night, their fifth-biggest crowd of the year. All fans received a special giveaway, a Talkin' Harry Doll. When the six-inch-high plush doll's belly was tapped, Harry's voice called out three of his famous calls: "Watch that baby, way outta here!" . . . "Struck him out!" . . . "Phils win!"

"Best promotion we had in years," Phillies chairman Bill Giles said.

By 2000, Giles was campaigning to get Harry Kalas into the broadcaster's wing of the Baseball Hall of Fame. Giles had previously written a few letters on Harry's behalf, and was disappointed when younger and lesser experienced announcers were chosen instead.

"Not that you're going to be selected based on the years that you serve, but Harry had been around so much longer than me and had maintained such a reputation in the industry and was so well-liked that I felt like he should have gone in before I did," said Marty Brennaman, who entered the Hall as the 2000 winner of the Ford C. Frick Award

Ford Frick served as the National League President from 1934 to 1951 and was baseball's third Commissioner from 1951 to 1965. As league president, he was praised for threatening to suspend St. Louis Cardinals players who were planning to protest Jackie Robinson breaking baseball's color barrier in 1947. As Commissioner, he was criticized for keeping Babe Ruth in the record books as baseball's single-season home run champion for a 154-game season alongside of Roger Maris, who broke the record in 1961 during a 162-game season. Frick also was instrumental in the founding of the National Baseball Hall of Fame and Museum in Cooperstown, N.Y., which was dedicated in 1939, three years after five all-time greats (Ty Cobb, Walter Johnson, Christy Mathewson, Honus Wagner and Ruth) were elected to its inaugural class.

The Hall of Fame launched the annual Ford C. Frick Award in 1978 to recognize a broadcaster for "major contributions to baseball." Mel Allen and Red Barber were elected the first season. One broadcasting great has followed every year since, including legends such as Ernie Harwell (1981), Vin Scully (1982), Jack Brickhouse (1983), Jack Buck (1985) and Harry Caray (1989).

"When you think of Harry Kalas, you think of the legends—Vin Scully, Harry Caray, Jack Brickhouse," said Merrill Reese, the popular voice of the NFL's Philadelphia Eagles since 1977. "He belongs right in that group, announcers as big as or bigger than the players they cover."

Harry Kalas just missed out on winning the Frick Award in 2001 when

Felo Ramírez, the Spanish-language radio voice of the Florida Marlins, was voted into the Hall. A month after Ramírez's induction, Harry and Jack Buck made a wager while dining together during a Phillies' visit to St. Louis.

"Harry, I bet you $100 that you get in next year," Buck said.

"That's $100 that I would love to lose," Harry said. "You're on."

January 29, 2002 started out a typical winter day for Harry Kalas, who made some horse racing bets and then followed the races on television. After taking an afternoon shower, Harry's wife Eileen told him that he'd missed a phone call from Hall of Fame President Dale Petroskey.

Harry called Petroskey back. At age 65, Harry the K finally was a Hall of Famer.

The first person Harry phoned was his buddy Jeff McCabe.

"Good news and bad news, pal," Harry told his friend. "I just missed the last race by two lengths and it would have paid off good. And . . . I just got off the phone with the Hall of Fame. I'm in."

Phillies and baseball fans throughout the country rejoiced when hearing the news that Harry was joining St. Louis Cardinals shortstop Ozzie Smith in the 2002 Hall of Fame class to be inducted on July 28 in Cooperstown. Filled with pride over the great honor, Harry immediately began adding the inscription "HOF 2002" below his autographs.

A few weeks after receiving word, Harry headed to spring training to begin a 2002 season that for him would be unlike any other. His fan mail multiplied, but Harry still answered every piece. A day didn't pass when he wasn't reminded in person of his new exalted status by friends, colleagues and fans.

During his last working day before being inducted, Harry was given a touching sendoff before leaving for Hall of Fame weekend. With the Phillies in Chicago, Harry was asked by the Cubs to carry on the tradition of the late Cubs broadcaster Harry Caray by singing "Take Me Out to the Ballgame" during the seventh-inning stretch. When Harry was announced to the Wrigley Field crowd, every Phillies player and coach stepped out of the dugout to tip his cap towards the press box. Harry received a rousing ovation from the Cubs fans that day for his lively delivery of the classic baseball song. The next month, Harry received a letter from the Cubs thanking him for his "riveting rendition."

Back in 1998, a few months after Harry Caray passed away, Harry had first sang "Take Me Out to the Ballgame" during Wrigley's seventh-inning stretch.

On that occasion, Harry purposely included the line "root, root, root for the Cubbies," which earned him some ribbing from Phillies personnel. He did it in tribute to Caray, an old drinking buddy. "He and my grandfather were very close," Chip Caray said. "When Harry Kalas did that, that was a real highlight to me. He had a great baritone voice, and he belted it out perfect."

Following their mid-week series at Wrigley Field, the Phillies headed from Chicago to Atlanta while Harry Kalas flew back to Philadelphia to pack for the Hall of Fame weekend. With his wife in the passenger seat, Harry then drove the 264 miles from his home to Cooperstown, a sleepy little village of 2,000 residents nestled along the Susquehanna River in upstate New York.

After arriving on Friday for the Sunday induction, Harry was kept extremely busy during his first two days in Cooperstown attending one official function after another. A lot of his family and friends were in town, but Harry didn't get much time with them. When touring the Hall on Friday morning, Harry did get a chance to mingle with some of the thousands of Phillies fans who had made the trip in his honor.

"It was neat to see Harry walk around Cooperstown and see all the people coming up to him," longtime *Philadelphia Daily News* baseball writer Paul Hagen said. "He never was in a hurry, always had time for an autograph or to have his picture taken. I remember thinking this is the way I would hope I would be or anyone would be if they made it big. Everybody wanted a little bit of his time. If 10 people want two or three minutes, it adds up. But somehow Harry always had time for everybody, and it was really fun to watch."

At the Hall, Harry made an emotional visit to Richie Ashburn's plaque. "My partner, Don Richard Ashburn," Harry said. Admiring the marker of immortality that Whitey had earned as a result of his stellar playing career. Harry reached out with his right hand and touched the plaque tenderly.

On Saturday, another Phillies legend was inducted into the Hall of Fame. Well, sort of. That morning, a mock induction ceremony was held at the Hall for a Phillie Phanatic costume which was being donated to the Hall. "He thinks he's going in for real," joked Tom Burgoyne, the man inside the suit.

Dressed in full Phanatic costume, Burgoyne was simply blown away seeing Harry Kalas, a good friend for years, sitting in the front row during the ceremony. He knew Harry had a lot going on that day, and certainly never expected him to show up for the Phanatic's comical event.

The Phillie Phanatic, big, green and furry, has been a fixture at every Phillies home game since debuting on April 25, 1978. Originally, Dave Raymond went from 22-year-old Phillies intern to playing the mascot for 15 years, and then Burgoyne took over in 1994 after serving as the backup Phanatic for six seasons. Burgoyne was very close with Harry, who was 30 years older. They did a lot of functions together over the years and often hung out together in the Veterans Stadium press club after home games. It was fitting that they "entered" the Hall together.

"I guess the Phanatic and Harry are linked a little bit," Burgoyne said. "Players come and go, but the Phanatic is always there. Harry was always there. I got a lot of pats on the back that weekend, but really it was all about Harry."

The Hall of Fame induction of Harry was so significant an event for the organization that the Phillies chartered busses to bring about 200 team employees and their families to Cooperstown. Everyone wanted to be there for Harry, who was as close to some of the Phillies secretaries and ticket sellers as he was to players and high-profile executives. The Phillies contingent was told it probably wouldn't get to see Harry until Sunday, but a big bash was held in his honor Saturday night on a private estate next to a lake about 12 miles outside of town. Just in case Harry made an appearance, the band was told to learn "High Hopes." Harry really wanted to be at the Phillies party, but he had a full schedule planned for him—dinner and then a private reception at the Hall of Fame.

"It's really a shame," Phillies President David Montgomery said early into the event. "Harry is the life of the party and here we are partying in his honor."

During the Hall of Fame dinner miles away, with Harry seated at a table of family members and friends, his son Todd Kalas put a plan into motion in order to get his father to the Phillies gathering for at least a few minutes. Todd first instructed everyone to eat quickly. The group then hopped into a van that he had rented. Around 9 p.m., three hours into the Phillies party, Harry walked in blowing kisses to a tremendous ovation.

"It was like a rock star showed up," Phillies videographer Dan Stephenson said. "Everyone was going nuts. It was insane."

Larry Andersen pointed to the band, which immediately broke into "High Hopes." Harry took a spot center stage, and with a mike in his hand, turned on his showmanship and delivered an enthusiastic fist-pumping, head-bobbing rendition. He'd sung "High Hopes" hundreds of times over the years, but probably never better than he did on that night. This performance, filmed by Dan Stephenson, later became the version of the song which was shown after Phillies victories at Citizens Bank Park following Harry's 2009 death.

When Harry finished singing his theme song, he received a bear hug from Andersen, then his right hand was grabbed and raised into the air like a champion boxer as the crowd repeatedly chanted, "Har-ry! Har-ry! Har-ry!"

"Everyone was so filled with joy and proud of Harry," Phillies business communications coordinator Deb Rinaldi said. "He was so deserving. You could feel the love for him, and the love that he felt for others came right through. He was emotional and in tears a little."

Harry could only stay for 30 minutes, but later called his Phillies party appearance the high point of the weekend. Later that night, Harry got his first look at his Hall of Fame plaque when attending the Hall's private reception. "He didn't say a word, but I know he was proud," Jeff McCabe said.

The next afternoon, Harry Kalas took his place with baseball greats as he was inducted into the Baseball Hall of Fame, along with 15-time All-Star shortstop Ozzie Smith and longtime Detroit Tigers beat writer Joe Falls, who entered as the annual J.G. Taylor Spink Award winner.

When Harry first ascended the podium, he looked out at the crowd and as far as he could see there was a sea of red. Some were St. Louis Cardinals fans in town for Ozzie Smith. Most were there for Harry Kalas, arguably the greatest ambassador the Phillies ever have had. Glenn Wilson, a Phillies outfielder in the 1980s, drove all the way from Houston with his youngest son, Andrew Kalas Wilson. Darren Daulton, the star catcher on the Phillies' 1993 World Series team, was there, too. "It was the first and only time I've ever been to the Hall of Fame," said Daulton, who brought his father and brother, both of whom flew in from Kansas. "I told Harry, 'If you make it, I'll go.'"

At the induction ceremony, Harry was introduced by Hall of Fame pitcher Tom Seaver. Dressed in a gray suit and pink tie with blue polka dots, Harry gave an emotional acceptance speech that lasted more than 6 minutes. He used this time to thank and honor the loves of his life—his family, Richie Ashburn and his friends. He closed with a poem that he had written specifically for another true love:

This is to the Philadelphia fan
To laud your passion as best I can
Your loyalty is unsurpassed
Be the Fightins in first or last
We come to the park each day
Looking forward to another fray
Because we know you'll be there
We know you really care
You give the opposing pitcher fits
Because as one loyalist shouts, 'Everybody hits!'
To be sure in Philly, there might be some boos
Because you passionate fans, like the manager, hate to lose
Your reaction to the action on the field that you impart
Spurs us broadcasters to call the game with enthusiasm and heart
We feel your passion through and through
Philadelphia fans, I love you

Harry's speech touched everyone. The next week, he received a letter from Jeff Idelson, the Baseball Hall of Fame Communications VP. "Dear Harry, just a short note of thanks for all that you did to make Hall of Fame weekend such a success. You did a great job with your speech and you should be proud. I am telling you the truth in that I've been here for nine induction ceremonies and your speech, by far, was one of the best I've ever heard."

Phillies fans were given another chance to show their love for Harry a few weeks later. August 18, 2002 was Harry Kalas Day at Veterans Stadium. The Phillies' average crowd in 2002 was 20,230. This game drew 58,493—by far the biggest crowd of the season and one of the largest for a baseball game in Veterans Stadium history. Harry was presented with a crystal microphone and miniature 1980 World Series trophy. He then entertained the crowd by singing a heartfelt rendition of "God Bless America."

Fans received a special treat, as they did at Harry's 30th anniversary tribute two years before. This time, everyone received a Harry & Whitey bobblehead. The six-inch-tall figurine featured Harry on the left in blue pants with a white jacket and white shoes, and Whitey on the right with a hat and carrying a pipe.

"His Whiteness used to say we were always joined at the hip, so he's probably a little surprised that we're not joined at the hip," Kalas said after eyeballing the giveaway item.

Dressed that evening in a white suit with a purple lei around his neck, Harry took a victory lap around the field at the end of the ceremony, riding on the back of a red convertible. To the crowd's amazement, former Phillie and then St. Louis Cardinals All-Star third baseman Scott Rolen popped out of the visiting dugout to graciously open the passenger door of the convertible in order to allow Harry to step in.

Once the face of the Phillies franchise, Rolen was traded to the Cardinals on July 29, 2002, after he rejected a lucrative contract extension. With free agency looming, Rolen was booed heavily in his final days with the Phillies. He then infuriated many fans in his first post-trade interview with ESPN's Peter Gammons. Asked about leaving Philadelphia for St. Louis, Rolen said, "It felt as if I'd died and gone to heaven." A mere 16 days after being traded, Rolen returned to Philadelphia with the Cardinals for a four-game series.

Though he had been showered with boos for three days, Rolen still couldn't say no when asked by the Phillies if he wanted to open the door for Harry during Sunday's pre-game ceremony. "Even after the trade, I wanted to be a part of this," Rolen said that day. "Harry has been a big part of my life. I wanted to shake his hand and tell him that I loved him."

Phillies fans responded to Rolen with more boos, which really ticked off one of Rolen's former teammates. "That was low class," Phillies first baseman Travis Lee said after the game. "That was a day to honor Harry. I thought it took a lot of balls for Scottie to come out and hold the door. They can boo him all they want when he's on the field, but not when we're honoring Harry. That was ridiculous."

The highlight of the day for Harry came in the third inning when his three sons joined him in the Phillies' television booth. Youngest son Kane Kalas did play-by-play and everyone got a kick out of the 13-year-old mispronouncing the last name of Cardinals superstar first baseman Albert Pujols. Standing next to his father, Kane stared at a lineup sheet in his hand, then said, *"Now batting is Albert . . . Pa-joel-is."*

Without missing a beat, and to everyone's amusement, Harry jumped in. *"His friends call him Pujols."*

That was vintage Harry, always quick with a quip and quick to help someone out of an embarrassing jam. Is it any wonder so many believe that Harry was a Hall of Famer in life long before his legendary broadcasting career was immortalized in Cooperstown?

Harry Kalas was in the spotlight again when the Phillies closed Veterans Stadium on September 28, 2003. All season long, the Phillies had a "countdown clock" on the Veterans Stadium right-field wall indicating the number of remaining games in their 33-year-old home. They had a special guest, often a former player, change the number each game after the fifth inning. Mike Schmidt and Steve Carlton, two of the Phillies' all-time greats, returned for the final game, but Harry Kalas changed the sign that day by pulling down No. 1, Richie Ashburn's number, and hanging up a zero. Harry was thinking of Whitey. At the wall, he pointed an index finger to the sky and blew a kiss.

Phillies broadcaster Tom McCarthy, working for the Eastern League's Trenton Thunder at the time, attended the Veterans Stadium finale as a fan. He was amazed hearing Harry Kalas get the loudest ovation during that special day in Phillies history.

"Oh, my goodness," McCarthy told himself. "Harry is one of the most popular sports figures in this city of all time."

CHAMPIONSHIP VOICE

Bundled up on a 44-degree October night in Philadelphia, a rowdy full house at Citizens Bank Park offered a rousing ovation as the seventh inning ended with the home team in front. Moments earlier, the Phillies had pulled ahead in this wild 2008 World Series Game 5, which started on a Monday and would end on a Wednesday due to a two-day postponement caused by rainstorms. Six more outs and Philadelphia would have a champion of its own for the first time in a quarter-century. Six more outs and the Phillies would be champions for the second time in 126 years.

As reliever J.C. Romero was taking his warm-up tosses for the eighth inning, the Phillies radio booth made a call to the bullpen. Scott Franzke, the radio play-by-play man, took off his headset and left his seat to make way for Harry Kalas. The legendary voice of the Phillies was six outs away, too. In his 44th year in the majors and 38th with the Phillies, Harry the K finally was closing in on a moment he'd been dreaming about since childhood. Harry did not do much radio in his twilight years—he worked only the fourth inning in his final seasons—but with network broadcasters assigned to the TV announcing, the Phillies wanted their legendary voice on the air for their 2008 postseason clinchers.

Harry was in the booth when the Phillies won their first two playoff rounds, and now was back there for Game 5 of the World Series hoping to call the final out to a championship, the one missing link in his great career. He was with the Phillies when they won their first title in 1980, but off the air because NBC-TV and CBS Radio had exclusive broadcasting rights.

The Tampa Bay Rays didn't score in the eighth, then the Phillies went down quietly in the bottom of the inning. It was on to the ninth. The Phillies' bullpen door beyond the center-field wall opened and Brad Lidge, a closer enjoying a perfect season in save situations, charged toward the mound as Drowning Pool's "Soldiers," his handpicked entrance song, blared from the ballpark sound system.

There are three swivel chairs in front of a counter in the Phillies radio booth. Scott Franzke always sits to the far right, radio color man Larry Andersen sits to the left. The middle chair sometimes is occupied by on-air guests, but often remains empty. That's where Harry always sat during his quick in-game visits to the radio booth.

Harry was in his usual spot for Game 5 and working with longtime partner Chris Wheeler, his former friend. The Phillies' lead television analyst, Wheeler has been in the club's broadcast booth since 1977 and, like Harry, missed out broadcasting the 1980 World Series. The Phillies wanted Wheels on the air for the 2008 ending, too.

Wheeler was seated to Harry's left in Andersen's chair. Jim Jackson, the team's pre-game and post-game radio host, was to the right of Harry in Franzke's chair, just watching. A few feet behind Harry, radio production engineer Joe Gaines surveyed the scene while standing on his elevated platform. In the back of the booth, Comcast SportsNet cameraman Jerry Hines sneaked in solely to shoot footage of Harry in his big moment. The booth normally has anywhere from three-to-five people in it during games. In the ninth inning of Game 5 of the 2008 World Series, it was jammed with at least a dozen bodies. The area was so crowded that Gaines eventually had to stand on a stool up in his perch to keep an eye on the guys calling the action.

Phillies broadcaster Tom McCarthy, off duty during the game, popped in for the ninth inning, too, and squeezed into a free space behind Harry up against the engineer's platform. "I'm a broadcast junkie and I wanted to see how Harry was going to call it," he said.

Harry Kalas seemed to be the calmest person in the booth.

Few broadcasters have matched his success and longevity. He was in Philadelphia for the glory years of the franchise — six playoff appearances, two pennants and a championship from 1976 to 1983—plus their 1993 World Series run. Even after being inducted into the broadcaster's wing of the Baseball Hall of Fame in 2002, Harry knew that there was a void in his broadcasting career. It wasn't something that he thought about a lot, but being on the air for a Phillies championship was something that he really had wanted for a long time.

Marty Brennaman, the Hall of Fame voice of the Cincinnati Reds since 1974, could relate to Harry's longing. When Cincinnati's Big Red Machine won the 1975 and 1976 World Series, Brennaman was shut out by the network's exclusivity rule. But he was fortunate. When the Reds returned to the World Series in 1990, they won and Brennaman finally got to make a championship call. A longtime Harry Kalas admirer, Brennaman was pulling hard for Harry to get his shot, too.

"You shouldn't have to go through your entire career without having an opportunity to broadcast a world championship, and there are many more of us who don't than those who do," Brennaman said. "For Harry to have the kind of career that he had and never to be able to be there on the microphone when your team is crowned world champions, it shouldn't be that way."

Following the 1993 season, one in which the Phillies fell two victories short of a championship, Harry would have a long wait for another shot at broadcasting fulfillment. The Phillies didn't make the playoffs again until 2007, but after winning their division on the final day of the regular season they were swept in the first round by the Colorado Rockies. For the sports fans of Philadelphia, this sobering defeat was another reminder that none of the city's four major franchises had won a championship since Julius Erving and Moses Malone led the 76ers to an NBA title in 1983.

The 2008 Phillies went back to the playoffs, this time clinching their division the day before their regular-season finale. With a year of playoff experience and the desire to avenge the previous season's quick playoff dismissal, the Phillies entered the 2008 postseason filled with confidence that this would finally be their year.

The Phillies made quick work of their first two playoff challengers, sweeping the Milwaukee Brewers in a best-of-five Division Series and taking care of the Los Angeles Dodgers in five games in the best-of-seven National League Championship Series.

The Fightins—that's what Harry Kalas called the Phillies—were World Series bound.

Their opponent was an unlikely foe. The Tampa Bay Rays ranked as one of the losingest franchises in baseball history until 2008. Since entering the league as an expansion team in 1998, the Rays had not even come close to posting a winning record for a season, averaging 97 losses per campaign over their first decade. Their 2008 team included a group of young, talented ballplayers, but a .500 record seemed a lofty-enough goal for a ballclub with a $43.7 million payroll, second-lowest in the majors and far below two of their two big-market division rivals—the New York Yankees ($209 million) and Boston Red Sox ($133 million).

Before the 2008 season, Tampa Bay made headlines in attempting to alter its image, and luck, by changing its name from Devil Rays to Rays. That change paled in significance to what then occurred on the field. The Rays shocked the baseball world by winning their division, then again by beating the Los Angeles Angels and Boston Red Sox in the first two rounds of the playoffs to secure the American League pennant.

No one was more excited than Harry Kalas, whose World Series opportunity came with a wonderful bonus that he never expected in his wildest dreams. To Harry, this was so much more than getting another shot at calling the final out to a championship because it would to be a Kalas-Kalas World Series. Todd Kalas, the oldest of Harry's two sons from his first marriage, joined the Rays' broadcast team in 1998 and was in his 11th season as an in-game television reporter for the club in 2008.

"It was a very special World Series from the time that we found out that we were going to be matched up against each other," Todd Kalas said. "The odds were one-in-a-million to have the Rays and Phillies playing each other. That was the coolest thing ever."

Harry and Todd joked about how the winner would have bragging rights forever. But deep down, both cherished the opportunity to professionally and personally share the World Series experience. Todd knew that his father was getting up there in age, perhaps nearing the end of his great career. Harry probably understood that, too.

"I want the Phillies to win, but if they don't the disappointment won't be quite as bad because somebody in the Kalas family will be celebrating," Harry said before Game 1.

Harry almost never asked for favors. But sensing a rare opportunity, he went to Rob Brooks, the Phillies' manager of broadcasting, to request the chance to work an inning with his son during the Series. Brooks thought it was a great idea. Father and son worked together on the Phillies broadcast team from 1994 to 1996 when Todd did Phillies home games for PRISM. But they never announced an inning together, much less a World Series inning.

Their big moment came in the opener at Tropicana Field in St. Petersburg, but first they were put in the national spotlight that night when FOX had Harry and Todd read off their respective teams' Game 1 starting lineups. When it was Todd's turn, he closed the middle three fingers on one of his hands, and then left the pinky and thumb open to give the "shaka" sign—a nonverbal Hawaiian greeting. Todd was sure his mother, a native Hawaiian, was watching from her home in Honolulu. Jasmine Kalas, a big baseball fan, indeed saw it.

"I cried," she said.

The Phillies were leading 2-0 when Harry got company in the Phillies radio booth for the fourth inning.

"Game 1, World Series, Phillies vs. Rays . . . that's pretty much the pinnacle," Todd Kalas said. "We knew how special it was the whole time, and it wasn't like we both got bogged down in our own worlds that we didn't try to appreciate it together. That's something that I'll always cherish."

During their inning together, Harry and Todd focused on the game, not themselves.

"We had done so many interviews because it was a popular side story that we pretty much had covered all that ground," Todd said. "Dad and I pretty much just talked about the two teams and the action on the field."

Outside of Philadelphia, the 2008 World Series won't go down in history as a classic. This best-of-seven meeting was over in five games and will be primarily remembered for its unusual Game 5. With the Phillies leading 3-games-to-1, their first chance to clinch came on a 47-degree Monday night at Citizens Bank Park in which a cold light rain was falling at first pitch. By the third inning, the rain was coming down harder, a strong wind was blowing and playing conditions became a mess. After the top half of the sixth inning, the game was stopped with the teams tied 2-2. A rain delay turned into a suspended game. More bad weather the next day pushed the conclusion of Monday's game to Wednesday.

"We'll stay here if we have to celebrate Thanksgiving here," baseball commissioner Bud Selig said.

Anticipating an eventual Phillies win, city officials began making plans for a victory parade. Comcast SportsNet, which televises most Phillies games, planned to cover the parade. Working ahead, Jon Slobotkin, their award-winning producer of Phillies telecasts from 1995 to 2005 and Harry's old boss, needed the intro to the possible parade coverage narrated even before the World Series was over. Of course, Slobotkin tapped Harry to perform the narration, which led to a potential problem.

Normally Harry would do anything for anyone, but he always had been incredibly superstitious. When Slobotkin would use in-game television graphics detailing a player's hot or cold streak and his luck suddenly changed, Harry playfully would get on him. He called his old boss 'Slo' and invented the term "Slo Jinx." For instance, if Chase Utley had a hitting streak end the same day it was detailed in a graphic for the opening of a telecast, Harry would tell people that Utley is suffering from the "Slo Jinx."

"Occasionally it would work its way onto the air,' Slobotkin said. "I'd say, 'Harry, I don't think the people at home know what the hell you're talking about when you say that.' He didn't care. He thought it was funny."

Knowing Harry, Slobotkin understood that he'd have to really push to get the parade voiceover completed during the Game 5 suspension. The day before the World Series resumed, they talked by phone.

"Harry, I need you to come in," Slobotkin told Harry. "I know the Phillies didn't win the championship yet, but we're preparing as if it's going to happen. And if they win, you may be hard to find."

"Don't worry, Slo, I'll take care of it," Harry responded.

Slobotkin was astonished. Harry didn't even put up a fight.

"The thing that struck me most was that Harry actually agreed to do it and not think this would cause the Phillies to lose," Slobotkin said. "In the past,

Harry might have said, 'I'm not doing anything until I know the victory's safe.'"

Harry met Slobotkin that day and put on a typical Kalas performance.

"After all that time of being incredibly superstitious and ripping me for preparing things that didn't happen, Harry came to me on the ultimate stage and delivered," Slobotkin said. "Harry did a masterful job with the 'tease,' which led off five-and-half hours of live parade coverage. I've gone back and watched that a couple times and it still gives me chills."

As Slobotkin walked Harry out of the building, he asked for a World Series prediction.

"I know we're going to do it this time, Slo," Harry said. "It's going to be great. The parade is going to be great and I just can't wait. It's their time and I know it's going to happen."

The next day, Game 5 resumed. Before the restart, *Philadelphia Daily News* baseball writer Paul Hagen asked Harry if he gave any thought about what he would say if and when the Phillies won.

"I'm trying not to think about it," Harry responded. "It's just going to happen the way it happens."

The Phillies scored a run in the long-delayed bottom of the sixth-inning to take a 3-2 lead, then the Rays scored in the seventh to pull even. But the Phillies came right back in the bottom of the seventh to take a 4-3 lead on a single by Pedro Feliz.

The game remained 4-3 at the end of the eighth inning. That's when Jerry Hines, the Comcast SportsNet cameraman, made his move. The previous inning, Hines had been standing near Harry while looking around to make sure no other competing cameramen moved in closer. Before the Rays hit in the top of the ninth, Hines slid his smallish frame into the narrow space between Harry's middle seat and the one to the right where Jim Jackson sat.

"I'm in your spot, but they kind of want me here," Hines told Jackson.

"Okay, but I can't promise you that I won't bump you if the Phillies win," Jackson said.

Hines propped the base of his 25-pound camera on the counter in front of the broadcasters, then tilted it so that the lens pointed towards Harry's face, which was a mere two feet away. Here was Harry preparing for his greatest baseball thrill and a super-sized television camera was staring at him from point-blank range. If Harry noticed it, he never let on. He was too focused on doing his job. In the ninth inning, Harry's eyes never left the field except for quick peeks at his scorecard.

The Rays' ninth started with Brad Lidge retiring Evan Longoria, the 2008 American League Rookie of the Year, on a popup to second base. But Rays catcher Dioner Navarro followed with a single to right, then pinch-runner Fernando Perez stole second base and the Rays suddenly had the tying run in scoring position with one out. After Ben Zobrist lined out to right field, the Phillies were one out away from their second championship in the franchise's 126-year history. With Phillies fans screaming, Eric Hinske, the Rays' last hope, stepped into the batter's box with the world championship on the line.

"Everyone was antsy, but Harry was calm," radio engineer Joe Gaines said. "He had a way of broadcasting when the moment became more intense. His inflection changed. The excitement in his voice raised just a little bit more. He gave that almost-classic feeling that something dramatic was about to happen."

With the tying run in scoring position, Phillies pitching coach Rich Dubee made a visit to the mound before Hinske saw a pitch. Dubee and Lidge decided to serve the left-handed pinch-hitter a steady diet of Lidge's best pitch: his 84-85 mph slider that starts out looking like a fastball before darting downward.

Hinske offered at Lidge's first pitch and tapped a weak grounder to the right side that was foul by two feet. Lidge walked behind the mound, scooped up a handful of dirt, and then threw it back to the ground and went into his stretch. Catcher Carlos Ruiz set up outside and Hinske took a checked swing for strike two.

Phillies fans were on their feet and their rally towels turned Citizens Bank Park into what looked like a sea of bouncing white waves.

Jim Jackson took a look at Harry. "Sitting there and seeing the intensity on his face, it was amazing," he said.

Harry was wearing a Phillies winter jacket, red wool with white leather sleeves. He had his chin down on the base of his neck, so that he could see over his reading glasses, which were on the edge of his nose. Harry's eyes zeroed in on Lidge. Harry then leaned in a little closer, waiting to react.

"One strike away; nothing-and-two, the count to Hinske. Fans on the their feet; rally towels are being waved. Brad Lidge stretches. The 0-2 pitch . . . Swing and a miss, struck him out! The Philadelphia Phillies are 2008 World Champions of baseball!

"Brad Lidge does it again, and stays perfect for the 2008 season . . . 48-for-48 in

save opportunities. And watch this city celebrate! Don't let the 48-hour wait diminish the euphoria of this moment and this celebration. And it has been 28 years since the Phillies have enjoyed a world championship, 25 years in this city without a team that has enjoyed a world championship. And the fans are ready to celebrate. What a night! Phillies winning 4-3, as Brad Lidge gets the job done once again. Wow! What a season for Lidge!"

At 9:58 p.m., on Oct. 29, 2008, Kalas had provided 18 seconds of ecstasy for Phillies fans. To no one's surprise, Harry had made the moment extra special with an emotion-filled call that was just perfect. Most Phillies fans were watching on television and didn't hear Harry's call live, but many got goose bumps hearing a replay for the first time.

"When you look at the call, there's nothing fancy," Paul Hagen said. "He doesn't use a lot of striking imagery or anything, but the way he delivered it, you could tell the excitement in his voice. He really felt it. I think a lot of broadcasters feel like they have to raise their voice and talk louder when something exciting happens, and it seems kind of forced. But with Harry, you could tell that he really did live and die with this team."

The television footage shows Kalas totally focused. He let his voice tell the story.

"I expected Harry to do something," Comcast cameraman Jerry Hines said. "You're waiting, waiting, waiting. His call was classic Harry, but his reaction came off like it was another game. He didn't move. It's almost like he didn't want to jinx it, even though it had just happened. I stayed for the next two or three minutes to make sure he didn't do something. He never did react like everyone else. He was too busy doing his job."

When seeing Hines' footage on television, Tom McCarthy noticed a change in Harry's face as he said, "The Phillies are 2008 World Champions of baseball."

"You can see the crack going up in his smile," McCarthy said. "That was unbelievable. If you just looked at that in itself, that was, 'I'm proud to call it because I didn't get a chance in '80. I'm glad to see it and I am the voice that needs to be on this call.' It's only appropriate."

As Harry was making his call, Hines' camera caught Chris Wheeler's furious fist-pumping and arm-shaking reaction to the Phillies triumph. What his footage missed was everyone else in the radio booth reacting similarly. Tom McCarthy, Jim Jackson, Joe Gaines, three Phillies employees and others did their own celebratory dances.

"I had no idea that I did that until I saw it." Wheeler said.

"Wheels' reaction was human," Tom McCarthy said. "I grew up a fan of the Mets. Scott Franzke grew up a fan of the Rangers and Harry grew up a fan of the Washington Senators. We fall in love with the teams that we follow, but Wheels is the purist of Phillies fans because he grew up rooting for them."

Wheeler received plenty of teasing over the next few months for his dramatic reaction. Harry and the other Phillies broadcasters even reenacted it on camera during spring training 2009. But during Wheeler's antics, he remained completely silent for more than a full minute, which he says was a calculated decision to allow Harry Kalas the opportunity to bask in the glory of his crowning achievement.

"People say, 'What happened there?'" Wheeler said in retrospect. "I consciously thought about that moment. I'd be lying if I said I didn't. I didn't know what was going to happen, but I was going to do everything in my power not to get in the way because that was Harry's moment. In 1980, he didn't have a chance to do it. I even thought about it at one point in the ninth inning. It entered my mind. It wasn't like it just happened that way, I didn't make any noise or do anything."

After letting Harry fly solo for over a minute, Wheeler finally chimed in.

"Hey, how about this game tonight? This is great. You think about all the things that happened since the resumption of play here tonight. And what a fabulous effort by this baseball team this year, the manager, Charlie Manuel, the coaching staff. And this city has a championship. It's been a long time."

After finally living his broadcasting dream, Harry sat silently in his chair with a smile, watching the Phillies celebrate on the field. Later, he accepted a few hugs in the booth.

"Great call," McCarthy told Harry during their embrace.

"You so deserved this," Jim Jackson said to Harry.

Harry thanked both for their compliments. Harry was a proud man on this night. So was his family.

Kane Kalas, a first-semester college freshman at the University of Miami, was watching the game with his buddies in Coral Gables, Fla. Before the ninth inning, the youngest of the three Kalas children turned down the sound on his television so that he could hear his father over the Internet.

Kane became emotional hearing his father call the final out. "I called him on his cell phone about 45 minutes after the game was over," Kane said. "He was so happy."

Brad Kalas, Harry's middle child, watched the game from his Southern California home with his girlfriend. He was excited for his dad, and absolutely ecstatic when Joe Buck sent FOX into the post-game commercial break with "Let's listen to Harry Kalas call the last out."

"Hearing that, I was so pumped up," Brad said. "Part of me was a little nervous because there had been so much hype on Dad calling the final out. I was hoping everything would go smoothly. Sure enough, it was amazing. That was the culmination of everything for my father, plus with Todd being on the other side with the Rays, it was just a magical year."

Todd didn't see or hear his father's call until the next day.

"That was incredibly gracious and generous of Wheels, as crazy and excited as he was in the background, to not interfere with the call," Todd said.

In the next year, Harry's call with Hines' footage was shown over and over in Philadelphia.

"Every time I see it or listen to it, it still fills you up with a lot of emotion because it was a pinnacle moment for him and a pinnacle moment for our franchise," said Phillies general manager Ruben Amaro, Jr. "Harry finally got to do what he wanted to do for so long."

Six months later, the Phillies' voice was gone.

"Thank God, Harry got to make that call," Jim Jackson said. "God works funny up there."

Perhaps believing his baseball resume was finally complete, Harry seriously considered retiring after the 2008 season. After Christmas 2008, Kalas phoned his agent Dion Rassias for help.

"I'm thinking about going out right now," Harry said. "I can go out on top. I'm done. I've got a lot of opportunities. I can do NFL Films forever. Why don't you call the Phillies to see if they'll buy out the last year on my contract?

Floored, Rassias pleaded with Harry to "sleep on it and get back to me."

Harry never called back, and was back in 2009 to broadcast his Fightins.

17

THE GOLDEN YEARS

The last Friday in October 2008 was Halloween, normally a time for trick-or-treating. But in Philadelphia, this special holiday was only about the treat for which Phillies fans had waited 28 years. Flatbeds filled with Phillies players paraded through the streets, providing eye candy for hooky-playing baseball fans lining the downtown sidewalks, up to 25-50 people deep in many spots. Two days after the Phillies won the World Series, city officials estimated that more than a million people attended a victory parade which stretched four miles from 20th & Market in Center City to Citizens Bank Park in South Philadelphia.

Mothers and fathers, blacks and whites, babies in strollers and grandfathers with canes turned the parade route into a sea of screaming people dressed in Phillies red. When it was hard to see, some improvised. Tots were given piggyback rides and teens climbed light posts. People hung out of windows and cheered from rooftops. Fans climbed street signs and hung in tree branches. The parade, scheduled for two hours, lasted over three due to the enormous turnout. An entire generation of Philadelphia fans had been waiting its whole life for this. The Phillies' first championship since 1980 and second in their long history also represented the city's first for any of its four major sports franchises in 25 years.

A string of police vehicles and two double-decker busses carrying media led the parade, followed by Pat Burrell, the team's longest-tenured player, riding in a Budweiser wagon pulled by six Clydesdales. Lined up behind Burrell, who rode with his wife, Michelle, and 125-pound English Bulldog, Elvis, was a fleet of six flatbed trucks equipped with confetti machines.

The lead flatbed carried the franchise's two biggest icons, Harry Kalas and the Phillie Phanatic. The Phillies' furry green mascot jumped for joy atop a makeshift platform that towered several feet above the cab of the super-sized truck. Down below in the back, Harry stood with his broadcast partners, Phillies ballgirls and Mayor Michael Nutter's office employees. Whenever the crowd spotted Harry in his gray jacket and black vest, their cheers grew in volume, and during those times that his flatbed slowed down, fans chanted—"Har-ry! Har-ry! Har-ry!" From start to finish, Harry was serenaded, then cheered, serenaded and cheered. Harry proved to be as big an attraction as any of the World Series champions' star players.

Riding next to Harry, Phillies radio announcer Scott Franzke pointed a video camera at his famous partner and asked, "What do you think, Harry?

"Breathtaking," he responded.

The day turned into a deeply moving experience for Harry Kalas. He loved Phillies fans with all his heart, and this latest show of affection was simply overwhelming. In return, Harry waved and blew kisses. Again and again, he walked from one side of the flatbed to the other in an attempt to acknowledge as many fans as he could.

"It was like Harry was the lead singer of a rock band and the crowd was trying to get him back out for an encore," said Jim Jackson, the Phillies' pregame and post-game radio host. "That's how loud it was."

The Phillies' flatbeds arrived in South Philadelphia for a pair of rallies attended by 100,000 fans. First, they made a quick stop at Lincoln Financial Field, home of the NFL's Philadelphia Eagles, then everyone headed to Citizens Bank Park, the Phillies' home since 2004. When introduced to the packed crowd at the Phillies ballpark, Harry again received some of the day's loudest cheers.

The most enduring memory from the ballpark victory rally for many fans was the first two sentences of Phillies second baseman Chase Utley's speech. With more than 40,000 in the stands and hundreds of thousands watching on live television, Utley shyly stepped up to a podium erected near second base and said, "World Champions . . . World F--king Champions!" Most fans cheered wildly, though a few parents with young children cringed at this unexpected obscenity from a star player with a reputation for being politically correct.

Harry Kalas cracked a smile.

From the outside looking in, everyone thought Harry was having a great day. He was, but he wasn't. Harry loved the parade, but he felt ill. His legs bothered him, and not because he was a 72-year-old man who had been on his feet for most of the day.

Harry had been living with a secret that no one other than his wife and closest friends knew. Harry was hurting during the Phillies parade because he had been postponing heart surgery to fix severe blood-flow issues in both his legs. Harry's doctors had reported that his left leg was nearly 100 percent blocked and his right leg 80 percent blocked.

About three months earlier, Harry had undergone surgery to repair a detached retina in his left eye. Prior to that July 18 procedure, Harry was given an EKG to make sure that his heart could handle the stress of the surgery. When the EKG showed an irregular heartbeat, Harry underwent a cardiac catheterization, and that test revealed the blockages in his legs. The blood flow was so poor in Harry's legs that the catheterization had to be done through one of his arms.

Harry's eye surgery had been reported in the local newspapers because it kept him away from the Phillies for nine days. During the week after he returned to work from that operation, Harry received an additional medical report that Phillies fans did not learn about. Harry was a few minutes from starting his broadcast of a road game when he made his usual pre-game phone call to his wife.

"Are you alone?" Eileen Kalas asked her husband at the start of their talk. "I have something that I want to talk to you about."

"Yeah, I'm alone," Harry responded.

Eileen Kalas had alarming news: A doctor had just called their home to let Harry know that recent tests showed that he had suffered a heart attack within the past year.

Harry's response to Eileen was more confusion than concern. "I had a heart attack? Wouldn't I know it if I had a heart attack?"

Eileen informed Harry that the doctor told her Harry had experienced a 'silent' heart attack. When Harry got off the phone with Eileen, he had a bewildered look on his face. "I had a heart attack, and I didn't even know it," Harry told Larry Andersen, his broadcast partner.

Medical studies show that one in four heart attacks don't cause chest pain and go unnoticed. Silent heart attacks, which result from a chronic shortage of blood to a portion of the heart, often cause permanent heart damage. Harry's attack, according to his doctors, left the muscle on the bottom portion of his heart "dead" and required surgery to address the blood-flow issues in his legs. Also, he needed to take care of an aortic aneurysm in his heart that was discovered 10 years earlier, but hadn't grown large enough to operate on until after his silent heart attack.

Harry took the phone call from Eileen about his silent heart attack in the visiting radio booth at Nationals Park in Washington, D.C. In an eerie coincidence, Harry's life would end nine months later from a heart attack suffered one room away in the Nationals Park visiting television booth.

In July 2008, Harry didn't seem too worried about this new, unexpected medical report. While the problem didn't need to be addressed immediately, his doctors encouraged him to take care of it as soon as possible. Believing the condition wasn't life-threatening, Harry decided to wait to undergo surgery until February 2009. He wanted to finish the baseball season, and then get through his football work with NFL Films and Westwood One radio. Eileen and friends tried to convince Harry to at least stop traveling with the Phillies and for Westwood One until he had the procedure done, but to no avail.

"Harry was very stubborn," close friend Bob Smith said. "He was going to do the Phillies run in the playoffs, then continue the ride afterward and do football. That was his No. 1 priority."

Eileen had worried about Harry's health for the previous several years. So had some of his close friends and co-workers. Harry was in his 70s, still smoking heavily and had been slowing down. Even in the booth, Harry wasn't quite the same. He had the same voice, enthusiasm and work habits, but in the early 2000s he began to make occasional on-air mistakes that were extremely out-of-character for him. He also had started to have some issues with his eyesight and his memory. As the years went on, the frequency of his errors increased. One night in Atlanta, he did a radio interview and got so mixed up that he talked about Mike Schmidt and Darren Daulton leading the 1993 Phillies to a World Series championship. Schmidt and the 1980 Phillies won the World Series, Daulton and the 1993 Phillies lost the World Series. Though Harry still was very good at calling baseball games and as beloved by Phillies fans as ever, his mistakes were noticed.

"I think we all saw him slowing down," Bob Smith said. "Near the end of his life, Harry wasn't as sharp as he was four or five years ago. He was 70-plus years of age. You could pick it up in his broadcasts with an occasional slip here and there."

Most everyone seemed to realize it wasn't the same old Harry except Harry himself.

"I think I'll be the first to know if I'm slipping, if I'm not seeing the field, if I'm not calling the games the way they should be called," Harry said in 2002. "At that point, I would hang them up. When that will come, I don't know."

No one dared complain. An imperfect but still terrific Harry was better than no Harry at all. Besides, Harry Kalas never came close to declining to the almost embarrassing point that Hall of Fame broadcaster Harry Caray did in his final years with the Chicago Cubs.

"I think everybody with age misidentifies flyballs and players," said Jon Slobotkin, who produced Phillies telecasts for Comcast SportsNet from 1998 to 2005. "I remember By Saam would have Luzinski flying out to Luzinski. Harry never ever got to that point. What we tried to do behind the scenes was help Harry in any way possible. No one wanted Harry to be ridiculed or exposed for his vision not being as good or miscalling some things."

According to Slobotkin, Chris Wheeler was a big help even though he no longer had an off-air friendship with Harry. Slobotkin was later informed that the practice continued after his former assistant Jeff Halikman succeeded him as lead producer for Phillies television games starting in 2006.

"Wheels was very, very helpful in transitioning Harry when things got a little tougher for him," Slobotkin said. "If Harry was having trouble seeing things or a lineup change was made that Harry might not have been aware of, Wheels was very, very proactive in pointing things out, both on the air politely and between innings."

Meantime, the same Philadelphia talk-radio hosts who had a national reputation for being very critical at times of all things related to Philadelphia sports refused to criticize Harry Kalas.

"I remember one day Harry miscalled a Tomas Perez non-home run," Slobotkin said. "Off the bat, it was, 'There it goes, long drive. . . .' But it was a routine flyball to right field. They played that cut on the radio the next day, but they talked about it almost in a way that you would say something about the uncle that you love. They were laughing, but not laughing at Harry. It was like, 'Even legends trip up once in awhile.' That solidified what I thought: Harry would never really be subject to massive criticism."

Philadelphia radio personality Howard Eskin lives by the same motto as the late, legendary sportscaster Howard Cosell—"Tell it like it is." Nicknamed "King" by Pete Rose, Eskin noticed Harry's on-air mistakes, but even he wouldn't harp on them during his show. When callers brought it up, he stuck up for Harry.

"You know why I did that?" Eskin said. "Because Harry gave us so much. I always said that we shouldn't tell star players when to retire. Did Steve Carlton have enough at the end? No, but he earned the right to tell us. Harry Kalas earned the right to tell us when he's done. When he kind of lost things a little bit, I said he's just a player. He wasn't what he was five years ago, but he's still the best broadcaster that the Phillies have ever had."

Philadelphian Joe Conklin is a skilled comedian and voice impersonator who does a very good Harry Kalas. During his comedy acts in concert and as a contributor to Angelo Cataldi's morning show on 610 WIP, Conklin has made fun of Eagles coach Andy Reid for his weight and Phillies manager Charlie Manuel for his speech, along with pretty much every other major sports figure in the city. Only one person has been off limits for Conklin.

"Harry Kalas was my idol," Conklin said. "I would never screw with Harry . . . never to the point where I had him drunk and driving, drunk and fighting. I just wouldn't do it. And I pretty much screwed with everybody on the air in our bits. He was definitely sacred. One of the reasons he was sacred was Harry was so beloved and the audience just didn't want to hear Harry being portrayed in a negative light. When Harry got his DUI, WIP wanted me to do something on it and I said, 'No, I can't do it. I just can't do it.'"

Harry became noticeably different in his final years to those who knew him outside the broadcast booth.

"In Harry's last two or three years, I don't think that he had the zest that he had before," said Frank Coppenbarger, the Phillies director of travel and clubhouse services. "He really got older. I noticed it."

Time and again, Eileen encouraged Harry to stop working so hard. She mentioned that Vin Scully, the great Los Angeles Dodgers broadcaster since 1950, had cut his schedule by working only home games and division road games in recent years. Harry refused to slow down. Rob Brooks, the Phillies' manager of broadcasting, had told Harry the same thing when mentioning that Scully was vacationing in Italy during one of the Dodgers' recent visits to Philadelphia.

"If you don't travel with the team, you can't do a good job broadcasting," Harry responded to all suggestions about slowing down.

Although living hard for a lot of years, Harry suffered only a few health problems until late in life.

He had one scare during a Hawaiian vacation in the late 1990s when he participated in the Maui Downhill Bicycle Tour with his buddy Joe Nunes. He was lucky to escape with only a left shoulder separation after losing control of his speeding bike and crashing a few feet from the edge of a high cliff. That trip had started with a bad omen. During his flight from Los Angeles to Hawaii, Harry was agitated by a young man sitting in front of him who was moaning nonstop. When the flight attendants provided oxygen for the passenger, Harry wound up sitting with the oxygen tank between his legs. Later in the week, when Harry ended up in a Maui emergency room after his bike crash, he heard a similar moaning noise coming from a man on a gurney next to him. Believe it or not, it was the same guy from the plane. "Get me outta here," Harry shouted. "I can't take any more of this."

Harry showed up in spring training with his arm in a sling, but recovered quickly and had no more serious health problems until his 2007 eye surgery.

As Harry grew older, he spent a lot more time at home when not at the ballpark, especially after he stopped drinking around 2003. Harry loved to spend time in his home office going through fan mail and watching sports on television. Day or night, visitors would often find Harry dressed in a robe at home.

"When I first moved to Philadelphia, Harry would get up in the morning and get all ready to go to work," Eileen Kalas said. "I said, 'I feel like I have to take a shower, put on my makeup and curl my hair. I hate this. If we don't go anywhere, then let's stay in our pajamas and be more comfortable.' He said, 'Could we?' He loved it. Harry would go out in his pajamas and get the paper and wave at a passerby. Some of our neighbors said they never saw Harry dressed unless he was going to work."

As Harry grew older, he often seemed to go out of his way to avoid using new technology.

"I think my father liked what he was used to," said Kane Kalas, Harry's youngest son. "He was kind of stuck in his own ways, and he liked his own routine. For instance, he never added his bills with a calculator. He did it by hand. I said, 'Why not use a calculator?' He said, 'A what?' Whenever he typed a document, it was on a typewriter. We never had a computer in the house. He used an old-fashioned razor. For a lot of other things, he wanted to stick with the old ways."

Early in the 2000s, Harry showed up to spring training in Florida one year with his first cell phone. There was, however, a learning curve for Harry. With Scott Graham's help, Harry set up his voicemail the day before the Phillies had a game in Fort Myers, which was a two-and-a-half-hour drive from the Phillies' facility in Clearwater. The night before the road trip, Graham and Andersen were having drinks at the Palm Pavilion in Clearwater Beach when they decided that they better start their drive the next morning at 8 a.m., instead of 8:30.

"I call Harry's condo," Graham said. "No answer. So I'm thinking, 'Do I bother calling his cell?' I call the cell, it rings four times and it goes to the voicemail. I say, 'Harry, I don't even know if you know how to retrieve the messages on this phone, but I'll try you again a little later on. We're going to leave at 8:00 tomorrow instead of 8:30.'"

A minute later, Graham's cell phone rings. It's Harry. "Scott Graham, I just want to let you know that I do know how to retrieve the messages on my cell phone. I just don't know how to answer it when it rings."

After cracking up, Graham said, "H, we'll teach you how to answer it tomorrow."

Harry definitely was set in his ways in other areas, as well. One thing he wasn't going to give up was his smoking habit. His wife and children, especially Brad and Kane, encouraged him to quit. He refused. He wasn't just hooked. He enjoyed it.

"Kane hates smoking," Eileen Kalas said. "Brad tied to get him to quit. Poor Brad always was worried about his health. He'd tell him to drink green tea, eat this, eat that . . . and it would always go in one ear and out the other."

When Harry first started using Dion Rassias as his agent in 2005, they would meet in Harry's Cadillac just outside of Rassias' downtown Philadelphia law office. Harry opted for this setting because he knew smoking wasn't permitted inside Rassias' prestigious workplace, The Beasley Firm.

"I don't even know why Harry needed to light up because as soon as you opened his car door, you needed a fire alarm to get in," Rassias said. "I don't know how he could see. It was like a cartoon. I couldn't work out there. I said, 'Hey, why don't we go indoors?'"

Soon thereafter, Dion broke office policy for Harry, who became the only person allowed to smoke in his building. Rick DiDonato made the same exception for Harry at Baker Sound.

When Harry had a doctor's exam about a month before his death, he was in the examination room with his wife and physician when he excused himself to go to the restroom. While Harry was gone, Eileen pleaded with the doctor to recommend that Harry give up a smoking habit that had started almost 60 years before.

Upon returning, the doctor spoke up. "You have to quit smoking," he told Harry.

Harry responded with a laugh. "Eileen told you to say that," he said.

The doctor fibbed and claimed it was his recommendation. Harry didn't buy it. Besides, Harry wasn't going to give up cigarettes for anyone. Once the doctor gave up his brief half-hearted attempt to break Harry's habit, he asked for an autograph. Harry signed a surgical glove with his name, then added an inscription: "Eileen told you to say that."

Although his body was slowing down, Harry refused to lighten his work schedule or prepare any less vigorously than he had for years. Before Phillies games, he continued to study statistics while peppering beat writers for information over dinner and tracking down information on visiting teams from their broadcasters. His mind and body were slowing down, but Harry was determined never to get by solely on his great voice.

In 2007, Harry was invited to work an inning in the ESPN *Sunday Night Baseball* booth with Jon Miller and Joe Morgan. When Harry entered, he was carrying a stack of books, including his scorebook, media guides, and record book.

"What's with all the books?" Jon Miller asked.

"In case I need them," Harry said.

Miller had to laugh.

"After 40 years, Harry wasn't phoning it in," Miller said years later. "He loved what he was doing and there was no other place that he'd rather be than the ballpark. I never heard Harry one time say to me, 'Let's hope that this game is a short one.' It bugs me when I hear broadcasters say that because we have the best job in the world. This is an imposition for you being at the ballpark? It wasn't for Harry."

By the late 2000s, still others saw signs that Harry was slowing down. NFL Films President Steve Sabol noticed it in May 2008 when he served as Harry's presenter for his enshrinement into the National Sportscasters & Sports writers Hall of Fame. Harry "didn't look good" and "seemed a little disengaged," Sabol said.

Jeff McCabe, Harry's old police officer friend, saw changes in Harry that concerned him greatly, too. "Harry always wanted to stay home. He had never been like that."

"Harry, you're just not yourself," McCabe told his friend in 2008. "You feeling okay? Your legs are like toothpicks. Talk to me."

Harry said he was fine.

McCabe knew about Harry's heart issue. He pleaded with him not to wait until baseball season was over to have heart surgery.

"Harry, get to the cardiologist," McCabe said. "Your heart's not pumping the way it should."

Harry didn't listen to his wife, and he didn't listen to his friends.

In August 2008, the Phillies made their only visit of the season to Chicago. Over the years, these trips had allowed Harry to visit with some of his high school friends in his hometown of nearby Naperville, Ill. Harry never forgot his roots or old pals such as Wally Baumgartner, and cousins Gene and Gib Drendel.

Naperville Community High School, Class of 1954, scheduled a 54th reunion for 2008. They'd picked the weekend of August 29-30 so that their most famous classmate could attend at least the first night's activities, just as he did for their 50th. The Phillies and Chicago Cubs had an early afternoon game that Friday, and then a late afternoon game on Saturday. Harry notified Baumgartner that he'd be free to socialize with his classmates on Friday night.

Baumgartner picked up Harry after Friday's game across the street from Wrigley Field at The Cubby Bear bar. In past years, this would have led to a few drinks, but Harry had given up alcohol by then, so the plan was to leave right away. But when Harry was recognized by most everyone in the bar, he ended up sticking around for a half-hour to sign autographs and pose for pictures with Phillies and Cubs fans.

During their drive to Naperville, Baumgartner almost immediately observed a different Harry. Wally was surprised when he made mention of one of Harry's past visits to town in order to be inducted into the school's Wall of Fame, and Harry had no recollection of the event. Harry still didn't remember it even after he was reminded that he had been inducted with another famous Naperville Central alum, one who also was in attendance.

"You were there," Wally said. "Paula Zahn of CNN was there."

Harry drew a blank.

At the reunion, other classmates noticed Harry had really aged. He was frail, quieter and struggled with his memory. Despite these increasing signs of age, Harry seemed rejuvenated at the ballpark in his final years. After no playoffs for 13 years, the Phillies won their division in 2007, then won it again in 2008 en route to going all the way to a world championship. Harry enjoyed the winning as much as anyone—maybe more than anyone—and the 2008 postseason was the crowning jewel to his great broadcasting career.

When the 2008 baseball season ended, Eileen Kalas hoped Harry might reconsider his stance on holding off on his heart surgery until after football season. He didn't. Two days after the Phillies victory parade, Harry did play-by-play on Westwood One radio for the New York Giants' 35-14 victory over the Dallas Cowboys in East Rutherford, N.J.

Harry then worked one game a week for the rest of the NFL season, sometimes having to take long flights to get there. He also traveled to Mount Laurel, N.J., every Wednesday morning for his NFL Films narrations.

Eleven days after the Pittsburgh Steelers won Super Bowl XLIII, Harry finally took care of his heart condition. His February 11, 2009 procedure at The Hospital of the University of Pennsylvania was considered successful. Doctors told Harry that the bottom of his heart was dead, but that the severe blockages in his legs had been opened with stents. Once again, he had a pulse in his legs. They told Harry that he would need a month to recover, but then he'd be medically cleared to head to Clearwater for the final few weeks of spring training and to work a full 2009 baseball season. His family and friends were relieved that the problem was resolved, but once again encouraged Harry to cut down on his traveling, at least during the beginning of the upcoming season. As usual, Harry said slowing down wasn't an option.

Family and friends knew details of Harry's surgery, but the public did not. Realizing that Harry's absence from the first two weeks of spring training games would be a red flag that something was up, Eileen Kalas instructed the Phillies to answer media inquiries about Harry's absence by saying he was recovering from undergoing a minor medical procedure.

"Eileen was very worried about what would be put out," Phillies President David Montgomery said. "I said, 'It's February. We don't need to make a statement right now about Harry. If he's recognized in the hospital, we'll say he's in for a procedure.' I was getting one level of concern from Eileen, then Harry would really soften it."

Harry was hospitalized for six days, but played down his situation to everyone. In his first public post-surgery comments, an interview with the *Bucks County Courier Times*, Harry shared the truth about his heart procedure.

"It's not the big casino," Harry said, referring to his terminology for cancer. "We're calling it minor surgery because I don't want people to worry. I'm feeling better and better all the time."

Kalas said he planned to be in spring training by mid-March. During that interview, Harry was asked for his thoughts about entering the final year of his contract in 2009. He said he hadn't had discussions with the Phillies about an extension, which didn't seem to be a big deal at the time. What potentially could be a big deal was his revelation during the interview that he wasn't sure if he'd return in 2010.

"We'll see how things go this year," said Harry, who didn't reveal to the reporter that he had pondered retirement only a few months earlier.

While Harry would only commit to working through 2009, Harry also said that every time he would ponder retirement, the same thought always ran through his head: "What would I do? What the heck would I do?"

As word of Harry's heart surgery spread to more of his friends, their level of concern grew.

"Harry, you gotta start taking care of yourself," longtime friend Joe Nunes advised him. "The last thing I want to happen is for me to turn the TV on and find out that you dropped dead."

Early in March 2009, Harry's first day back to work since his surgery was for an NFL Films narration project. Harry performed 15 pages of voiceovers, a much longer read than usual, for the 2008 Arizona Cardinals' highlight film. It took an exhausting 80 minutes to complete. Dave Plaut, a longtime NFL Films producer, quietly observed his friend looking old and tired during the session. "Harry didn't look great, but he sounded OK," Plaut said. "I could tell he wasn't himself."

Harry missed the start of spring training to continue recovering from his surgery. But by mid-March, he was getting antsy and seemed to be perking up physically, just as the doctors had predicted. On March 21, 11 days before the Phillies would leave spring training for Philadelphia, Harry showed up for work in Clearwater, Fla. That morning, Tom McCarthy walked into the broadcaster's office at Bright House Field and found Harry, dressed in a white jacket, sitting in a chair reading up on the team.

Two days later, Harry and his partners did a broadcasting roundtable interview together for the Phillies website in the Hooters VIP Diamond Dugout area at Bright House Field. With a slight breeze blowing through his bangs, Harry looked good and sounded good. He was smiling. He appeared healthy and happy.

"Well, it's a pleasure to be here and I'm looking forward to the season because last year was the most exciting, most fun season that I've ever experienced with the Philadelphia Phillies," Harry said during the group interview hosted by Scott Palmer, the team's director of public affairs. "The fact that that team came together and brought us a world championship, I will never forget."

Harry initially had no health problems while working the Phillies' final spring games. He even found some time to take walks on Clearwater Beach, and was thrilled that his legs felt great. On March 26, the weekend before spring training ended, Harry celebrated his 73rd birthday the way he'd celebrated past birthdays. He met his oldest son, Tampa Bay Rays broadcaster Todd Kalas, at Derby Lane for dinner and gambling on the greyhounds. This was Harry's old spring stomping ground, a place that he loved for years. But this time, Harry cut their visit short. After the sixth race, he told Todd that he was tired and wanted to leave.

"OK, we'll come back next year," Todd told his father.

"Nah," Harry replied. "I think this is the last time I come to Derby Lane."

At the time, Todd didn't think much of the surprising comment. "I wasn't overly worried," he said. "Obviously, he had lost some weight and was a little bit frailer than he had been. I assumed that he still was in recovery mode from that offseason surgery. So I didn't anticipate anything more than that was on the horizon. Listening back to some of his calls in 2008, I don't think he had lost much off his fastball. I thought that he still was calling a pretty good game. As long as he loved what he was doing and the doctors had cleared him to travel for the season, I just assumed it was another 162 games. I figured HK would figure out a way to get it done."

Harry may have somehow realized that he didn't have long to live. In the final two months of his life, he would often get emotional while saying goodbye to a friend, either over the phone or in person.

"It was almost like Harry was saying goodbye without realizing it," Atlanta Braves broadcaster Chip Caray said of a conversation that he had with Harry before a Phillies game in the first week of the 2009 season

Rick DiDonato of Baker Sound thought it was strange when Harry called out of the blue in March 2009 to thank him for 22 years of working together on voiceovers. Former Phillies outfielder Glenn Wilson was freaked out when Harry ended their last call with "Willie, I love you." Did Harry know what was coming? For years, he'd not only talked about dying during conversations with his wife, but he did so with a chilling premonition.

"I'm going to die in the booth," Harry said on more than one occasion.

Harry believed it, but the way it came out seemed comical to Eileen Kalas.

"That's just great," Eileen once said. "Little kids are watching the game and Harry Kalas dies in the booth."

"I wouldn't do that," Harry responded.

"Why don't you die someplace else?" Eileen said.

"No, I'm going to die in the booth," Harry said. "I'll wait for a commercial or wait until the game's over, but I'm going to die in the booth."

The Phillies left 2008 spring training after a Thursday game in Florida. The club had two more exhibition games scheduled at Citizens Bank Park in Philadelphia for Friday night and Saturday afternoon against Tampa Bay before opening the 2009 regular season against Atlanta on *Sunday Night Baseball.*

Harry had intended on broadcasting both Tampa Bay exhibition games but wound up missing the first. He'd gotten a touch of the flu in his final days of spring training, then felt a lot worse after returning to Philadelphia. Upon his returning home, Harry was tired, weak and had no appetite. He also was losing a lot of weight.

Eileen insisted that Harry visit a doctor. Thinking that he needed to get better in a hurry, Harry reluctantly agreed.

Harry planned to skip the Friday night game against Tampa Bay, which would be aired only on radio, and then return for Saturday's exhibition, a television game.

A medical exam revealed Harry was dehydrated and had lost 10 percent of his body weight, dropping from 170 to 151 pounds. The doctor ordered Harry to go to a hospital immediately for treatment. Again, Harry begrudgingly followed orders and was driven by Eileen to Lankenau Hospital in Wynnewood, Pa. Harry figured that he'd be administered an IV to get some fluids into his system, and then head home a few hours later.

On the way to the hospital, Eileen phoned David Montgomery. Both believed that it was a no-brainer for Harry to skip Saturday's exhibition game in order to rest up further. With Sunday's season opener to be televised on ESPN, not on the Phillies' network, and with Monday being an off day, Harry easily could have had three days to get better. While Eileen and David were talking, Harry shouted from the passenger seat, "Tell Monty, it's a TV game."

"I know it's a TV game," David said into the phone to Eileen.

Harry insisted on working the next day. "It's a TV game tomorrow. I'm coming in," he said.

The plan changed when Harry was admitted to the hospital, which infuriated him. In his mind, Harry felt he would be letting down the Phillies and his fans by missing Saturday's game, even though it was a meaningless exhibition. A few minutes after Harry was admitted, as he was about to doze off, Eileen headed home. "I figured he was in good hands, and I told him that I'd be back that night," she said. About five hours later, Eileen was home when she received a surprising phone call from Harry.

"They're releasing me," he said. "I'm feeling only perfect."

Thinking Harry had talked the doctors into sending him home, Eileen was livid driving back to the hospital to pick up her husband. "I was very angry because I knew he was really sick," she said.

Upon arriving at the hospital, Eileen learned the truth. Harry hadn't been released. "A nurse met me in the hall and said, 'Eileen, we want to keep him overnight. He will not stay.'"

When Eileen entered Harry's hospital room, her husband was out of his bed and in a chair.

"I'm not missing tomorrow's game," Harry said.

"You're staying," Eileen shot back with anger.

"I'm leaving, and if you don't take me home I'm walking," Harry said sternly.

Ignoring his wife's pleas, Harry started to change from hospital garb into his clothes with an IV still in his arm. "They wouldn't let me get dressed until you got here," he told Eileen.

As Harry was fiddling with his clothes, a nurse noticed the IV and said, "Harry, sit down, you have to let me take out the IV."

Laughing, Harry said, "Yeah, that wouldn't look good during the game."

Against medical advice, Harry discharged himself. On their way back home, Harry phoned Rob Brooks, the Phillies manager of broadcasting.

"H, don't worry about coming in tomorrow," Brooks told Harry. "We have it covered."

"No, I'm going to do the game," Harry said, forcefully.

Harry got his way. He worked that Saturday and told everyone that he was feeling fine. Come Wednesday, Harry pulled one of his colorful sports jackets out of his closet for a matinee game, the Phillies' opening-series finale against the Atlanta Braves. He wanted to dress up because Phillies players and coaches were to be receiving their World Series rings in an on-field, pre-game ceremony that, naturally, he would emcee. Harry also was to be given the honor of throwing out the ceremonial first pitch.

But when Harry tried on his sports jacket, a size 42 regular, it appeared to be falling off him because he had lost so much weight during his recent illness. He ended up borrowing one of his son Kane's loud, red sports jackets, which amazingly fit him perfectly even though it was a size 39 regular.

"Kane likes bright colors just like his dad, and Harry was so proud to wear that jacket," Eileen said.

At the ballpark, Harry's emcee performance was flawless, and then when he took the pitcher's mound to throw out the first pitch, he received a spectacular ovation that just seemed to go on and on.

Standing in front of the mound, Harry leaned forward pretending to get a sign from Phillies catcher Carlos Ruiz. With the crowd still cheering, Harry broke his concentration to wave and blow a kiss. Harry then leaned in again for a sign, wound up and found enough strength only to throw a one-hopper that bounced right in front of the plate and into Ruiz' glove. Playing umpire, the Phillie Phanatic called the pitch a strike. With a smile, Harry held out both arms with his hands facing up, as if to say, "What do you expect from a 73-year-old?"

During the Phillies game that day, Harry left the booth during his normal fifth-inning break to have a quick smoke. Billy Atkinson, the man who runs the Citizens Bank Park press elevator, picked Harry up and rode him down to the basement. Atkinson made small talk with Harry about the Phillies' upcoming road trip, a weekend in Denver followed by three games and a scheduled trip to the White House during a four-day visit to Washington.

"This trip will be one to remember," Harry Kalas told the elevator man.

A LEGEND DEPARTS

Many in the Phillies traveling party took particular notice when Harry Kalas boarded the team charter, Delta flight 9836. For the first road trip of the 2009 baseball season, a 4 p.m. flight from Philadelphia to Denver, the Hall of Fame announcer took a seat up front with the other broadcasters and the coaches, instead of his usual spot in the back row. Harry loved sitting in the back with the veterans players. He had been there since the 1970s, minus those few months in 2002 when he was booted out. In recent years, Harry hadn't been drinking on the plane with players—he gave up alcohol around 2003—but he still enjoyed the conversation, and watching guys play cards a row or two ahead of him.

Phillies broadcaster Tom McCarthy observed that Harry had been looking tired, but then thought to himself, "He is 73 years old."

Other than his unusual seat location on the plane, there seemed to be nothing else out of the ordinary for Harry or the Phillies during their weekend in Colorado. After opening the season by dropping two of three games at home, the Phillies seemed to be experiencing what had become for them a typical early season run of mediocre baseball, as they were whipped 10-3 in their series opener at Coors Field before winning 8-4 the next day.

On Sunday morning, Harry Kalas packed his bags, checked out of the Ritz-Carlton hotel and took the team bus to the ballpark. The Phillies would head from Denver to Washington immediately after the game, then return to Philadelphia after that series ended.

While in Denver, Harry took a call from his older brother. Jim Kalas was extremely worried about Harry's health. He thought Harry had returned to work too soon from the February heart surgery.

"Won't the Phillies just let you do home games?" Jim asked.

"I can't do that," Harry said.

Harry had greatly enjoyed the Phillies' series finale with the Rockies. Down 5-3 after seven innings, the Phillies scored two in the eighth to tie and then two in the ninth to pull ahead, the go-ahead runs coming on a homer by Matt Stairs. Harry had no way of knowing it at the time, but his home run call would become a footnote to his great career, and by all accounts, it was perfect. *"Long drive into deep right-center field, this ball is . . . Outta here! Matt Stairs with a two-run, pinch-hit home run, and the Phillies have taken a 7-5 lead here in the ninth inning."*

From there, Phillies closer Brad Lidge worked his way into a two-on, two-out jam in the bottom of the ninth before Troy Tulowitzki hit into a game-ending groundout. Harry's voice filled with excitement as he called the final out. *"Bouncing ball to Chase Utley, this should be the game, Chase throws him out and that will be it as the Phils win two out of three here at Coors Field, coming back to take this one by a score of 7-5."*

Following the game, the Phillies headed to the airport for a long night flight to Washington, D.C.

Once again, Harry opted for a seat in the front of the plane, an obvious sign that he wasn't himself. He took a Row 3 window seat on the right side of the plane, a row ahead of Phillies batting practice pitcher Ali Modami. Harry ate a bison burger and made small talk with Modami. "He looked and sounded good. It was the same old Harry."

While the team was still in the air, Julie Vanwey, Harry's stepdaughter, drove from her home in Elsmere, Del., to the Phillies' hotel in Arlington, Va. Vanwey, 40 years old and single, recently had begun working as a personal assistant to Harry. She planned to go along with her step-dad on some Phillies road trips during the 2009 season, to make sure that Harry was eating and taking care of himself.

On this particular trip, Julie was hoping to enjoy a special perk. The Phillies were scheduled to play games in Washington on Monday, Wednesday and Thursday. On the Tuesday off day, the reigning World Series champions had accepted an invitation to the White House in order to be congratulated by President Barack Obama. Harry very much wanted Julie to accompany him to the White House even though he had been told by the Phillies that only players could bring guests with them.

According to Phillies President David Montgomery, "We had a very limited list because of security clearance reasons. It wasn't us saying no. The goal was to stay around 70 guests and we ended up under 100 by three."

Apparently 27 over their limit was the limit.

Eileen Kalas, Harry's wife and Julie's mother, wasn't happy about Harry not being able to take Julie to the White House. She and Phillies management had had their differences over the years concerning Harry, and the Phillies' decision this time, in her opinion, was grossly unfair.

"The Phillies have one Hall of Famer going to the White House and he's not allowed to bring a guest?" she told Harry. "It's not right."

Showing his inventive side, Harry concocted a plan to get around the Phillies' decree. He asked Jimmy Rollins, the team's star shortstop, to see if every Phillies player was bringing a guest.

Harry was looking forward to visiting the White House, too. He brought three basketball books from his library as a gift to the President, who had just entered office two-and-a-half months earlier.

Julie arrived at the Ritz-Carlton, Pentagon City in Arlington late at night, but before the Phillies checked in after 1 a.m., the next morning. She thought about greeting Harry in the lobby, but figured he'd be too tired to talk. She intended to shop for a new dress to wear to the White House the next day while the Phillies were playing the Nationals in an afternoon game. She and Harry planned to then dine together on Monday night.

When the Phillies finally arrived at their hotel, Harry indeed was beat from the long day and night. He went straight to bed and hoped to get to sleep in a hurry. It already was very late and the team bus was scheduled to depart the hotel at 11:30 the next morning for Monday's game.

Lying in bed, Harry started experiencing chest pains. He should have called for medical attention, but instead waited for the pain to just go away. They didn't. He tossed and turned all night, possibly in great fear. His father had died of a heart attack. Richie Ashburn, his best friend, died of a heart attack. Harry had a bad heart.

The next morning Harry's good friend Jeff McCabe noticed a missed blocked call on his phone at 2:30 a.m. McCabe wondered if it had been Harry, who always called him when something was wrong.

Harry did place a call to Eileen a few moments before leaving for the ballpark that Monday morning, April 13, 2009. He told his wife that he didn't sleep well, but not about the chest pains. Eileen hadn't wanted Harry to go on this road trip because she worried that the change in altitude in Denver would be rough on his heart. When Harry told Eileen that he didn't get a good night's rest, she said, "I told you not to go to Denver."

"It's not the altitude," Harry said, trying to calm his wife. "I just didn't sleep well."

"It's probably your heart." Eileen said.

"I gotta go," Harry said. "The bus is here."

"Okay, but promise me the minute you get there you'll go see the Phillies trainer," Eileen said. After some coaxing, Harry agreed.

"I have to go," he said again. "Eileen, I love you. I have to go."

Harry left his room, took an elevator to the lobby and then walked to the team bus. He took a seat near the back with most of the other broadcasters—Larry Andersen, Tom McCarthy, Scott Franzke and Chris Wheeler.

"He seemed fine to me," Franzke said.

He wasn't. During the ride to the ballpark, Harry confessed to Andersen that he had a bad night.

"I'm not doing so hot," Harry said. "I didn't get much sleep. I was having chest pains."

"Why didn't you call somebody?" Andersen said.

Kalas didn't answer, but Andersen figured that he knew the answer. Harry probably didn't want to bother anybody, even at the expense of his own life. He also might have been afraid of what the doctors would tell him. He certainly didn't want to be told to take some time off. He had made that clear enough.

During the bus ride to Nationals Park, Harry approached Jimmy Rollins about the White House visit. Rollins told Harry that Ryan Howard, the Phillies' star first baseman, was going alone.

"Do you think Julie can be his guest?" Harry asked.

"I think it's cool, but I can't ask him for you," Rollins said.

Howard wasn't on the team bus, so Harry headed for the clubhouse once he arrived at Nationals Park. He didn't keep his promise to Eileen about talking to the Phillies trainer during his clubhouse visit. Nobody noticed if he even made an attempt.

Harry did go looking for Ryan Howard, who wasn't at his locker.

Seeing Harry during his pre-game appearance in the Phillies clubhouse, *Philadelphia Daily News* baseball writer Paul Hagen offered a warm greeting. "Hey Harry, how was Denver?"

"Coooooold," Harry said in a friendly voice, stretching out the "o" to emphasize his point.

Phillies manager Charlie Manuel remembers seeing Harry that morning and thinking that he "didn't look good."

Waiting out Howard in the clubhouse, Harry wrote down the starting lineups, which were posted on a wall. Within a few minutes, Harry spotted the man he was searching for in the food room, seated at a table with outfielder Jayson Werth and Rollins.

"Ryan, can you take my stepdaughter to the White House," Harry asked.

"Sure, H, no problem," Howard said right away.

Harry thanked Howard and Rollins, then went on his way.

"I hope we don't get into trouble for this," Rollins thought to himself.

Before he forgot, Howard right away went looking for Frank Coppenbarger, the Phillies' director of team travel and clubhouse services, so that Julie Vanwey could be added to the White House guest list.

"We can't do it," Coppenbarger told Howard. "It's only for spouses and fiancées."

Coppenbarger then contacted Rob Brooks, the Phillies' manager of broadcasting, and asked him to give Harry the bad news about Julie and the White House visit.

Coppenbarger was simply relaying the decision that he had received from his superiors in Phillies management. Frank loved Harry Kalas, but he had been told that the White House visitor list was set in stone.

"It was kind of weird that he couldn't bring somebody," Rollins said in retrospect.

On his way from the clubhouse level to the press box, Harry ended up on the elevator with Larry Andersen and Brooks, who was en route to deliver the message to Harry privately. The elevator stopped to pick up CSNPhilly.com reporter John Finger, who had just arrived at the ballpark. Finger expected the usual friendly hello and small talk with Harry, whom he'd known since he started covering the Phillies in 2001. During their brief ride, Harry didn't say a word to him.

"It was so noticeable when I got on the elevator that I was like 'Oh, wow, he looks tired,'" Finger recalled.

When the elevator reached the sixth floor, the broadcast media level, everyone got off, even Finger, who had forgotten to hit the button for the fifth floor, the print media level. As Finger was realizing his mistake and returning to the elevator, Andersen and Brooks entered the Phillies radio booth and Harry went into the visiting television booth.

Wearing a sports coat over his Phillies television jersey, Harry took a seat in front of the booth and set his briefcase on the counter. He opened it up and pulled out a Phillies media guide, scorecard, pencil and his reading glasses. He then started jotting down the lineups. Harry neatly wrote in the Phillies' starting nine, then began with the Nationals. He penciled in the first four names, getting through cleanup hitter Adam Dunn.

Tragically and ironically, Harry was done after Dunn. Once he'd printed those four letters, his 73-year-old heart gave out. A massive attack sent him crashing from his seat to the floor.

Over in the radio booth, Andersen and Brooks had a brief conversation. Harry was alone for maybe two minutes when Brooks excused himself.

"I need to go talk to Harry about the White House," Brooks told Andersen before heading to the television booth, which was the next room over.

When Brooks entered around 12:30 p.m., Harry was lying on the floor unconscious. Brooks was terrified. Despite being half Harry's age, Brooks was very close to Harry. They had worked together for 17 years. He knew Harry's medical history. Brooks phoned 911, then went down to his knees and started administering CPR.

"I think he was with us at that point," Brooks said.

Not for long. The CPR wasn't working. Harry stopped breathing. Shaking, Brooks hustled over to the next booth to tell Andersen, who frantically ran to see Harry.

Harry was on his back with his legs straight out. His left arm was at his side, his right arm bent at the elbow and next to his head in a Statue of Liberty position. His eyes were open. Blood was dripping from one of his ears. Knowing Harry was in big trouble, Andersen gave his friend another round of CPR.

"Come on H, come on H!" he shouted while pumping on Harry's chest.

Within a few minutes, medical help arrived. EMTs worked on Harry in the booth, then placed him on a gurney and headed for George Washington University Hospital.

Chris Wheeler was standing by the elevator when Harry was rushed out. He'd heard the EMTs working on his longtime partner. Seeing Harry on the stretcher, Wheeler could tell right away that the situation was extremely critical. Harry had an oxygen mask over his face and EKG leads dotting his chest. His chest wasn't moving.

"This doesn't look good," Wheeler told himself.

As the EMTs were working on Harry in the press box, Brooks phoned Eileen Kalas and then Phillies president David Montgomery. When her phone rang, Eileen was drinking coffee, watching television and paying bills in Harry's home office as two handymen worked in her kitchen putting in a new part for her electric stove.

"Harry passed out in the booth," Brooks told Eileen. "We've called the ambulance. They're on their way."

Montgomery had traveled from Philadelphia to Washington by train early that morning with his wife. He was going to go to the game that afternoon, but really was in town to accompany the Phillies to the White House the following day. He checked into the hotel at 11:30 a.m., did a little unpacking and was headed to a food court across the street for lunch. He made it only as far as the hotel lobby when Brooks called. Instead of eating, he caught a cab and rushed to the ballpark.

Julie Vanwey, Harry's stepdaughter, was in her room getting ready to go shopping when she received a panicked phone call from her mother. Eileen told Julie to get to the hospital right away.

Once he arrived at Nationals Park, Montgomery took charge of the chaotic situation. Montgomery closed the Phillies clubhouse to alert the team, and then gathered the Philadelphia media together for an initial briefing. Within minutes, websites were posting information that Harry had collapsed in a press box. During the short wait for an update that most everyone feared would not be good news, Montgomery was approached by Nationals management. The club offered to postpone the game. Montgomery appreciated the gracious gesture, but declined. It was, after all, the Nationals' home opener. Besides, Montgomery was sure that Harry would want the game to be played.

At the hospital, Julie Vanwey was led to a small chapel. Rob Brooks was there. They talked about Harry's condition, and also briefly about the White House visit problem. They had been there only a few minutes when a doctor entered with an update.

Harry Kalas, legendary broadcaster, had been pronounced dead at 1:20 p.m.

Julie was asked if she wanted to see Harry's body. She did. But first, she called her mother.

"He didn't make it," Julie said, breaking the terrible news.

"Oh, my baby!" Eileen cried out.

Julie was numb being led into the room where Harry's body lay. He had been in her life since she was a teen, and they cared deeply for each other. She stayed with Harry for 20 minutes before finally saying a tearful goodbye.

Although feeling as if he were in shock, Rob Brooks headed back to the ballpark. The Phillies had a game to play in 90 minutes. He had a job to do, and he knew he'd be directing a radio broadcast on this day that would be like none other.

After Montgomery had learned in a call from Brooks that Harry had died, he passed along the sad news to the team. Upon exiting the Phillies clubhouse, Montgomery approached a group of waiting media and said softly, "We lost our voice today."

Harry's oldest sons, Todd and Brad, received word quickly, but Kane, a freshman at the University of Miami, was in class. When he turned on his cell phone, he too learned the tragic news in a text message from a friend who had picked up reports of Harry's death from an online news outlet.

Jeff McCabe, Harry's close friend, raced to the Kalas home to console Eileen, who was distraught and dealing with a constant stream of phone calls.

She also had a funeral to plan. McCabe turned on the television, which seemed to have nonstop Harry Kalas coverage on all the local stations.

"Do you want to see how they're honoring Harry?" he asked.

"No, I don't know if I can handle it," she said.

Jasmine Kalas, Harry's first wife, took the news extremely hard, after getting a call from Todd, the older of her two children. She hadn't talked to Harry in many years, but never stopped loving him. Within minutes, she started to receive phone calls and emails from her many Phillies friends whom she had kept after she and Harry separated in 1987 and divorced in 1993.

Montgomery immediately called off the next day's visit to the White House. The players were stunned by Harry's passing, but had a game to play. The media was kept away from Phillies players before the game, but not from the Phillies broadcasters, who tearfully shared their emotions.

Chris Wheeler appeared to be taking the loss as hard as anyone. He had been a very good friend to Harry for many years before things turned ugly between them. Maybe five feet from where Harry died, Wheeler was sitting on a counter in the press box 30 minutes later when two reporters entered.

"His glasses were sitting right here," Wheeler said, his eyes red and his voice cracking. "I packed his bag. That was spooky. Somebody had to do it. I was the only one around and we're getting to the point where we have to do the game."

Wheeler stopped talking for a minute, then shook his head in disgust. "You know, he and I have been down a lot of roads. Thirty-nine years. A lot of good times."

With wet eyes, Scott Franzke told a story from March 2006. He'd just joined the Phillies that season. "My first day on the air in spring training, we were in Kissimmee doing an exhibition game with the Astros. I came on in the fourth inning to work with Harry. Ryan Howard hit an opposite-field home run and Harry did the 'Outta here!' All I could think of was, 'Wow, I'm sitting next to Harry Kalas.'"

A few minutes later, Harry's broadcasting team was still trying to cope while simultaneously trying to help Phillies fans make it through the day.

"I broke Harry's No. 1 rule, and that's to be prepared," Franzke said months later. "There was no preparing for that game."

Franzke and his color man Larry Andersen opened on radio, while Tom

McCarthy, Chris Wheeler and Gary Matthews were in the TV booth.

"This will be the most impossible of days to broadcast a baseball game, but just as Harry had to do when he lost his good friend Whitey 12 seasons ago, we have a first pitch at 3:05," Franzke said during his opening. "Harry and Whitey, together once again, will be listening and hopefully enjoying the game along with the rest of us."

Larry Andersen spoke next. "There's no words. I can't even talk. . . . It's just a sad day and it's going to be sad for a long time to come to the ballpark and not see Harry and not hear his little jabs that he could do behind the scenes, his 'High Hopes,' everything about him. It's just not the same already."

Both the Phillies radio and television broadcasts developed into tributes to Harry. Wheeler told stories about the 1993 Phillies, Harry's favorite team. Tom McCarthy talked about Harry's special relationship with fans. On one of the saddest days in franchise history, the broadcasters tried to look back on all the great memories Harry left during his 39 years with the club.

Phillies players were having a tough time, too. They knew what he meant to the franchise and to the fans, and to them. He was a generation or two older than all of them, but a trusted friend.

The National Anthem was preceded by a moment of silence for Harry. Right before the first pitch, Harry was given another tribute by Phillies center fielder Shane Victorino. In the dugout and with television cameras rolling, Victorino lit up a cigarette in honor of Harry, who had been a heavy smoker since high school. Victorino took a drag, then passed it to his teammates. Ryan Howard, Scott Eyre and others participated in sharing four cigarettes. All of the players are non-smokers, but they did it for Harry.

"I just thought it would be neat because that's what Harry liked to do," Victorino said. "When we got off the bus, he would always stop and light one up."

Victorino provided another touching tribute during the game. In the third inning of a 9-8 Phillies victory, Victorino hit a leadoff homer. After circling the bases, he held up his left hand and pointed to the broadcast booth while jogging from home plate to the Phillies dugout.

Despite winning the game, the Phillies' mood stayed deeply somber.

"Coming back in the clubhouse, there wasn't much more than a whisper, no music, no shaking hands, no nothing," Frank Coppenbarger said. "Winning is very important every day, but I thought winning was more important that day. It was really important for the guys, important for Harry and important for Philadelphia to come out ahead that day."

Back in Philadelphia, Phillies employees working at Citizens Bank Park cried at their desks and hugged one another. Phone calls and emails started pouring in from alumni, baseball executives, fans and friends of Harry. Jean Ashburn, Whitey's widow, left a message expressing her family's love for Harry. Outside the ballpark, Phillies fans dropped off cards, flowers, teddy bears, homemade signs and, fittingly, beer. Harry didn't have a statue of his own and Richie Ashburn's was inside the ballpark at Ashburn Alley, so they flocked to the 10-foot-high bronze likeness of one of Harry's favorite players and close friends, Michael Jack Schmidt.

Phillies fans everywhere were in shock. Harry Kalas' sudden death was one of the biggest stories to hit Philadelphia in decades, maybe even bigger than the Phillies winning the 2008 World Series. The next day, the *Philadelphia Daily News* devoted 14 of its 72-page tabloid to Kalas, including the front and back covers.

Among the thousands of fans in mourning was a 60-year-old Marlton, N.J., man who suffers from severe multiple sclerosis, and whose days were always brightened listening to Harry. Bruce Savateri, no longer able to walk and barely capable of speaking, was in his wheelchair crying when his wife returned home from an errand that day. "He died!" Bruce said between sobs, pointing to the living room television. Harry Kalas, Bruce's window to the world, was gone.

Around the country, Harry's friends and colleagues went into mourning. VIPs from all over the nation sent condolences.

"People in Philadelphia feel a personal sense of loss right now," famed sportscaster Bob Costas said when hearing of Kalas' death. "This was a voice that took them from childhood to adulthood through all stages of life. Things change . . . but Harry Kalas is always calling the games. This is a civic loss."

Baseball commissioner Bud Selig called Kalas "one of the great voices of our generation."

Vin Scully and Jon Miller, two of baseball's broadcasting giants, were sharing laughs before a Dodgers-Giants game at Dodger Stadium when someone approached. "I've got bad news, Harry Kalas just died in Washington," the stranger told them.

"Ooooooh, nooooo," Scully said, his voice sounding like a shriek.

The voice of the Dodgers since 1950, Scully was visibly upset about losing a friend he'd known since Harry first started broadcasting Major League Baseball with Houston in 1965. Scully paid a special tribute to Harry during his telecast. Six months later, Vin said, "I was horrified when I heard he passed. He was such a sweet, sweet man. And he said goodbye in the booth. I never spent the time I wish I had with him, but I sat around with him before every game in each other's booth. I knew Philadelphia loved him, and as well they should have. He was a wonderful human being. I really do miss him."

Around the country, Harry's friends tried to deal with the terrible news, each in their own way.

Former Phillies outfielder Glenn Wilson was watching an Astros baseball game from his home in Houston when Harry's death was reported during the broadcast. A born-again Christian, Wilson got on his knees and started praying.

"I got a call that he passed out in the press box," said Rick Walker, who broadcasted NFL games with Harry for Westwood One radio. "Never in a million years did I imagine it was fatal because I didn't think he would die. I just thought the guy was bionic."

ESPN *Baseball Tonight* host John Kruk, a star player for the Phillies in the 1990s, heard from a co-worker that Harry had collapsed. When he phoned the Phillies public relations department for an update, the woman answering the phone was sobbing. "Don't tell me, don't tell me," Kruk cried out.

Even the Philadelphia media struggled to cope. Comcast SportsNet's Michael Barkann had trouble talking on the air when first reporting news of Harry's death. At 610 WIP radio, Howard Eskin did his afternoon talk show in tears.

From his home in Los Angeles, Brad Kalas, the second of Harry's three sons, found some comfort watching ESPN, which aired many kind words about his father. "Having a famous dad helped out the healing process," he said.

Everyone was devastated, but those whom Harry knew best decided that, if he had to die, Harry at least went out in his home away from home.

"There was no place Harry would rather be than the booth," said Howard Deneroff, Harry's Westwood One boss. "I hate to say this, but there are worse places you can pass away. We all want to die in our sleep painlessly. But if baseball is your life—and it was Harry's life—then dying in a broadcast booth makes perfect sense."

A CITY WEEPS

The day after Harry Kalas died in a baseball press box, the Phillies' scheduled trip to the White House was postponed. They had a day off in Washington, D.C., but nobody felt like doing much of anything.

They were in mourning.

Shane Victorino, the team's center fielder, couldn't get Harry off his mind. While roaming the lobby of the Phillies' hotel in Arlington, Va., he spotted Frank Coppenbarger, the team's director of team travel and clubhouse services. Speaking for the team, Victorino said, "We want to do something to honor Harry."

Coppenbarger briefed Victorino on the honors that the Phillies were planning for Harry for the remainder of the 2009 season, which had begun a week earlier. A black circular patch with a white "HK" would be stitched over the hearts of game jerseys for players and coaches. Harry's "Outta here!" call would play over the Citizens Bank Park sound system after every Phillies home run. An "HK 1939-2009" billboard would be added to the outfield wall in left field, below the Harry the K's restaurant. The Phillies home television booth would be renamed in honor of Harry. "High Hopes," Harry's theme song, would be played at Phillies home games—first during the seventh-inning stretch of every game, and then after the initial homestand following every Phillies victory.

Victorino was impressed by all the Harry tributes planned by Phillies management. But he told Coppenbarger that the Phillies players wanted to create their own tribute. Harry had always been so much more than a broadcaster to Phillies players, even in his final years when most were less than half his age.

"Why don't we get his sports coat and white shoes, and put them in the dugout?" Victorino asked.

"If that's what you want to do, let me ask the family," Coppenbarger said.

Before checking with the Kalas family, Coppenbarger phoned Phillies President David Montgomery to run Victorino's request past him. Montgomery loved the idea. "To the players, that was Harry's uniform," Montgomery said.

Victorino's suggestion touched Harry's widow, Eileen Kalas, who picked out a light blue sports jacket and a pair of size nine white leather loafers to drop off at Citizens Bank Park before the Phillies returned home later in the week.

Phillies management then decided to do even more for Harry. They added a pre-game ceremony to honor Kalas during their next home series, and came up with another idea based on an earlier commemoration for Harry's beloved broadcast partner. In 1997, thousands of Phillies fans walked past Richie Ashburn's coffin at Philadelphia's Fairmount Park. The Phillies wanted to give their fans a similar opportunity to say goodbye to Harry. The morning after Harry Kalas died, David Montgomery phoned Eileen to discuss tribute plans.

"Eileen and I had a lengthy conversation and talked about her wishes," Montgomery said. "Originally, we talked about doing something off site. Then the more we thought about it . . . Citizens Bank Park, the ballpark was the right place for Harry."

Eileen told Montgomery that she wanted to talk things over with Harry's three sons Todd, Brad and Kane. Soon thereafter, Phillies management and the Kalas family agreed on a two-day weekend tribute for Harry at Citizens Bank Park. On Friday night, Harry would be honored before the Phillies' first home game since his passing. On Saturday morning, Citizens Bank Park would host a public memorial service, an event that would start only after fans received the opportunity to go onto the playing field and pass Harry's closed casket to pay their final respects.

The day after Harry's death, a spokeswoman from the Washington D.C., chief medical examiner's office released a statement listing Harry's official cause of death: high blood pressure and atherosclerotic cardiovascular disease—a hardening of the arteries and leading cause of heart attacks. Hearing the report, Eileen Kalas told friends and family, "There was nothing anybody could have done for him."

James A. McCafferty Funeral Home in Philadelphia was chosen by the Kalas family to conduct Harry's funeral.

Funeral director Mark McCafferty, 37, was one of Harry's biggest fans. He was honored beyond words upon learning that his funeral home was selected to bury Harry. "You bury someone like that once in your career," said McCafferty, who has handled about 200 burials annually since joining the family business at age 14. "I couldn't believe Harry was dead. I grew up listening to the guy my whole life. I'd met him about 10 times. I felt pressure to make him look good for everybody in the whole Delaware Valley."

McCafferty soon learned that that there would be no open-casket viewing. "I thought Harry wouldn't want me to see him dead," Eileen Kalas said. "I wanted to remember him smiling and happy. We talked about it, too. He did not want an open casket."

The funeral home's first duty was to make a three-hour trip to Washington D.C., to bring Harry back to Philadelphia. Brian McCafferty, Mark's brother, drove a 2009 black Cadillac hearse to pick up the body, leaving Philadelphia at 3 p.m., the next day. Along for the ride was Frank Bachmayer, police captain of the 15th district in northeast Philadelphia. Both are big Phillies fans, too. Both revered Harry Kalas.

"It definitely was an emotional time," Captain Bachmayer said. "You do this all the time, especially having 28 years in law enforcement. But when it's somebody that you knew a lot about and was so important to everybody, it was very sad. I was a fan of Harry's."

In Washington D.C., only Maryland or Virginia licensed funeral directors legally can pick up bodies. A Virginia funeral director was contracted to claim Harry's body in D.C., and then transfer it to McCafferty.

Captain Bachmayer was asked to identify the body.

"It was an emotional moment," he said. "All the workers that were there were silent. Usually everybody is walking around and talking. The emotion for me is always there, whether it's a kid on the street. . . . You have to try to control it and be aware of what you're doing. I usually go in slow motion when I do those things."

When the stretcher was rolled in front of him, Captain Bachmayer picked up Harry's right hand. A wrist band had Harry's name on it. Then the police officer looked at Harry's face. He braced himself, remembering that Harry had fallen to the ground during his fatal heart attack.

"Everything looked very peaceful," he said. "His hair was not messed up. It looked like he was sleeping. He looked normal. I said to Brian, 'This is him.' We put him in back of the hearse."

"Can you believe this?" Brian McCafferty said.

"It's going to be a long ride home," Captain Bachmayer said.

Neither said much as they started their drive back to Philadelphia in the rain. Knowing they were carrying a Philadelphia icon was very upsetting even for a mortician who has done this his entire life and for a police officer who has identified countless bodies during his career. Driving back, the silence finally was broken by the ring of the police officer's cell phone. Coincidentally, his outgoing ring happened to be Harry's 2008 World Series final-out call.

"You hear Harry saying, 'Here's the 0-2 pitch,'" the officer said. "It was just a surreal moment. I apologized to Brian for not putting it on vibrate."

When the hearse approached Philadelphia, Captain Bachmayer, who was behind the wheel for the return trip, phoned for a police escort. Three squad cars met them at the Bridge Street exit of I-95. "It was still raining and I wanted to make sure I got Mr. Kalas there as safely as possible," he said. "And I thought that he deserved an escort."

Around 11 p.m., the day after Harry Kalas died, the hearse pulled into McCafferty's on Frankford Avenue in northeast Philadelphia.

Before long, McCafferty realized that Eileen Kalas and the Phillies weren't totally in sync. While they did work out details for the tributes at Citizens Bank Park, the Phillies were completely in the dark about what would take place during the private graveside funeral that Eileen was planning.

"As a funeral director, you can tell when there's an issue and I knew there was an issue right way," Mark McCafferty said. "I could tell there was tension. Just getting them on the same page wasn't the easiest thing in the world."

"If there was tension, we didn't know it," Eileen Kalas said. "We weren't arguing with the Phillies. They knew all of our plans and helped execute them."

Eileen set the graveside funeral for late Saturday afternoon, immediately after the Phillies ballpark memorial. She decided that the first event would be for the Phillies and Harry's fans, but that the burial would be just for the Kalas family and a few close friends. No one from the Phillies organization was invited to the graveyard funeral, not even Harry's last broadcast partners. "It was for family," Eileen Kalas said.

She made a few exceptions. Scott Graham, let go from his Phillies broadcasting job after the 2006 season, got invited, along with several other close Kalas friends, such as Jeff McCabe, Joe Nunes, and agent Dion Rassias.

Harry's three sons, his brother and other relatives made plans to attend the Phillies ballpark event, but Eileen Kalas opted to skip it. "I couldn't have gone out there that day and had people talk to me and tell me they're sorry, because I wouldn't have been able to give anything back to them," Eileen said. "The burial with the hymns and Harry's three boys, his brother, his nieces and nephews . . . that's what I needed."

The task of finding a proper burial spot fell to funeral director Mark McCafferty. "You've got to find a place that's befitting," Dion Rassias told McCafferty after passing along the same message from the office of Philadelphia Mayor Michael Nutter.

Before making a final recommendation to the family, McCafferty looked into the possibility of burying Harry in several notable Philadelphia locations. His first thought was Christ Church Burial Ground, a 290-year-old cemetery in downtown Philadelphia that serves as the final resting place of Benjamin Franklin and four other Declaration of Independence signers. Unfortunately, there were no available plots. After striking out at several other potential locations, McCafferty ended up choosing another historic graveyard, which was within the Philadelphia city limits but sits several miles from downtown Philadelphia.

At a cost of $20,000, the Kalas family purchased a double gravesite, overlooking the Schuylkill River, at Laurel Hill Cemetery, a National Historic Landmark that acts as the final resting place for an estimated 100,000 people, many from the 1700s and 1800s. A great many are memorialized with enormous monuments. Buried at Laurel Hill are Declaration of Independence signer Thomas McKean and 42 Civil War generals, the most famous being George Meade, who defeated Robert E. Lee at the Battle of Gettysburg in

1863. Other Laurel Hill notables include portrait painter Thomas Sully; Henry Deringer, a gunsmith who gave his name to the famous pistol; architect Frank Furness; and first U.S. Mint director David Rittenhouse, after whom Philadelphia's exclusive Rittenhouse Square was named.

Kalas also rests in the company of three 19th-century professional baseball players—Lon Knight, Henry Luff and Jack McFetridge. A former Phillie, McFetridge pitched a complete-game shutout for the 1890 club in his pro debut at age 20 and then never played another professional game until 1903, his final season, when he was 1-11, again for the Phillies.

"When Harry died, obviously we heard, and we were surprised when we got the call," said Gwendolyn Kaminski, Laurel Hill's director of development and programming. "The funeral director said the Kalas family wanted Harry buried in the city and at the best cemetery. From a historical standpoint, we're the best."

Laurel Hill was so pleased with the Kalas family's choice that the cemetery donated four plots adjoining Harry's gravesite so that no one ever can be buried immediately in front of him.

While tending to the endless funeral details, Eileen Kalas became overcome with grief again when one of the family dogs reacted dramatically to the return home of Harry's suitcase from Washington, D.C. During Harry's last stay at home, his five-year-old, 120-pound golden retriever Scout started acting oddly. Usually, Scout slept outside Harry's bedroom. But a few days before Harry died, Scout insisted on sleeping in a tiny area next to Harry's nightstand, curling up as close as possible to Harry. Eileen tried to move the dog, thinking Harry would trip over Scout if he got up to go to the bathroom in the middle of the night. But Scout wouldn't budge.

"Just let him sleep there," Harry said. "He's protecting me."

After Harry's death, Scout acted normally until Julie Vanwey, Harry's stepdaughter, entered the Kalas house with Harry's belongings. When she placed Harry's suitcase in his bedroom, Scout entered the room and started howling next to it. When the door was shut, the dog's cries grew even louder. After the suitcase had been put into a closet, Eileen was awakened by "a horrible sound" in the middle of the night. "It was Scout," she said. "I thought he died. That dog wanted Harry's suitcase. He must have known. His heart was broken. Harry was so good to him."

Sadly, Scout's behavior then became more erratic. The dog stopped eating and drinking. Eventually, Eileen made the agonizing decision that Scout would be better off in a new home with a man around. Jerry Roth, a friend of Harry's, agreed to take in the dog.

"I really believe Scout would have died if I kept him," Eileen said.

While the Kalas family and Phillies were planning their respective memorial events, the late broadcasting legend received an outpouring of love from every direction. Doug Glanville, a scholarly former Phillies outfielder, grew up in northern New Jersey rooting for the Phillies even though Yankee Stadium was only a few minutes from his childhood home in Teaneck. In April 2009, Glanville wrote an op-ed column for the *New York Times* in which he described how much Harry's calls meant to Phillies ballplayers.

"When I hit my only career inside-the-park home run, I knew as I rounded those bases that the moment was being immortalized by Harry's description—even if I couldn't hear it live," Glanville wrote. "Players could go their entire careers without ever experiencing Harry calling their great moments, and that is a great loss for them. But I knew that my home run story was being told, so that anyone listening would not only understand what was happening, but feel every spike hit the turf as I rounded second. Harry also gave meaning to these events. And I found meaning in some of my achievements not so much by looking at my trophy collection, but because I could step back to watch the video . . . and so I got to hear Harry conveying something I'd done on the field to our fans. Harry didn't provide just a walk-through of a great play, he embodied a convergence of perspective and emotion and approached it all as if it was his duty to share every morsel of it."

The Phillies received dozens of similar stories from their alumni, most of whom loved Harry Kalas like a teammate. Harry's colleagues from around the country also expressed their great loss in a variety of forums.

Ernie Harwell, the retired Hall of Fame voice of the Detroit Tigers, remembered Harry during an ESPN Radio appearance. "It's a great blow to baseball. He was very popular from a personal standpoint and he was very popular from a public standpoint. And I think everybody that ever heard that great voice of Harry Kalas felt that he was a very close friend of theirs."

The week of Harry's death, Eileen Kalas received a moving letter from a former President of the United States:

Dear Eileen,

Laura and I are deeply saddened by the loss of Harry. Our hearts ache and our prayers are with you and your family. Your husband was a remarkable man whose distinctive voice, passion for sports, and optimistic and compassionate spirit lifted the hearts of millions. I was honored to have met him and I hope the memories you have of him bring you strength and comfort during this difficult time. May God bless you.

Sincerely,
George W. Bush

During the days leading up to the public tributes, Eileen discussed the arrangements with Harry's three sons. As Harry's eldest, Todd assumed that he would be speaking for the family at the public memorial, but said, "If anyone would like to speak, that's fine."

"I'd kind of like to, unless you have something prepared," said Kane Kalas, then a month shy of his 20th birthday and a college freshman at the University of Miami.

Surprised, Todd paused momentarily, then said, "That'll be tough, Kane."

"I want to speak," Kane said. "If anybody else wants to, they can, too."

Todd went along with his younger half-brother's wishes. "Go ahead and take this one. I have a lot of commitments to do on radio and television. If you feel passionate about it, I want you to speak."

Kane had done a lot of public speaking in high school, so he knew that he wouldn't have stage fright. But he understood that this speech would likely be the most important one he would make in his life. He started searching that night to find exactly the right words to honor his late father and hero.

"I told myself that I wanted it to be one of the most authentic speeches that I've ever made, so I didn't write it out word for word," Kane said. "Instead, I jotted down points of what I wanted to talk about, and I rehearsed it a couple times by myself in my room, just to see how I would feel."

Meanwhile, during his first day back in Philadelphia, Todd Kalas made a visit to Citizens Bank Park to meet with the media. There, he tearfully observed the impromptu shrine for his father at the Mike Schmidt statue outside the third-base gate. He nearly choked up upon seeing Miller Lite cans scattered among the messages, flowers, teddy bears and hats. "It was nice that they had a beer there for him," Todd said with a hint of a smile. "He's able to have his cocktails again now, where he is."

On Friday, April 16, three days after Harry's passing, the Quaker City String Band, longtime friends of Harry Kalas, performed and sang "We're Just Wild About Harry" outside Citizens Bank Park prior to the Phillies game that evening.

Inside, the Phillies began their two days of tributes. The Kalas boys were at Friday's game for an emotional pre-game ceremony that included Todd, Brad and Kane throwing out the first pitches in unison. Hall of Famer Mike Schmidt spoke to the crowd about his good friend Harry Kalas. "If you can look past Ben Franklin and William Penn, Harry Kalas might have been the greatest person to ever grace Philadelphia," Schmidt said. "As many lives as he affected over the time that he lived in Philadelphia and this area, who would have a bigger impact on this city? I can't think of anybody."

With the Phillies' flag in Ashburn Alley flying at half-staff, Kane closed the pre-game event with an unforgettable rendition of the National Anthem. Just like his father, he showed that he was putting good use to his wonderful baritone voice.

A highlight of the night came during the seventh-inning stretch when the stadium's PhanaVision replayed a video of Harry singing the first verse of "High Hopes" on the night before his 2002 Hall of Fame induction. The sellout crowd at Citizens Bank Park rose and sang along with Harry. Afterward, fans gave Harry a standing ovation, which prompted a chant: "Har-ry! Har-ry! Har-ry!"

After Friday's game, an 8-7 Phillies loss to the San Diego Padres, a group of broadcasters, media members and ballpark workers gathered in the press dining room. The Phillies departure from Veterans Stadium after the 2003 season had brought an end to the nightly post-game drinking sessions in the Phillies' press club, at which Harry had been a regular. For one night, the tradition was renewed.

As Harry was being toasted in the ballpark's press club, a 45-year-old Phillies fan started forming a line for the next morning's public memorial. Mark Such of Warminster, Pa., arrived at 9:30 p.m., outside the third-base gate through which fans would be let into the ballpark to file past Harry's coffin. Wearing a Phillies batting practice jersey, Such camped out all night so that he could become the first fan to pay respects to Harry, whom he'd met a few times. "He treated everybody the same, and if I could do that I would be a better person," the Phillies fan said.

At midnight, Such got company when another 45-year-old man became the second in line. Michael Aldridge of Blackwood, N.J., arrived with a sign that read: "No crying in baseball until now." The men talked the night away, then assisted ballpark workers in setting up police barricades for fan control.

Meanwhile, inside the McCafferty Funeral Home, funeral director Mark McCafferty was saying goodbye to Harry in his own special way. Before coffins are closed, funeral directors typically cover the body up to the shoulders in a six-foot-long casket blanket. For Harry's burial, McCafferty ordered a white velvet blanket embroidered in red with Harry's name, the year of his birth and death, four baseball players, and his famous home run call, "That Ball's Outta Here!" In his entire career, this was the first time McCafferty had ever custom-ordered such a blanket. As one of his final tributes to Harry, he paid for it himself.

Before sealing the casket, McCafferty, a practicing Catholic, said three quick prayers—Our Father, Hail Mary and Glory Be.

At 5:30 a.m., on Saturday, with a full moon helping light their way, six police motorcycles and four police cars led a McCafferty hearse carrying Harry's body as it left the funeral home for Citizens Bank Park. "When we approached the ballpark around 6 a.m., the moment was surreal," McCafferty said. "We knew very shortly that all of Philadelphia would be watching this."

By 7 a.m., hundreds of fans were lined up at Citizens Bank Way, the street adjoining the ballpark. The gates were not scheduled to open until 8 a.m., but the Phillies moved it up to 7:30 in an effort to make sure everyone who attended the free event would get a chance to pass by Harry's casket. Inside, the club set up memorial books and offered complimentary donuts and drinks.

Ten minutes after the gates opened, Phillies President David Montgomery was there shaking hands and thanking fans for coming. Chairman Bill Giles arrived shortly thereafter wearing white shoes in honor of Harry.

"We were subbing for Harry," Montgomery said. "If it was any other occasion, nobody put the fans more in the forefront than Harry did. He would have been there."

Down on the playing field, about 30 feet behind home plate, a white coffin with gold trim rested on a stand perched three feet off the ground. A spray of 100 red roses mixed with baby's breath and leatherleaf decorated the coffin lid. Stands on both sides of the coffin displayed pictures of Harry, one a black-and-white head shot, the other a color photo of Harry throwing out the first pitch during his last Phillies home game.

The weather for the public tribute was perfect. The average temperature for Philadelphia in April is 52 degrees. But for Harry's public memorial, mourners were treated to a 72-degree day with sunshine and a clear blue sky.

This degree of memorial tribute, with a baseball figure lying in state at a ballpark, had been staged only twice before—for the wildly popular New York Yankees slugger Babe Ruth in 1948, and in 2002 for St. Louis Cardinals broadcasting legend Jack Buck, a close friend of Harry's.

More than 9,000 Phillies fans showed up for Harry Kalas' public memorial. A steady stream of fans slowly and quietly filed past Harry's coffin for over five hours. Most people reached out and placed a hand on the casket. Many snapped pictures. There were a lot of tears. After saying their goodbyes, most fans took a seat in the lower level between first and third base, and patiently waited for the memorial service to begin. The early arrivals had to wait for several hours, but nobody seemed to be bothered. In a fitting tribute to Harry, a spirit of friendship and generosity flowed through the crowd.

At 1 p.m., Comcast SportsNet began live television coverage of the tribute, which opened with Harry's family, friends and colleagues passing by the casket. Harry's three sons were there. So was Jim Kalas, Harry's older brother and only sibling. Back in Hawaii, Jasmine Kalas, Harry's first wife, sat at a friend's home watching the ceremony over the Internet.

True to her word, Eileen Kalas opted not to attend. Some Phillies employees whispered that she was boycotting the event. David Montgomery said that that he had only learned the night before that Eileen had scheduled Harry's private funeral to follow the public event.

"I didn't boycott," Eileen said. "I didn't go because that was for the fans. It was very personal between the fans and Harry. I wanted the boys to have their time. I also wanted to be strong for the private funeral. I was focusing on getting Harry buried. I watched some of it on TV. I thought the Phillies did it beautifully and the fans were wonderful."

Bill Campbell, the man whom Harry controversially replaced in the Phillies booth in 1971, showed up, as did Philadelphia Eagles announcer Merrill Reese,

St. Joseph's basketball coach Phil Martelli, Temple basketball coach Fran Dunphy and Dave Raymond, the original Phillie Phanatic.

Twenty-two former Phillies were in attendance, including Hall of Famers Steve Carlton, Robin Roberts and Mike Schmidt, plus notables such as Dick Allen, Ricky Bottalico, Larry Christenson, Darren Daulton, Dallas Green, John Kruk, Garry Maddox and Mitch Williams.

After the Phillies' alumni passed by the casket, the 2009 team, led by manager Charlie Manuel, appeared from its dugout. The players were dressed in their game uniforms, minus hats as a sign of respect, and slowly walked past the coffin, some taking longer than others to reflect. From there came a baseball rarity as an entire uniformed team joined fans in the stands.

Phillies broadcaster Tom McCarthy, the unofficial successor to Harry as the club's lead television announcer, emceed the ballpark memorial.

"The voice of our tributes was our subject," said longtime PR man Larry Shenk, remembering how Harry had officiated so many previous Phillies events.

The public memorial included nine speakers, each of whom offered their own unique and moving eulogy. Richard Ashburn, Whitey's son, led off by reading a poem his wife Lisa had written for Harry, who had done the same for Whitey's Hall of Fame induction.

HARRY THE K
His voice would melt butter
There could be no other
To replace our Harry the K
He was a kind man, would engage any fan
And never turn someone away
He had a great smile and plenty of style
High Hopes was his motto and song
When he'd shout "Outta here," we'd all stand and cheer
To know that the ball was long gone
With his partner and friend, he's reunited again
And they'll call all the plays from above
Though our voice is now gone, you'll grace heaven with your song
Harry, know that you go with our love

Joe O'Loughlin, who wrote Harry a touching condolence letter after Richie Ashburn died, represented Phillies fans at the Kalas family's request. David Montgomery, Mike Schmidt and Jamie Moyer represented Phillies management, alumni and the 2009 team, respectively. Also speaking were Pennsylvania Governor Ed Rendell, Philadelphia Mayor Michael Nutter, NFL Films President Steve Sabol and Kane Kalas.

Schmidt showed a side of himself that Phillies fans had never seen during an emotional six-minute eulogy that ironically fell 22 years to the day on which Harry Kalas famously called Michael Jack's 500th career home run.

"Our Harry Kalas is gone," Schmidt told the crowd. "We can't bring him back. We must grieve, but we must also not allow our grief to overpower our ability to celebrate his beautiful life. Nothing describes Harry's life better than 'bountiful.' There was nothing about Harry that suggested anything but good times, smiles, fun, simply making people happy. Think about this man: millions of people from March until October for 40 years depended upon Harry every day for entertainment—working people, construction workers, cab drivers, office workers, the elderly, the hospitalized and homebound, even children. Everybody's lives were made better by Harry Kalas."

Kane Kalas displayed composure beyond his years while delivering a moving eulogy, a highlight of the memorial.

"One of my father's greatest strengths in the booth . . . was his ability to convey emotion using his velvety voice," Kane told the crowd. "When the Phillies were down, the calmness and the assuredness of my father's voice let us know that there was still hope and that no matter what happens, tomorrow is another day. When the Phillies were winning, however, the excitement in my father's voice inspired us all. It excited us, and it raised our spirits. Similarly, as I grew up, my father's voice has been there for me. . . . The encouragement of my father instilled in me a deep-rooted desire to approach everything in my life with passion and with commitment, just as my father had done.

"My fondest memory of my father occurred five years ago, the first time that I sang the National Anthem here at a Phillies game. I still remember the look of honor, joy and pride in my father's eyes when he looked at me and said, 'Son, I'm proud of you.' Today, the only thing that I'd like to say is we are all deeply and profoundly proud of you, Dad. I love you."

When the eulogies were finished, Baseball Chapel President Vince Nauss said a prayer. Then the past and present Phillies were called back to the field, along with members of the front office and Harry's broadcast partners. The hearse, parked all morning far down the right-field foul line, slowly backed up. The vehicle stopped about 30 feet beyond first base, then the back door opened. Starting from home plate, next to Harry's coffin, everyone formed parallel lines leading to the hearse.

Dan Baker, the Phillies public address announcer since 1972, broke the silence. "Led by Bill Giles, who brought Harry Kalas to Philadelphia 38 years ago, it is only fitting that Harry Kalas pass through the people whose lives he touched so much."

Bill Giles and David Montgomery were at the front of the line to receive the casket. Eventually the casket was passed down the line, but initially the old guard struggled to keep the heavy coffin level. "Don't drop Harry," former Phillies pitcher Larry Christenson yelled. Funeral director Mark McCafferty quickly moved in to help by grabbing the back end of the casket.

"I didn't want to be in the front page of the newspaper with the casket on the ground," McCafferty said. "As soon as I saw the first guys pick up Harry, I knew they were in trouble because the average age was about 67. Nobody was carrying him. I call them 'hand-dressers.' They were putting their hands on the handle of the casket."

While Harry's casket was being passed along on its way to the hearse, Harry's two oldest sons suddenly appeared together in a taped message played on the left field PhanaVision scoreboard.

"Hi, I'm Brad Kalas, and when Dad would always be driving to the ballgames, he would listen to Frank Sinatra, Broadway tunes and also Simon & Garfunkel. One of his favorite songs was 'Bridge Over Troubled Water.'"

"And I'm Todd Kalas, and back in the day in the early-to-mid '70s, in those times of the eight-track player . . . we had an eight-track player in our car. So on the way to the game, we would hear 'Bridge Over Troubled Water' and he would sing along. And he said a couple of times, 'When I reach my final resting place, this is the song I want to hear.'"

Brad Kalas appeared again. "Dad, this one is for you!"

Listening to the angelic voice of Art Garfunkel singing "Bridge Over Troubled Water," the 1970 Grammy Awards Song of the Year, most everyone in the ballpark became teary. A day or two earlier, Todd Kalas had mentioned his father's love for that song to Phillies manager of broadcasting Rob Brooks, who then told Dan Stephenson, the team's video production manager. Video Dan rushed to put together a moving video tribute that followed Todd and Brad's introduction.

As the coffin passed the first-base box seats, fans began cheering and whistling. Single voices from all over the ballpark called out, "We love you, Harry!" When the coffin finally reached the end of the line, eight members of the 2009 Phillies roster and staff—Carlos Ruiz, Lou Marson, Ryan Howard, Jamie Moyer, Milt Thompson, Brett Myers, Jimmy Rollins and manager Charlie Manuel—walked it the last few steps to the hearse and placed Harry's body inside. The back door shut and the hearse slowly exited the stadium, with the Simon & Garfunkel tune still going strong over the PA system.

"All of it was the most emotional moment of my life," Todd Kalas said.

With most everyone still wiping tears from their eyes, the memorial service concluded in the only way it could. Local entertainer Eddie Bruce, a friend to Harry, entered the field and led everyone in a "High Hopes" sing-along. After the first verse, Harry finished the rest of the song on the enormous PhanaVision screen as Phillies fans continued to sing along as a final goodbye to their old friend.

"I was sort of Harry's opening act," Eddie Bruce said. "It was just an unbelievable experience."

Closing with "High Hopes" offered an upbeat ending for an upbeat man's funeral. The rousing finale also gave Harry's close friends and family a few minutes to exit the ballpark before everyone else. By the time the crowd began filing out, six limos were lined up behind the hearse and already heading for Harry's private graveside tribute at Laurel Hill Cemetery.

"When we left Citizens Bank Park, there were very few people that knew Harry was being buried that day," funeral director Mark McCafferty said. "Otherwise we would have had helicopters following us."

Despite their preparations, Harry's funeral procession hit bumper-to-bumper traffic crossing through town. A large group of highway patrol escorts quickly took care of that problem.

"The police were able to clear a path wide enough to get our cars through," said Mark McCafferty, who led the funeral procession. "If President Obama comes to Philadelphia, he'd be lucky to get an escort like that."

With the weather great, people had their car windows down and maybe figured out what was gong on. "People were cheering," McCafferty said. "It was an unbelievable tribute to an unbelievable man."

Eileen Kalas opted against being driven from her home to the graveyard service alone. Terry Kline, the attorney for Harry's Estate, accompanied her. "Terry is real easygoing and understood how I felt, and that's why I wanted to go with him," Eileen said.

The burial service began with Eddie Bruce and Charlene Holloway, a singer at Sharon Baptist Church, leading everyone in three of Harry's favorites hymns—"Wonderful Words of Life," "Joyful, Joyful, We Adore Thee" and "Angels We Have Heard on High."

Reverend Ed Rust led the service and Phillies broadcaster Scott Graham offered a eulogy. From there, several other friends and family members took turns speaking. "It was kind of an open field for people to get up and say something," Graham said. "It was certainly a format that Harry would have enjoyed."

Following the graveside service, most of the invited guests returned to Harry's house in Media. After six days filled with tears and grieving, Harry's family and close friends shared a lot of laughter that evening. They ate Chinese food, and then spent much of the night singing Harry's favorite songs, retelling memorable stories and watching old videos. Jim Kalas called the night a form of "comic relief."

"Everybody was sad, but we were remembering the good times," Kane Kalas said. "We put some happiness in the midst of what happened."

Harry certainly would have been very pleased with the way the day ended. After all was said and done, Harry the K was a man who had lived most of his life with a smile on his face and a song on his lips.

LONG LIVE HARRY THE K

Putting words in the mouth of the President of the United States is a high-profile, high-pressure profession. Curt Smith lived that life from 1989 to 1993 as a speechwriter for President George Herbert Walker Bush. Working in the White House and traveling everywhere with the President had its perks, but the hours were long, sometimes around the clock. And it wasn't easy attempting to elegantly capture the President's voice and message while storytelling in an uplifting and realistic way.

"The words that you write will be heard around the world," Smith said. "You try to fashion them in as exact and literate a way as you can. Many times I would get to the White House at 6:30 in the morning and they would need a political speech by noon, which was news to me."

By the weekend, Smith usually needed to relax. He often took a long summer drive with his wife from their home in Alexandria, Va., to his Uncle Charles' place in West Chester, Pa. Curt and his uncle, a former college professor, would spend the afternoon listening to Harry Kalas broadcast Philadelphia Phillies games, either from the living room television or back porch radio.

"During the White House years, I'm working 24/7," Smith said. "I needed my sanity restored, so I would drive to West Chester. I'd have a couple cold ones and there would be Harry the K talking ball."

Smith never was a Phillies fan—he grew up in the 1950s and '60s in upstate New York following the Yankees—but he loved baseball. In particular, he appreciated hometown announcers calling games and their unique relationships with their fan bases. Smith has authored 10 baseball books and is considered the foremost expert on the history of baseball broadcasting. In *Voices of Summer*, released in 2005, he ranked the Top 101 baseball announcers of all time using 10 criteria—continuity with a team, knowledge, longevity, kudos, language, network coverage, persona, popularity, voice and miscellany.

"In my view, Harry was as fine a broadcaster as I've ever heard," Smith said. "What was marvelous about Harry Kalas was that he and Mel Allen had the most distinctive voices in the history of baseball broadcasting. I grew up an admirer of Allen calling Yankees games and I became an admirer of Kalas. Their styles were quite different, but both their voices were extraordinary. Even until Harry was in his 50s and 60s, he had this wonderful baby face with a voice that resembled a wrecker demolishing cars. It had that deep penetrating baritone that absolutely commanded radio or television.

"The ordinary announcer blessed with the ordinary voice could not broadcast baseball as Harry did. Harry had an almost Spartan way of speaking. I would bet you that Harry probably said fewer words during a game than most baseball broadcasters. I've talked to other broadcasters about this. They agree that Harry was an aberration in the best sense of the term. He didn't need to fill dead air with mindless happy talk and endless blather as some announcers do.

"You sat there and were listening to a friend, a companion around the stove or the bar talking a little ball. You related to Harry's rhetoric because he didn't overwhelm you. He had a very laconic sort of style, almost Gary Cooper, in essence. He was not as profuse, thankfully, as many announcers are. He didn't need to be. He knew the game. He was beloved by his community. He understood baseball's lineage and poetry, and above all, he had a voice that could only be given to him by God."

Vin Scully, the subject of Smith's 2009 book *Pull up a Chair*, was rated first in *Voices of Summer*, followed by Mel Allen, Ernie Harwell, Jack Buck and Red Barber. Harry Kalas ranked 25th. Since Smith considered more than 1,000 broadcasters for his rankings, Harry's Top 25 rating is high praise. But probably to many baseball fans, especially Phillies fans, Harry deserved to be higher on the list, perhaps in the Top 10.

Curt Smith agrees. "If the book was re-released today, Harry would rank between 10th and 15th place," he said.

In the 2005 edition, Harry scored high across the board except for one category—network baseball coverage. When opportunities to do national baseball work presented themselves, Harry generally passed. He did call the Chicago Cubs-San Diego Padres' 1984 National League Championship Series for CBS Radio.

Smith, who in November 2009 served as a presenter for Harry's posthumous induction into the Radio Hall of Fame during a banquet in Chicago, is planning to update his rankings for a revised edition by 2014. He predicts Harry will move up significantly due to more points accumulated in his longevity, continuity and kudos categories.

"Keep in mind, it's just my ranking—it's not sacrosanct and people can agree or not—but I tried to be as objective as possible," Curt Smith said. "I didn't want this to be an arbitrary list of 'Here's who I like and the hell with you.' No, this is why I set up strict category criteria and tried to be as honest and fair as I could. Having said that, I wrote that this list would be constantly evolving because the criteria would change, and Harry is a good example of that."

Harry Kalas' enormous popularity has seemed only to increase since he died in April 2009. Jim Kalas, Harry's older brother, was amazed seeing all the attention and love Harry received in the first few months following his death. "I always thought that Harry was a big name in Philadelphia, but not anywhere else. But since Harry's death, my God. I didn't realize that he was a national figure."

Harry's voice was indeed well-known around the nation. But in Philadelphia, Harry rose to the level of a sports giant. Many considered him among the last of a dying breed of baseball broadcasting greats around the country who became hometown institutions.

"When you talk about local baseball broadcasters, there's the connection to the community and then there's the objective ranking of a broadcaster, and sometimes they're not separable," Bob Costas said. "If you grew up in Philadelphia, that's what you want a baseball game to sound like. If you grew up in Detroit, you want it to sound like Ernie Harwell. If you grew up in St.

Louis, you want it to sound like Jack Buck or Harry Caray, or maybe both. If you grew up in Los Angeles, it's unthinkable that anybody but Vin Scully would call a ballgame. So Harry was a great announcer with a distinctive baritone voice, but if it was just that and you happened to be passing through town, you'd say that's a very good announcer. What made Harry Kalas an all-time announcer was all the years in Philadelphia, all the connection to all the moments that people associate him with.

"And from everything I understand, unlike a whole lot of broadcasters, Harry was just really one of the guys. Not just friendly or acquainted with the guys, but he hung out with the guys. He went out with them. He was on the back of the plane with them. He played cards with them. At various times, he drank with them. He went to dinner with them and swapped stories with them. He's a presence both around the team and the city. Once it gets to that level of connection, then we're not making broadcasting school judgments."

Nationally, a lot of people didn't know Harry's name or face, but most every sports fan knew his voice.

Shortly after Harry's death, ESPN baseball analyst and former Phillie John Kruk asked a professional football player, "Did you know Harry was the voice of NFL Films?"

"That's the guy?" the player said. "Oh my God, that's the greatest voice I've ever heard. That voice gave me chills."

"We got that every day," Kruk shot back with civic pride.

Kruk, a star on the Phillies 1993 World Series team, considers Harry the franchise's greatest ambassador. For four decades, Harry was a 24/7 walking-talking poster boy for the Phillies.

"There was nobody that could represent the Phillies better," Kruk said. "Mike Schmidt, Steve Carlton, Robin Roberts . . . all the great players in the Phillies past and present can't add up to what Harry brought to that team. He brought viewership, loyalty and fans. They can't bring in fans like Harry."

Esteem for Harry reached as far as the Oval Office. In May 2009, the Phillies finally visited the White House after having canceled their scheduled April visit because Harry had died the day before. During a warm Friday morning on the South Lawn of the White House, Phillies players and coaches were honored for winning the 2008 World Series.

President Obama, standing on a platform with the Phillies behind him, began his nine-minute speech in their honor by paying tribute to the ballclub's late broadcaster.

"Welcome to the White House, and congratulations to the World Champion Philadelphia Phillies. We originally planned to do this last month, but we postponed after the loss of the legendary voice so familiar to any sports fan, Hall of Fame announcer, the great Harry Kalas. Harry left us as he lived, in the ballpark preparing to call another game for his beloved Phillies, and I know a season without the comfort of his voice is difficult. But I also know that Harry is here with us in spirit today and he is proud of all of you. He waited 28 years to call another World Series championship run, and what an unbelievable run it was."

One month after that rescheduled White House visit, Harry's 2008 World Series ring was given to the family. Julie Vanwey, the stepdaughter whom Harry had wanted to take to the White House, was given his championship ring without fanfare. She drove to Citizens Bank Park, double-parked her car and ran inside to pick up the 14-karat white gold ring with 103 diamonds.

"Seeing the Kalas name is what I liked more than anything," said Eileen Kalas, Harry's wife.

During Julie's brief stop at Citizens Bank Park to retrieve Harry's ring, the Phillies also handed over a stack of sympathy cards. Eileen read them all carefully, and one written by a 13-year-old Phillies fan from Bensalem, Pa., particularly touched her.

"His voice always gave me inspiration," Tyler Fortna wrote. "I always wanted to be like him when I grow up . . . but I know that I will never be like him. When I watched Phillies games, Harry made me feel like they were winning when they were losing. I met him when I was 7, and he asked me what I wanted to be when I grow up. I said, 'Baseball.' Then he said, 'Long drive, deep to center, that ball is outta here. Home run, Tyler Fortna.' Thank you for all of Harry's memories, the great calls. He's the best broadcaster ever. He's up in heaven now and still calling the Phillies."

Eileen not only wrote Tyler a thank you letter, she included four tickets to a September Phillies game from Harry's season ticket allotment. Tyler was shocked at Eileen's thoughtfulness and generosity. "I'm so thankful that Harry's wife took the time to read my letter and respond. When Harry died, it was a tough day for me and I just wanted to share with Harry's family what he meant to me. I never expected anything back."

Throughout the year, it seemed like everyone was trying to give back to a man who had spent his life giving so much to others. For instance, Pennsylvania Congressman Joe Sestak honored the life of Harry Kalas by reading an extensive tribute into the Congressional Record. In August, Phillies broadcasters founded The Kalas Award, which will fund an annual college scholarship for an area student with broadcasting aspirations.

Another big honor came about in August. Since 1978, the Phillies annually have inducted one of their greats to their Wall of Fame, now located in the Ashburn Alley section of Citizens Bank Park. Harry became the first non-uniformed member of this exclusive club.

As always, the Wall of Fame induction ceremony was held on Alumni Weekend, so more than 40 former Phillies players returned to be part of Harry's night, including Hall of Famers Jim Bunning, Steve Carlton, Robin Roberts and Mike Schmidt. Eileen Kalas made a rare appearance to the ballpark for the ceremony, too. When spotting Carlton, Eileen approached. "I looked Lefty straight in the eyes and said, 'Thank you for talking me into going out with Harry,'" she said. Indeed, Carlton had helped play matchmaker in 1985 when Harry, married to Jasmine Kalas at the time, expressed interest in a cocktail waitress whom he had just met.

Phillies videographer Dan Stephenson dug into his video archives to add a special touch to the Wall of Fame ceremony in Harry's honor. Harry had been the master of ceremonies for this event in past years, so Dan put together old tapes of Harry's introductions to welcome the 11 returning Wall of Famers onto the field for Harry's posthumous induction.

This time, Mike Schmidt filled in for Harry during the ceremony and Todd Kalas, Harry's oldest son, spoke for the family.

"Dad lived about the perfect life," Todd told the crowd. "He had an incredible generosity and time for each and every person that he would meet, and an unwavering spirit of 'High Hopes.' While he's not here with us physically, we can carry those passions with us in our daily lives. And in that way, we'll always have a part of Harry Kalas in our hearts. And I know that as he's looking down upon on us right now, that will complete his perfect life."

Following his father's passing, Todd Kalas has been asked if he'd someday like to follow Harry as the Phillies' lead announcer. Todd has been a member of the Tampa Bay Rays' broadcast team for years, but most of his duties have involved hosting the pre-game and post-game television shows. From 1994 to 1996, however, he had done play-by-play for Phillies home games on PRISM.

"Honestly, I've been conflicted," Todd said about his future plans. "I am humbled that people think of me as a possibility as a successor there, but I don't think it's the right thing now. If five years down the road an opportunity comes up and I don't feel like I'm coming right in on the coattails of Dad, that would be a possibility."

Jasmine Kalas, Todd's mother, says it's "her greatest wish" that Todd get an opportunity to return "to carry on the matrix of his dad's love of the Phillies."

"I'd hate to have to follow Harry in Philadelphia," said Jon Miller, the voice of the San Francisco Giants and ESPN *Sunday Night Baseball*.

Tom McCarthy, who began his second stint with the Phillies in 2008, took over for Harry, promising that he would remain true to Harry's standards.

"I don't think there's pressure," McCarthy said. "I'm going to try to honor Harry in whatever it is that I do the rest of my career. The right thing to do is respect the game and respect the position, and I'm going to do that. That's what I think Harry would want me to do."

McCarthy has a lot of company in wanting to honor Harry. To many tourists, the Philadelphia Museum of Art is an attraction as much for what's outside as inside. Every day, visitors run up the same front steps as fictional boxer Rocky Balboa famously did in *Rocky*. In addition, next to the steps, pictures routinely are snapped of the 10-foot-high bronze Rocky statue that originally served as a prop in *Rocky III*.

"I guarantee you that you could do a Kalas statue right next to the Rocky statue and it would be as noted . . . because Harry was Philadelphia and he was damn proud of it," said Rick Walker, who broadcasted NFL games with Harry for Westwood One radio.

Apparently a young Phillies fan from Center City in Philadelphia had the same thought. The day after Harry died, a 20-year-old college student started an online petition on Facebook to convince the Phillies to erect a Kalas statue outside Citizens Bank Park.

"Philadelphia has a Rocky statue," Antonio Jose, a junior at Community College of Philadelphia, wrote on the front page of his petition. "Don't you think Harry has done more for this city than Rocky did? I say he deserves the same if not more."

Over the summer, Jose temporarily forgot about his posting. "I thought it was going to be a Facebook group that didn't go anywhere," he said.

Nine months later, to Jose's surprise, more than 20,000 Phillies fans had joined his club, and by then, things were really taking off with one of the country's top sculptors joining the cause.

Lawrence Nowlan, a 44-year-old Philadelphia native and lifelong Kalas admirer, volunteered his services to make a bigger-than-life Harry statue for cost—about $80,000 including the base.

"My thought is what a great thing to be involved in as a fan," said Nowlan, who hopes to have a seven-foot-high bronze statue with white shoes and colorful jacket completed by late 2010 or early 2011. "Harry's like your buddy. He was more of a fan than an employee of the Phillies. We're going to give it to the Phillies from the fans, and they'll have to let us put it somewhere outside the ballpark."

By Christmas 2009, Nowlan, who now lives in New Hampshire, had completed a 24-inch prototype of Harry standing with his legs crossed and leaning on a baseball bat.

When the Kalas family pledged their support for the project, Mike Schmidt and Richard Ashburn followed and $15,000 was raised within the first few weeks. Chris Wheeler was among the first to make a donation.

Another person doing his best to keep Harry's memory alive is Pat Hughes, the longtime and well-respected radio voice of the Chicago Cubs. As much as anyone, Hughes appreciates the all-time greats in his line of work. He's honored some of his favorites including Red Barber, Marty Brennaman, Jack Buck, Harry Caray, Bob Uecker and Harry Kalas—in his series of *Baseball Voices* CDs. These treasures offer audio tours down memory lane for fans with interviews and vintage play-by-play calls—some famous and others obscure.

When Harry's CD first debuted in 2007, it included his call of Schmidt's 300th, 400th and 500th career homers, plus an entire half-inning from his first big-league game in 1965. After the 2009 season, it was updated and reissued with Harry's 2008 postseason calls.

"When I received the final production of Harry's, I pulled one out to make sure it was good to go," recalled Hughes, who does the writing, narrating and producing for the CD series. "I put the first track on and his beautiful voice comes booming through the speakers. I played that for my wife and she said, 'Honey, and I thought *you* had a good voice.'"

Harry's voice still resonates in Philadelphia when comedian Joe Conklin does his Kalas impersonations on WIP Radio or in concert. "It's a little touchy now, but when I open my mouth with Harry, I have instant credibility. I'd see Harry at banquets and he was always congenial with me . . . 'Joe, you're the best. Just keep doing what you're doing.' He didn't have a problem with anything. He'd laugh at it."

Even "The Boss" took time to pay tribute to Harry the K. Two weeks after Harry's death, Bruce Springsteen played two nights at the Spectrum in Philadelphia. During the second show, he offered a special treat for the crowd thanks to WIP Radio sports-update anchor Rob Charry.

In August 1985, Charry worked as an overnight disc jockey for WIOQ-FM in Philadelphia when Springsteen came to town on his *Born in the USA* tour. Charry came up with the idea of producing a spoof in which Harry would call a fabricated Springsteen homer against Clarence Clemons, The Boss' saxophone player. Harry, of course, agreed to do it.

"He kind of looked at it and took the microphone and embellished the whole thing that I wrote," Charry said. "The only thing he didn't say was 'Outta here!'"

Charry used it on the air, then threw the tape in with many of the others that he'd kept over the years. The Springsteen tape was put away for almost a quarter-century until Harry died.

"I was thinking, 'There's got to be something I can do to help contribute to Harry,'" Charry said. "Then I remembered I had this tape. I had hundreds of cassette tapes, and most aren't labeled, but I found it, edited out what didn't need to be on and played it at WIP."

Charry later learned that Springsteen was scheduled for another performance in Philly. He emailed an MP3 of his clip to Ike Richman, head of public relations for Comcast Spectator, and then it was forwarded to Springsteen's people. The Boss heard it and liked it. On April 29, 2009 Springsteen broke it out in concert.

"All right, we're going to send this one out to the late Phillies announcer of 39 years, Harry Kalas. . . . Harry the K," Springsteen enthusiastically told the crowd. "Hard to believe, Harry, hard to believe! Quite awhile back he recorded this. I don't know if you're going to able to hear ... we'll give it a shot."

At that point, Harry's 1985 home run call boomed over the sound system.

"We're going to have a pinch-hitter here with the bases loaded and two outs in the ninth inning. It looks like Bruce Springsteen. Just called up. They call him 'The Boss.' He'll be facing 'The Big Man' [Clarence Clemons], who is getting it up there at 95 mph. The wind-up and the pitch. . . . Swing and a long drive, deep right-center, it's got a chance. A grand slam home run, Bruce Springsteen!"

With a guitar strapped over his shoulder, Bruce reacted to Harry's home run call by pretending to circle the bases with his hands in the air. He paused for a moment, then pulled out his harmonica for the opening of one of his legendary tunes, "Thunder Road."

Brad Kalas, Harry's son, watched the clip on YouTube. "I was like, 'Wow.' Stuff like that keeps me going."

One of the things that helped former Phillies broadcaster Scott Graham cope with Harry's passing was their last talk. Graham, who succeeded Harry as the lead voice of NFL Films, fondly remembers the Phillies' 2009 season opener, a nationally televised Sunday night game against the Atlanta Braves. Working a pre-game show for XM Radio, Graham was at Citizens Bank Park for the first time since being let go by the Phillies following the 2006 season. Eight days before his death and just out of the hospital, Harry Kalas had light radio duties that night because ESPN was televising the game.

While eating in the press dining room as the game was beginning, Graham ran into Harry.

"Harry had a constant thing where if you were on radio and things went the wrong way for the Fightins, he felt that you were not doing your job scoring enough runs or keeping the opposition off the board," Graham recalled. "Then Harry would come into the radio booth, and with a disdainful look, he'd 'wave' you off. Now if he left the radio booth with a lead after the fourth inning and you gave it up in the fifth, God help you."

Shortly after Graham's visit with Harry had ended, the Braves took a 2-0 first-inning lead with Scott Franzke at the radio mike. "Harry returned and says, 'I gotta go wave off Franzke.' So he goes running down the hall, and I see him walking into the radio booth with his arm in the air. That's the last thing he ever said to me. That's perfect."

Hearing stories like Graham's helped Eileen Kalas get through the first few months after Harry died. But it hasn't been easy for her.

Although Harry made a very good living for many years, Eileen made a quick decision to sell their the 41-year-old ranch home in Media, Pa., and move into a fixer-upper in Delaware. She and Harry originally had purchased the Delaware home for their retirement. By July 2009, less than three months after Harry's death, their Media home went on the market for $625,000. Ten days later, it sold for $575,000.

With a lot of renovation work needed on the Delaware house, Eileen put most of her belongings into storage and moved into Homestead Studio Suites in Newark. She had a roommate, Deena Williams, an old friend from California who was there for most of the last seven months of 2009 to help Eileen. The two friends worked day and night for months turning her Delaware property into a livable space.

On December 3, 2009, Eileen began a new chapter of her life by finally moving into her Delaware house. While she intended to keep her residence in Delaware, her immediate plans were to "get away for a while" and continue the painful process of moving on without Harry. Eileen hoped to spend the first part of 2010 with her 90-year-old father, who lives alone in a log cabin in northern California and sells fruit to fishermen from the side of a road. From there, Eileen planned to go to Hawaii for "six months or so" to relax, read and do some soul-searching.

If Eileen gets to Hawaii, there will be two Mrs. Kalases in the state.

Jasmine, Harry's first wife, left Philadelphia in 2003 to return to Hawaii, her homeland. She'd always remained close to many people in the Phillies organization and cherishes memories of her many years with Harry, although their marriage ended in a drawn-out divorce. Even after all the intervening years, however, when Harry died, Jasmine received an email from a woman who works for the Phillies that included the line, "You're the real Mrs. Harry Kalas."

Eileen Kalas laughs when hearing comments like that. Unlike Jasmine, she never became close to the Phillies' front office personnel or players' wives. Eileen knows that she never was accepted by some Phillies employees, and insists that this never bothered her.

Surprisingly, Jasmine Kalas never remarried. "No thank you," she said. "I still have my love for Harry."

She's in good company there.

Curt Smith marvels at all the ways that Harry was honored during Phillies games in 2009—with the players' uniform patch, the "Outta Here" call after home runs, Harry singing "High Hopes" after games, etc.

"You've got all that, then something that has never happened in history for a broadcaster," Smith said. "The players themselves took it upon themselves to put Harry's sports coat and shoes in the dugout every game. There are five or six concrete ways within a year of how Harry has been honored. What does that tell you about the respect and love accorded to Harry by the tri-state area? It tells you everything that you need to know. No broadcaster has ever been honored in such a variety of ways. Harry Caray allegedly died in 1997, but his shadow, like Banco's ghost, hovers over Chicago. It's amazing. I would think that Harry Kalas' situation is precisely the same."

During the final week of the 2009 season, the tributes continued when the Phillies launched a celebration at Citizens Bank Park following a 10-3 win over Houston that clinched their third consecutive division title. The players sprayed champagne in the clubhouse, then came back outside to celebrate with fans, just as they did when winning the last two division titles and the 2008 World Series at home. Each of those earlier parties ended with Harry Kalas on the field singing "High Hopes."

This time, with music playing and the crowd cheering, Phillies center fielder Shane Victorino looked out at left field and realized that Harry needed to be made a part of the festivities. Victorino pointed to the HK billboard on the outfield wall and told shortstop Jimmy Rollins, "Let's go to HK."

With Victorino and Rollins leading the way, a pack of Phillies players followed. Believing that Harry was with them in spirit, one by one they laid a hand on the HK tribute, which is located on the wall in left-center field near the 374-foot marker. "He's definitely part of this whole situation," Victorino later recalled. "We can't forget about Harry. He's still a big part of this team. He did more than commentate on our games."

After the group had finished their tribute, second baseman Chase Utley and right fielder Jayson Werth appeared from the Phillies clubhouse. "We were a little late, but we still wanted to go out there and pay our respects," Werth said.

With lit cigars hanging from their lips, Utley and Werth headed to the sign carrying two beers apiece. Once they got there, they shook up their

Budweisers, opened the cans and sprayed the sign. "I wanted to make sure we doused HK right," Werth said, speaking as if the wall really was Harry. "We know that's what he'd want. He was a big part of this franchise for a long time. It was our responsibility to pay Harry respect."

The next day, Rollins revealed his potential future plans. If the Phillies repeated as World Series champions in 2009, he wanted to wear Harry's sports jacket and white shoes to the victory parade. Rollins unfortunately never got the chance. The Phillies reached the World Series, but lost in six games to the New York Yankees.

If the Phillies had won it all again, Eileen Kalas was going to drop off the worst of Harry's large collection of bad ties for players to wear in the parade, too.

Larry Andersen already had a sampling. "Harry's ugly ties went to LA," Eileen said with a laugh.

Eileen gave away most of Harry's clothes right away. Jeff McCabe, Harry's longtime confidant, has the jacket that Harry wore the night the Phillies won the 2008 World Series. Agent Dion Rassias has another of Harry's jackets.

No matter how much or little she keeps of Harry's things, Eileen always will treasure their memories so much more. Over the years, she had made two-dozen scrapbooks and photo albums chronicling Harry's career in broadcasting, some of which include fan mail.

As was to be expected, the final nine months of 2009 were tough on the Kalas family, especially Eileen Kalas. During one of her depressed days, Eileen started wondering where Harry was. Was he okay? Eileen may not be particularly religious, but she is very spiritual.

"Harry, if you're out there, give me a sign," she said looking to the ceiling. "Tell me that you're okay. Please let me know."

The next day, while absentmindedly running the vacuum over the living room rug, Eileen looked down and was startled. Staring at the rug, Eileen noticed a "P" just like the Phillies "P."

"It was their logo, perfect," she said.

She wondered if she had unconsciously vacuumed a certain way. The more that she thought about it, the more Eileen was convinced that it was a sign from her deceased husband.

"Harry was telling me that he was okay," Eileen said. "It figures Harry would do it this way."

SOURCES

Associated Press

Baseball Digest

Baseballhalloffame.org

Baseball-Reference.com

BaseballLibrary.com

Bucks County Courier Times

Carchidi, Sam. *Bill Campbell: The Voice of Philadelphia Sports*. Moorestown, N.J.: Middle Atlantic Press, 2006.

Carfagno, Mark. *Hardball & Hardship*. Washington, D.C.: U.S. Library of Congress, 2009.

Cincinnati Enquirer

Comcast SportsNet

ESPN.com

ESPN Radio

Giles, Bill; Myers, Doug. *Pouring Six Beers at a Time*. Chicago: Triumph Books, 2007.

Honolulu Advertiser

Hughes, Pat. *Harry Kalas: Voice of the Phillies* audio CD. (Baseballvoices.com)

Los Angeles Times

Naperville Sun

Philadelphia Bulletin

Philadelphia Daily News

Philadelphia Inquirer

Phillies Memories: The Greatest Moments in Philadelphia Phillies History. DVD. Major League Baseball Productions, 2009

Philadelphia Phillies Media Guides (1971-2009)

Suehiro, Arthur. *Honolulu Stadium: Where Hawaii Played*. Honolulu: Watermark Publishing, 1995.

The New York Times

The Road to the Championship: The Philadelphia Phillies Video Yearbook. Box Set, 2001-2008. Written and Produced by Dan Stephenson, 2009.

Trenton Times

USA Today

Vaclavone.blogspot.com

Westcott, Rich. *Mickey Vernon: The Gentleman First Baseman*. Philadelphia: Camino Books, Inc., 2005.

Wheeler, Chris; Gullan, Hal. *A View from the Booth*. Philadelphia: Camino Books, Inc., 2009.

Wolfe, Rich. *Remembering Harry Kalas*. Phoenix: Lone Wolfe Press, 2009.

WHYY.org

Wikipedia.org

INDEX